The Epistles of Paul the Apostle to the Thessalonians

G. G. Findlay

BAKER BOOK HOUSE
Grand Rapids, Michigan 49506

Reprinted 1982 by

Baker Book House Company

First published in 1904 as part
of the Cambridge Greek New Testament
for Schools and Colleges

ISBN: 0-8010-3503-1

PHOTOLITHOPRINTED BY CUSHING - MALLOY, INC.
ANN ARBOR, MICHIGAN, UNITED STATES OF AMERICA

PREFACE
BY THE GENERAL EDITOR.

THE General Editor does not hold himself responsible, except in the most general sense, for the statements, opinions, and interpretations contained in the several volumes of this Series. He believes that the value of the Introduction and the Commentary in each case is largely dependent on the Editor being free as to his treatment of the questions which arise, provided that that treatment is in harmony with the character and scope of the Series. He has therefore contented himself with offering criticisms, urging the consideration of alternative interpretations, and the like; and as a rule he has left the adoption of these suggestions to the discretion of the Editor.

The Greek Text adopted in this Series is that of Dr Westcott and Dr Hort. For permission to use this Text the thanks of the Syndics of the University Press and of the General Editor **are** due to Messrs Macmillan & Co.

THE LODGE,
    QUEENS' COLLEGE, CAMBRIDGE.
       27 *October*, 1904.

EDITOR'S PREFACE.

THIS is substantially a new work, designed for the Greek Testament student as the previous volume from the same hand, in the *Cambridge Bible for Schools and Colleges* (1891), was written for the student of the English Bible. The first four chapters of the Introduction, and the Appendix, bear indeed identical titles in each book; but their matter has been rewritten and considerably extended. The Exposition is recast throughout. Literary illustration from English sources has been discarded, so that full attention might be given to the details of Greek construction and verbal usage. The train of thought in the original text is tracked out as closely as possible—the analyses prefixed to the successive sections will, it is hoped, be useful for this purpose; and the historical and local setting of the Epistles is brought to bear on their elucidation at all available points. In particular, the researches made of recent years into Jewish apocalyptic literature have thrown some fresh light on the obscurities of St Paul's eschatology.

Two Commentaries of first-rate importance have appeared during the last dozen years, of which the writer has made constant use: viz. the precious *Notes on the Epistles of St Paul* bequeathed to us by the late Bishop Lightfoot, in which 123 out of 324 pages are devoted to 1 and 2 Thessalonians; and Bornemann's interpretation contained in the fifth and sixth editions of Meyer's *Kommentar*, a work as able and judicious as it is laborious and complete. At the same time, one reverts with increasing satisfaction to the old interpreters; frequent quotations are here made from the Latin translators—Erasmus, Calvin, Beza, Estius, Bengel, beside the ancient Versions—who in many instances are able to render the Greek with a brevity and nicety attainable in no other tongue.

GEORGE G. FINDLAY.

TABLE OF CONTENTS.

		PAGES
PREFACE		v
MAP		viii

I. INTRODUCTION

I.	The City of Thessalonica	ix
II.	The Coming of the Gospel to Thessalonica	xiv
III.	The Gospel of St Paul at Thessalonica	xxiii
IV.	The Origin and Occasion of the Epistles	xxxii
V.	The Authorship of the Epistles	xlii
VI.	Vocabulary, Style, and Character of the Epistles	lv
VII.	The Greek Text of the Epistles	lxv
VIII.	Analysis of the Epistles	lxix

II.	TEXT	1—11
III.	NOTES	13—214
IV.	APPENDIX	215—232
V.	INDICES	233—248

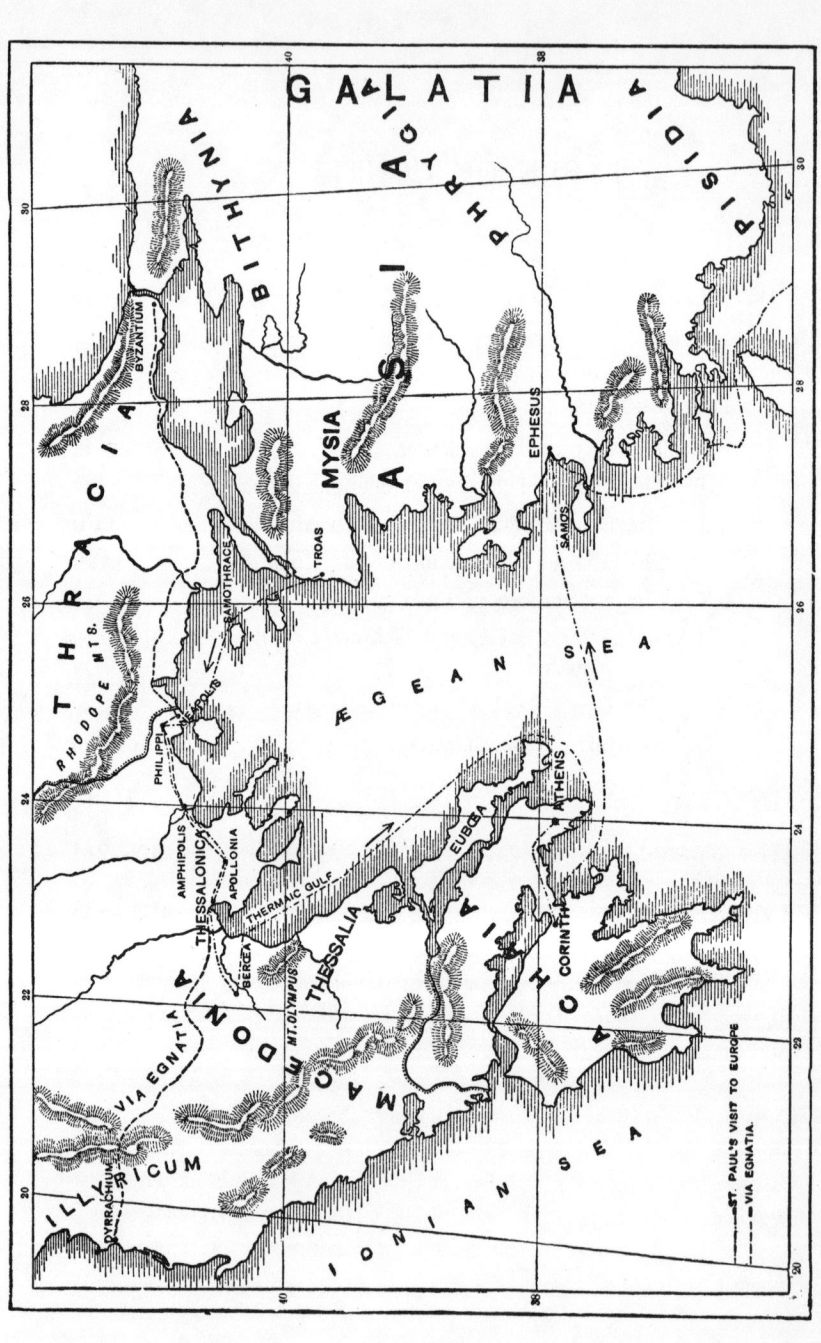

INTRODUCTION.

CHAPTER I.

THE CITY OF THESSALONICA.

AMONGST the great cities of the ancient world in which the Apostle Paul lived and laboured, two still remain as places of capital importance—Rome and Thessalonica. The latter has maintained its identity as a provincial metropolis and an emporium of Mediterranean traffic, with singularly little change, for above two thousand years. Along with its capital, the province of Macedonia to this day retains the name and the geographical limits under which St Paul knew it sixty generations ago. At the present moment (May, 1903) "Salonika" (or *Saloniki*, Σαλονίκη in vulgar Greek, Turkish *Selanik*) supplies a conspicuous heading in our newspapers, being the focus of the renewed struggle between the Cross and the Crescent, and a mark of the political and commercial ambitions which animate the Great Powers of Europe and the Lesser Powers of the Balkan Peninsula, in the disturbed condition of the Turkish Empire.

This town first appears in Greek history under the name of *Therma* (Θέρμα, Θέρμη), "Hot-well," having been so entitled from the springs found in its vicinity (cf. Κρηνίδες, the older name of Philippi). According to Herodotus (VII. 121), Xerxes when invading Greece made its harbour the head-quarters of his fleet. On the site of Therma Θεσσαλονίκη (Θεσσαλονίκεια in Strabo) was built in the year 315 B.C. by Cassander, the brother-in-law of Alexander the Great, who seized the throne of Macedonia soon after the conqueror's death. Cassander named the new foundation, probably, after his royal wife (see Diodorus Siculus,

xix. 52). The new title first appears in Polybius' *Histories* (XXIII. 4. 4, &c., as Θετταλονίκη). On the Roman conquest of Macedonia in 168 B.C., the kingdom was broken up into four semi-independent republics, and Thessalonica was made the capital of one of these. In the year 146, when the province was formally annexed to the Empire, the four districts were reunited, and this city became the centre of Roman administration and the μητρόπολις of the entire region. The Romans made of its excellent harbour a naval station, furnished with docks (Livy XLIV. 10). Through this city passed the Via Egnatia, the great military highway from Dyrrachium which formed the land-route between Rome and the East, and ran parallel to the maritime line of communication crossing the mid-Ægean by way of Corinth. On the termination of the civil war which ended with the defeat of Brutus and Cassius at Philippi in 42 B.C., when it had fortunately sided with the victors, Thessalonica was declared a *libera urbs* or *liberæ condicionis* (Pliny *N. H.* IV. 10 [17]); hence it had its recognized δῆμος and its elective πολιτάρχαι[1] (Acts xvii. 5-8). Its coins bear the inscription Θεσσαλονικέων ἐλευθερίᾳ. "The whole city was essentially Greek, not Roman as Philippi was" (Lightfoot). At the same time the city depended on the imperial favour, and was jealous of anything that might touch the susceptibilities of the Government; the charge of treason framed against the Christian missionaries was the most dangerous that could have been raised in such a place.

At this epoch Thessalonica was a flourishing and populous city. The geographer Strabo, St Paul's contemporary, describes it as the one amongst Macedonian towns ἡ νῦν μάλιστα τῶν ἄλλων εὐανδρεῖ (VII. 7. 4); and Lucian writes, a century later, πόλεως τῶν ἐν Μακεδονίᾳ τῆς μεγίστης Θεσσαλονικῆς (*Asinus*, 46);

---

[1] On this term see the article "Rulers of the City" in Hastings' *Dict. of the Bible*, and E. D. Burton, "The Politarchs," in *Amer. Journal of Theology*, July 1898. The title was one of limited application; it appears on the inscription still to be seen on the arch at the western gate of the city, which is given in Böckh's *Corpus Inscr. Graec.* II. p. 53 [1967]. Its use affords a fine test of the circumstantial accuracy of St Luke.

Theodoret refers to it in similar terms in the fifth century. At the beginning of the tenth century it is computed to have held 200,000 souls. To-day its population numbers something under 100,000; but it is in size the third, and in importance quite the second, city of Turkey in Europe. The Jews count for more than half its inhabitants, and have about 30 synagogues; Thessalonica is, in fact, the most Jewish of all the larger towns of Europe. The bulk of these however form a modern settlement, dating from the expulsion of this people by Ferdinand of Spain toward the end of the 15th century. The Christians—mainly Greeks or Bulgars—amount to only a fifth of the present population, the Turks being equally numerous. The people are largely occupied, as in the Apostle's time (I. iv. 11), in small manufactures along with commerce.

Thessalonica owes its commercial and political importance to the 'coign of vantage' that it holds in the Balkan peninsula. "So long as nature does not change, Thessalonica will remain wealthy and fortunate." Situated midway by land between the Adriatic and the Hellespont and occupying the sheltered recess of the Thermaic Gulf (now the Gulf of Saloniki) at the northwestern corner of the Ægean Sea, it formed the natural outlet for the traffic of Macedonia and the point toward which the chief roads from the north through the Balkan passes converged; hence it supplies the terminus of the modern line of railway running south to the Mediterranean from Vienna through Belgrade. This was one of those strategic points in the Gentile mission whose value St Paul's keen eye at once discerned and whose occupation gave him the greatest satisfaction—"Thessalonicenses positi in gremio imperii nostri," says Cicero. From Thessalonica "there sounded out the word of the Lord in every place" (I. i. 8); here many ways met, and from this centre "the word of the Lord" was likely to "run and be glorified" (II. iii. 1).

The site of the town is fine and commanding. It rises from the harbour like an amphitheatre, covering a sloping hill-side from which it looks out to the south-west over the waters of the Gulf, with the snowy heights of Mount Olympus, the fabled home of the Greek gods, closing its horizon, while it is guarded by high mountain ridges upon both sides. From the time of its occupation by the Romans, the historical associations of the city become numerous and interesting. Cicero spent some months at Thessalonica in exile during the year 58 B.C., and halted here on the way to and from his province of Cilicia (51—50 A.D.), dating from this place some characteristic letters, which might profitably be compared with these of the Apostle addressed to the same city. At Thessalonica he was found again in the winter of 49—48 with Pompey's army, which pitched its camp there before the fatal battle of Pharsalus. Six years later Octavian and Antony encamped in the same spot, preparing to encounter the republican leaders, whom they defeated at Philippi. The most notable disaster of Thessalonica was the massacre of 15,000 of its inhabitants ordered by Theodosius the Great in revenge for some affront inflicted upon him during an uproar in the city (390 A.D.), for which crime St Ambrose, the great Bishop of Milan, compelled the Emperor to do abject penance, refusing him absolution for eight months until he submitted.

In Church history Thessalonica bears the honourable name of "the orthodox city," as having proved itself a bulwark of the Catholic faith and of the Greek Christian Empire through the early middle ages[1]. It was an active centre of missionary labour amongst the Goths, and subsequently amongst the Slavonic invaders of the Balkan peninsula, from whose ravages the city suffered severely. In the roll of its Bishops there is one name of the first rank, that of *Eustathius* († 1198 A.D.), who was the most learned Greek scholar of his age and an enlightened Church reformer; it is still a metropolitan Greek see, claiming a succession continuous from the Apostolic days. The Norman Crusader, Tancred of Sicily, wrested the city from the Greek Emperor in 1185, and it remained for a considerable

---

[1] It must be said, however, that Tafel (*de Thessalonica ejusque agro*, 1839), the chief authority on the history of the city, conjectures that this epithet was conferred on Thessalonica because of its obstinate defence of *image-worship* in the 8th and 9th centuries.

time under the Latin rule ; in 1422, after several vicissitudes, it passed into the hands of the Venetians. They in turn were compelled in 1430 to yield it to the Turks, who effected here their first secure lodgement in Europe, half a century before the fall of Constantinople. The city had been captured by the Saracens, in a memorable siege, as early as the year 904, but was only held by them for a while.

Thessalonica till lately possessed three ancient and beautiful Greek churches turned into mosques,—those of St Sophia, St George, and St Demetrius. The first of these, which as a monument and treasury of Byzantine art was inferior only to St Sophia of Constantinople, was destroyed in the great fire of September 4th, 1890.

CHAPTER II.

The Coming of the Gospel to Thessalonica.

It was in the course of his second great missionary expedition that the Apostle Paul planted the standard of the Cross in Europe, in the year of our Lord 51[1] or thereabouts. Setting out from Antioch in Syria, he had taken the prophet Silas of Jerusalem (Silvanus of the Epistles) for his companion, on the occasion of the παροξυσμός between himself and Barnabas which arose at this juncture (Acts xv. 32—41). The young Timothy was enlisted as their assistant, in place of John Mark, a little later in the journey (Acts xvi. 1—3). The province of Asia, with Ephesus for its centre where St Paul afterwards spent three fruitful years, was the primary objective of this campaign. But after traversing South Galatia and revisiting the Churches founded in this region (by Paul and Barnabas) on the previous journey, the Apostles were "forbidden by the Holy Ghost to speak the word in Asia," so that, instead of continuing their travels further west, they struck across the peninsula to the north; and being again checked by the Spirit when crossing into Bithynia, they changed their route a second time and finally arrived at Troas, the north-western port of Asia Minor. It has been commonly supposed that during this part of his travels St Paul founded in Galatia proper (i.e. in the north or north-west of the extensive Roman province then known by this

[1] The date "53 (or 52)" was given in the *Cambridge Bible for Schools* (1890); but the writer has since been led to believe that the Conference of Paul and Barnabas with the "pillars" of the Judean Church at Jerusalem took place in the year 49 rather than 51, so that all the Pauline dates from this point onwards to the release from the imprisonment at Rome are thrown back two years in comparison with the former estimate. See the article on *Paul the Apostle* in **Hastings'** *Dict. of the Bible*, **1. 5,** *Chronology*.

THE JOURNEY TO THESSALONICA.

name[1]) the Churches addressed in the Epistle πρὸς Γαλάτας; but St Luke's indications in Acts xvi. 6—8 are slight and cursory, so that both the route followed and the time occupied on this part of the tour are uncertain. If the evangelization of the "Galatians" of the Epistle was effected at this period, through the delay caused by the illness of the Apostle Paul in their country (Gal. iv. 12—15), we must allow for a considerable period, perhaps the winter of 50—51, spent in North Galatia before the three missionaries reached the terminus of their journey through Asia Minor and St Paul heard the cry of the "man of Macedonia" which summoned him to cross the sea into Europe (Acts xvi. 9—12). It was at Troas that the true goal of this decisive journey disclosed itself, the reason of God's repeated interference with His servant's designs. In Macedonia the Gospel was to find a congenial soil and a prepared people; and Thessalonica was to furnish a centre, far in advance of any post hitherto occupied by the Gentile mission, from which the new faith would spread widely and rapidly through the adjacent provinces situated at the heart of the Roman Empire.

The story of the missionaries' voyage across the Ægean, their journey inland to Philippi, their success and their sufferings in that city, so graphically related by St Luke who had joined the company at Troas and writes Acts xvi. 10—40 as an eye-witness, need not be repeated. Only one reference the Apostle makes in these Letters to his experience at Philippi; it is such as to show that he and Silas, instead of being daunted by their rough handling in that town, entered on their mission at Thessalonica with high spirit and in the assurance that the hand of God was with them (I. ii. 1, 2). From the allusion made in Phil. iv. 16, written many years later, we gather that St Paul received help twice over from his friends in Philippi during the time of his first visit to Macedonia. "Even in Thessalonica," he writes, "you sent to supply my need both once and twice."

Thessalonica lay a hundred miles west of Philippi along the

---

[1] See W. M. Ramsay's *Historical Geography of Asia Minor*, pp. 252 ff., 453; or his *Church in the Roman Empire*[3], pp. 13 ff.; or article *Galatia* in Hastings' *Dictionary of the Bible.*

Via Egnatia, at a distance of three days' journey. "Amphipolis and Apollonia" appear in Acts xvii. 1 as the chief towns and halting-places on the way. These were both inland towns,—the former a place of importance, which had played a considerable part in earlier Greek history. Probably neither contained a Jewish colony, such as might have supplied a starting-point for missionary work. Entering the streets of Thessalonica the Apostle found himself in a Greek commercial city with a large infusion of Jewish immigrants, resembling Tarsus, his native town, and Antioch where he had ministered for so long. At the western (Vardar) gate, by which the travellers must have left the city, an arch may still be traced[1] commemorating the victory of Philippi; this monument, if not so old as St Paul's time, dates but little later.

We have described in chapter I. the position of Thessalonica and its growing importance as a centre of trade and population. There was another circumstance which gave the missionaries of Christ a vantage-ground here. At Philippi the Jews were not numerous or wealthy enough to boast a synagogue: they only had a προσευχή, a retired oratory "by the river-side," probably open to the air (Acts xvi. 13). But in Thessalonica "there was a synagogue of the Jews"; and the Israelite community had gathered about it a number of attached proselytes, and exerted considerable influence over its compatriots in other districts of the province: see Acts xvii. 1—4, 13. Paul and Silas might not expect to gain many converts from the synagogue itself; the readiest hearers of the Gospel were found in the circle of devout and enlightened Gentiles who had been attracted toward Judaism, and yet were only half satisfied by it, men weary of heathen superstition and philosophy and more or less instructed in the Old Testament, but not prepossessed by the ingrained

---

[1] This triumphal arch, now built into the city street, bore an inscription, which has been removed to the British Museum, giving the names of the Politarchs in office when it was erected. It is curious that three of these are identical with names of St Paul's Macedonian friends, *Sopater* of Berœa, *Gaius* the Macedonian, and *Secundus* of Thessalonica (Acts xix. 29, xx. 4): see Conybeare and Howson's *Life and Epp. of St Paul*, new ed. (1880), pp. 258 f.

CONVERSION OF THE THESSALONIANS. xvii

prejudice, the pride of Abrahamic descent, and the scorn of a crucified Messiah, which closed the ears of the Jews everywhere against the apostolic message. From this outlying constituency of proselytes and synagogue-frequenters, amongst which not seldom there were found, as at Thessalonica (Acts xvii. 4), a number of the more refined and intelligent Greek women of the upper classes, St Paul gathered the nucleus of his Churches. His success in this field and the fact that he robbed Judaism thereby of its most valued and liberal adherents, who were the evidence of its power and religious value to the eyes of the Gentile world, explain the bitter resentment, the blind hatred and rancour, with which St Paul was pursued wherever he moved by the Hellenist Jews (see Acts xxi. 28, xxiv. 5). Here in Thessalonica, while "some" of the Jews "were persuaded and consorted with Paul and Silas," a "great multitude of the devout Greeks[1]" accepted the Gospel, "and of the first women (*the ladies*, as we should say, *of the city* : γυναικῶν τῶν πρώτων) not a few." The Apostles felt it a duty—and to this they were prompted by the best feelings of their hearts (Rom. ix. 1—3)— to appeal "to the Jew first," however often they were repelled in doing so ; hence "according to Paul's custom he went in unto them [the Jews], and for three sabbaths discoursed with them from the Scriptures" (Acts xvii. 2). Considering the three heads of discourse indicated by the historian in conjunction with

[1] Ramsay prefers here the reading of **AD**, the Coptic, and Latin Vulgate, which distinguish "the devout" (or "God-fearing"): i.e. the Proselytes) and "the Greeks" (τῶν σεβομένων καὶ Ἑλλήνων), the latter being understood as mere heathen, previously unattached to the Synagogue. 1 Thessalonians certainly implies that most of the readers had been brought out of idolatry into the knowledge of Christ by the ministry of Paul and Silas (I. i. 9 f.). But *v.* 4 of Acts xvii. does not sum up the whole result of the mission in Thessalonica; it describes the immediate effect of the three weeks' preaching in the Synagogue, which resulted in the adhesion to Paul and Silas of a few only of its Jewish members, but of quite a crowd of Greek proselytes. The wider extension of the Apostles' work, to Greeks outside the Synagogue, naturally followed upon this separation. The text of the great MSS., τῶν τε σεβομένων Ἑλλήνων, therefore approves itself; while the reading of **AD**, cop vg, appears to be an emendation due to the very reflexion which leads Ramsay to prefer it as the original.

the "three sabbaths" over which St Paul's Scriptural argument extended (ἐπὶ σάββατα τρία), it looks as though he had advanced his proof in three successive stages : " opening and laying before" his fellow Israelites (1) the general doctrine of *a suffering Messiah* (ὅτι τὸν χριστὸν ἔδει παθεῖν), and (2) of *the Messiah's resurrection* (καὶ ἀναστῆναι ἐκ νεκρῶν) ; then proceeding (3) to identify "this Jesus whom I proclaim to you" with the suffering and risen Christ, whose image he had drawn from Scripture (καὶ ὅτι οὗτός ἐστιν ὁ χριστός, ὁ Ἰησοῦς ὃν ἐγὼ καταγγέλλω ὑμῖν). For two sabbaths the Synagogue listened with toleration, perhaps with curiosity, to the abstract exegetical theorem ; but when it came to clinching the matter by evidence given that the suffering and rising Christ of the prophets is none other than Jesus of Nazareth, the man who was twenty years before condemned by the Sanhedrin at Jerusalem as a blasphemer and crucified by the Roman Governor at the people's request, their patience was at an end. Yet it was not so much the advocacy of the claims of the Nazarene addressed to themselves, as the successful proclamation of His name to the Gentiles and the alienation of their own proselyte supporters, which inflamed "the Jews" to the pitch of anger described in Acts xvii. 5 : they "burst into jealousy, and, enlisting certain scoundrels amongst the loafers of the city, they gathered a mob and raised a riot." The house of Jason (this name is probably equivalent to *Jesus*), where St Paul and his companions lodged, was attacked with a view to seizing the Apostles and "bringing them before a public meeting" (προαγαγεῖν εἰς τὸν δῆμον). Jason was, presumably, a Jew of property who had accepted the faith of Christ. Failing to find the leaders, the mob "dragged Jason," and certain other Christians who came in their way, "before the politarchs" (ἐπὶ τοὺς πολιτάρχας).

The accusation brought against the Apostles was adapted to prejudice the magistrates of an imperial city like Thessalonica : they were charged (1) with being *revolutionaries*—"these that have turned the world upside down (οἱ τὴν οἰκουμένην ἀναστατώσαντες, v. 6)[1] have come hither also"; and (2) *with rebellion against*

[1] This charge is easy to understand in the light of subsequent events; it is not easy to see what suggested it to St Paul's opponents

the *Emperor*—"the whole of them contravene the decrees of Cæsar, asserting that there is another king, namely Jesus" (*v.* 7). On these outrageous charges legal conviction was of course impossible; but the mere bringing of them "alarmed the multitude and the politarchs" (*v.* 8), knowing as they did with what undiscriminating severity the Romans were accustomed to suppress even the appearance of rebellion. The Politarchs were, however, content with "taking security from Jason and the rest" for their good behaviour, and so dismissed the complaint (*v.* 9). Paul and Silas were compelled by these proceedings to leave the city at once (*v.*10)—probably the security given by their friends included a promise to this effect; they had become marked men, in the eyes both of the Government and of the populace, in such a way that their return was barred for many months afterwards (I. ii. 18). "The brethren immediately, by night, sent away both Paul and Silas to Berœa" (*v.* 10).

The impeachment for treason against Rome reminds us of the charge brought against our Lord Himself by the Jews before Pilate: "If thou release Him, thou art not Cæsar's friend. Every one who maketh himself a king, contradicteth Cæsar" (John xix. 12). Cæsar was the master of the world, and could brook no rival kingship. To employ the terms "king" or "kingdom," in any sense, within his empire was calculated to rouse fatal suspicion. The accusations were a distortion of what Paul and Silas had actually preached. They did publish a "kingdom of God" that claimed universal allegiance (I. ii. 12, II. i. 5, 8),

in Thessalonica at so early a date as this. The disturbance in Philippi was not serious enough to give colour to language of this kind, nor to lead any one to think of "the world" (τὴν οἰκουμένην) as affected by the preaching of these wandering Jewish visionaries. If however the news had recently come to Thessalonica of the riots at Rome resulting in the expulsion of the Jews from that city, on the occasion of which Aquila and Priscilla migrated to Corinth (Acts xviii. 2), and if, as the words of Suetonius suggest (*Claudius*, 25: "Judaeos impulsore Chresto [Christo] assidue tumultuantes Roma expulit"), these dangerous riots were connected with the preaching of Christianity in Rome and had advertised there its existence as a disturbing force in the Empire, we can better account for the adoption of this sweeping indictment and for the sensitiveness of the public authorities in the provincial capital.

and "another king" than the world-ruler of Rome, "even Jesus," whom God had set at His right hand and crowned with glory and honour, who should one day "judge the world in righteousness" (Acts xvii. 31). The language of II. ii. 3—12 (see Expository Notes) indicates certain aspects of St Paul's eschatological teaching in Thessalonica out of which a skilful accuser would not find it difficult to make political capital against him. The prejudice excited against the Gospel at Thessalonica by the phrase "the kingdom of God" or "of Christ," and by the forms of doctrine connected with it, suggests a practical reason for the comparative disuse of this terminology in St Paul's Epistles, which is often thought surprising and is mistakenly alleged as a matter of contrast between the doctrine of the Apostle and that of Jesus Himself.

The work accomplished by the missionaries in Thessalonica, and the nature and extent of the opposition they had aroused, imply a period of labour of greater duration than the three weeks referred to in Acts xvii. 2. St Luke surely intends that datum to apply only to the preaching of St Paul in the Synagogue, leaving undefined the much longer time over which his ministry outside the Synagogue was extended. The two Epistles indicate a degree of Christian knowledge and a settled fellowship and discipline among St Paul's adherents, and moreover a close personal acquaintance and attachment between themselves and him, which presuppose months rather than weeks of intercourse[1]. The allusion of Phil. iv. 16, already noticed, implies a continued sojourn. Paul and Silas left their infant flock prematurely, under circumstances causing them great concern as to its safety and an intense desire to return and complete its indoctrination (I. ii. 17—iii. 13). But the work, though wrought in a comparatively brief time and so hurriedly left, was well and truly done. The foundation laid was sure, and bore the shock of persecution. The visit of Timothy, sent

---

[1] "Paul evidently refers to a long and very successful work in Thessalonica...December 50—May 51 seems a probable estimate" of the length of his residence there (Ramsay, *St Paul the Traveller*, &c., p. 228). This is, perhaps, an extreme view.

LATER VISITS TO THESSALONICA. xxi

from Athens soon after St Paul's arrival from Berœa, found the Church unshaken in its faith and loyalty and abounding in works of love, while it was strengthened and tested through trial, so that it was able to send back to the Apostle on Timothy's return, with expressions of sorrow for his continued absence, assurances which were to him as life from the dead (I. iii. 8) amid his heavy trials and toils at Corinth.

Of St Paul's later associations with Thessalonica the traces are slight. This city had, doubtless, a principal place in his thoughts when in 1 Cor. xvi. 5 f. he speaks of "passing through Macedonia" on the way from Ephesus to Corinth toward the close of the third missionary tour, and when in 2 Cor. viii. and ix., written a few months later (56 A.D.), he commends to the Corinthians the signal liberality of "the churches of Macedonia" amongst whom he was travelling at that time. During this visit, as in his first residence at Thessalonica, the Apostle's life was one of peril and agitation : he writes of this period in 2 Cor. vii. 5, $\dot{\epsilon}\nu$ $\pi\alpha\nu\tau\dot{\iota}$ $\theta\lambda\iota\beta\acute{o}\mu\epsilon\nu\sigma\iota\cdot$ $\ddot{\epsilon}\xi\omega\theta\epsilon\nu$ $\mu\acute{a}\chi\alpha\iota$, $\ddot{\epsilon}\sigma\omega\theta\epsilon\nu$ $\phi\acute{o}\beta\sigma\iota$; cf. the $\pi\sigma\lambda\grave{\upsilon}\varsigma$ $\dot{a}\gamma\acute{\omega}\nu$ of I. ii. 2. On his return from Corinth eastwards, in the spring of 57, St Paul again traversed Macedonia (Acts xx. 3—6) and associated with himself, in carrying the collection made by the Gentile Churches for the Christian poor in Jerusalem, two Thessalonians named "Aristarchus and Secundus." The former of these remained with the Apostle for several years, sharing in his voyage to Rome (Acts xxvii. 2) and in his imprisonment there. In Col. iv. 10 and Phm. 24 the Apostle sends greetings from Aristarchus, calling him $\dot{o}$ $\sigma\upsilon\nu\alpha\iota\chi\mu\acute{a}\lambda\omega\tau\acute{o}\varsigma$ $\mu\sigma\upsilon$. During his latest travels, in the interval between the first and second Roman imprisonment, St Paul describes himself as "on my journey ($\pi\sigma\rho\epsilon\upsilon\acute{o}\mu\epsilon\nu\sigma\varsigma$) to Macedonia" (1 Tim. i. 3) on the occasion of his meeting Timothy shortly before writing the first extant Epistle to him, when the Apostle gave him orders "to stay on ($\pi\rho\sigma\sigma\mu\epsilon\hat{\iota}\nu\alpha\iota$) in Ephesus " as his commissioner. Thus a third time, as it appears, St Paul crossed from Asia Minor into Macedonia. Once we have clear evidence of his traversing the same route in the opposite direction (Acts xx.); in all probability he did so a second time, on his release from the first Roman captivity, if he fulfilled the intention, implied in Phil. ii. 24 and Phm. 22, of revisiting the Churches of Macedonia and Asia so soon as he should be set at liberty.

The last reference to this city in St Paul's history is the sad note of 2 Tim. iv. 10: "Demas hath forsaken me, having loved the present world, and hath taken his journey to Thessalonica." This deserter is referred to at an earlier time in Col. iv. 14, and therefore was with St Paul in his former imprisonment. Whether Demas was a Thessalonian or not we cannot tell. His name is probably short for *Demetrius*. A martyr of the latter name, suffering in the reign of Maximian, has become the patron saint of the city.

CHAPTER III.

THE GOSPEL OF ST PAUL AT THESSALONICA.

IT is now time to ask, What, precisely, was the Gospel brought by Paul and Silvanus and Timotheus to Thessalonica, which produced amongst its people so powerful and enduring an effect? Was there anything, we may further enquire, that was special to the place and the occasion in the form which their message assumed, anything that may explain the peculiar tone of Christian feeling, the mould of thought and of experience revealed by the two Letters and characterizing the faith of this great Macedonian Church in its beginning? The data of the Epistles, compared with the hints given us by the story of the Acts, enable us to furnish some answer to these questions.

(1) The starting-point of St Paul's teaching, as it addressed itself in the first instance to orthodox Jews, must be found in *the proof of the Messiahship of Jesus*, which was derived from the prophecies of Scripture compared with the historical facts of the life, death and resurrection of the Saviour. The method of this proof, briefly but very significantly indicated in Acts xvii. 3 (see p. xviii. above), is largely set forth in St Luke's report of the Apostle's discourse at the Pisidian Antioch (Acts xiii.).

(2) But in turning to the Gentiles, and especially when their preaching caught the ear of Greeks hitherto uninfluenced by the teaching of the Synagogue—and this seems to have been the case to a remarkable degree at Thessalonica—the missionaries of Christ had much to say about *the falsity and sin of idolatry*. This fact is strongly reflected in the account given by the writers in I. i. 9 f. of their readers' conversion: ἐπεστρέψατε πρὸς τὸν θεὸν ἀπὸ τῶν εἰδώλων κ.τ.λ. Their faith was emphatically a "faith

toward God" (ἡ πίστις ὑμῶν ἡ πρὸς τὸν θεόν, I. i. 8): see Expository Notes. As "God's Son, whom He raised from the dead," they recognized Jesus; in this character they "await Him from the heavens" for their "deliverer." The gods of their forefathers, whose images occupy the temples and public places of the city, and other minor deities adored in domestic or more private worship, they renounced as being "nothing in the world" (1 Cor. viii. 4), mere "shows" (εἴδωλα) of Godhead. Henceforth they acknowledge but "one God the Father, of whom are all things and we for Him" (1 Cor. viii. 6). That they "know not God" is the misery of the heathen; with this guilty ignorance their base moral condition, and the peril of eternal ruin in which they stand, are both connected (I. iv. 5; II. i. 8 f.). This "living and true God," the Father of the Lord Jesus, they had come to know and to approach as "our Father" (I. i. 3, iii. 11, 13; II. ii. 16); He is to them "the God of peace" (I. i. 1, v. 23; II. i. 2), who had "loved them and given them eternal comfort and good hope in grace" (II. ii. 16), had "chosen" them and "called them to enter His own kingdom and glory" (I. i. 4, ii. 12), who "would count them worthy of their calling and accomplish in them every desire of goodness and work of faith" (II. i. 11), whose "will" is their "sanctification" and who had "called them in sanctification" and "not for uncleanness" (I. iv. 3, 7), whose "word" is now "working" in them to these great ends (I. ii. 13), who can and will "comfort and strengthen their hearts in every good work and word," so that they may be found "unblamable in holiness" before Him at the Redeemer's coming (I. iii. 13; II. ii. 17), who "will bring" back "with Him" and restore to their communion those who have "fallen asleep" in death (I. iv. 14—17), who will recompense those who have "suffered for His Kingdom" with "rest" at the last while He sends "affliction on their afflicters" (II. i. 5—7). Such was the God and Father to the knowledge of whom the readers of these Epistles had been brought a few months ago out of the darkness and corruption of Paganism: it must be their one aim to serve and to please Him; the Apostle's one desire for them is that they may "walk worthily" of Him who called them (I. ii. 12, iv. 1; II. ii. 13 f.). The good news brought to

Thessalonica is spoken of repeatedly, and with peculiar emphasis, as "the gospel *of God*"; at the same time, it is "the gospel of our Lord Jesus Christ" (II. i. 8), since He is its great subject and centre: cf. Rom. i. 3, "the gospel of God...concerning His Son."

In this typical Græco-Roman city there were evidently in various ranks of society, both within and without the range of Jewish influence, a large number of minds prepared for "the good news of God." While the ancestral cults long maintained their hold of the rural population, in the great towns of the Empire scepticism was generally prevalent. The critical influence of philosophy, the moral decay of Paganism and the disgust excited amongst thoughtful men by many of its rites, the mixture and competition of conflicting worships tending to discredit them all, the spread of a uniform civilization breaking the spell of the old local and native religions, had caused a decided trend in the direction of monotheism and laid the more receptive natures open to the access of a simpler and purer faith. It is interesting to observe the prominence of *God* in these Epistles, and the manifold ways in which the Divine character and the relations of God to Christian men had been set forth to the Thessalonian Church. Such teaching would be necessary and specially helpful to men emerging from heathen superstition or unbelief; these Letters afford the best example we have of St Paul's earliest instructions to Gentile converts. The next report furnished to us in the Acts of his preaching to the heathen (xvii. 22—31: the discourse at Athens), represents the Apostle as dwelling mainly on two things—*the nature of the true God*, and *the coming of Jesus Christ to judge the world.*

(3) In proclaiming to the Jews a suffering and dying Messiah, the Apostle Paul must needs have shown *how* "it behoved the Christ to suffer" (Acts xvii. 3). *The purpose of the Redeemer's death, its bearing upon human salvation,* was explained by him "to the Jew first, and also to the Greek." This we infer from the central position of this topic in other Epistles, and from the prominence given to it in the Address of Acts xiii. 38 f., where the announcement of the forgiveness of sins and of justification

by faith forms the climax of the sermon, belonging to St Paul's earlier ministry, and where these great gifts of salvation are referred to the dying and rising from the grave of the rejected "Saviour, Jesus." The language of 1 Thess. v. 8—10 leaves us in no doubt that the same "word of the cross" was proclaimed at Thessalonica as everywhere else. Here "salvation" comes "through our Lord Jesus Christ, *who died for us*,"—a salvation in part received already, in part matter of "hope," and which belongs to those who "have put on the breastplate of *faith* and love." This salvation is the crying need of the Gentile world, which in its ignorance of God is enslaved to idolatry and shameful lusts, and is exposed to "the anger of God" that is "coming" and will break suddenly upon the "sons of night and of darkness," who are "perishing" in their refusal to "receive the love of the truth" (cf. I. i. 9 f., iv. 5, v. 2—9; II. i. 8 f., ii. 8—12).

We can understand all this in the light of the evangelical teaching of the Epistle to the Romans (see i. 16—25, iii. 23—26, v. 1—11, &c.: cf. the kindred passages in Galatians and 2 Corinthians); but without such knowledge the Apostle's allusions in these Letters would have been unintelligible to ourselves; and without oral instruction to the same effect, they would have been meaningless to Thessalonian readers. It must be admitted—and the fact is remarkable—that very little is said here upon the subject of the Atonement and Salvation by Faith. To suppose, however, that the Apostle Paul avoided such themes in his first ministry in Macedonia, or that, before the outbreak of the Legalist controversy, he had not yet arrived at his distinctive doctrine of Justification by Faith, is the least likely explanation of the facts. It stands in contradiction with the testimony given by 1 Cor. ii. 1 f., i. 17—24, where, referring to his work at Corinth going on at the very time when the Thessalonian Epistles were written, the Apostle tells us that "Jesus Christ crucified" formed the one thing he "had judged it fit to know," finding in this "the testimony of God" charged with "God's power and God's wisdom" for men; and where he identifies "the gospel Christ had sent" him "to preach" with "the cross of Christ," for which he is supremely jealous "lest it should be made void."

As in Corinth later, so amongst the Galatians earlier in the same missionary tour[1], "Jesus Christ had been placarded (or painted up), crucified" (Gal. iii. 1). That in the interval the Apostle should have lapsed at Thessalonica into another gospel—that of the Second Coming substituted for the gospel of the Cross (Jowett)—is historically and psychologically most improbable. In justice to the writer we must bear in mind the limited scope of these seemingly unevangelical Letters, and their strictly "occasional" nature. From the absence of argument and direct inculcation on the theme of the Atonement and the Forgiveness of Sins we should infer, not that St Paul was indifferent to these matters when he thus wrote, nor that these were points of minor importance in his preaching at Thessalonica, but that they were here received without demur or controversy and that the ὑστερήματα τῆς πίστεως (I. iii. 10) which he desired to make good in this community lay in other directions—that in fact the Thessalonian Church was not less but *more* loyal to the cross of Christ than some others. This conclusion is in harmony with the general tone of commendation characterizing both Epistles.

(4) The most conspicuous and impressive theme of the Apostolic preaching in Thessalonica, so far as it is echoed by the Letters, was undoubtedly *the coming of the Lord Jesus in His heavenly kingdom.* These writings are enough to show that the second advent of Christ was an important element in the original Gospel, the good news which God has sent to mankind concerning His Son. "One is apt to forget that the oldest Christianity was everywhere dominated by eschatological considerations" (Bornemann). The religion of the Thessalonian Christians is summed up in two things, viz. their "serving a living and true God" and "awaiting His Son from the heavens" (I. i. 9 f.). In the light of Christ's *parousia* they had learned to look for that "kingdom and glory of God" to which He had called them, for the sake of which they are so severely suffering (I. ii. 12; II. i. 5, 10—12, ii. 13 f.). "The coming of our Lord Jesus with all His saints"

---

[1] Or, according to W. M. Ramsay, earlier still, in St Paul's first missionary journey along with Barnabas, when the Churches of South Galatia were founded (Acts xiii., xiv.).

was an object of intense desire and fervent anticipation to the Apostle himself; he had impressed these feelings on his disciples at Thessalonica to an uncommon degree. His appeals and warnings throughout rest on this "hope in our Lord Jesus Christ" as upon their firmest support. "Each section [of the First Epistle] in turn runs out into the eschatological prospect" (Bornemann). It was, moreover, upon this subject that the misunderstandings arose which the Apostle is at so much pains to correct—the first (in I. iv. 13) touching the share of departed Christians in the return of the Lord; the second (in II. ii. 2) concerning the imminence of the event itself.

What may have been the train of thought in St Paul's mind which led him to dwell on the *parousia* with such emphasis at this particular time, we cannot tell. There were however two conditions belonging to his early ministry in Europe that might naturally suggest this line of preaching:—

For one thing, the Christian doctrine of final judgement was calculated to rouse the Greek people from its levity and moral indifference and to awaken in sleeping consciences the sense of sin; moreover, it had impressive analogies in their own primitive religion. Hence the Apostle, with a practical aim, advanced this truth at Athens, declaring that "God, having overlooked the times of ignorance, now commands men that all everywhere should repent; *because He has appointed a day* in which He will judge the world in righteousness, by the man whom He ordained." From such passages as 1 Cor. i. 7 f., iii. 12—15, iv. 3—5, ix. 27, xv. 23—28, 51—57, 2 Cor. v. 10, it appears that the thought of the Second Coming and the Last Judgement had been impressed with similar force on St Paul's Corinthian converts; this expectation was a fundamental axiom of the earliest Christianity. To the busy traders of Corinth and Thessalonica, or to the philosophers and dilettanti of Athens, he made the same severe and alarming proclamation. Indeed, St Paul regarded the message of judgement as an essential part of his good tidings: "God will judge the secrets of men," he wrote, "*according to my gospel*, through Jesus Christ" (Rom. ii. 16). But the announcement of Christ's **coming in** judgement involves the whole doctrine of the Second Advent. In what they said on this solemn subject, the writers tell us, they had been both exact and full (I. v. 2, II. ii. 5 f.). Yet its bearings are so mysterious and its effect on the mind, when fully entertained, is so exciting, that one is not surprised at the agitations resulting from this teaching in the young Christian community of Thessalonica.

But further, it should be observed that the Apostle Paul, as he entered Macedonia and set foot on the Via Egnatia, was brought more directly under the shadow of the Roman Empire than at any time before. Philippi, a Roman colony and a memorial of the victory by which the Empire was established; Thessalonica, a great provincial capital of Western aspect and character; the splendid military road by which the missionaries travelled and along which troops of soldiers, officers of state with their retinues, foreign envoys and tributaries were going and coming—all this gave a powerful impression of the "kingdom and glory" of the great world-ruling city, to which a mind like St Paul's was peculiarly sensitive. He was himself a citizen of Rome, and by no means indifferent to his rights in this capacity; he held a high estimate of the prerogatives and functions of the civil power (Rom. xiii. 1—7). As the Apostle's travels extended and his work advanced, he became increasingly sensible of the critical relations that were coming into existence between Christianity and the Roman dominion and state-fabric; he recognized the powerful elements both of correspondence and of antagonism by which the two systems were associated.

What the Apostle now saw of the great kingdom of this world, prompted new and larger thoughts of that spiritual kingdom of which he was the herald and ambassador (cf. 1 Tim. ii. 7; 2 Tim. iv. 17; Acts ix. 15, xxiii. 11, xxvii. 23). He could not fail to discern under the majestic sway of Rome signs of moral degeneracy and prognostics of ruin. He remembered well that by the sentence of Pontius Pilate his Master had been crucified (1 Tim. vi. 13); in his own outrageous treatment by the Roman officials of Philippi, as in the sufferings that the Christian flock of Thessalonica endured from their $\sigma\upsilon\mu\phi\upsilon\lambda\acute{\epsilon}\tau\alpha\iota$ (I. ii. 14), there were omens of the conflict that was inevitable between secular tyranny and the authority of Christ. The charge made against himself and his fellow-believers, like that framed against our Lord before Pilate, put *Cæsar and Jesus* in formal antithesis (see p. xix., above; and notes on II. ii. 3—9, bearing upon the Cæsar-worship of the Provinces). At the bottom and in the ultimate verdict of history, the accusation was true; the struggle between Christianity and Cæsarism was to prove internecine. If the Apostles preached, as they could do without any denunciation of the powers that be, a universal, righteous and equal judgement of mankind approaching, in which Jesus, crucified by the Roman State, would be God's elected Judge; if they taught that "the fashion of this world passeth away" (1 Cor. vii. 31), and that the world's enmity to God would culminate one day in the rule of a universal despot aping Divinity, the master of Satanic imposture, whom the Lord will swiftly "consume by the breath of His mouth and the manifestation of His coming" (II. ii. 3—11), there were grounds plausible enough for accusing the preachers of treasonable doctrine, even though no overt political offence had been committed. The prophetic portrait too closely approached historic actuality. That such a judgement was reserved, in the near or farther future, for "the man of lawlessness" and his like, was "good news" for all good and honest men; but it was of fatal import to the imperialism of the Caligulas and Neros, and to much that was flourishing in the social and political order of which the deified Cæsars were the grand impersonation. In this far-reaching consequence lies the most significant and distinctive, though not the most obvious, feature of the Gospel of St Paul at Thessalonica.

In its more immediate bearing, it is manifest that the hope of Christ's return in glory was the consolation best suited to sustain the Church, as it sustained the Apostle himself, under the "great conflict of sufferings" through which both are passing.

(5) *The moral issues* of the Gospel inculcated by St Paul and his companions at Thessalonica, the new duties and affections belonging to the life of believers in Christ, are touched upon at many different points and brought out incidentally in a very natural and instructive way; but they are not developed with

the fulness and systematic method of subsequent Epistles. Most prominent here are the obligation to *chastity*, as belonging to the sanctity of the body and dictated by the indwelling of the Holy Spirit (I. iv. 1—8); and the claims of *brotherly love*, with the good order, the peace, and mutual helpfulness that flow from it (I. iv. 9f., v. 12—15; II. iii. 14f.). What is singular in these Epistles is the repeated and strong injunctions they contain on the subject of *diligence* in secular labour and in the common duties of life (I. iv. 10—12; II. iii. 6—15).

A striking moral feature of the Gospel taught in Thessalonica is manifest in *the conduct of the missionaries of Christ* themselves, —their incessant toil, their unbounded self-denial, the purity and devoutness of their spirit, and their fearless courage (I. i. 6f., ii. 1—12; II. iii. 7f.). Chiefly in order to spare expense to the Christian society, but partly also by way of example, they maintained themselves during this mission by manual labour (I. ii. 9; II. iii. 9).

CHAPTER IV.

THE ORIGIN AND OCCASION OF THE EPISTLES.

I. WHEN St Paul and his companions left Thessalonica, they counted upon it that the separation would last only "for the season of an hour," ἀπορφανισθέντες ἀφ' ὑμῶν πρὸς καιρὸν ὥρας (I. ii. 17 f.). The Apostle had laid his plans for a prolonged sojourn in this important centre, and greatly wished to have given his converts a more complete course of instruction (I. iii. 10). He had removed to Berœa, which lay 50 miles to the south-west, with the full intention of returning so soon as the storm blew over. But the Thessalonian Jews, instead of being appeased by his removal, pursued him, and he was compelled to quit the Province altogether (Acts xvii. 13 f.). Silas and Timothy were however able to remain in Berœa, while the Apostle sailed from the Macedonian coast to Athens. On landing at Athens, he appears to have sent enquiries again to Thessalonica to see if the way was open for his return, which received a discouraging reply; or Silas and Timothy, arriving from Berœa, brought unfavourable news from the other city; for he relates in I. ii. 18 that "we had resolved to come, both once and *twice*, but Satan hindered us"—a hindrance doubtless found in the malicious influence of the Jews, at whose instigation the Politarchs still kept "Jason and the rest" bound over to prevent Paul and Silas again disturbing the peace of the city. On the failure of this second attempt and now that the three missionaries are reunited at Athens (Acts xvii. 15), since their anxiety for the Thessalonians is so keen, the other two send Timothy thither (*his* presence had not been proscribed: see I. iii. 1—5), in order to comfort and strengthen the infant Church in its distress. Silas must afterwards have left St Paul's side also while he was still in Athens, possibly revisiting Philippi or Berœa, for we find "Silas and Timothy" a little later "coming down" together "from Macedonia" to rejoin their leader at Corinth (Acts xviii. 5). It seems that some members of the Thessalonian Church, listening perhaps to malignant insinuations and not appreciating St Paul's consideration for "Jason and the rest" who would have suffered if he and Silas returned to the forbidden city, had complained of the Apostle's failure to keep his promise; he dwells on this failure at such length and so earnestly in 1 Thess. ii. and iii., that one feels sure there was a very definite reason for the exculpation.

St Paul soon left Athens, which he found a sterile soil for his Gospel, and he had been but a short time in Corinth (for he was still preaching in the Synagogue: Acts xviii. 4—6) when Timothy in company with Silvanus reached him. The report he brought was a veritable $εὐαγγέλιον$ to the much-tried Apostle, who had entered on his mission at Corinth under an unusual dejection of mind (cf. 1 Cor. ii. 3). He was relieved and cheered; the encouragement gave new life to his present work (cf. Acts xviii. 5 and 1 Thess. iii. 8). The Thessalonians are "standing fast in the Lord"; they "long to see" him as much as he does to see them (I. iii. 6). They continue to be "imitators of the Lord" and of His Apostles, following steadily the path on which they had so worthily set out (I. i. 5 ff.). Their faith has stood without flinching the test of prolonged persecution. By their activity and courage, and their exemplary Christian love, they have commended the Gospel with telling effect throughout Macedonia and Achaia (I. i. 7 ff., iv. 10 f.). The expectations the Apostles had formed of them have been even surpassed; they know not how to thank God sufficiently "for all the joy wherewith" they "rejoice before Him" on this account (I. iii. 9). The New Testament contains nowhere a more glowing or unqualified commendation than that bestowed on the character and behaviour of the Thessalonian Church at this time.

What Paul and Silas have heard from their assistant increases their longing to see the Thessalonians again; for if their anxiety is relieved, their love to this people is greatly quickened, and they "are praying night and day with intense desire" that the obstacle to their return may be removed (I. iii. 10). Indeed St Paul's primary object in writing the First Epistle is *to express his eager wish to revisit Thessalonica*. This purpose dominates the first half of the Letter (chh. i.—iii.). Associated with this desire, there are two aims that actuate him in writing. In the first place, the Apostle wishes *to explain his continued absence* as being involuntary and enforced, and in doing so *to justify himself from aspersions* which had reached his readers' ears. Ch. ii. 1—12 is a brief *apologia*. We gather from it that the enemies of Christianity in Thessalonica (*Jewish* enemies[1], as the denunciation of *vv.* 14—16, together with the probabilities of the situation, strongly suggests) had made use of the absence of the missionaries to slander them, insinuating doubts of their courage (I. ii. 2), of their disinterestedness and honesty (*vv.* 3, 6, 9), and of their real affection for their Thessalonian converts (*vv.* 7 f., 11 f.). The slanderers said, "These so-called apostles of Christ are self-seeking adventurers. Their real object is to make themselves a reputation and to fill their purse at your expense[2]. They have beguiled you by their flatteries and pre-

[1] The opponents whom St Paul denounces in I. ii. 15 f. are unconverted Jews, altogether hostile to the Gospel he preaches. The Jews of Thessalonica, after driving him from their own city, followed him to Berœa and attacked him there; their compatriots at Corinth imitated their example, though fortunately not with the same success (Acts xvii. 5, 13, xviii. 12—17). Of the Jewish Christians opposed to the Apostle's Gentile mission, the "false brethren" who afterwards troubled him at Corinth and in Galatia, we find no trace whatever in these Epistles. They were written in the interval between the first rise of the legalist controversy, composed by the Council of Jerusalem (Acts xv; Gal. ii. 1—10), and its second outbreak some years later. To this renewed crisis probably the contention of St Paul with St Peter, as well as the four Epistles of the Second Group, belongs. See A. Sabatier's *The Apostle Paul*, pp. 10 f.; also the writer's *Epistles of Paul*, pp. 61—64, and the article in Hastings' *Dict. of the Bible* on 'Paul,' I. 4 (*a*).

[2] One is at a loss to think what can have given any handle to the reproach of πλεονεξία, unless it were that St Paul had during his stay at Thessalonica on two occasions received contributions of some kind from Philippi (Phil. iv. 15).

tence of sanctity (*vv.* 4 f., 10) into accepting their new-fangled faith; and now that trouble has arisen and their mischievous doctrines bring them into danger, they creep away like cowards, leaving you to bear the brunt of persecution alone. And, likely enough, you will never see them again!" Chapter ii. is a reply to innuendoes of this kind, which are such as unscrupulous Jewish opponents were sure to make. Timothy reported these charges floating about in Thessalonian society; perhaps the Church, while earnestly disowning them, had made in writing some allusion to the taunts levelled at its Apostles, which rendered it still more necessary that they should be confronted[1]. Considering the short time that Paul and Silas had been in this city, and the influence which the Synagogue-leaders had formerly possessed over many members of their flock, considering also the disheartening effect of continued persecution upon a young and unseasoned Church, one cannot wonder at the danger felt lest its confidence in the absent missionaries should be undermined. Happily that confidence had not been shaken,—"You have good remembrance of us at all times" (I. iii. 6): so Timothy had assured the Apostle; so, it may be, their own letter now testifies for the Thessalonians. Yet it is well that everything should be said that may be to repel these poisonous suspicions.

In the second place, and looking onward to the future, the Apostles write in order *to carry forward the instruction of their converts in Christian doctrine and life*—καταρτίσαι τὰ ὑστερήματα τῆς πίστεως ὑμῶν (I. iii. 10). With this further aim the First Epistle is extended to chh. iv. and v. (Λοιπὸν οὖν, ἀδελφοί, iv. 1), when in its first intention it had been already rounded off by the concluding prayer of iii. 11—13. In passing westward from Asia Minor into Europe, St Paul's mission has entered upon a new stage. He is no longer able quickly to visit his Churches, now numerous and widely separated, and to exercise amongst them a direct oversight. The defect of his presence he must supply

---

[1] On the probability that the Thessalonian Church *had written a letter* to St Paul, to which he is replying in 1 Thessalonians, see J. Rendel Harris, "A Study in Letter-writing," *Expositor*, V. VIII., pp. 161—180.

INTRODUCTION.

by messenger and letter. Moreover, he may have found in the case of the Macedonian, as afterwards in that of the Corinthian Church (see 1 Cor. vii. 1, &c.; cf. Phil. iv. 15; also 1 Thess. iv. 9, v. 1—passages which almost suggest that the Thessalonians had *asked* the Apostles to write to them if they could not come), that the Greek Christian communities were apt for intercourse of this sort and took pleasure in writing and being written to. Anyhow, these (with the possible exception of the Epistle of James) are the earliest extant N.T. Letters; and when the writers describe themselves as "longing to see you and to complete the deficiencies of your faith," we perceive how such Epistles became necessary and to what conditions we owe their existence. The Apostle Paul found in epistolary communication a form of expression suited to his genius and an instrument that added to his power (see 2 Cor. x. 9 ff.), while it extended the range and sustained the efficacy of his pastoral ministry.

The ὑστερήματα which had to be supplemented in the faith of this Church, were chiefly of a practical nature. (1) On the moral side, St Paul emphasizes the virtue of *chastity*, notoriously lacking in Greek city-life, in respect of which the former notions of Gentile converts had commonly been very lax; and *brotherly love*, with which, in the case of this Church, the duty of *quiet and diligent labour* was closely associated (iv. 1—12). (2) On the doctrinal side, a painful misunderstanding had arisen, which Timothy had not been able to remove, touching *the relation of departed Christians to Christ on His return*; and there was in regard to the Last Things a restlessness of mind and an over-curiosity unfavourable to a sober and steadfast Christian life (iv. 13—v. 11). (3) With this we may connect symptoms of *indiscipline* in one party, and of *contempt for extraordinary and emotional spiritual manifestations* in another, which the closing verses of the Epistle indicate (v. 12—22). These latter contrasted indications resemble the antagonisms which took a more pronounced and reprehensible form in the Corinthian Church some six years later.

II. After writing their First Epistle, "Paul and Silvanus and Timotheus" received further tidings from Thessalonica (by what

TOPICS OF THE SECOND EPISTLE. xxxvii

channel we know not) which moved them to write a *Second.* The Second is a supplement or continuation, and in many of its phrases almost an echo, of the First. (The relations of the two will be discussed more narrowly in the next chapter.) The freshness of colouring and liveliness of personal feeling which characterize the former Epistle, are comparatively wanting in this. We gather from the opening Act of Thanksgiving that the storm of persecution is still more violent and the fidelity of the Church even more conspicuous than when the Apostles wrote some months before: "Your faith grows exceedingly, and your love multiplies. We make our boast in you among the churches of God, because of your faith and endurance in persecution" (i. 3 f.). St Paul says nothing further, however, of his intention to return; his hands are by this time tied fast at Corinth (Acts xviii. 5—18), and his thoughts preoccupied by the exacting demands of his work in this new sphere: he commends them to "the Lord, who will stablish them and keep them from the Evil One" (iii. 3—5). Nor does he enter on any further defence, nor indulge in renewed reminiscences, of his conduct toward the Thessalonians and his experiences amongst them. It is almost entirely the latter (chh. iv., v.) and not the earlier part (chh. i.—iii.) of 1 Thessalonians that is reflected in 2 Thessalonians.

There are two topics of the former Epistle to which it is necessary to advert again; on these the writers find that they must be more explicit and more urgent than before. First and chiefly, *about the Second Advent*—ὑπὲρ τῆς παρουσίας τοῦ κυρίου ἡμῶν Ἰησοῦ Χριστοῦ καὶ ἡμῶν ἐπισυναγωγῆς ἐπ' αὐτόν (ii. 1). A rumour is abroad, claiming prophetic origin and alleged to be authenticated by the founders of the Church, to the effect that "the day of the Lord has arrived" and He must be looked for immediately (*v.* 2). The report is pronounced a deception (*v.* 3). St Paul states reasons, partly recalled from his oral teaching, why so speedy a consummation is impossible. This gives occasion to his memorable prediction of the advent of ὁ ἄνθρωπος τῆς ἀνομίας, whose appearance and rise to supreme power will give, he predicts, the signal for Christ's return in glory (*vv.* 3—12). This prophecy is the one great difficulty which meets the student of these Epistles, and is amongst the most mysterious passages in the Bible. It will be dealt with at length in the *Notes*, and further in the *Appendix* to this volume.

The other object the Apostles have in writing this Letter is *to reprove the disorderly fraction of the Church* (ch. iii. 6—15). The First Epistle intimated the existence of a tendency to idleness and consequent insubordination (I. iv. 11 f., v. 12—14), to which reference was there made in a few words of kindly and guarded censure. This gentle reproof failed to check the evil, which had become aggravated and persistent, endangering the peace of the whole Church. It was connected, presumably, with the excitement on the subject of Christ's advent. This expectation furnished an excuse for neglecting ordinary labour, or even an incentive to such neglect. The Apostles take the offenders severely to task, and direct the brethren to refuse support to such as persist in idleness and to avoid their company. This discipline, it is hoped, will bring about their amendment.

That this Letter is the *second* of the two, and not the first (as Grotius, Ewald, F. C. Baur, and some others, have contended), is apparent from the course of affairs and the internal relationship of the two documents, as we have just examined them. 2 Thessalonians, whoever wrote it, presupposes and builds upon 1 Thessalonians. It deals more fully and explicitly with two principal points raised in the former Letter, as they present themselves in their further development. Certain disturbing influences, which had begun to make themselves felt when Timothy left Thessalonica bringing the news that elicited the former Epistle, have by this time reached their crisis. The thanksgiving of II. i. 3—12 implies an advance both in the severity of persecution and in the growth and testing of Thessalonian faith; for which faith acknowledgement is made to God in terms even stronger than before. The personal recollections and explanations, which form so interesting a feature of the other Epistle, are suited to St Paul's *first* communication of the kind with this beloved Church. The absence of such references in the shorter Epistle marks it as a supplement to the other, following this after a brief interval. The expression of ch. ii. 2, "neither through word nor *through letter*, as on our authority" (ὡς δι' ἡμῶν), is most naturally explained as alluding to some misunderstanding or misquotation (see Expository Note) of the language of 1 Thessalonians on the subject of the Parousia.

The two Epistles were written, as we have seen, *from Corinth;* not "from Athens," as it is stated in the "subscription" attached to each of them in the MSS. followed by the Authorized English Version: Πρὸς Θεσσαλονικεῖς...ἐγράφη ἀπὸ 'Αθηνῶν. They were both composed during St Paul's residence of eighteen months in Corinth (Acts xviii. 11), extending perhaps from Autumn 51 to Spring 53, A.D. They belong, therefore, as nearly as we can judge, to *the winter of* 51—52, A.D., in the eleventh or twelfth year of the Emperor Claudius; being twenty-one years after our Lord's Ascension, two years after the Council at Jerusalem, five years before the Epistle to the Romans, fifteen years, probably, before the death of St Paul, and nineteen years before the Fall of Jerusalem.

NOTE ON THE PLURAL AUTHORSHIP.

The question of the use of the *pluralis auctoris* in St Paul's Letters is one of considerable difficulty; no summary answer can be given to it. It is exhaustively discussed in the Essay of Karl Dick (Halle, 1890), entitled *Der schriftstellerische Plural bei Paulus*, who comes to the conclusion that the authorial "we" (for a singular *ego*) was a recognized usage of later Greek, and may therefore be looked for in St Paul; that one cannot without violence or over-subtlety force upon the *we* a uniformly multiple significance; that St Paul's use of the first person plural is not stereotyped and conventional, and must be interpreted according to circumstances in each case; that the context frequently indicates a real plurality in his mind—and this with various nuances of reference and kinds of inclusion; and that the inclusive (or

INTRODUCTION.

collective) and the courteous "we" shade off into each other, making it impossible to draw a hard and fast line between them. In the Thessalonian Epistles one would suppose the plural of the first person to have its maximum force. Three writers present themselves in the Address, who had been companions in their intercourse with the readers; and while the third of the trio was a junior, the second had an authority and importance approximating to that of the first. Παῦλος καὶ Σιλουανός stood side by side in the eyes of the Thessalonian Church (cf. Acts xvi., xvii.); and nothing occurs in the course of either Epistle to suggest that one of the two alone is really responsible for what is written. In other instances of a *prima facie* joint authorship (viz. 1 and 2 Corinthians, Galatians, Colossians, Philippians), there existed no such close associations of the persons appearing in the Address, and no such continuous use of the plural is found, as we recognize here. The two Letters give utterance, for the most part, to the recollections, explanations, and wishes of *the missionaries and pastors of the Thessalonian Church as such*; and their matter was therefore equally appropriate to Paul and Silas, if not to their attendant Timothy in the same degree. The distinction between μηκέτι στέγοντες κ.τ.λ. and ἐγὼ μηκέτι στέγων κ.τ.λ., in I. iii. 1 and 5 (see Expository Notes), can hardly be explained without assuming *Paul and Silas* to be intended in the former instance; and if so, then in the general tenor of the Epistle. Against the prevailing ἡμεῖς, the ἐγὼ μὲν Παῦλος of I. iii. 18, and the τῇ ἐμῇ χειρί Παύλου of II. iii. 17, stand out in relief; with less emphasis, the first singular of II. ii. 5 betrays the individuality of the leading author, as it recalls doctrine of a pronounced individual stamp; and the ἐνορκίζω ὑμᾶς τὸν κύριον κ.τ.λ. of I. v. 27 is the outburst of strong personal feeling.

The master spirit of St Paul and his emotional idiosyncrasy have impressed themselves on the First Epistle, of which we cannot doubt that he was, in point of composition, the single author, though conscious of expressing and seeking to express the mind of his companions, and more particularly of Silas, throughout. In the less original paragraphs of the Second

THE PLURAL AUTHORSHIP   xli

Epistle, there may be some reason for conjecturing (see the next chapter) that one of the other two—Silas more probably than Timothy—indited the actual words, while St Paul supervised, and endorsed the whole with his signature.

In the exposition the plural authorship will be assumed, accordingly, to embrace St Paul's companions—one or both.

CHAPTER V.

THE AUTHORSHIP OF THE EPISTLES.

THAT these Letters were written by the author whose name heads the Address of each, was doubted by no one until the beginning of the last century. The testimony of the Early Church to their antiquity, and to the tradition of Pauline authorship, is full and unbroken; it is even more precise and emphatic in the case of the Second Epistle than in that of the First. See the catena of references given by Bornemann in the *Kritisch-exegetischer Kommentar*, pp. 319 f. 2 Thessalonians was used by Polycarp (*ad Philipp.* xi. 4) and by Justin Martyr (*Dial.* xxxii., cx.),—in iii. 15 and ii. 3 ff. respectively; Justin's references touch its most peculiar and disputed paragraph. There are passages moreover in the *Epistle of Barnabas* (iv. 9, xviii. 2), and in the *Didaché XII. Apostolorum* (v. 2, xii. 3, xvi. 3—7), in which the ideas and imagery of this Epistle seem to be echoed.

The German writer Christian Schmidt first raised doubts respecting 2 Thessalonians in the year 1801, and Schrader respecting 1 Thessalonians in 1836. Kern, in the Tübingen *Zeitschrift für Theologie* (1837), and de Wette in the earlier editions of his *Exegetisches Handbuch des N. T.* (retracting his adverse judgement in the later editions), developed the critical objections against the Second Epistle. F. C. Baur, the founder of the 'Tendency' School of N. T. Criticism, restated the case against the traditional authorship of both Epistles, giving to it extensive currency through his influential work on "Paul the Apostle of Jesus Christ" (1845: Eng. Trans., 1873). Baur supposed the two Letters to have been written about the year 70, the "Second"

1 THESSALONIANS A HOMOLOGUMENON. xliii

earlier than the "First,"—by some disciple of St Paul with the Apocalypse of St John in his hand, wishing to excite renewed interest in the Parousia amongst Pauline Christians, in whose minds the delay had by this time bred distrust.

In their rejection of 1 Thessalonians Schrader and Baur have remained almost alone; Holsten and Steck in Germany, van der Vies, Pierson-Naber, and van Manen[1] in Holland, are the only names of note amongst their supporters. Along with Philippians, 1 Thessalonians may be added to 1 and 2 Corinthians, Romans, and Galatians, as counting for all practical purposes amongst the undisputed Epistles of St Paul. Not only Lightfoot, Ramsay, Bornemann, Zahn, Moffatt, but critics who are most sceptical about other documents—such as Hilgenfeld, Weizsäcker, Holtzmann, Pfleiderer, Jülicher, Schmiedel—pronounce this Letter to be unmistakably St Paul's.

I. The internal evidence for the authorship of 1 THESSALONIANS is such as to disarm suspicion.

(1) *The picture the Apostle Paul gives of himself* and of his relations to the Church in chh. i.—iii. is a delicate piece of self-portraiture; it bears the marks of circumstantial truth and unaffected feeling; it harmonizes with what we learn of St Paul and his companions from other sources (see the Expository Notes for details); and it is free from anything that suggests imitation, or interpolation, by another hand. *Nemo potest Paulinum pectus effingere* (Erasmus).

(2) The same air of reality belongs to *the aspect of the Thessalonian Church*, as it here comes into view. It exhibits the freshness, the fervour and impulsive energy of a newborn faith, with much of the indiscipline and excitability that often attend the first steps of the Christian life, so full at once of joy and of peril. The Church of Thessalonica has a character distinctly its own. It resembles the Philippian Church in the frankness, the courage, and the personal devotion to the Apostle, which so greatly won his love; also in the simplicity and thoroughness of

---

[1] See the article of the last-named on "Paul" in the *Encyclopædia Biblica*.

its faith, which was untroubled by the speculative questions and tendencies to intellectual error that beset the Corinthian and Asian Churches. These traits agree with what we know of the Macedonian temperament. At the same time there was at Thessalonica a disposition to run into morbid excitement and an unpractical enthusiasm, that we do not find in any other of the communities addressed in the Pauline Epistles.

(3) *The absence of* any allusion to *Church organization* and to the existence of *a specialized ministry*, beyond the general category of the officers who are spoken of in I. v. 12—14, points to a simple and elementary condition of Church-life. This remark applies to both documents; and the Thessalonian are parallel to the Corinthian Epistles in this respect. Both at Thessalonica and Corinth difficult points of discipline had arisen, which would surely have involved reference to the responsible officers of the community, had these possessed the established status and well-defined powers which accrued to them in early Post-apostolic times.

(4) The attitude of the writers toward *the Parousia* is such as no disciple or imitator, writing in St Paul's name, could possibly have ascribed to him after his death. He is made to write as though Christ were expected to come within his own lifetime: "we the living, we who survive until the coming of the Lord," I. iv. 15, 17. Taken in their plain sense, these words at least leave it an open question whether the Lord would not return while the writers and their readers yet lived. That a later author, wishing to use the Apostle's authority for his own purposes, should have ascribed such words to his master is hardly conceivable. In doing this he would be discrediting the very authority on which he builds; for by this time *St Paul had died, and Christ had not returned.*

(5) Observe the manner in which the writer speaks in the passage just referred to of "those falling asleep" (οἱ κοιμώμενοι: see Expository Note upon the tense), in such a way as to show that the question concerning the fate of believers dying before the Lord's return is a *new* one, that has arisen in the Thessalonian Church for the first time. This being the case, the Letter

DOUBTS RESPECTING 2 THESSALONIANS. xlv

can only have been written within a few months of this Church's birth. For it is never long in any community, of size beyond the smallest, before death has made its mark.

II. The suspicions against the authenticity of 2 THESSALONIANS are more persistent; they are not so ill-founded as in the case of the First Epistle. Baur maintained that the two Letters are of the same mint, and that both must be regarded as spurious or both authentic; his followers have generally separated them, regarding the Second as a reproduction of the First dating about twenty years later and addressed to an altered situation, composed by way partly of imitation and partly of qualification and correction of 1 Thessalonians (see pp. xxxvii. ff.). H. J. Holtzmann, however, the most eminent of Baur's successors, admits in the last edition of his *Einleitung*[3] (p. 216) that "the question is no longer as to whether the Epistle should be pushed down into the Post-apostolic age, but whether, on the other hand, it does not actually reach back to the lifetime of the Apostle, in which case it is consequently genuine and must have been written soon after 1 Thessalonians, about the year 54."

Jülicher, a pupil of the same school, concludes his examination by saying (*Einleitung*[1], p. 44), "If one is content to make fair and reasonable claims on a Pauline Epistle, no occasion will be found to ascribe 2 Thessalonians to an author less original or of less powerful mind than Paul himself." Harnack and Moffatt (*Introd. to Liter. of N. T.*) decide for authenticity. Bahnsen (in the *Jahrbuch für prot. Theologie*, 1880, pp. 696 ff.) advanced a theory which identified ὁ ἀντικείμενος and ὁ ἄνθρωπος τῆς ἀνομίας with the antinomian and libertine Gnosticism of the period of Trajan (about 110 A.D.); he saw τὸ κατέχον in the rising Episcopate of that epoch. Bahnsen had been anticipated by Hilgenfeld, in his *Einleitung*, pp. 642 ff. (1875), and was followed by Hase (*Lehrbuch d. Kirchengeschichte*, I. p. 69) and Pfleiderer (*Urchristenthum*, pp. 78, 356 ff.); but this far-fetched and artificial construction has found few other adherents. The opinion prevalent amongst those who contest the Pauline authorship (so Kern, in the work above specified; Schmiedel, in the *Handcommentar;* Holtzmann's *Einleitung,* and article in the *Zeitschrift für N. T. Wissenschaft,* 1901, pp. 97—108) is that 2 Thessalonians dates from the juncture between the assassination of the emperor Nero in June 68 A.D. and the fall of Jerusalem in August 70 (cf. Expository Note on II. ii. 4) and is contemporary with and closely parallel to Rev. xiii., xvii., and that by ὁ ἀντικείμενος and ὁ ἄνθρωπος τῆς ἀνομίας is meant *the dead Nero,* who was then and for long afterwards supposed by many to be living concealed in the East, the fear of his return to power adding a further element of horror to the confusion of the time (cf. pp. 222 f. in the Appendix). The readers of the first century, had they suspected the *Nero redivivus* in the Antichrist of ch. ii. 3 f., would hardly have given unquestioning circulation to a prediction that had thus missed its mark, and whose supposititious character a little enquiry would have enabled them to detect.

The above theory brings the origin of the document to within a very few years (or even months) of the Apostle's death. Now the Apostle Paul had not spent his days in some corner of the Church, amongst a narrow circle of disciples; no Christian leader was known so widely, none at that time had so many personal followers surviving, so many intimate and well-informed friends and acquaintances interested in his work and his utterances, as the martyr Apostle of the Gentiles. There is a strong antecedent presumption against the possibility of any writing otherwise than genuine finding currency under St Paul's name at this early date, especially one containing a prediction that stands isolated in Pauline teaching and that proved itself (*ex hypothesi*) completely mistaken. Were it conceivable that a composition of this nature, invented throughout or in its principal passages, could have been accepted in the second century, that it should have been palmed upon the Thessalonian Church within six years of St Paul's death—for this is what we are asked to believe, on the assumption of non-authenticity—is a thing incredible in no ordinary degree. **Wrede,** the latest opponent of the traditional view, admits the fictitious authorship to be incompatible with the date 68—70 (see his pamphlet, *Die Echtheit des zweiten Thessalonicher-briefes,* pp. 36—40).

DEFENCE OF PAULINE AUTHORSHIP. xlvii

The nearer this Epistle is brought to St Paul's lifetime, the more improbable and gratuitous becomes the theory of spurious authorship. Moreover, the language of ch. ii. 2 and of iii. 17 makes an explicit protest against literary personation—a protest which at least implies some measure of conscience and of critical jealousy on such points in early Christian times. Professing in his first word to be "Paul" and identifying himself in ii. 15 with the author of the first Epistle, the writer warns his correspondents against this very danger; to impute the Letter to some well-meaning successor, writing as though he were Paul in the Apostle's vein and by way of supplement to his teaching, is to charge the writer with the offence which he expressly condemns. The Epistle is no innocent pseudepigraph. It proceeds either from "Paul and Silvanus and Timotheus," or from someone who wished to be taken for these authors and who attempts to cover his deception by denouncing it! Schmiedel's apology for this "abgefeimten Betrüger" (*Handcommentar zum N. T.*, II. i., p. 12) is more cynical than successful.

The fact is that no real trace of the Nero-legend is discoverable in 2 Thessalonians (see Weiss' *Apocalyptische Studien*, 2, in *Studien und Kritiken*, 1869); this groundless speculation of Kern and Baur should be dismissed from criticism. As Klöpper says in his able defence of the authenticity (Essay on 2 Thessalonians in the *Theolog. Studien aus Ostpreussen*, 1889, Heft 8, p. 128): "Nothing has done more to confuse the situation than the idea that the author of our Epistle could not have conceived and propounded his prophecy, in the form which it assumes, without having before his eyes by way of historical presupposition the person of Nero, or (to speak more precisely) the figure of *Nero redivivus* as this is incorporated in the Johannine Apocalypse." Granting that the traits of the personality of the emperor Nero have left their mark on the Apocalypse of St John, they are not to be found here. 2 Thessalonians belongs to pre-Neronian Apocalyptic, and falls therefore within the period of St Paul's actual career. The true historical position is that of Spitta (*Urchristenthum*, I. p. 135 ff.; similarly von Hofmann in his Commentary, Klöpper in the Essay cited above, Th. Zahn in his *Einleitung*), viz. that in ὁ ἄνομος of ch. ii. the image of Antiochus Epiphanes idealized in the Book of Daniel, and of Gaius Caligula as known to St Paul, have been "smelted together" (see Appendix, pp. 217—222), and that the emperor Gaius represented to the writers the furthest development which "the mystery of lawlessness" in its continuous "working" had attained up to their time. Spitta's hypothesis, propounded in the first volume of his valuable Essays *Zur Geschichte und Litteratur des Urchristenthums* (1893), pp. 109—154, proceeds upon the datum just stated. He conceives the real author of 2 Thessalonians to have been *Timothy*, writing by St Paul's side at Corinth under the Apostle's suggestion and in his name, but writing out of his own mind and as the member of the missionary band who had been most recently present and teaching in Thessalonica. Spitta thus seeks to account both for the singular *resemblance* of the Second Epistle to the First, and for its singular *difference* therefrom. (1) Under the former head, it is observed that, outside of ii. 2—12, there are but nine verses in 2nd which do not reflect the language and ideas of 1 Thessalonians. In its whole conception as well as in vocabulary and phrasing, apart from the peculiar eschatological passages, the later Epistle is an echo of the earlier; the spontaneity and freshness that one expects to find in the Apostle's work are wanting; indeed it is said that St Paul, had he wished to do so, could not have repeated himself thus closely without reading his former Letter for the purpose. Such imitation, it is argued, would be natural enough in Timothy with the First Epistle before him for a model, when writing to the same Church shortly afterwards on his master's behalf and in their joint name. Amid this sameness of expression we miss the geniality and lively play of feeling, the *Paulinum pectus*, which glows in the First Epistle and which vindicates it so strongly for the Apostle. The tone is more cool and official throughout. There is a measured, almost laboured and halting, turn of language, which (it is said) betrays the absence of the master mind and the larger part played by the secretary—presumably Timothy—in the composition of this Letter. In comparing II. i. 3—7, ii. 13 f., with I. i. 2—5, iii. 9 f.; II. i. 10—

CONTRAST BETWEEN THE TWO EPISTLES. xlix

12 with I. ii. 19 f., iii. 11 ff.; II. iii. 7 ff. with I. ii. 7 ff., one cannot escape the impression of a certain blunting of St Paul's incisive touch and a weakening of his firm grasp in passing from one Letter to the other. Wrede (*op. cit.*) finds in this effacement of style the chief reason for denying the Pauline authorship; he regards the Second Epistle as a carefully adapted imitation of certain sections of the First.

Bornemann accounts for the contrast thus described by pointing out that by the date of the Second Epistle St Paul was immersed in Corinthian affairs, and that his heart was no longer away at Thessalonica as when he first wrote; moreover, the intense and critical experience out of which the First Epistle sprang had stamped itself deeply on the soul of the Apostle, so that in writing again, after a brief interval, to a Church whose condition gave no new turn to his reflexions, the former train of thought and expression recurred more or less unconsciously and the Second Letter became to a certain extent a rehearsal of the First. To this explanation may be added two considerations: (1) That the occasion of this supplement, viz. the continuance of the unwholesome excitement about the Parousia and of the disorder touched upon in I. iv. 10 ff., v. 14, involved a measure of surprise and disappointment, which inevitably chilled the writer's cordiality and made the emphasis of affection and the *empressement* of the First Epistle impossible in this. Galatians, with 1 or 2 Corinthians, exhibits fluctuations of feeling within the same Letter not unlike that which distinguishes the two Epistles to the Thessalonians. (2) The visions rising before the Apostle's mind in II. i. 5—10, ii. 2—12, were of a nature to throw the writer into the mood of solemn contemplation rather than of familiar intercourse.

When all has been said, the suspicion remains, strengthened by renewed and closer comparison of the parallel verses of the two Epistles, that some other hand beside St Paul's had to do with the penning of 2 Thessalonians. Since *three* writers address the Thessalonians (cf. pp. xxxix—xlii), and the matter-of-fact plurality of the prevailing "we" on their part is vouched for by the passages in which the chief author speaks for himself as "I" or

INTRODUCTION.

"I, Paul" (I. ii. 18, iii. 5, II. ii. 5, iii. 17), it is a possibility conceivable under the circumstances and consistent with the primary authorship on St Paul's part, that one of his companions —preferably *Silvanus*, as the coadjutor of the Apostle—was the actual composer of the large portion of 2 Thessalonians which traverses the ground of 1 Thessalonians, and in which the language is moulded on that of the earlier Letter with added touches of a more prolix style. Silas was an inspired "prophet" (Acts xv. 32; cf. 1 Pet. v. 12).

When Spitta comes to the original part of 2 Thessalonians— ch. ii. 1—12 (the signs premonitory of the Day of the Lord) and iii. 6—15 (the excommunication of idlers)—his theory breaks down. He sees in ii. 5 a reminder of *Timothy's* teaching at Thessalonica, supposing that St Paul's young helper had views about the Last Things more definite in some respects, and more Jewish in their colouring, than those of his leader who had spoken of the coming of "the day" as altogether indeterminate in time (see I. v. 1 f.). He suggests that Timothy had adopted some *Jewish* apocalypse of Caligula's time (he was conversant with "sacred writings," 2 Tim. iii. 15,—an expression possibly including non-canonical books; and 2 Thessalonians, though quotations are wanting in it, is steeped in O. T. language beyond other Pauline Epistles); and that he gave to this a Christian turn, shaping it into his prophecy of "the mystery of iniquity," which lies outside St Paul's doctrine and is nowhere else hinted at in his Epistles. But considering the chasm separating the Pauline mission from Judaism, it is improbable that either Timothy should have borrowed, or St Paul endorsed, a non-Christian apocalypse; granted that the conception of *vv.* 3—5 goes back to the epoch of Caligula, there is no reason why it should not have originated either in St Paul's mind, since by the year 40 he was already a Christian, or amongst the numerous "prophets and teachers" at Jerusalem and Antioch between 40 and 50 A.D. Caligula's outrage on the Temple[1] was a sign of the times that could hardly fail to stir the prophetic spirit in the Church, while it roused the passionate anger of the Jewish people.

[1] 40—41 A.D.

ANTICHRIST IN CHRISTIAN APOCALYPTIC. li

The expressions of 2 Thess. ii. 5—7 suggest that ὁ ἄνθρωπος τῆς ἀνομίας was no new figure to Christian imagination; his image, based on the Antiochus-Caligula pattern, had become a familiar object in Christian circles before the Apostles preached in Thessalonica. Jewish Apocalyptic had produced from its own soil, it seems likely, representations parallel to that of ὁ ἀντικείμενος in the 2nd Thessalonian Epistle and of not dissimilar features: so much may be granted to Spitta's theory. The fact that "Antichrist" does not appear in his subsequent Epistles, does not prove that St Paul at no time held the doctrine attaching thereto, nor even that he ceased to hold it at a later time. The circumstances calling for its inculcation at Thessalonica were peculiar to the place and occasion. In later Epistles, from 2 Corinthians v. onwards, the Parousia recedes to a distant future, and a glorious intervening prospect opens out for humanity in Romans xi.; but this enlargement of view in no way forbids the thought of such a finale to human history and such a consummate revelation of Satanic power preceding the coming of the Lord in judgement, as this Epistle predicts. Our Lord's recorded prophecies of the end of the world cannot be understood without the anticipation of a last deadly struggle of this nature.

Chap. ii. 1—12 supplies the crucial test to every hypothesis of the origin of 2 Thessalonians. Timothy being the last of the trio whose names figure in the Address and quite the subordinate member of the party (see I. iii. 2; Acts xvi. 2 f.; 1 Tim. i. 2, &c.), had this young assistant written *v.* 5 *propria persona*, he would have been bound to mark the distinction—by inserting ἐγὼ Τιμόθεος or the like (cf. I. ii. 18)—the more so since this Letter expressly purports to come from the Apostle Paul himself (iii. 17). The whole deliverance is marked by a loftiness of imagination, an assurance and dignity of manner, and a concise vigour of style, that one cannot well associate with the position and the known qualities of Timothy. Whatever may be said of other parts of the Letter, this its unique paragraph and veritable kernel comes from no second-hand or second-rate composer of the Pauline school, but from the fountain-head.

INTRODUCTION.

The other original section of the Epistle, ch. iii. 6—15 (where, however, echoes of Epistle I. are not wanting), speaks with the decision and tone of authority characteristic of St Paul in disciplinary matters. The readers could never have presumed that a charge so peremptory proceeded from the third and least important of the three missionaries ostensibly writing to them, that "we" throughout the passage meant in reality Timothy alone, and that St Paul, who immediately afterwards puts his signature to the document, had allowed his assistant to give orders—and to advance eschatological speculations—which did not in reality issue from himself.

The alleged discrepancies between the two Epistles present no very serious difficulty. It is true that 1 Thessalonians seems to represent the Parousia as *near and sudden*, 2 Thessalonians as *more distant and known by premonitory signs*. But the latter is written on purpose to qualify the former and to correct an erroneous inference that might be drawn from it (II. ii. 2: see Expository Note); this being the case, a *prima facie* disagreement on the point is only to be expected. The premonitory sign afforded by the coming of Antichrist shows that the end, though it may be near, is not immediate. On the other hand, no date is given for the appearing of Antichrist, so that "the times and seasons" remain uncertain after the 2nd Epistle as before it; it is still true that "the day of the Lord comes as a thief in the night," though the first alarm of the thief's coming has been particularly described. The like contrast, easily exaggerated into discrepancy, is found in our Lord's predictions recorded in St Matthew: on the one hand, uncertainty of date (ch. xxiv. 36); on the other, a premonitory sign for the faithful (*v.* 33).

There is not even the appearance of contradiction between the reason given in II. iii. 9 and that stated in I. ii. 9 (as elsewhere—Acts xx. 34; 1 Cor. ix. 15—19; 2 Cor. xi. 7 ff.) for *the practice of manual labour* on the part of the missionaries. To save expense to his converts was always an object of importance with St Paul; at Thessalonica another necessary end was served by this policy, viz. to set an example of hard work and independence. In Acts xx. 33—35 the second of these motives is

THEORIES OF INTERPOLATION.   liii

again hinted at, though with a somewhat different application, along with the first; later, in 2 Cor. xi. 12, St Paul discloses a third motive for this self-denying rule. There are minor differences of expression distinguishing the two Letters—such as the reference to "the Lord" (Christ) in a series of expressions of the 2nd Epistle, where "God" appears in the parallel sentences of the 1st Epistle; but each of St Paul's Epistles has idiosyncrasies due to passing circumstances or moods of thought too fine for us to trace; the variations of this kind here occurring are, in consideration of the pervasive resemblance of the two documents, of a nature altogether too slight for one to build any distinction of authorship upon them.

Outside ch. ii. 1—12 there is nothing to lend colour to the notion of a post-Pauline origin for the Second Epistle; and there is nothing in that central passage that can with plausibility be set down as later than 70 A.D. The directions given for the treatment of the "brother walking disorderly" (iii. 6—15) belong to the incipient stage of Church organization. To suppose this passage written in the second century, or even in the last quarter of the first, is to attribute to the author a peculiar power of ignoring the conditions of his own time. But these instructions harmonize well enough with those addressed to the Corinthians (1 Cor. v.) respecting the extreme case of disorder in that Church.

The theories of *interpolation* have found but little acceptance. They account for the striking difference between 2 Thess. ii. 2—12 (to which i. 5—12 might be added) and 1 Thessalonians, and the equally striking correspondence to the 1st which the 2nd Epistle in other parts presents, by attributing to the two sections an entirely different origin. Thus P. W. Schmidt (in his *Der 1 Thess.-Brief neu erklärt, nebst Excurs über den 2ten gleichnamigen Brief*; also in the *Short Protest. Commentary*, by Schmidt and others, translated) would distinguish a genuine Epistle of Paul consisting of II. i. 1—4, ii. 12 *a*, ii. 13—iii. 18, treating the rest as an interpolation made about the year 69 by some half-Judaistic Christian akin to the author of Rev. xiii., who wished to allay the excitement prevailing in his circle respecting the Parousia, and who worked up the idea of the *Nero redivivus* into an apocalypse, employing an old and perhaps neglected letter of the Apostle as a vehicle for this prophecy of his own. S. Davidson, in his *Introduction to the Study of the N.T.*[2], vol. I., pp. 336—348, elaborated a similar view. But this compromise, while open to most of the objections brought against the theory of personation, raises others peculiar to itself. It ascribes to St Paul a Letter from which the pith has been extracted—little more than a shell without the kernel—weak and disconnected in its earlier part, and a Second to the Thessalonians following hard upon the First yet wanting in reference to the Parousia which fills the horizon of the previous Letter. If a partition must be made upon these lines, one would rather adopt Hausrath's notion (in his *Die Zeit der Apostel*[2], II., p. 198; translated under the title *History of the Times of the Apostles*), that 2 Thess. ii. 1—12 is a genuine Pauline fragment, which some later Paulinist has furnished with an epistolary framework in order to give it circulation amongst his master's writings.

The text and tradition of the Second Epistle afford no ground for conjecture that it ever existed in any other form than that which we know. Where the Apostle has the same things to say and the same feelings to express which found utterance in the First Epistle, he writes (or one of his companions for him) in the same strain, but in a manner more ordinary and subdued as the glow of emotion which dictated the first Letter has cooled, and his mind has become engrossed with other interests. Where new ideas and altered needs on the part of his readers require it, as in II. i. 5—12, ii. 2—12, iii. 6—15, he strikes out in new directions with characteristic force and originality.

On the whole subject, comp. the articles on *Thessalonians I.* and *II.* in Hastings' *Dictionary of the Bible*, vol. IV. The article in Smith's *Dict. of the Bible, ad rem*, by J. B. Lightfoot, is still valuable. Bornemann, in Meyer's *Kritisch-exegetischer Kommentar*[6], gives a complete and masterly discussion of the above questions, summing up decisively in favour of the authenticity of both Epistles. See also Askwith's vindication of the genuineness of the 2nd Epistle: *Introduction to the Thess. Epistles*, ch. v.

As to the relations of 2 Thess. ii. 1—12 to the Apocalypse, there will be something to say in the Appendix.

CHAPTER VI.

Vocabulary, Style and Character of the Epistles.

VOCABULARY. There are, as nearly as possible, 5,600 Greek words used in the New Testament. Out of these, 465 are in requisition for the Epistles to the Thessalonians,—a fairly extensive vocabulary, considering their limited scope and the amount of repetition in them. To this total of 465, the 2nd Epistle contributes 105 words, out of its 250, wanting in the 1st: half of these appear in the two peculiar eschatological sections (in chh. i. and ii.); not a few of the remainder—such as αἱρέομαι, ἀτακτέω, διωγμός, ἐκδίκησις, ἐνκαυχάομαι, εὐδοκία, κλῆσις, κρατέω, περιεργάζομαι, ὑπεραυξάνω—are variants or synonyms of expressions employed in Epistle I. That, notwithstanding, 2 Thessalonians should be distinguished from 1 Thessalonians in *two-fifths* of its vocabulary, is a fact somewhat singular in view of the large measure of dependence it exhibits (see pp. xlviii. ff. above), while e.g. Galatians holds all but *a third* of its lexical content in common with Romans, and Colossians shares its words with Ephesians and Philippians jointly in almost the same proportion. 1 Corinthians with its 963, and 2 Corinthians with its 762 words, disclose however a greater verbal dissidence.

These Epistles contain but a small proportion of *hapax-legomena*—21 in the First and 9 in the Second, amounting to less than a fifteenth of their entire vocabulary and an average of rather more than four to the chapter. It is observable that the habit of using new and singular words grew upon St Paul; this tendency is most marked in his latest writings, the Epistles to Timothy and Titus, with a proportion of some thirteen hapax-legomena to the chapter, constituting a fifth of their lexical contents; these ratios steadily increase as we proceed from the earlier to the later groups of Epistles. To the Thessalonian hapax legomena 24 words may be added which are peculiar in the N.T. to these with the other Pauline Epistles (including the Pastorals): 4 of these occur in both Letters, 14 in First, and 6 in Second Thessalonians. This raises the total number of Pauline hapax-legomena found in 1 and 2 Thessalonians to 54, out of the 848 words specific to St Paul amongst New Testament writers—a fraction not much smaller than the relative length of the two Epistles would lead us to expect. Of the above 54 locutions, it may be noted that 13 range no further than the second group of the Epistles (viz. 1 and 2 Corinthians, Galatians, Romans)—ἁγιωσύνη, ἀδιαλείπτως, ἔκδικος, ἐπιβαρέω, εὐσχημόνως, μόχθος, πλεονεκτέω, προλέγω, στέγω, στέλλομαι, συναναμίγνυσθαι, ὑπεραίρομαι, φιλοτιμέομαι; ἄρα οὖν, so characteristic of Romans, is only found once (in Ephesians) outside the first two groups; ἀγαθωσύνη and πάθος each occur in the first, second, and third groups; ἐνέργεια is the one prominent word peculiar to the first with the third (Eph., Col., Phil., Phm.) groups; ὑπερεκπερισσοῦ recurs only in Eph. iii. 20; ἐξαπατάω, ὄλεθρος, προΐστημι are found, outside of 1 and 2 Thess., in the second and fourth (1 and 2 Tim., Titus) groups; μνεία in the third and fourth; ἐπιφάνεια and ἤπιος (? I. ii. 7) reappear only in the fourth, and form a significant link between the first and last of Paul's extant Letters.

The hapax-legomena proper to the two Epistles present no marked peculiarities. The majority of them are compounds, of the types prevailing in later Greek. Ἀμέμπτως recurs twice (or thrice), and is paralleled by ἄμεμπτος in Philippians and elsewhere; ἔνδειγμα is a variant of ἐνδείκνυμι, ἔνδειξις, both Pauline, and all classical; ὑπερεκπερισσῶς (eminently Pauline) is all but the same as -οῦ; ἀναμένω, ἄτακτος &c., ἐκδιώκω, κέλευσμα, κολακία, ὁσίως, περιεργάζομαι, περιλείπομαι, προπάσχω, τίνω, ὑπερβαίνω are classical words of everyday speech, incidentally employed here; ἀπορφανίζω, ἐνορκίζω, ὑπεραυξάνω are rare intensives, due to the occasion; ἐνκαυχάομαι, ἐξηχέω, καλοποιέω, ὀλιγόψυχος, ὁλοτελής, περικεφαλαία, σημειόω, συμφυλέτης, may be distinguished as

VOCABULARY. lvii

words of the κοινή, most of them found in the LXX but not confined to Biblical Greek. Of ἐνδοξάζω there is no other example outside the LXX. Σαίνεσθαι, if meaning "to be shaken," would be a hapax-legomenon in sense; but see the Expository Note on I. iii. 3. The only absolutely unique expressions of the two Epistles are ὀμείρομαι—supposed to be a dialectic variant of ἱμείρομαι (see Expository Note on I. ii. 8)—and the obvious compound θεοδίδακτος, the elements of which are given by Isaiah liv. 13 (Jo. vi. 45; cf. Expository Note on I. iv. 9). There is nothing in the Greek of these Epistles that would present any difficulty to a contemporary reader moderately acquainted with the Hellenistic phraseology of the Jewish synagogues and schools of the Diaspora. Beyond a few Hebraistic locutions, such as υἱὸς σκότους, ἀπωλείας, &c., στέφανος καυχήσεως, δοκιμάζειν and στηρίζειν τὰς καρδίας, and perhaps εἰς ἀπάντησιν, there is little or nothing of distinctively "Biblical" Greek to be found in them, and few technical terms of theology: in this respect they resemble 1 and 2 Corinthians, and differ from Romans and Galatians. As Deissmann shows in his "Bible Studies," the amount of this element in the language of the N.T. has been exaggerated; many expressions formerly supposed to be peculiar to the Greek of the Bible are proved by Inscriptions and the Papyri to have been current in the vernacular of New Testament times.

The Epistles betray no special linguistic associations with other N.T. writings beyond St Paul's, apart from the connexion of certain passages in 1 Thessalonians with the prophecies of Jesus, to which reference will be made later, and the striking manner in which the Apocalyptic imagery and phrases of O. T. prophecy are woven into the tissue of 2 Thessalonians. The difficulties of structure and expression marking II. i. 6—10 indicate the introduction by the original writer of some non-Pauline, and probably liturgical, sentences (see Expository Notes). I. iv. 13—18 has a number of verbal correspondences with the parallel passage in 1 Corinthians. In point of syntax, there is nothing really exceptional to note. The Pauline periodic structure of sentences prevails throughout both Epistles.

In STYLE the Epistles are almost identical—a statement to be understood, however, with the qualification stated in the previous chapter, that in the large part of the 2nd Epistle in which it repeats the substance of the 1st, the freshness and point of the earlier Letter are somewhat to seek. The characteristic features of St Paul's dialect and manner are very apparent; but they have not yet assumed the bold and developed form presented by the Epistles of the second group. In wealth of language, in rhetorical and literary power, as in force of intellect and spiritual passion, these writings do not rise to the height of some of the later Epistles. Nor should we expect this. The Apostle's style is the most natural and unstudied in the world. It is, as Renan said, "conversation stenographed." In Galatians and 2 Corinthians, where he is labouring under great excitement of feeling, face to face with malignant enemies and with his disaffected or wavering children, his language is full of passion and grief, vehement, broken, passing in a moment from rebuke to tenderness, from lofty indignation to an almost abject humility—now he "speaks mere flames," but the sentence ends in pity and tears; "yea, what earnestness, what clearing of" himself, "what indignation, what yearning, what jealousy, what avenging!" In Romans and Galatians, again, you watch the play of St Paul's keen and dexterous logic, sweeping and massive generalization, daring inference, vivid illustration, swift retort, and an eagerness that leaps to its conclusion over intervening steps of argument indicated by a bare word or turn of phrase in passing. But these Epistles afford little room for such qualities of style. They are neither passionate nor argumentative, but practical, consolatory, prompted by affection, by memory and hope. Hence they represent "St Paul's normal style" (Lightfoot), the way in which he would commonly talk or write to his friends. For this reason, as well as for their historical priority, 1 and 2 Thessalonians form the best introduction to the writings of St Paul.

In general character and tone, in the simplicity and ease of expression which especially marks 1 Thessalonians, and in the absence of the dialectic mannerisms, the apostrophes and

STYLE.   lix

ellipses, distinguishing the polemical Epistles, these Letters resemble that to the Philippians. But it is remarkable that the Epistle to the Philippians, without any cause for this in its subject-matter, contains twice as many hapax-legomena to the chapter as are found in our Epistles. For Philippians was written nearly ten years later (see pp. lv. f.).

I. i. 2—5, ii. 14—16, II. i. 6—10, ii. 8—10, are good examples of St Paul's characteristic practice of extending his sentences to an indefinite length in qualifying and explanatory clauses, by the use of participles and relative pronouns and conjunctions. Later Epistles (*Ephesians* especially) show how this feature of style also grew upon him. In the third of the above instances the paragraph is so disjointed, that some further explanation appears necessary (see p. lvii. above, and Expository Notes). In I. i. 8, ii. 11, iv. 4—6, 14, II. i. 9, ii. 7, iii. 6, we find instances of *ellipsis* and *anacoluthon*—of those altered or broken sentences, and dropped words left to the reader's understanding, to which the student of St Paul is accustomed. II. ii. 7 gives an example of *inverted structure* resembling Gal. ii. 10. I. ii. 14, 15 (*the Jews*—who killed the Lord Jesus, &c.); v. 8, 9 (*salvation*—for God did not appoint us to wrath, &c.); II. i. 10 (that *believed*—for our testimony addressed to you was believed), illustrate St Paul's curious fashion of "going off upon a word," where some term he happens to use suddenly suggests an idea that draws him aside from the current of the sentence, which he perhaps resumes in an altered form. In I. ii. 4, 19—20, iii. 6—7, iv. 3 and 7, v. 4, 5, II. ii. 9 and 11, 10 and 12, we see how expressions of the Apostle are apt to return upon and repeat themselves in a changed guise. In 2 Thessalonians the repetition of the same word or phrase is so frequent as to constitute a distinct mannerism of the Epistle; 42 doublets of this nature are counted. I. iii. 5, v. 23, II. iii. 2—3, iii. 11 (ἐργαζομένους...περιεργαζομένους) exemplify the fondness, shared by St Paul with many great writers, for *paronomasia*.

Beside the hapax-legomena enumerated on pp. lvi. f., there are a number of verbal usages characteristic of these Letters and not recurring later in St Paul's writings: viz. αὐτὸς δὲ ὁ θεός (or κύριος)

INTRODUCTION.

at the beginning of prayers (I. iii. 11, v. 23, II. ii. 16); the use of the bare optative in *prayers to God* (add II. iii. 16 to the above), Rom. xv. 5 affording the only other Pauline example; αὐτοὶ οἴδατε, καθὼς (καθάπερ) οἴδατε (I. i. 5, ii. 1 f., 5, 11, iii. 3 f., v. 2, II. iii. 7); ἔργον πίστεως (I. i. 3, II. i. 11); εἶναι πρός (I. iii. 4, II. ii. 5, iii. 10 : elsewhere γίνομαι and παρεῖναι πρός); στέγω in the sense of I. iii. 1, 5; κατευθύνω (I. iii. 11, II. iii. 5); ἅμα σύν (I. iv. 17, v. 10); παρακαλεῖτε ἀλλήλους (I. iv. 18, v. 11); τοῦτο γὰρ (ἐστιν) θέλημα (τοῦ) θεοῦ (I. iv. 3, v. 18); στηρίζειν τὴν καρδίαν (I. iii. 13, II. ii. 17 : the verb St Paul only uses in Romans besides); ὀφείλω εὐχαριστεῖν (II. i. 3, ii. 13) ; περιποίησις in the active sense (I. v. 9, II. ii. 14); παρουσία (of the Second Advent), only in 1 Cor. xv. 23 besides. Phil. iv. 3 gives the only other Pauline instance of ἐρωτάω employed in the sense of I. iv. 1, v. 12, II. ii. 1.

Not one quotation from the Old Testament, nor from any other literary source, is found in the Thessalonian Epistles. The writers are addressing Gentile converts, and in such a way that Scriptural proof and illustration are not required. But allusions to O. T. teaching are rife. The writer of 2 Thessalonians has his mind full of the apocalyptic ideas of the Books of Isaiah and Daniel, to a less extent of Ezekiel and the Psalter; his prophetical and hortatory passages are so steeped in the O. T., beyond what is common with St Paul, that this fact is even urged as evidence for inauthenticity. Compare

I. ii. 4 with Ps. xvi. 3[1], &c.;
ii. 12 with 4 (2) Esdras ii. 37;
ii. 16 with Gen. xv. 16;
ii. 19 with Isai. lxii. 3, Ezek. xvi. 12, Prov. xvi. 31;
iv. 5 with Ps. lxxviii. 6, &c.;
iv. 8 with Isai. lxiii. 11;
v. 8 with Isai. lix. 17;
v. 22 with Job i. 1, 8.
II. i. 8 with Isai. lxvi. 15;
i. 9, 10 with Isai. ii. 10 f., 17, 19—21;

[1] The Old Testament references in this list are made to the Greek Version.

VERBAL PARALLELS. lxi

also with Isai. xlix. 3, Ps. lxxxviii. 8;
and Mal. iii. 17 (*in that day*);
i. 12 with Isai. lxvi. 5;
ii. 4 with Dan. xi. 36, Isai. xiv. 14, Ezek. xxviii. 2, &c.;
ii. 8 with Isai. xi. 4, Dan. vii. 9—11;
ii. 11 with Ezek. xiv. 9;
ii. 13 with Deut. xxxiii. 12;
iii. 16 with Num. vi. 26.

Bornemann traces through 2 Thessalonians a chain of resemblances in language and idea to Isai. xxiv. ff., also to Ps. lxxxviii., xciii., cv.

Quite unusual in St Paul are the repeated and sustained *echoes of the words of Jesus* to be found in 1 Thessalonians in the passages relating to the Judgement and Second Coming. Compare

I. ii. 15 f. with Mat. xxiii. 29—39, Lk. xi. 45—52, xiii. 33 ff.;
iv. 16 f. with Mat. xxiv. 30 f.;
v. 1—6 with Mat. xxiv. 36—44, Lk. xii. 38—40, 46;
also II. ii. 2 with Mat. xxiv. 4—6.

The general form of the Letters of St Paul is moulded on the Epistolary style of the period; and this is especially evident in their commencement and conclusion. The Egyptian Greek Papyri afford numerous parallels to his opening εὐχαριστία, in which μνεία, προσευχή, ἀδιαλείπτως recur—the two former words *passim*. In ordinary correspondence it was a usual thing to begin with pious expressions of gratitude and references to prayer. The Apostle fills out the conventional formulæ of greeting, giving to them a new sacredness and weight of meaning. See Deissmann's *Bible Studies*, pp. 21 ff.; and J. Rendel Harris in *Expositor*, V. VIII. 161—180, "A study in Letter-writing." The argumentative and hortatory parts of his Epistles resemble the διατριβή of the contemporary Stoic schools, and may be illustrated from the *Dissertationes* of Epictetus.

In their CHARACTER these oldest extant Epistles of the Apostle Paul may now be easily described. They are *the letters of a missionary*, written to an infant Church quite recently brought

INTRODUCTION.

from heathen darkness into the marvellous light of the Gospel. They lie nearer, therefore, to the missionary preaching of St Paul (Acts xiv. 15—17, xvii. 22—31, &c.) than do any of the later Epistles. This accounts for their simplicity, for the absence of controversy and the elementary nature of their doctrine, and for the emphasis that is thrown in 1 Thessalonians upon the relation of the readers through the gospel *to God*.

They are addressed to *a Macedonian Church*, and they manifest in common with the Epistle to the (Macedonian) Philippians a peculiar warmth of feeling and mutual confidence between writer and readers. The first of the two is a singularly *affectionate* Letter. (For the second, see the observations on pp. xlviii. ff.) From 2 Cor. viii. 1—6 we gather that the generosity which endeared the Philippians to St Paul (Phil. iv. 14—17) distinguished Macedonian Christians generally. The writers can hardly find words tender enough or images sufficiently strong to express their regard for the Thessalonians (I. ii. 7, 11, 17, 19, 20, iii. 9). St Paul feels his very life bound up with this community (iii. 8). The missionaries boast of their Thessalonian converts everywhere (II. i. 4). If they exhort them, their warnings are blended with commendations, lest it might be thought there is some fault to find (I. iv. 1, 9 f., v. 11 ; II. iii. 4). Again and again the Apostle repeats, more than in any other Letter, "You yourselves know," "Remember ye not?" and the like,—so sure is he that his readers bear in mind the teaching at first received and are in hearty accord with it. In like fashion, when writing to the Philippians, the Apostle gives thanks to God "for your fellowship in the Gospel from the first day until now" (Phil. i. 5).

Further, these two are especially *cheering and consolatory letters*. St Paul had sent Timothy to "encourage" the Thessalonians "concerning their faith" (I. iii. 2); in writing the First Epistle on Timothy's return he pursues the same object. Persecution was the lot of this Church from the beginning (I. iii. 4 ; Acts xvii. 5—9), as it continued to be afterwards (2 Cor. viii. 2 : cf. what was written to Philippi ten years later, Phil. i. 28 ff.); death had visited them, clouding their hopes for the future lot of departing kindred. The Apostle bends all his efforts to encourage his distressed friends. He teaches them to glory in tribulation; he makes them smile through their tears. He reveals the "weight of glory" that their afflictions are working out for them; he describes the Christian dead as "fallen asleep through Jesus," and coming back to rejoin their living brethren on His return (I. iv. 13 ff.). He shows them—and to a generous Christian nature there is no greater satisfaction—how much their brave endurance is furthering the cause of Christ and of truth (I. i. 6—8; II. i. 3 f.), and how it comforts and helps himself and his companions in their labours. The Second Epistle is designed to allay causeless agitation respecting the advent of Christ, to recall to the ranks of industry some who had taken occasion to neglect their avocations, so disturbing the peace of the community and burdening it with their support. But along with these reproofs, and with the most solemn denunciation of future judgement for persecutors and rejecters of the truth, the commendatory and consolatory strain of the First Epistle is maintained in the Second.

Finally, these are *eschatological Epistles*: they set forth "the last things" in Christian doctrine—the Second Coming of the Redeemer, the restoration of the dead and transformation of the living saints, the final judgement of mankind; they announce the coming of Antichrist as the forerunner and Satanic counterpart of the returning Christ. Chap. ii. 1—12 in 2 Thessalonians is called the Pauline Apocalypse, since it holds in St Paul's Epistles a place corresponding to that of the Book of Revelation in the writings of St John. We have previously suggested (chap. III.) circumstances which may have led the Apostle Paul to dwell upon this subject. The prolonged persecution under which the Thessalonians laboured, served to incline their thoughts in the same direction—toward the heavenly kingdom which, they hoped, would soon arrive to put an end to the miseries of "this present evil world." In the comparative ease and pleasantness of our own lives, we perhaps find it difficult to understand the degree to which the minds of Christians in early times were absorbed in thoughts of this nature.

By their eschatological views and teachings these Letters are linked to chap. xv. of 1 Corinthians, the next of the Epistles in order of time. Subsequently the subject of the *parousia* retreats into the shade in his writings. For this, two or three causes may be suggested. Between the writing of 1 and 2 Corinthians St Paul suffered from a sickness which brought him to the gates of death (2 Cor. i. 8—10, iv. 7—v. 8), and which profoundly affected his inner experience: from this time he anticipated that death would end his earthly career (Phil. i. 20 f.; Acts xx. 24; 2 Tim. iv. 6—8, 18). Beside this, the disturbing effect of preoccupation with the Second Advent at Thessalonica, and the morbid excitement to which it gave rise in some minds, may have led him to make this subject less prominent in later teaching. As time went on and the kingdom of Christ penetrated the Roman Empire and entered into closer relations with existing society, the Apostle came to realize the need for a longer development of Christianity, for a slower and more pervasive action of the "leaven" which Christ had put into "the kneading" of human life, than could be counted upon at an earlier stage. In St Paul's last Letters, however, to his helpers Timothy and Titus, he reverts frequently and fondly to "that blessed hope and appearing of the glory of our great God and Saviour Jesus Christ" (Tit. ii. 13). Long ago he had reconciled himself, with reluctance, to the fact that he must first indeed be "absent from the body" in order to be "present with the Lord." Still "the coming of the Lord Jesus," whether it should be in the first or fourth watch of the night, was the mark of his labours; it was the summit, to his eyes, of all Christian hope. These two fervent Epistles, with their bright horizon of promise crossed by lurid thunder-clouds, breathe the constant desire of the Church with which the book of Scripture closes:

COME, LORD JESUS!

CHAPTER VII.

THE GREEK TEXT OF THE EPISTLES.

THE text of 1 and 2 Thessalonians stands on the same footing as that of the other Pauline Epistles. It has been faithfully preserved, and comes down to us amply attested by witnesses of the first rank in each of the three orders—Greek Codices, Versions, and Patristic writers. Westcott and Hort find occasion in their critical edition to mark only a single word, viz. ἐπιστεύθη in II. i. 10, as a case of "primitive corruption" which raises suspicion of error in all the oldest witnesses. The five primary Greek Uncials, of the fourth and fifth centuries, are available: the Vaticanus (**B**), the Sinaiticus (ℵ), the Alexandrinus (**A**), Codex Ephraemi rescriptus (**C**)—this with lacunæ, and Codex Claromontanus (**D**). Of secondary but considerable importance are Boernerianus (**G**); **H**, surviving in detached leaves variously designated, extant here only in two fragments, viz. I. ii. 9—13 and iv. 5—11; Porfirianus (**P**), defective in I. iii. 5—iv. 17. The inferior uncials—D^c, Moscuensis (**K**), and Angelicus (**L**)—contain a text purely of the later ("received") type. **E** (Sangermanensis) is a mere copy of **D** and its correctors; **F** (Augiensis) is practically identical with **G** above: it is idle to quote these two, where they bring no new evidence. Amongst the Minuscules several are approved by the critics as containing ancient readings, and deserve to rank with **GHP** above-mentioned; 17, 37, 47, 73 are those chiefly adduced in the Textual Notes below, along with the precious readings of the annotator of 67, known as 67**.

The various copies of the pre-Hieronymian Latin Version and recensions (**latt**) come into court along with the Vulgate (**vg**):

MSS. of special note are occasionally discriminated—as am, the Codex Amiatinus; fu, Fuldensis; harl, Harleianus, &c. The three Egyptian Versions appear as cop (Coptic or Memphitic), sah (Sahidic or Thebaic), and basm (Bashmuric). In Syriac, there is the Peshitto (pesh) or Syriac Vulgate, conformed to the later, settled mould (called by Westcott and Hort the "Syrian" recension) of the Greek original; and the Harclean (hcl)—later in date but largely older in substance—with its *text* and *margin*. The Gothic (go), Æthiopic (aeth), and Armenian (arm) are outlying Versions, which furnish readings of confirmatory value, as they indicate the trend of the Greek text in different regions at the time of their making. The Greek Fathers—Irenæus (through his Latin interpreter), Clement of Alexandria, Hippolytus, Origen, Didymus, Eusebius, Euthalius, Athanasius, John Chrysostom, Theodore of Mopsuestia, Theodoret, Cyril of Alexandria, Theophylact, Oecumenius; and the Latins—Tertullian, Cyprian, Ambrose, 'Ambrosiaster,' Jerome (Hieronymus), Damasus, Augustine, Lucifer of Calaris, Vigilius—are cited by the recognized abbreviations.

The characteristics of the different groups, and of the more strongly featured Codices and Versions, stand out with some prominence in the text of these Epistles[1]. I. iii. 2 (the description of Timothy) affords a signal example of the "conflate" nature of the Syrian recension, exemplified in **KL** and prevailingly in **P**, in the bulk of the minuscules, in the Peshitto Syriac and Chrysostom; I. iv. 1 (the omission of $καθὼς καὶ περιπατεῖτε$) illustrates its tendency to smooth out the creases of St Paul's style. The idiosyncrasies of the "Western" clan (**DG**, latt, and Latin Fathers frequently) reveal themselves again and again: see, in this connexion, the Textual Notes on I. ii. 12, 14 ($ἀπό$), 16 ($ὀργὴ τοῦ θεοῦ$), iii. 2 (where the Western recension is suspected of having caused the confusion by adding $τοῦ θεοῦ$ to $συνεργόν$), iv. 13, 16, 17, v. 13 ($ἐν αὐτοῖς$), II. i. 4 ($καυχᾶσθαι$), ii. 2 (repeated $μηδέ$), 3 ($ἁμαρτίας$), 8 ($ἀναλοῖ$), 10 ($ἀληθείας Χριστοῦ$), iii. 4, 14 ($-μίσγεσθαι$), 16. **G** has some glaring Latinisms, indicating a reaction of the Western versions on the Greek text:

[1] In regard to the examples here given, see the Textual Notes.

DIFFICULT READINGS. lxvii

see I. ii. 3, 17, v. 12, II. ii. 4. Erroneous Syrian readings are often traceable to a "Western" invention. Instances may be noted in which the tendencies of Alexandrian copyists to smoothness and classicalism of expression, and to harmonistic agreement, seem to be in evidence: I. i. 1 (the completion of the form of salutation, Alexandrian and Western), 5 (τοῦ θεοῦ), ii. 2 (the reading (a) of the Textual Notes), iv. 1 (cancelling of first ἵνα), 8, 11, v. 12, 21, 27 (insertion of ἁγίοις), II. iii. 6 (? -οσαν[1], belonging to the Alexandrian vernacular). The unique value of B is shown by the fact that it records alone, or nearly alone, a series of readings which intrinsic and transcriptional probability point out as possibly original, notwithstanding the solitary attestation: see I. ii. 16 (ἔφθακεν), iii. 2, iv. 9, v. 9 (ὁ θεὸς ἡμᾶς and omission of Χριστοῦ), II. i. 4 (ἐνέχεσθε), ii. 8 (om. Ἰησοῦς), iii. 4 (καὶ ἐποιήσατε καὶ ποιήσετε), 6, 13. On the other hand, the palpable mistakes of B in iii. 1 (διότι), 9 (ἡμῶν), iv. 17 (ἐν for σὺν κυρίῳ), II. iii. 14 (ἐπιστολῆς ὑμῶν), prove this great MS. to be far from impeccable. It is betrayed in I. v. 12, II. ii. 2, by its habitual itacism, -ε for -αι.

Decision between alternative readings of the Greek text is very difficult in the case of ἤπιοι—νήπιοι, I. ii. 7; συνεργόν—συνεργὸν τοῦ θεοῦ—διάκονον τοῦ θεοῦ, iii. 2; ἐνέχεσθε—ἀνέχεσθε, II. i. 4; ἐν φλογὶ πυρός—ἐν πυρὶ φλογός, i. 8; the omission or retention of Ἰησοῦς in ii. 8; ἀναλοῖ—ἀνελεῖ in same verse; the retention or omission of καί in ii. 14; the reading of the duplicate ποιέω-forms in iii. 4; παρελάβοσαν—παρελάβετε in iii. 6. There is hesitation or difference amongst the critics in some other instances: e.g. in I. i. 5 (ἐν before ὑμῖν), 7 (τύπον—τύπους), 9 (ἡμῶν—ὑμῶν), ii. 12 (καλοῦντος—καλέσαντος), 16 (ἔφθακεν—ἔφθασεν), iii. 4 (the augment of ηὐδοκήσαμεν), 13 (ἀμέμπτους or -ως, and the final ἀμήν), iv. 1 (? οὖν), 10 (? τούς), v. 3 (? δέ), 4 (κλέπτης—κλέπτας), 10 (περί—ὑπέρ), 13 (ὑπερεκπερισσοῦ or -ῶς), 15 (? καί), 21 (? δέ), 25 (? καί), 27 (? ἁγίοις); in II. i. 10 (ἐπιστεύθη—ἐπιστώθη), ii. 3 (ἀνομίας—ἁμαρτίας), 12 (ἅπαντες—πάντες), 13 (ἀπ' ἀρχῆς—ἀπαρχήν), iii. 6 (? ἡμῶν after κυρίου).

[1] On the ending -οσαν, see J. H. Moulton in *Expositor*, May 1904, p. 366; and *Classical Review*, March 1904, p. 110.

lxviii   *INTRODUCTION.*

The conspectus of readings furnished in the Textual Notes hereafter will indicate the grounds of judgement in disputed cases; it may serve also to illustrate the peculiarities of the chief ancient witnesses, and, as it is hoped, to interest the student in questions of the Lower Criticism. The material is drawn mainly from the digest of critical evidence found in Tischendorf's 8th edition. Kenyon's or Nestle's Manual will supply a full Introduction to the science of N. T. Textual Criticism; on a smaller scale, Warfield's *Introduction* lays down clearly and skilfully the leading principles. Scrivener's *Introduction* (the last edition), and C. R. Gregory's *Prolegomena* to Tischendorf's *Novum Testamentum Grœce*, contain the best accessible catalogues and descriptions of the documents.

CHAPTER VIII.

ANALYSIS OF THE EPISTLES.

I. In 1 Thessalonians there are two clearly marked main divisions: chh. i.—iii., *personal*; iv., v., *moral and doctrinal*. (1) The first and chief part of the letter is an outpouring of the heart of the writers—i.e. of St Paul's own heart especially—to their brethren in Thessalonica. The Apostle tells them *what he thinks of them*, how he prays for them and thanks God for what they are, for all they have attained and all they have endured as Christian believers. Then *he talks about himself and his fellow-missionaries*, reminding the readers of their work and behaviour at Thessalonica, informing them of his repeated attempts to return thither, of the circumstances under which Timothy had been sent instead, and the inexpressible delight given to himself and Silvanus by Timothy's good report of their state and of their love for the absent Apostles.

(2) In *v.* 1 of ch. iv. the author passes from narrative and prayer to exhortation. His homily bears chiefly *on Christian morals*,—"how you ought to walk and to please God." In the midst of this condensed and powerful address there is introduced the great passage relating to the παρουσία (ch. iv. 13—v. 11), informing the readers more definitely *what they should believe* on this vital matter of faith, to them so profoundly interesting, respecting which they had gathered defective and misleading notions. The misunderstandings and the agitations existing in the Church upon this subject affected its "walk"; they were disturbing to the Church's peace and prejudicial to its soberness of thought and joy of faith. Hence

the introduction of the doctrinal question at this stage and in this form.

II. The Second Epistle contains but little personal matter, and is in this respect strikingly different from the First. After the Thanksgiving, occupying the first chapter, which enlarges on the punishment in store for the Church's persecutors in contrast with the rest and glory destined for Christ's faithful sufferers, the author proceeds at once to the questions of *doctrine and discipline* which called for this further instruction. This Epistle bears therefore a supplementary character, dealing more at large with certain matters that were treated incidentally in the First and setting them in a somewhat different light. Chaps. ii. and iii. of the 2nd Epistle correspond to chaps. iv. and v. of the 1st; but they do not range over the same variety of topics. (1) Ch. ii. 1—12 disposes of *the false alarm about the parousia*, which was producing, it appears, quite a demoralizing excitement; (2) ch. iii. 6—15 is addressed to the case of *certain idlers and busybodies*, whose obstinate indiscipline compels the Apostles to take severe measures for their correction. The intervening part of the Letter, ch. ii. 13—iii. 5, is taken up with thanksgiving, prayer, and exhortation of a general character; these paragraphs echo the thoughts and expressions of 1 Thessalonians in a manner quite unusual with the Apostle Paul, even in the case of Epistles most nearly allied in their subject and time of composition.

The exposition of the two Letters is based upon the following plan:

1*st Epistle.*

§ 1. Address and Salutation, i. 1.

§ 2. Thanksgiving for the Thessalonian Church, i. 2—10.

§ 3. The Conduct of the Apostles at Thessalonica, ii. 1—12.

§ 4. Fellowship in Persecution with the Judæan Churches, ii. 13—16.

§ 5. The Separation of the Apostles from their Converts, ii. 17—iii. 5.

ANALYSIS. lxxi

§ 6. The Good News brought by Timothy, iii. 6—13.
§ 7. A Lesson in Christian Morals, iv. 1—12.
§ 8. Concerning them that Fall Asleep, iv. 13—18.
§ 9. The Coming of the Day, v. 1—11.
§ 10. The Church's Internal Discipline, v. 12—15.
§ 11. Directions for Holy Living, v. 16—24.
§ 12. The Conclusion, v. 25—28.

2nd Epistle.

§ 1. Salutation and Thanksgiving, i. 1—4.
§ 2. The Approaching Judgement, i. 5—12.
§ 3. The Revelation of the Lawless One, ii. 1—12.
§ 4. Words of Comfort and Prayer, ii. 13—iii. 5.
§ 5. The Case of the Idlers, iii. 6—15.
§ 6. Conclusion of the Letter, iii. 16—18.

The scheme of Epistle II., it will be observed, is much simpler than that of Epistle I. In other words, 1 Thessalonians is an unconstrained, discursive *letter*; 2 Thessalonians is more of a calculated *homily*.

ΠΡΟΣ ΘΕΣΣΑΛΟΝΙΚΕΙΣ Α

1 ¹Παῦλος καὶ Σιλουανὸς καὶ Τιμόθεος τῇ ἐκκλησίᾳ Θεσσαλονικέων ἐν θεῷ πατρὶ καὶ κυρίῳ Ἰησοῦ Χριστῷ· χάρις ὑμῖν καὶ εἰρήνη. ²Εὐχαριστοῦμεν τῷ θεῷ πάντοτε περὶ πάντων ὑμῶν μνείαν ποιούμενοι ἐπὶ τῶν προσευχῶν ἡμῶν, ³ἀδιαλείπτως μνημονεύοντες ὑμῶν τοῦ ἔργου τῆς πίστεως καὶ τοῦ κόπου τῆς ἀγάπης καὶ τῆς ὑπομονῆς τῆς ἐλπίδος τοῦ κυρίου ἡμῶν Ἰησοῦ Χριστοῦ ἔμπροσθεν τοῦ θεοῦ καὶ πατρὸς ἡμῶν, ⁴εἰδότες, ἀδελφοὶ ἠγαπημένοι ὑπὸ [τοῦ] θεοῦ, τὴν ἐκλογὴν ὑμῶν, ⁵ὅτι τὸ εὐαγγέλιον ἡμῶν οὐκ ἐγενήθη εἰς ὑμᾶς ἐν λόγῳ μόνον ἀλλὰ καὶ ἐν δυνάμει καὶ ἐν πνεύματι ἁγίῳ καὶ πληροφορίᾳ πολλῇ, καθὼς οἴδατε οἷοι ἐγενήθημεν ὑμῖν δι᾽ ὑμᾶς· ⁶καὶ ὑμεῖς μιμηταὶ ἡμῶν ἐγενήθητε καὶ τοῦ κυρίου, δεξάμενοι τὸν λόγον ἐν θλίψει πολλῇ μετὰ χαρᾶς πνεύματος ἁγίου, ⁷ὥστε γενέσθαι ὑμᾶς τύπον πᾶσιν τοῖς πιστεύουσιν ἐν τῇ Μακεδονίᾳ καὶ ἐν τῇ Ἀχαίᾳ. ⁸ἀφ᾽ ὑμῶν γὰρ ἐξήχηται ὁ λόγος τοῦ κυρίου οὐ μόνον ἐν τῇ Μακεδονίᾳ καὶ Ἀχαίᾳ, ἀλλ᾽ ἐν παντὶ τόπῳ ἡ πίστις ὑμῶν ἡ πρὸς τὸν θεὸν ἐξελήλυθεν, ὥστε μὴ χρείαν ἔχειν ἡμᾶς λαλεῖν τι· ⁹αὐτοὶ γὰρ περὶ ἡμῶν ἀπαγγέλλουσιν ὁποίαν εἴσοδον ἔσχομεν πρὸς ὑμᾶς, καὶ πῶς ἐπεστρέψατε πρὸς τὸν θεὸν ἀπὸ τῶν εἰδώλων

δουλεύειν θεῷ ζῶντι καὶ ἀληθινῷ, ¹⁰καὶ ἀναμένειν τὸν υἱὸν αὐτοῦ ἐκ τῶν οὐρανῶν, ὃν ἤγειρεν ἐκ [τῶν] νεκρῶν, Ἰησοῦν τὸν ῥυόμενον ἡμᾶς ἐκ τῆς ὀργῆς τῆς ἐρχομένης.

2 ¹Αὐτοὶ γὰρ οἴδατε, ἀδελφοί, τὴν εἴσοδον ἡμῶν τὴν πρὸς ὑμᾶς ὅτι οὐ κενὴ γέγονεν, ²ἀλλὰ προπαθόντες καὶ ὑβρισθέντες καθὼς οἴδατε ἐν Φιλίπποις ἐπαρρησιασάμεθα ἐν τῷ θεῷ ἡμῶν λαλῆσαι πρὸς ὑμᾶς τὸ εὐαγγέλιον τοῦ θεοῦ ἐν πολλῷ ἀγῶνι. ³ἡ γὰρ παράκλησις ἡμῶν οὐκ ἐκ πλάνης οὐδὲ ἐξ ἀκαθαρσίας οὐδὲ ἐν δόλῳ, ⁴ἀλλὰ καθὼς δεδοκιμάσμεθα ὑπὸ τοῦ θεοῦ πιστευθῆναι τὸ εὐαγγέλιον οὕτως λαλοῦμεν, οὐχ ὡς ἀνθρώποις ἀρέσκοντες ἀλλὰ θεῷ τῷ ΔΟΚΙΜΆΖΟΝΤΙ ΤᴀϹ ΚᴀΡΔΊᴀϹ ἡμῶν. ⁵οὔτε γάρ ποτε ἐν λόγῳ κολακίας ἐγενήθημεν, καθὼς οἴδατε, οὔτε προφάσει πλεονεξίας, θεὸς μάρτυς, ⁶οὔτε ζητοῦντες ἐξ ἀνθρώπων δόξαν, οὔτε ἀφ' ὑμῶν οὔτε ἀπ' ἄλλων, δυνάμενοι ἐν βάρει εἶναι ὡς Χριστοῦ ἀπόστολοι· ⁷ἀλλὰ ἐγενήθημεν νήπιοι ἐν μέσῳ ὑμῶν, ὡς ἐὰν τροφὸς θάλπῃ τὰ ἑαυτῆς τέκνα· ⁸οὕτως ὀμειρόμενοι ὑμῶν ηὐδοκοῦμεν μεταδοῦναι ὑμῖν οὐ μόνον τὸ εὐαγγέλιον τοῦ θεοῦ ἀλλὰ καὶ τὰς ἑαυτῶν ψυχάς, διότι ἀγαπητοὶ ἡμῖν ἐγενήθητε· ⁹μνημονεύετε γάρ, ἀδελφοί, τὸν κόπον ἡμῶν καὶ τὸν μόχθον· νυκτὸς καὶ ἡμέρας ἐργαζόμενοι πρὸς τὸ μὴ ἐπιβαρῆσαί τινα ὑμῶν ἐκηρύξαμεν εἰς ὑμᾶς τὸ εὐαγγέλιον τοῦ θεοῦ. ¹⁰ὑμεῖς μάρτυρες καὶ ὁ θεός, ὡς ὁσίως καὶ δικαίως καὶ ἀμέμπτως ὑμῖν τοῖς πιστεύουσιν ἐγενήθημεν, ¹¹καθάπερ οἴδατε ὡς ἕνα ἕκαστον ὑμῶν ὡς πατὴρ τέκνα ἑαυτοῦ παρακαλοῦντες ὑμᾶς καὶ παραμυθούμενοι καὶ μαρτυρόμενοι, ¹²εἰς τὸ περιπατεῖν ὑμᾶς **ἀξίως** τοῦ θεοῦ τοῦ καλοῦντος ὑμᾶς εἰς τὴν ἑαυτοῦ **βασιλείαν** καὶ δόξαν.

¹³Καὶ διὰ τοῦτο καὶ ἡμεῖς εὐχαριστοῦμεν τῷ θεῷ ἀδιαλείπτως, ὅτι παραλαβόντες λόγον ἀκοῆς παρ' ἡμῶν τοῦ θεοῦ ἐδέξασθε οὐ λόγον ἀνθρώπων ἀλλὰ καθὼς ἀληθῶς ἐστὶν λόγον θεοῦ, ὃς καὶ ἐνεργεῖται ἐν ὑμῖν τοῖς πιστεύουσιν. ¹⁴ὑμεῖς γὰρ μιμηταὶ ἐγενήθητε, ἀδελφοί, τῶν ἐκκλησιῶν τοῦ θεοῦ τῶν οὐσῶν ἐν τῇ Ἰουδαίᾳ ἐν Χριστῷ Ἰησοῦ, ὅτι τὰ αὐτὰ ἐπάθετε καὶ ὑμεῖς ὑπὸ τῶν ἰδίων συμφυλετῶν καθὼς καὶ αὐτοὶ ὑπὸ τῶν Ἰουδαίων, ¹⁵τῶν καὶ τὸν κύριον ἀποκτεινάντων Ἰησοῦν καὶ τοὺς προφήτας καὶ ἡμᾶς ἐκδιωξάντων, καὶ θεῷ μὴ ἀρεσκόντων, καὶ πᾶσιν ἀνθρώποις ἐναντίων, ¹⁶κωλυόντων ἡμᾶς τοῖς ἔθνεσιν λαλῆσαι ἵνα σωθῶσιν, εἰς τὸ ἀναπληρῶσαι αὐτῶν τὰς ἁμαρτίας πάντοτε. ἔφθασεν δὲ ἐπ' αὐτοὺς ἡ ὀργὴ εἰς τέλος.

¹⁷Ἡμεῖς δέ, ἀδελφοί, ἀπορφανισθέντες ἀφ' ὑμῶν πρὸς καιρὸν ὥρας, προσώπῳ οὐ καρδίᾳ, περισσοτέρως ἐσπουδάσαμεν τὸ πρόσωπον ὑμῶν ἰδεῖν ἐν πολλῇ ἐπιθυμίᾳ. ¹⁸διότι ἠθελήσαμεν ἐλθεῖν πρὸς ὑμᾶς, ἐγὼ μὲν Παῦλος καὶ ἅπαξ καὶ δίς, καὶ ἐνέκοψεν ἡμᾶς ὁ Σατανᾶς. ¹⁹τίς γὰρ ἡμῶν ἐλπὶς ἢ χαρὰ ἢ στέφανος καυχήσεως—ἢ οὐχὶ καὶ ὑμεῖς—ἔμπροσθεν τοῦ κυρίου ἡμῶν Ἰησοῦ ἐν τῇ αὐτοῦ παρουσίᾳ; ²⁰ὑμεῖς γάρ ἐστε ἡ δόξα ἡμῶν καὶ ἡ χαρά. 3 ¹Διὸ μηκέτι στέγοντες ηὐδοκήσαμεν καταλειφθῆναι ἐν Ἀθήναις μόνοι, ²καὶ ἐπέμψαμεν Τιμόθεον, τὸν ἀδελφὸν ἡμῶν καὶ διάκονον τοῦ θεοῦ ἐν τῷ εὐαγγελίῳ τοῦ χριστοῦ, εἰς τὸ στηρίξαι ὑμᾶς καὶ παρακαλέσαι ὑπὲρ τῆς πίστεως ὑμῶν ³τὸ μηδένα σαίνεσθαι ἐν ταῖς θλίψεσιν ταύταις. αὐτοὶ γὰρ οἴδατε ὅτι εἰς τοῦτο κείμεθα· ⁴καὶ γὰρ ὅτε πρὸς ὑμᾶς ἦμεν, προελέγομεν ὑμῖν ὅτι μέλλομεν θλίβεσθαι, καθὼς καὶ ἐγένετο καὶ οἴδατε.

⁵διὰ τοῦτο κἀγὼ μηκέτι στέγων ἔπεμψα εἰς τὸ γνῶναι τὴν πίστιν ὑμῶν, μή πως ἐπείρασεν ὑμᾶς ὁ πειράζων καὶ εἰς κενὸν γένηται ὁ κόπος ἡμῶν. ⁶Ἄρτι δὲ ἐλθόντος Τιμοθέου πρὸς ἡμᾶς ἀφ' ὑμῶν καὶ εὐαγγελισαμένου ἡμῖν τὴν πίστιν καὶ τὴν ἀγάπην ὑμῶν, καὶ ὅτι ἔχετε μνείαν ἡμῶν ἀγαθὴν πάντοτε ἐπιποθοῦντες ἡμᾶς ἰδεῖν καθάπερ καὶ ἡμεῖς ὑμᾶς, ⁷διὰ τοῦτο παρεκλήθημεν, ἀδελφοί, ἐφ' ὑμῖν ἐπὶ πάσῃ τῇ ἀνάγκῃ καὶ θλίψει ἡμῶν διὰ τῆς ὑμῶν πίστεως, ⁸ὅτι νῦν ζῶμεν ἐὰν ὑμεῖς στήκετε ἐν κυρίῳ. ⁹τίνα γὰρ εὐχαριστίαν δυνάμεθα τῷ θεῷ ἀνταποδοῦναι περὶ ὑμῶν ἐπὶ πάσῃ τῇ χαρᾷ ᾗ χαίρομεν δι' ὑμᾶς ἔμπροσθεν τοῦ θεοῦ ἡμῶν, ¹⁰νυκτὸς καὶ ἡμέρας ὑπερεκπερισσοῦ δεόμενοι εἰς τὸ ἰδεῖν ὑμῶν τὸ πρόσωπον καὶ καταρτίσαι τὰ ὑστερήματα τῆς πίστεως ὑμῶν; ¹¹Αὐτὸς δὲ ὁ θεὸς καὶ πατὴρ ἡμῶν καὶ ὁ κύριος ἡμῶν Ἰησοῦς κατευθύναι τὴν ὁδὸν ἡμῶν πρὸς ὑμᾶς· ¹²ὑμᾶς δὲ ὁ κύριος πλεονάσαι καὶ περισσεύσαι τῇ ἀγάπῃ εἰς ἀλλήλους καὶ εἰς πάντας, καθάπερ καὶ ἡμεῖς εἰς ὑμᾶς, ¹³εἰς τὸ στηρίξαι ὑμῶν τὰς καρδίας ἀμέμπτους ἐν ἁγιωσύνῃ ἔμπροσθεν τοῦ θεοῦ καὶ πατρὸς ἡμῶν ἐν τῇ παρουσίᾳ τοῦ κυρίου ἡμῶν Ἰησοῦ μετὰ πάντων τῶν ἁγίων αὐτοῦ.

4 ¹Λοιπόν, ἀδελφοί, ἐρωτῶμεν ὑμᾶς καὶ παρακαλοῦμεν ἐν κυρίῳ Ἰησοῦ, [ἵνα] καθὼς παρελάβετε παρ' ἡμῶν τὸ πῶς δεῖ ὑμᾶς περιπατεῖν καὶ ἀρέσκειν θεῷ, καθὼς καὶ περιπατεῖτε,—ἵνα περισσεύητε μᾶλλον. ²οἴδατε γὰρ τίνας παραγγελίας ἐδώκαμεν ὑμῖν διὰ τοῦ κυρίου Ἰησοῦ. ³Τοῦτο γάρ ἐστιν θέλημα τοῦ θεοῦ, ὁ ἁγιασμὸς ὑμῶν, ἀπέχεσθαι ὑμᾶς ἀπὸ τῆς πορνείας, ⁴εἰδέναι ἕκαστον ὑμῶν τὸ ἑαυτοῦ σκεῦος

κτᾶσθαι ἐν ἁγιασμῷ καὶ τιμῇ, ⁵μὴ ἐν πάθει ἐπιθυμίας καθάπερ καὶ τὰ ἔθνη τὰ ΜΗ ΕἰΔΌΤΑ ΤῸΝ ΘΕΌΝ, ⁶τὸ μὴ ὑπερβαίνειν καὶ πλεονεκτεῖν ἐν τῷ πράγματι τὸν ἀδελφὸν αὐτοῦ, διότι ἔΚΔΙΚΟC ΚΎΡΙΟC περὶ πάντων τούτων, καθὼς καὶ προείπαμεν ὑμῖν καὶ διεμαρτυράμεθα. ⁷οὐ γὰρ ἐκάλεσεν ἡμᾶς ὁ θεὸς ἐπὶ ἀκαθαρσίᾳ ἀλλ' ἐν ἁγιασμῷ. ⁸τοιγαροῦν ὁ ἀθετῶν οὐκ ἄνθρωπον ἀθετεῖ ἀλλὰ τὸν θεὸν τὸν ΔιΔΌΝΤΑ ΤῸ ΠΝΕῦΜΑ ΑὐΤΟῦ ΤῸ ἅγιον Εἰc ἡΜᾶc. ⁹Περὶ δὲ τῆς φιλαδελφίας οὐ χρείαν ἔχετε γράφειν ὑμῖν, αὐτοὶ γὰρ ὑμεῖς θεοδίδακτοί ἐστε εἰς τὸ ἀγαπᾶν ἀλλήλους· ¹⁰καὶ γὰρ ποιεῖτε αὐτὸ εἰς πάντας τοὺς ἀδελφοὺς [τοὺς] ἐν ὅλῃ τῇ Μακεδονίᾳ. Παρακαλοῦμεν δὲ ὑμᾶς, ἀδελφοί, περισσεύειν μᾶλλον, ¹¹καὶ φιλοτιμεῖσθαι ἡσυχάζειν καὶ πράσσειν τὰ ἴδια καὶ ἐργάζεσθαι ταῖς χερσὶν ὑμῶν, καθὼς ὑμῖν παρηγγείλαμεν, ¹²ἵνα περιπατῆτε εὐσχημόνως πρὸς τοὺς ἔξω καὶ μηδενὸς χρείαν ἔχητε.

¹³Οὐ θέλομεν δὲ ὑμᾶς ἀγνοεῖν, ἀδελφοί, περὶ τῶν κοιμωμένων, ἵνα μὴ λυπῆσθε καθὼς καὶ οἱ λοιποὶ οἱ μὴ ἔχοντες ἐλπίδα. ¹⁴εἰ γὰρ πιστεύομεν ὅτι Ἰησοῦς ἀπέθανεν καὶ ἀνέστη, οὕτως καὶ ὁ θεὸς τοὺς κοιμηθέντας διὰ τοῦ Ἰησοῦ ἄξει σὺν αὐτῷ. ¹⁵Τοῦτο γὰρ ὑμῖν λέγομεν ἐν λόγῳ κυρίου, ὅτι ἡμεῖς οἱ ζῶντες οἱ περιλειπόμενοι εἰς τὴν παρουσίαν τοῦ κυρίου οὐ μὴ φθάσωμεν τοὺς κοιμηθέντας· ¹⁶ὅτι αὐτὸς ὁ κύριος ἐν κελεύσματι, ἐν φωνῇ ἀρχαγγέλου καὶ ἐν σάλπιγγι θεοῦ, καταβήσεται ἀπ' οὐρανοῦ, καὶ οἱ νεκροὶ ἐν Χριστῷ ἀναστήσονται πρῶτον, ¹⁷ἔπειτα ἡμεῖς οἱ ζῶντες οἱ περιλειπόμενοι ἅμα σὺν αὐτοῖς ἁρπαγησόμεθα ἐν νεφέλαις εἰς ἀπάντησιν τοῦ κυρίου εἰς ἀέρα· καὶ οὕτως

πάντοτε σὺν κυρίῳ ἐσόμεθα. ¹⁸Ὥστε παρακαλεῖτε ἀλλήλους ἐν τοῖς λόγοις τούτοις.

5 ¹Περὶ δὲ τῶν χρόνων καὶ τῶν καιρῶν, ἀδελφοί, οὐ χρείαν ἔχετε ὑμῖν γράφεσθαι, ²αὐτοὶ γὰρ ἀκριβῶς οἴδατε ὅτι ἡμέρα Κυρίου ὡς κλέπτης ἐν νυκτὶ οὕτως ἔρχεται. ³ὅταν λέγωσιν Εἰρήνη καὶ ἀσφάλεια, τότε αἰφνίδιος αὐτοῖς ἐπίσταται ὄλεθρος ὥσπερ ἡ ὠδὶν τῇ ἐν γαστρὶ ἐχούσῃ, καὶ οὐ μὴ ἐκφύγωσιν. ⁴ὑμεῖς δέ, ἀδελφοί, οὐκ ἐστὲ ἐν σκότει, ἵνα ἡ ἡμέρα ὑμᾶς ὡς κλέπτας καταλάβῃ, ⁵πάντες γὰρ ὑμεῖς υἱοὶ φωτός ἐστε καὶ υἱοὶ ἡμέρας. Οὐκ ἐσμὲν νυκτὸς οὐδὲ σκότους· ⁶ἄρα οὖν μὴ καθεύδωμεν ὡς οἱ λοιποί, ἀλλὰ γρηγορῶμεν καὶ νήφωμεν. ⁷οἱ γὰρ καθεύδοντες νυκτὸς καθεύδουσιν, καὶ οἱ μεθυσκόμενοι νυκτὸς μεθύουσιν· ⁸ἡμεῖς δὲ ἡμέρας ὄντες νήφωμεν, ἐνΔΥϹΆΜΕΝΟΙ θώρακα πίστεως καὶ ἀγάπης καὶ περικεφαλαίαν ἐλπίδα ϲωτηρίαϲ· ⁹ὅτι οὐκ ἔθετο ἡμᾶς ὁ θεὸς εἰς ὀργὴν ἀλλὰ εἰς περιποίησιν σωτηρίας διὰ τοῦ κυρίου ἡμῶν Ἰησοῦ [Χριστοῦ], ¹⁰τοῦ ἀποθανόντος περὶ ἡμῶν ἵνα εἴτε γρηγορῶμεν εἴτε καθεύδωμεν ἅμα σὺν αὐτῷ ζήσωμεν. ¹¹Διὸ παρακαλεῖτε ἀλλήλους καὶ οἰκοδομεῖτε εἷς τὸν ἕνα, καθὼς καὶ ποιεῖτε.

¹²Ἐρωτῶμεν δὲ ὑμᾶς, ἀδελφοί, εἰδέναι τοὺς κοπιῶντας ἐν ὑμῖν καὶ προϊσταμένους ὑμῶν ἐν κυρίῳ καὶ νουθετοῦντας ὑμᾶς, ¹³καὶ ἡγεῖσθαι αὐτοὺς ὑπερεκπερισσοῦ ἐν ἀγάπῃ διὰ τὸ ἔργον αὐτῶν. εἰρηνεύετε ἐν ἑαυτοῖς. ¹⁴Παρακαλοῦμεν δὲ ὑμᾶς, ἀδελφοί, νουθετεῖτε τοὺς ἀτάκτους, παραμυθεῖσθε τοὺς ὀλιγοψύχους, ἀντέχεσθε τῶν ἀσθενῶν, μακροθυμεῖτε πρὸς πάντας. ¹⁵ὁρᾶτε μή τις κακὸν ἀντὶ κακοῦ τινὶ ἀποδῷ, ἀλλὰ πάντοτε τὸ ἀγαθὸν διώκετε εἰς ἀλλήλους καὶ εἰς

πάντας. ¹⁶Πάντοτε χαίρετε, ¹⁷ἀδιαλείπτως προσεύχεσθε, ¹⁸ἐν παντὶ εὐχαριστεῖτε· τοῦτο γὰρ θέλημα θεοῦ ἐν Χριστῷ Ἰησοῦ εἰς ὑμᾶς. ¹⁹τὸ πνεῦμα μὴ σβέννυτε, ²⁰προφητείας μὴ ἐξουθενεῖτε· ²¹πάντα [δὲ] δοκιμάζετε, τὸ καλὸν κατέχετε, ²²ἀπὸ παντὸс εἴδους πονηροῦ ἀπέχεсθε. ²³Αὐτὸς δὲ ὁ θεὸς τῆς εἰρήνης ἁγιάσαι ὑμᾶς ὁλοτελεῖς, καὶ ὁλόκληρον ὑμῶν τὸ πνεῦμα καὶ ἡ ψυχὴ καὶ τὸ σῶμα ἀμέμπτως ἐν τῇ παρουσίᾳ τοῦ κυρίου ἡμῶν Ἰησοῦ Χριστοῦ τηρηθείη. ²⁴πιστὸς ὁ καλῶν ὑμᾶς, ὃς καὶ ποιήσει.
²⁵Ἀδελφοί, προσεύχεσθε [καὶ] περὶ ἡμῶν.
²⁶Ἀσπάσασθε τοὺς ἀδελφοὺς πάντας ἐν φιλήματι ἁγίῳ. ²⁷Ἐνορκίζω ὑμᾶς τὸν κύριον ἀναγνωσθῆναι τὴν ἐπιστολὴν πᾶσιν τοῖς ἀδελφοῖς.
²⁸Ἡ χάρις τοῦ κυρίου ἡμῶν Ἰησοῦ Χριστοῦ μεθ' ὑμῶν.

ΠΡΟΣ ΘΕΣΣΑΛΟΝΙΚΕΙΣ Β

1 ¹Παῦλος καὶ Σιλουανὸς καὶ Τιμόθεος τῇ ἐκκλησίᾳ Θεσσαλονικέων ἐν θεῷ πατρὶ ἡμῶν καὶ κυρίῳ Ἰησοῦ Χριστῷ· ²χάρις ὑμῖν καὶ εἰρήνη ἀπὸ θεοῦ πατρὸς καὶ κυρίου Ἰησοῦ Χριστοῦ.

³Εὐχαριστεῖν ὀφείλομεν τῷ θεῷ πάντοτε περὶ ὑμῶν, ἀδελφοί, καθὼς ἄξιόν ἐστιν, ὅτι ὑπεραυξάνει ἡ πίστις ὑμῶν καὶ πλεονάζει ἡ ἀγάπη ἑνὸς ἑκάστου πάντων ὑμῶν εἰς ἀλλήλους, ⁴ὥστε αὐτοὺς ἡμᾶς ἐν ὑμῖν ἐνκαυχᾶσθαι ἐν ταῖς ἐκκλησίαις τοῦ θεοῦ ὑπὲρ τῆς ὑπομονῆς ὑμῶν καὶ πίστεως ἐν πᾶσιν τοῖς διωγμοῖς ὑμῶν καὶ ταῖς θλίψεσιν αἷς ἀνέχεσθε, ⁵ἔνδειγμα τῆς δικαίας κρίσεως τοῦ θεοῦ, εἰς τὸ καταξιωθῆναι ὑμᾶς τῆς βασιλείας τοῦ θεοῦ, ὑπὲρ ἧς καὶ πάσχετε, ⁶εἴπερ δίκαιον παρὰ θεῷ ἀνταποδοῦναι τοῖς θλίβουσιν ὑμᾶς θλίψιν ⁷καὶ ὑμῖν τοῖς θλιβομένοις ἄνεσιν μεθ᾽ ἡμῶν ἐν τῇ ἀποκαλύψει τοῦ κυρίου Ἰησοῦ ἀπ᾽ οὐρανοῦ μετ᾽ ἀγγέλων δυνάμεως αὐτοῦ ἐν πυρὶ φλογός, ⁸διδόντος ἐκδίκησιν τοῖς μὴ εἰδόσι θεὸν καὶ τοῖς μὴ ὑπακούουσιν τῷ εὐαγγελίῳ τοῦ κυρίου ἡμῶν Ἰησοῦ, ⁹οἵτινες δίκην τίσουσιν ὄλεθρον αἰώνιον ἀπὸ προσώπου τοῦ κυρίου καὶ ἀπὸ τῆς δόξης τῆς ἰσχύος αὐτοῦ, ¹⁰ὅταν ἔλθῃ ἐνδοξασθῆναι ἐν τοῖς ἁγίοις αὐτοῦ καὶ θαυμασθῆναι ἐν πᾶσιν

τοῖς πιστεύσασιν, ὅτι ἐπιστεύθη τὸ μαρτύριον ἡμῶν ἐφ᾽ ὑμᾶς, ἐν τῇ ἡμέρᾳ ἐκείνῃ. ¹¹Εἰς ὃ καὶ προσευχόμεθα πάντοτε περὶ ὑμῶν, ἵνα ὑμᾶς ἀξιώσῃ τῆς κλήσεως ὁ θεὸς ἡμῶν καὶ πληρώσῃ πᾶσαν εὐδοκίαν ἀγαθωσύνης καὶ ἔργον πίστεως ἐν δυνάμει, ¹²ὅπως ἐνδοξασθῇ τὸ ὄνομα τοῦ κυρίου ἡμῶν Ἰησοῦ ἐν ὑμῖν, καὶ ὑμεῖς ἐν αὐτῷ, κατὰ τὴν χάριν τοῦ θεοῦ ἡμῶν καὶ κυρίου Ἰησοῦ Χριστοῦ.

2 ¹Ἐρωτῶμεν δὲ ὑμᾶς, ἀδελφοί, ὑπὲρ τῆς παρουσίας τοῦ κυρίου [ἡμῶν] Ἰησοῦ Χριστοῦ καὶ ἡμῶν ἐπισυναγωγῆς ἐπ᾽ αὐτόν, ²εἰς τὸ μὴ ταχέως σαλευθῆναι ὑμᾶς ἀπὸ τοῦ νοὸς μηδὲ θροεῖσθαι μήτε διὰ πνεύματος μήτε διὰ λόγου μήτε δι᾽ ἐπιστολῆς ὡς δι᾽ ἡμῶν, ὡς ὅτι ἐνέστηκεν ἡ ἡμέρα τοῦ κυρίου. ³μή τις ὑμᾶς ἐξαπατήσῃ κατὰ μηδένα τρόπον· ὅτι ἐὰν μὴ ἔλθῃ ἡ ἀποστασία πρῶτον καὶ ἀποκαλυφθῇ ὁ ἄνθρωπος τῆς ἀνομίας, ὁ υἱὸς τῆς ἀπωλείας, ⁴ὁ ἀντικείμενος καὶ ὑπεραιρόμενος ἐπὶ πάντα λεγόμενον θεὸν ἢ σέβασμα, ὥστε αὐτὸν εἰς τὸν ναὸν τοῦ θεοῦ καθίσαι, ἀποδεικνύντα ἑαυτὸν ὅτι ἔστιν θεός—. ⁵Οὐ μνημονεύετε ὅτι ἔτι ὢν πρὸς ὑμᾶς ταῦτα ἔλεγον ὑμῖν; ⁶καὶ νῦν τὸ κατέχον οἴδατε, εἰς τὸ ἀποκαλυφθῆναι αὐτὸν ἐν τῷ αὐτοῦ καιρῷ· ⁷τὸ γὰρ μυστήριον ἤδη ἐνεργεῖται τῆς ἀνομίας· μόνον ὁ κατέχων ἄρτι ἕως ἐκ μέσου γένηται. ⁸καὶ τότε ἀποκαλυφθήσεται ὁ ἄνομος, ὃν ὁ κύριος [Ἰησοῦς] ἀνελεῖ τῷ πνεύματι τοῦ στόματος αὐτοῦ καὶ καταργήσει τῇ ἐπιφανείᾳ τῆς παρουσίας αὐτοῦ, ⁹οὗ ἐστὶν ἡ παρουσία κατ᾽ ἐνέργειαν τοῦ Σατανᾶ ἐν πάσῃ δυνάμει καὶ σημείοις καὶ τέρασιν ψεύδους ¹⁰καὶ ἐν πάσῃ ἀπάτῃ ἀδικίας τοῖς ἀπολλυμένοις, ἀνθ᾽ ὧν τὴν ἀγάπην τῆς ἀληθείας οὐκ ἐδέξαντο εἰς τὸ σωθῆναι αὐτούς· ¹¹καὶ διὰ τοῦτο πέμπει αὐτοῖς ὁ θεὸς ἐνέργειαν πλάνης εἰς τὸ πιστεῦσαι αὐτοὺς τῷ ψεύδει, ¹²ἵνα κριθῶσιν πάντες οἱ μὴ πιστεύσαντες τῇ ἀληθείᾳ ἀλλὰ εὐδοκήσαντες τῇ ἀδικίᾳ.

¹³Ἡμεῖς δὲ ὀφείλομεν εὐχαριστεῖν τῷ θεῷ πάντοτε περὶ ὑμῶν, ἀδελφοὶ ἨΓΑΠΗΜΈΝΟΙ ὑπὸ Κγρίογ, ὅτι εἵλατο ὑμᾶς ὁ θεὸς ἀπ' ἀρχῆς εἰς σωτηρίαν ἐν ἁγιασμῷ πνεύματος καὶ πίστει ἀληθείας, ¹⁴εἰς ὃ ἐκάλεσεν ὑμᾶς διὰ τοῦ εὐαγγελίου ἡμῶν, εἰς περιποίησιν δόξης τοῦ κυρίου ἡμῶν Ἰησοῦ Χριστοῦ. ¹⁵Ἄρα οὖν, ἀδελφοί, στήκετε, καὶ κρατεῖτε τὰς παραδόσεις ἃς ἐδιδάχθητε εἴτε διὰ λόγου εἴτε δι' ἐπιστολῆς ἡμῶν. ¹⁶Αὐτὸς δὲ ὁ κύριος ἡμῶν Ἰησοῦς Χριστὸς καὶ [ὁ] θεὸς ὁ πατὴρ ἡμῶν, ὁ ἀγαπήσας ἡμᾶς καὶ δοὺς παράκλησιν αἰωνίαν καὶ ἐλπίδα ἀγαθὴν ἐν χάριτι, ¹⁷παρακαλέσαι ὑμῶν τὰς καρδίας καὶ στηρίξαι ἐν παντὶ ἔργῳ καὶ λόγῳ ἀγαθῷ.

3 ¹Τὸ λοιπὸν προσεύχεσθε, ἀδελφοί, περὶ ἡμῶν, ἵνα ὁ λόγος τοῦ κυρίου τρέχῃ καὶ δοξάζηται καθὼς καὶ πρὸς ὑμᾶς, ²καὶ ἵνα ῥυσθῶμεν ἀπὸ τῶν ἀτόπων καὶ πονηρῶν ἀνθρώπων, οὐ γὰρ πάντων ἡ πίστις. ³Πιστὸς δέ ἐστιν ὁ κύριος, ὃς στηρίξει ὑμᾶς καὶ φυλάξει ἀπὸ τοῦ πονηροῦ. ⁴πεποίθαμεν δὲ ἐν κυρίῳ ἐφ' ὑμᾶς, ὅτι ἃ παραγγέλλομεν [καὶ] ποιεῖτε καὶ ποιήσετε. ⁵Ὁ δὲ κύριος κατευθύναι ὑμῶν τὰς καρδίας εἰς τὴν ἀγάπην τοῦ θεοῦ καὶ εἰς τὴν ὑπομονὴν τοῦ χριστοῦ.

⁶Παραγγέλλομεν δὲ ὑμῖν, ἀδελφοί, ἐν ὀνόματι τοῦ κυρίου Ἰησοῦ Χριστοῦ στέλλεσθαι ὑμᾶς ἀπὸ παντὸς ἀδελφοῦ ἀτάκτως περιπατοῦντος καὶ μὴ κατὰ τὴν παράδοσιν ἣν παρελάβετε παρ' ἡμῶν. ⁷αὐτοὶ γὰρ οἴ-

δατε πῶς δεῖ μιμεῖσθαι ἡμᾶς, ὅτι οὐκ ἠτακτήσαμεν ἐν ὑμῖν ⁸οὐδὲ δωρεὰν ἄρτον ἐφάγομεν παρά τινος, ἀλλ' ἐν κόπῳ καὶ μόχθῳ νυκτὸς καὶ ἡμέρας ἐργαζόμενοι πρὸς τὸ μὴ ἐπιβαρῆσαί τινα ὑμῶν· ⁹οὐχ ὅτι οὐκ ἔχομεν ἐξουσίαν, ἀλλ' ἵνα ἑαυτοὺς τύπον δῶμεν ὑμῖν εἰς τὸ μιμεῖσθαι ἡμᾶς. ¹⁰καὶ γὰρ ὅτε ἦμεν πρὸς ὑμᾶς, τοῦτο παρηγγέλλομεν ὑμῖν, ὅτι εἴ τις οὐ θέλει ἐργάζεσθαι μηδὲ ἐσθιέτω. ¹¹ἀκούομεν γάρ τινας περιπατοῦντας ἐν ὑμῖν ἀτάκτως, μηδὲν ἐργαζομένους ἀλλὰ περιεργαζομένους· ¹²τοῖς δὲ τοιούτοις παραγγέλλομεν καὶ παρακαλοῦμεν ἐν κυρίῳ Ἰησοῦ Χριστῷ ἵνα μετὰ ἡσυχίας ἐργαζόμενοι τὸν ἑαυτῶν ἄρτον ἐσθίωσιν. ¹³Ὑμεῖς δέ, ἀδελφοί, μὴ ἐνκακήσητε καλοποιοῦντες. ¹⁴εἰ δέ τις οὐχ ὑπακούει τῷ λόγῳ ἡμῶν διὰ τῆς ἐπιστολῆς, τοῦτον σημειοῦσθε, μὴ συναναμίγνυσθαι αὐτῷ, ἵνα ἐντραπῇ· ¹⁵καὶ μὴ ὡς ἐχθρὸν ἡγεῖσθε, ἀλλὰ νουθετεῖτε ὡς ἀδελφόν. ¹⁶Αὐτὸς δὲ ὁ κύριος τῆς εἰρήνης δῴη ὑμῖν τὴν εἰρήνην διὰ παντὸς ἐν παντὶ τρόπῳ. ὁ κύριος μετὰ πάντων ὑμῶν.

¹⁷Ὁ ἀσπασμὸς τῇ ἐμῇ χειρὶ Παύλου, ὅ ἐστιν σημεῖον ἐν πάσῃ ἐπιστολῇ· οὕτως γράφω. ¹⁸ἡ χάρις τοῦ κυρίου ἡμῶν Ἰησοῦ Χριστοῦ μετὰ πάντων ὑμῶν.

NOTES.

1 THESSALONIANS.

CHAPTER I.

TITLE. The received form of the titles of St Paul's Epistles has no MS. authority. It appeared first in Beza's printed editions, and was adopted by the Elzevirs; the A.V. took it from Beza. προς Θεσσαλονικεις α´ is the heading of the Epistle in ℵABK 17, also in cop basm goth; similarly throughout the Paúline Epp. in ℵAB and C (where extant); D prefixes αρχεται, from 2 Cor. onwards. This form of title belongs to the earliest times, when St Paul's Epistles formed a single and separate Book, entitled O ΑΠΟCΤΟΛΟC, within which the several Letters were distinguished by the bare address. The two to the Thessalonians appear to have always stood last in the second group of those addressed to Churches, consisting of smaller Epistles (Eph. Phil. Col. 1 and 2 Thess.).

B* spells Θεσσαλονεικεις, a characteristic itacism; G -νικαιους.

1. DG^gr read Σιλβανος, as regularly in the Papyri.

BG 47 73, and the Gr. text of Cramer's Catena, g r vg syrr (except hcl^mg) basm aeth, conclude the greeting without the clause απο Θ. πατρ. ημων και κυριου I. X., which is added in 2 Thess., and almost uniformly in later Epp. The shorter reading is sustained by Chr, in his Commentary ad loc., Thphyl, and expressly by Or^{4, 468} (Lat. interpr.): "Ad Thess. vero prima ita habet, *Gratia vobis et pax*, et nihil ultra"; similarly Lucifer^brug, "Non addas, *a Deo patre nostro et domino J. C.*" The T.R., with minor variations, is found in all other witnesses, including ℵACDKLP, the old latt (except f g r) cop, &c. The tendency to assimilate formulæ of salutation was irresistible; cf. Col. i. 2, where BD vg syrr (except hcl^mg) Or Chr, against the vast majority, support the shorter text. A case for the maxim, "Brevior lectio præferenda."

2. ℵ^cCDKP &c., latt cop syrr, add to μνειαν the complement υμων, which is wanting in ℵ*AB 17 67**—a Western and Syrian insertion. Cf. Eph. i. 16, where D* is against the addition and ℵ shows no variation. In each of these instances the pronoun has just previously

occurred. Versions are of little or no weight where points of grammatical usage are involved.

3. The reading του εργου...τον κοπον...την υπομονην, of D*, exhibits the carelessness of Western transcribers; G has the accusative throughout. *et laboris et caritatis* (as if τ. κοπου και τ. αγαπης) in vg.

4. BDG omit, ℵACKP insert, the article του before θεου: cf. ii. 4. Possibly the art. is an Alexandrian insertion, due to *v*. 3 (εμπροσθεν του θεου). See the note next but two; cf. II. ii. 13; also Heb. vi. 18, where the same group (ℵ*ACP) insert the article.

5. C reads ευαγγ. του θεου (instead of ημων); ℵ του θεου ημων, by conflation: this aberrant variation may be due to the influence of ii. 2, 8 f.

ACDGKP, &c., influenced by the context, repeat εν before πληροφορια—wanting in ℵB 17.

εν before υμιν is supported by BDG and the T.R., against ℵACP 17 67** in which it is wanting; cf. note on *v*. 4 above. Here εν might easily be dropped after εγενηθημεν, and would hardly be officiously inserted: transcriptional probability favours its genuineness. In ii. 10 εν is absent in construction with this verb; but εγενηθημεν has there a different turn of meaning (see Expository Note), while in this place δι' υμας suggests the antithetical εν υμιν: see iii. 7, iv. 14; 2 Cor. i. 11, 20, iii. 18; Rom. i. 17, for the like Pauline *play* upon prepositions.

7. τυπον in BD* 17 47 67**, latt vg sah cop. τυπους, in ℵACGKLP, &c., assimilated to υμας. Cf. II. iii. 9; but the plural in 1 Pet. v. 3.

The T.R. omits second εν (τη Αχ.) after KL and many minuscules; other minuscules omit τη also—in both instances assimilating *v*. 7 to *v*. 8. See next note.

8. On the other hand, ℵACDGP, &c., latt vg, insert εν τη before Αχαια, copying *v*. 7; while B 17 37 47 sah cop preserve the shorter reading. On the grammatical difference see Expository Note.

εχειν ημας (in this order): all pre-Syrian uncials; B* reads υμας, as in next note.

9. B, with 20 minuscules, sah cop, Thdrt Dam Oec, reads περι υμων (for ημων), a mistake due perhaps to the prominent υμων of *v*. 8; WH place υμων in the margin.

The εχομεν of T.R. is found only in a few minuscules; εσχομεν in all uncials and best versions. Present and 2nd aorist forms of this verb are often confused, through the resemblance of uncial ε and c.

10. ACK omit των before νεκρων: Pauline usage varies.

Before της οργης, εκ is read by אABP 17 73: απο by CDGKL, &c., Western and Syrian; vg *ab ira*.

§ 1. 1. 1. ADDRESS AND GREETING.

1. Παῦλος κ. Σιλουανὸς κ. Τιμόθεος—so in II. i. 1—now together at Corinth (see *Introd.* pp. xxxii. f.), write as joint-founders and pastors of this Church: cf. 2 Cor. i. 19. St Paul betrays himself as the actual composer in ii. 18 and iii. 5, and speaks in his own person again, with strong feeling, in v. 27. Timothy is distinguished from his senior companions in iii. 6 ff.; Silvanus' share throughout is passed over in silence. St Paul's practice varies in the Letters of associate authorship: in 1 and 2 Thess. the body of the Epistle runs in the 1st person *plural*, and the 1st *plural* prevails in 2 Cor. i.—ix. (otherwise in x.— xiii.); but 1 Corinthians, Galatians, Philippians, Colossians, despite the associated names in the Address, run in the 1st *singular*. In the latter instances St Paul's companions share in the greeting only; in the former they are parties to the matter of the Epistle. Cf. Note on the Plural Authorship, *Introd.* p. xxxix.

For the association of Silvanus with St Paul see Acts xv. 27, 40,— xviii. 5; the Silvanus of 1 Pet. v. 12 is almost certainly the same person—an important link between St Peter and St Paul, and between the latter and the Judæan Church (cf. note on ii. 14). Silvanus appears always as *Silas* in Acts: the latter name was supposed to be a Greek abbreviation of the former (Latin); but Th. Zahn makes out (*Introd. to N.T.*, Vol. I, pp. 31, 32) that Σίλας is of Aramaic origin (שְׁאִילָא, שְׁאִילָא, or שִׁילָא,—Jewish personal names found in the Inscriptions, and in the Talmud: from root שְׁאַל), and that *Silvanus* was Silas' (Shila's) adopted name of Roman citizenship (see Acts xvi. 37), chosen presumably from resemblance of sound; cf. Jesus-Jason, Joseph-Hegesippus, &c. Σιλουανός, shortened, should have made Σιλουᾶς or Σιλβᾶς (cf. Josephus, *Jewish War*, VII. 8), rather than Σίλας. His Roman surname, and his established position in the mother Church (Acts xv. 22, 32), suggest that Silvanus was amongst the ἐπιδημοῦντες Ῥωμαῖοι of Acts ii. 10 converted on the day of Pentecost; or possibly, had belonged to the συναγωγὴ Λιβερτίνων (Acts vi. 9) in Jerusalem. St Paul had "selected Silas" (ἐπιλεξάμενος, Acts xv. 40)—"elegit socium non ministrum" (Blass)—on setting out for his second Missionary Expedition; Timotheus was enlisted later (Acts xvi. 1—3) to replace John Mark (xiii. 5), in a subordinate capacity; hence "Paul and Silas" figure in the narrative of Acts xvi., xvii. For Timothy's relations with the Thessalonian Church see iii. 2—6, and notes below. In 1 and 2 Thess. St Paul distinguishes himself by no title; similarly in Phil. i. 1 he and Timothy are alike δοῦλοι Χριστοῦ 'Ιησοῦ; in Phm. 9 he styles himself δέσμιος Χρ.'Ιησ.: in all other Epistles the designation ἀπόστολος, or κλητὸς ἀπόστολος, is attached to his name. He stood on a homelier footing with the Macedonian Churches than with others (see ii. 7—12, and *Introd.* pp. xliii., lxii.). In ii. 6 (see note) the three missionaries rank together as 'apostles.' The Judaistic attacks on St Paul's authority, which engaged the Apostle on the third missionary tour, had not yet commenced: contrast Gal. i. 1, 11—20; 1 Cor. ix. 1 ff.; 2 Cor. x. 8, &c.; Rom. i. 1—6.

The three names—Paul, Silvanus, Timothy—typify the mixed condition of Jewish society at this time, and of the primitive Christian constituency. Paul and Silvanus are Jews (Hebrew *Saul*, and *Sila* or *Shila*), with Roman surname and citizenship; Timotheus had a Greek name and father, but a Jewish mother (Acts xvi. 1). So the Church was a Græco-Roman superstructure, resting on a Jewish foundation.

The Letter is addressed τῇ ἐκκλησίᾳ Θεσσαλονικέων ἐν θεῷ πατρὶ καὶ κυρίῳ 'Ιησοῦ Χριστῷ—a form of description confined to 1 and 2 Thessalonians, freely rendered: "To the assembly of Thessalonians acknowledging God as Father and Jesus Christ as Lord, gathered in this twofold Name." Τῇ ἐκκλησίᾳ receives its local limitation; then τῇ ἐκκλησίᾳ Θεσσαλονικέων receives the necessary spiritual definition, ἐν θεῷ κ.τ.λ.

In later Epistles St Paul writes "To the church (or saints) *in* Corinth, Rome, &c."; only in 1 and 2 Thess. does he use in his Address the name of the *people* (citizens)—in Gal. i. 2, however, "To the churches of Galatia" (cf. i. 22; 1 Cor. xvi. 1, 19; 2 Cor. viii. 1). The later style of expression—" Church in," &c.—superseded this as the Christian community spread and the Church came to be thought of as an extended whole ' in ' many places : thus it is already conceived in 1 Cor. i. 1; cf. ii. 14 below.

ἐν θεῷ πατρὶ κ.τ.λ. might be attached grammatically to the predicate χάρις ὑμῖν κ.τ.λ.; so Hofmann construes, with a few others. But the ἀπό-clause following εἰρήνη, which is genuine in 2 Thess. i. 2 (though spurious here), excludes the reference of ἐν θεῷ κ.τ.λ. to the predicate *there*, making it very unlikely here. Moreover, the foregoing designation requires this limitation; there were many ἐκκλησίαι Θεσσαλονικέων, meeting for manifold purposes—civil and religious (including the Synagogue), regular or irregular (cf. Acts xix. 32, 39); this "assembly of Thessalonians" is constituted "in God the Father and the Lord Jesus Christ." It is a stated religious society, marked off from all that is Pagan or Jewish as it is grounded "in God" confessed as "Father," and "Jesus Christ" adored as "Lord": cf. carefully 1 Cor. i. 2 with viii. 5, 6. Everything this ἐκκλησία Θεσσαλονικέων rests upon and exists for is centred in those two Names, which complement each other and are bound by the vinculum of the single ἐν. "In God the Father," its members know themselves to be His children (cf. v. 4, ii. 12, iii. 13, v. 23 f.; II. ii. 16); "in the Lord," discerning their Saviour's divine Sonship and authority (v. 10, ii. 15, see note, iv. 15—17, &c.); "in Jesus," His human birth and history (ii. 15, iv. 14, &c.); "in Christ," His living presence and relationship to His people (ii. 7, iv. 16, &c.).

The doubly anarthrous θεῷ πατρί (cf. v. 9, and contrast iii. 13, &c.) is the rule in epistolary formulæ, occurring besides in Eph. vi. 23 and Phil. ii. 11, where, as here, the phrase carries a quasi-confessional force: "in a God (known as) Father, and (as) Lord, Jesus Christ." "In Christ," "in the Lord," is St Paul's characteristic definition of Christian acts or states; "in God" occurs, in like connexion, only in ii. 2 and Col. iii. 3 besides—the latter an instructive parallel.

χάρις ὑμῖν echoes, more in sound than in sense, the χαίρειν, χαίρετε, of every-day Greek salutation (cf. Acts xv. 23, xxiii. 26; James i. 1, &c.), while εἰρήνη reproduces the Eastern שָׁלוֹם, *salaam* (cf., beside the Epp., Dan. iv. 1, vi. 25; Lk. x. 5, xxiv. 36, &c.): here the Pauline greeting has its earliest and briefest form, enlarged already in 2 Thess. This formula may well have been St Paul's own coinage, passing from him to other Christian writers (see the greetings of 1 and 2 Peter, 2 John, and Revelation); his whole gospel is enfolded in the wish χάρις ὑμῖν καὶ εἰρήνη, as the whole faith of his readers in the definition ἐν θεῷ πατρὶ κ. κυρίῳ Ἰησοῦ Χριστῷ. Χάρις is the sum of all Divine blessing bestowed in Christ on undeserving men; εἰρήνη (the fruit of χάρις received in faith), the sum of all blessing thus experienced by man. "Grace," in its full import, begins with the coming of Christ (Rom. v. 15; Tit. ii. 11; Jo. i. 17); "Peace," including the inner tranquillity and health flowing from reconciliation with God, begins with the sense of justification (Rom. v. 1; Eph. ii. 14). Both, received as bounties of God, become habits and qualities of the soul itself (see Rom. v. 1, 2; 2 Cor. viii. 7; Phil. iv. 7); but χάρις naturally leans to the former (objective) and εἰρήνη to the latter (subjective) sense. Both centre in the cross of Christ, where God exhibits His grace and Christians find their peace (see v. 9 f.; Gal. ii. 21; Col. i. 20; Eph. ii. 14—18; Rom. v. 10: cf. Heb. ii. 9, xiii. 20 f.). GRACE is St Paul's watchword, occurring twice as often in his writings as in all the rest of the N.T.; in this Epistle however it will only meet us again in the final greeting, v. 28. Cf. the note on χάρις in II. i. 12.

§ 2. 1. 2—10. THANKSGIVING FOR THE THESSALONIAN CHURCH.

This εὐχαριστία is one long sentence spun out in a continuous thread (cf. Eph. i. 3—14; and see *Introd.* p. lix.). It affords a good example of the writer's characteristic style (see Jowett's or Lightfoot's Commentary *ad loc.*). St Paul's sentences are not built up in orderly and balanced periods (as e.g. those of the Epistle to the Hebrews); they grow like living things, putting forth processes now in this direction now in that, under the impulse of the moment, and gathering force as they advance by the expansion in each successive movement of the thought of the previous clause. On the *epistolary form* of Thanksgiving, see *Introd.* p. lxi.

Εὐχαριστοῦμεν is buttressed by three parallel participles (*vv.* 2—4), in which μνείαν ποιούμενοι supplies *the occasion*, μνημονεύοντες *the more immediate* and εἰδότες κ.τ.λ. *the ultimate ground* of the Apostle's thanksgiving: "We give thanks...in making mention...as we remember...since we know," &c. The above fundamental ground of thanksgiving is made good by *proof* in the ὅτι-sentence beginning in *v.* 5, which, covering the rest of the chapter, gives an account (*a*) of the bringing of the gospel to Thessalonica (*v.* 5), (*b*) of its reception by the readers (*v.* 6); finally, of the effect of all this upon others, as evidenced (*c*) in the impression made on them by the conversion of the Thessalonians (*vv.* 7 f.), and (*d*) in the report which is everywhere current of the success of the Apostles' mission in this city (*vv.* 9 f.). We are thus brought round at the conclusion to the starting-point of the doxology, viz. ὑμῶν τοῦ ἔργου τῆς πίστεως.

2. **εὐχαριστοῦμεν τῷ θεῷ**. Except in writing to "the churches of Galatia," the Apostle always begins with thanksgiving (cf. v. 18); here expressed with warmth and emphasis: see *Introd.* pp. xxxiii., lxii. Εὐχαριστέω (classical χάριν ἔχω, 1 Tim. i. 12, &c.)—with its cognates in -τος, -τία, confined to St Paul's amongst the Epistles—is infrequent in the N.T. elsewhere; the compound first occurs in Demosthenes, *de Corona* p. 257, with an earlier sense, 'to do a good turn to' (Lightfoot).

μνείαν ποιούμενοι, *making mention* rather than *remembering*; *mentionem* (Beza), not *memoriam* (Vulg.), *facientes*—the latter the sense of μνημονεύω in v. 3 cf. Plato, *Protag.* 317 E and *Phaedrus* 254 A (Lightf.); also Rom. i. 9; Eph. i. 16; Phm. 4. Μνείαν ἔχω, in iii. 6, is different (see note). ἐπὶ τῶν προσευχῶν ἡμῶν, *on occasion of our prayers*; so ἐπ' ἐμοῦ, *in my time* (Herodotus); ἐπ' ἐμῆς νεότητος (Aristophanes); ἐπὶ δείπνου (Lucian): 'recalling your name when we bend before God in prayer'; observe the union of prayer and thanksgiving in v. 17 f.

3. **ἀδιαλείπτως μνημονεύοντες**: *indesinenter memores* (Calvin)—or still better, *indesinenter memoria recolentes* (Estius: for μνημονεύω = μνήμων εἰμί), *being unremittingly mindful of your work*, &c. The rhythm and balance of the participial clauses seem to speak, however, for the attachment of the adverb to v. 2—*making mention of you in our prayers unceasingly*; St Paul uses ἀδιαλ. characteristically of *prayer*: see ii. 13, v. 17; Rom. i. 9 f.; 2 Tim. i. 3. Μνημονεύω is capable of the same double use as μνείαν ποιοῦμαι above; but it is construed with περί in the sense of *mentioning* (cf. Heb. xi. 22); the bare genitive suits the sense *remembering*: cf. Gal. ii. 10; Col. iv. 18; and note the different shade of meaning conveyed by the *accusative* in ii. 9. On the grammatical construction, see Winer-Moulton, *Grammar*, pp. 256 f.

ἔμπροσθεν τοῦ θεοῦ κ.τ.λ. at the end of this clause balances τῷ θεῷ and ἐπὶ τῶν προσευχῶν of the preceding clauses: "in the presence (or sight) of our God and Father" St Paul and his companions ever bear in mind the Christian worth of the Thessalonians. Ἔμπροσθεν in this connexion is peculiar to this Epistle: ii. 19, iii. 9, 13; cf. 2 Cor. v. 10; Acts x. 4; 1 Jo. iii. 19. Grammatically, the ἔμπροσθεν clause might adhere to the nearer verbal nouns ἔργου, κόπου, ὑπομονῆς, or **to** the last alone (so Lightf.: cf. iii. 13; and, for the idea, 2 Cor. iv. 18; Heb. xi. 27), much as ἐν θεῷ πατρί is attached to ἐκκλησίᾳ in v. 1; but ἡμῶν points back to the subject of μνημονεύοντες, and through the first part of the Letter there runs a tone of solemn protestation on the writers' part (see *Introd.* pp. xxxiv. f.) with which this emphatic adjunct to the participle is in keeping: see ii. 4 ff., 19 f., iii. 9; and cf. Rom. ix. 1 f.; 2 Cor. i. 23, xi. 31.

ὑμῶν τοῦ ἔργου τῆς πίστεως καὶ τοῦ κόπου τῆς ἀγάπης καὶ τῆς ὑπομονῆς τῆς ἐλπίδος τοῦ κυρίου κ.τ.λ. On occasion of mentioning *persons* (v. 2), one recalls their *character and deeds*. The three objects of remembrance—ἔργου, κόπου, ὑπομονῆς (for the trio, cf. Rev. ii. 2)—are parallel and collectively introduced by the possessive ὑμῶν, each being expressed by a verbal noun with subjective genitive, on which genitive in each case—πίστεως, ἀγάπης, ἐλπίδος—the emphasis rests: "remembering how your faith works, and your love toils, and your hope endures"; see Blass' *Gram. of N.T. Greek*, p. 96. The third of the latter three is defined by the objective genitive, τοῦ κυρίου ἡμῶν Ἰησοῦ Χριστοῦ: Hope fastens on "our Lord Jesus Christ" (1 Jo. iii. 3)— thus named under the sense of the majesty of His παρουσία (cf. *v.* 10, v. 9, 23; II. i. 12, ii. 14, 16; also 1 Cor. i. 7—9, &c.)—while in this context Faith looks, through Christ, "toward God" (*v.* 8 f.), and Love has "the brethren" for object (iv. 9 f.; II. i. 3). The familiar Pauline triad first presents itself here—*fides, amor, spes: summa Christianismi* (Bengel); they reappear in v. 8: cf. the thanksgiving of II. i. 3 f.; also 1 Cor. xiii. 13 (where *love* predominates, as against Corinthian selfishness and strife; here *hope*, under the pressure of Thessalonian affliction); Gal. v. 5 f.; Col. i. 4 f.; in 1 Pet. i. 3 ff. *hope* again takes the lead. Faith and Love are constantly associated (see iii. 6, &c.), Faith and Hope frequently (Rom. v. 1 ff., xv. 13, &c.), Love and Hope in 1 Jo. iv. 17 f. These formed the three "theological virtues" of Scholastic Ethics, to which were appended the four "philosophical virtues," *Wisdom, Courage, Temperance, Justice.*

τοῦ ἔργου τῆς πίστεως, *faith's work* (activity; cf. Ja. i. 4)—a wide expression (cf. ii. 13 below; II. i. 11, ii. 17; Gal. v. 6) corresponding to "the fruit of the Spirit" or "of the light" (Gal. v. 22; Eph. v. 9), which embraces the whole practical outcome of Thessalonian faith indicated immediately afterwards in *vv.* 7—10. The commendation is characteristic of this Church (see *Introd.* p. xxxiii.). This connexion of "faith," on its first appearance in St Paul's writings (cf. πίστις ἐνεργουμένη, Gal. v. 6), with "work," shows that he was as far from approving a theoretical or sentimental faith as St James (see Ja. ii. 14 ff.). In the second group of his Epistles "faith" indeed is opposed to (Pharisaic) "works *of law*" (see Rom. iv. 1—5; Gal. ii. 16, iii. 10—14), for these "works" were put by the legalists *in the place of faith* and were built upon as affording in their own right a ground of salvation; the "work" of this passage and of James ii. is *the offspring of faith*, and affords not the ground but the aim and evidence of salvation. The distinction comes out very clearly in Eph. ii. 8—10: οὐκ ἐξ ὑμῶν, θεοῦ τὸ δῶρον· οὐκ ἐξ ἔργων...αὐτοῦ γάρ ἐσμεν ποίημα... ἐπὶ ἔργοις ἀγαθοῖς. Since πίστις is the root-virtue of Christianity, Christians as such are styled οἱ πιστεύοντες (ii. 13; II. i. 10, &c.).

τοῦ κόπου τῆς ἀγάπης κ.τ.λ. The *faith* of this Church shone in its *toil of love* (see iv. 9 ff.; II. i. 3) *and endurance of hope* (*vv.* 6, 10,

ii. 14, v. 4 f.; II. i. 4 ff., ii. 14). Κόπος signifies *wearing toil*, labour carried to the limit of strength, and differs from ἔργον as effort and exertion from activity: St Paul refers both to his manual labour (ii. 9; II. iii. 8) and to his missionary toil (iii. 5; 2 Cor. vi. 5) as κόπος; cf. κοπιάω, Jo. iv. 6; Rev. ii. 3. In 1 Cor. iii. 8 κόπος gives the measure for Divine *reward*: here it is the expression of human *love*; thus parents task themselves for their children (cf. ii. 7—9; also Eph. iv. 28, κοπιάτω). On ἀγάπη, the specific N.T. word for (spiritual) Love—to be distinguished from φιλία and ἔρως—see Trench's *N.T. Synonyms*, § 12, or Cremer's *Bibl.-Theological Lexicon*.

Ὑπομονή is a more positive, manful virtue than *patience* (see Trench, *Syn.* § 53); it corresponds to the classical καρτερία or καρτέρησις (Plato, Aristotle), and embraces *perseverantia* as well as *patientia* (Old Latin) or *sustinentia* (Vulg.); hence it suits with ἔργον and κόπος: see Rom. ii. 7, καθ' ὑπομονὴν ἔργου ἀγαθοῦ; cf. also II. i. 4—7, and (including ὑπομένω) II. iii. 5; Rom. v. 4, viii. 25; Col. i. 11; Heb. xii. 1 ff.; Matt. x. 22. *Hope in our Lord Jesus Christ* inspired the brave patience in which Thessalonian virtue, tried from the first by severe persecution (v. 6, iii. 2—6), culminated.

V. 4 discloses the deeper ground of the Apostles' thanksgiving, lying in their conviction, formed at the beginning of their ministry to the Thessalonians (v. 5) and confirmed by subsequent experience (vv. 6 ff., ii. 13), that the readers are objects of God's electing love. **εἰδότες**—*siquidem novimus* (Estius)—implies settled knowledge; contrast this with γνῶναι of iii. 5 (see note).

ἀδελφοὶ ἠγαπημένοι ὑπὸ [τοῦ] θεοῦ. The parallel construction of II. ii. 13 (see note) proves ὑπὸ θεοῦ to belong to the participle, for which otherwise ἀγαπητοί would have served (see ii. 8; Phil. iv. 1, and *passim*; cf. Rom. i. 7); the *ordo verborum* forbids attachment to τὴν ἐκλογήν (A.V.). This phrase occurs in Sirach xlv. 1, used of Moses (with καὶ ἀνθρώπων added); cf. Rom. ix. 25 (Hos. ii. 23, LXX). The perf. participle marks the readers as objects of an abiding, determinate love (cf. 1 Jo. iii. 1, ἀγάπην δέδωκεν), which has taken expression in their election.

εἰδότες...τὴν ἐκλογὴν ὑμῶν. St Paul's doxologies commonly look behind the human worth of the subjects to some gracious action or purpose on God's part towards them; cf. e.g. 1 Cor. i. 4 ff.; Phil. i. 6; Col. i. 4 f. Ἐκλογή (*picking out, selection*), from ἐκλέγομαι (= αἱρέομαι, II. ii. 13), denotes the act of God in choosing a man or community to receive some special grace or to render some special service (e.g., in Acts ix. 15), or for both intents at once; more particularly, as here and in II. ii. 13, to salvation in Christ (see Rom. ix. 11, xi. 5, 28). In Rom. xi. 7, by metonymy, it signifies a body of *chosen persons* (=ἐκλεκτοί: for which usage cf. Rom. viii. 33; Tit. i. 1). Rom. xi. shows how St Paul's doctrine of "election," "the elect of God," grew out of the O.T. conception of Israel as "the people of Jehovah" chosen and separated from the nations: see e.g. Ps. xxxiii. 12, cxxxv. 4; Deut. xiv. 2; Isai. xliii. 1—7; and cf. further with these passages Rom. viii. 28—39; 1 Cor. i. 26—31; Eph. i. 4 ff.; also 1 Pet. ii. 9 f. This election, in the case of Israel or of the N.T. Churches, implied *selection* out of the mass who, for whatever reason, are put aside—"the rest" (iv. 13, v. 6, below); and *appropriation* by God. Under the "call" of the Gospel the national gives place to a spiritual election, or ἐκλογὴ χάριτος (Rom. xi. 5), of individual believers who, collectively, constitute henceforth "the Israel of God" (Gal. vi. 16); this is formed οὐ μόνον ἐξ Ἰουδαίων (λεῖμμα, xi. 5) ἀλλὰ καὶ ἐξ ἐθνῶν (Rom. ix. 24; Eph. iii. 6), the latter being grafted into the "garden-olive" (Rom. xi. 24) of God's primitive choice. In Rom. viii. 28—30 the Divine ἐκλογή is represented as an orderly πρόθεσις—love *planning* for its chosen—with its successive steps of πρόγνωσις, προόρισις, &c.; in Eph. i. 4 it is carried back to a date πρὸ καταβολῆς κόσμου (see note on II. ii. 13 below). Our Lord's parable of the Marriage-Supper (Matt. xxii. 1—14) distinguishes the ἐκλεκτοί from the κλητοί, 'the invited'; otherwise in the N.T. the two terms are equal in extent: see note on ii. 12; and cf. κλῆσις and ἐκλέγομαι as they are associated in 1 Cor. i. 26 ff. God's choice of men does not preclude effort on their part (see *v.* 3), nor even the contingency of failure; though the Apostle "*knows* the election" of his readers, he "sends *in order to know*" their "faith...lest" his "toil should prove vain" (iii. 5; cf. 2 Tim. ii. 10; Jo. vi. 70). The missionaries are practically certain that their converts are of God's elect, not absolutely sure of the final salvation of every individual thus addressed.

Of God's special favour to this people the writers were persuaded (*a*) by *the signal power attending their ministry at their first preaching to them* (*v.* 5), and (*b*) by *the zeal and thoroughness with which they had accepted the gospel* (*vv.* 6 ff.).

5. ὅτι τὸ εὐαγγέλιον ἡμῶν οὐκ ἐγενήθη εἰς ὑμᾶς κ.τ.λ. Ὅτι—introducing the coordinate and corresponding sentences of *vv.* 5, 6 (τὸ εὐαγγ. ἡμῶν οὐκ ἐγενήθη εἰς ὑμᾶς...καὶ ὑμεῖς μιμ. ἡμῶν ἐγενήθητε)—is explicative of εἰδότες, not τὴν ἐκλογήν, signifying *in that, seeing that,* rather than *how that* (**R.V.**); for ὅτι of the *ground*, not *content*, of knowledge, cf. Jo. vii. 29, xviii. 2; otherwise in 1 Cor. i 26. The other view is strongly stated in Lightfoot's Note *ad loc.*

For γίνομαι εἰς of local direction, cf. Acts xx. 16; but ethical direction (cf. iii. 5) is implied: "*our Good News reached you*, arrived at your hearts." The "good news" is *ours* as "we proclaim" it (ii. 4, 9; II. ii. 14; 2 Cor. iv. 3; Rom. i. 15, ii. 16, &c.), but *God's* as He originates and sends it (ii. 2, 9, 12; Rom. i. 2, &c.), and *Christ's* as He constitutes its matter (iii. 2; II. i. 8; Rom. i. 2; 1 Cor. i. 23, &c.). Ἐγενήθην, the Doric aorist of the κοινή, is frequent in this Epistle.

οὐκ...ἐν λόγῳ μόνον ἀλλὰ καὶ ἐν δυνάμει κ.τ.λ. Εἰς gives the persons *to* whom, ἐν the influence *in* which the εὐαγγέλιον came. Its bearers in delivering their message at Thessalonica were conscious of a supernatural power that made them at the time sure of success. For the antithesis λόγος—δύναμις, familiar in the Epistles, see 1 Cor. ii. 1, 4 f., iv. 19 f.; 2 Cor. x. 11 (ἔργον); 1 Jo. iii. 18: in ii. 13 below the same contrast appears in the form λόγος ἀνθρώπων and θεοῦ (see note). For the phrase ἐν δυνάμει, cf. II. i. 11, ii. 9.

Behind the *effective power* (δύναμις) with which the Good News wrought on its Thessalonian hearers there lay certain *personal influences* operative therein, **ἐν πνεύματι ἁγίῳ καὶ πληροφορίᾳ πολλῇ**: the single ἐν (cf. note on ἐν, v. 1) combines these adjuncts as the two faces, objective and subjective, of one fact. The πνεῦμα ἅγιον reappears in *v.* 6, iv. 8, v. 19; the Thessalonians knew "the Holy Spirit" as an invisible power attending the Gospel and possessing the believer with sanctifying effect, which proceeds from God and is God's own Spirit (τὸ πνεῦμα αὐτοῦ τὸ ἅγιον, iv. 8). See 1 Cor. ii. 9—16; 2 Cor. i. 22; Rom. viii. 1—27; Gal. iii. 14, iv. 4—7; Eph. iv. 30, for St Paul's later teaching; and Lk. xi. 13, Jo. xiv.—xvi., for the doctrine of our Lord respecting the Spirit. The *power* of the Gospel was ascribed to the Holy Spirit in the original promise of Jesus (Lk. xxiv. 49; Acts i. 8); cf. Lk. i. 35, iv. 14; Matt. xii. 28; Acts x. 38; Gal. iii. 5; Rom. xv. 13, 19, for various powerful activities of the Spirit. *Physical miracles* (δυνάμεις, see note, **II. ii. 9**) are neither indicated nor excluded here.

Πληροφορία has two meanings: (*a*) *fulness* (R.V. marg.), i.e. *full issue* or *yield*, as from πληροφορέω in 2 Tim. iv. 5 or Lk. i. 1; (*b*) or *full assurance* (A.V., R.V. text, *much assurance; certitudo et certa persuasio*, Erasmus), as from πληροφορέω in Rom. iv. 21, xiv. 5. According to (*a*) the thought is that the Good News came to the hearers "in the plenitude" of its effect and bore rich fruit (cf. ii. 13); according to (*b*), that it came with "full conviction" and confidence on the part of preachers and hearers (cf. ii. 2 ff.). The foregoing subject, εὐαγγέλιον ἡμῶν, sustained by οἷοι ἡμεῖς ἐγενήθημεν in the sequel, speaks for the latter interpretation, which accounts for the combination ἐν πν. ἁγ. καὶ πληροφ. (see note above) in this connexion: "We delivered our message and you received it under the mighty influence of the Holy Spirit, and so in full assurance of its efficacy." Πληροφορία bears the subjective sense in the other N.T. exx.—Col. ii. 2; Heb. vi. 11, x. 22; so in Clemens Rom. *ad Cor.* xlii, μετὰ πληροφορίας **πνεύματος ἁγίου** ἐξῆλθον εὐαγγελιζόμενοι, which echoes this passage; to the like effect πν. ἅγιον is associated with παρρησία in Acts iv. 31, and with μαρτυρία in Acts i. 8 and Jo. xv. 26 f. The warm convictions attending the proclamation of the Gospel at Thessalonica reflected themselves in the χαρὰ πνεύματος ἁγίου of its recipients (*v.* 6).

For confirmation of what the writers assert about their preaching, they appeal, in passing, to the knowledge of the readers: **καθὼς οἴδατε οἷοι ἐγενήθημεν [ἐν] ὑμῖν δι᾽ ὑμᾶς,** *as you know the sort of men that we proved (were made to be) to* [or *amongst*] *you on your behoof*,—how confidently full of the Spirit and of power. In this connexion, δι᾽ ὑμᾶς refers not to *the motives of the preachers* (shown in ii. 5—12), but to *the purpose of God* toward their hearers, who for their sake inspired His servants thus to deliver His message (cf. Acts xviii. 9 f.; also 1 Cor. iii. 5 f., 21 f.; 2 Cor. i. 6, iv. 7—15): proof is being adduced of God's electing grace towards the Thessalonians (*v.* 4). For collocation of different prepositions (ἐν, διά) with the same pronoun, cf. iv. 14; see Textual Note, preferring ἐν ὑμῖν. The repeated and varied references made in the Epistle, by way of confirmation, to *the readers' knowledge* (ii. 1 f., 5, 9 f., iii. 4, iv. 2, v. 2) are explained in the *Introd.* p. lxii.

The relative οἷος should be distinguished from the indirect interrogative ὁποῖος, as used in *v.* 9: there strangers are conceived as asking, "What kind of entrance had Paul, &c.?" and receiving their answer; here it is no *question* as to what the Apostles were like at Thessalonica, but *the fact of their having been so and so* is reasserted from the knowledge of the readers. For similar exx. of the relative pronoun apparently, but not really, substituted for the interrogative, cf. 2 Tim. i. 14; Lk. ix. 33, xxii. 60; Mk v. 33: see Kühner's *Ausführliche Grammatik d. griech. Sprache*², II. § 562. 4, "Dass das Relativ (ὅς, οἷος, ὅσος) in abhängigen Fragesätzen an der Stelle des Fragepronomens ὅστις oder τίς, ὁποῖος oder ποῖος, u. s. w., gebraucht werde, wird mit Unrecht angenommen"; also Rutherford's *First Greek Syntax*, § 251.

A colon, not a full-stop, should close *v.* 5.

V. 6 supplies the other side to the proof given in *v.* 5 of the election of the readers (*v.* 4), **ὅτι...καὶ ὑμεῖς** (in contrast to τὸ εὐαγγ. ἡμῶν, *v.* 5) **μιμηταὶ ἡμῶν ἐγενήθητε κ.τ.λ.** The internal construction of the verse is open to doubt, as to whether the δεξάμενοι clause (*a*) explains the μιμηταί,—"in that you received the word, &c."; or (*b*) supplies the antecedent fact and ground of the imitation,—"after that," or "inasmuch as, you had received the word," &c. According to (*a*), the Thessalonians imitated the Apostles and their Lord *in their manner of receiving the word*: such a narrowing of μιμηταί is not in keeping with *v*. 3 nor *vv*. 9 f., which describe the general Christian behaviour of the readers, as in the parallel instances of μιμητής—ii. 14; 1 Cor. iv. 16, xi. 1; Eph. v. 1; Ph. iii. 17—20. According to (*b*), the Thessalonians *in their changed spirit and manner of life* on receiving the Gospel, had copied "the ways in the Lord" (1 Cor. iv. 14—17) of their teachers (1 Cor. xi. 1; cf. Eph. iv. 20—24, 1 Jo. ii. 6, Jo. xiii. 34, &c.)—*since you gave a welcome to the word*: the good beginning accounts for the worthy course. By their cordial reception of the Divine message they entered bravely and joyfully upon the way of life marked out by the example of the Apostles and their Lord— a decisive evidence of God's loving choice of this people (*v*. 4).

δεξάμενοι τὸν λόγον ἐν θλίψει πολλῇ μετὰ χαρᾶς πνεύματος ἁγίου. The welcome given to the Gospel was enhanced at once by the adverse conditions attending it (*in much affliction*) and by the gladness which surmounted these conditions (*with joy of—inspired by—the Holy Spirit*). Cf. the case of Berœa: ἐδέξαντο τὸν λόγον μετὰ πάσης προθυμίας, Acts xvii. 11. For the *warmth* of reception implied in δέχομαι, see ii. 13, and note; also II. ii. 10, 1 Cor. ii. 14, Lk. viii. 13, Ja. i. 21, &c. For the association of *joy* with *receiving the word*, see Lk. ii. 10, viii. 13, Acts viii. 8, 39, xiii. 48; of Christian *joy* with *affliction*, Rom. v. 3, xii. 12, 2 Cor. vi. 10, Col. i. 24, Acts v. 41, &c.; of *joy* with *the Holy Spirit*—a conjunction as characteristic as that of *power* and the Spirit (*v*. 5)—Rom. xiv. 17, xv. 13, Gal. v. 22, Phil. iii. 3, Lk. x. 21, Acts xiii. 52. The genitive is that of *source* connoting *quality*—a joy that comes of the Spirit and is spiritual. Acts xvii. 5—13 shows the kind of θλίψις "amid" which this Church was founded.

7. ὥστε γενέσθαι ὑμᾶς τύπον πᾶσιν, κ.τ.λ. Infinitive clause of *result*, heightening the appreciation of the Thessalonian Church in *v*. 6, and thus adding to the evidence of its "election" (*v*. 4). The readers had followed the example set them so well, that they had become in turn "a pattern to all" Christians around them. Τύπον is intrinsically better than τύπους (see Textual Note); for the Church collectively—**not** its individual members—was known at a distance.

πᾶσιν τοῖς πιστεύουσιν, a substantival designation (cf. note on τὸν ῥυόμενον, v. 10)—*to all believers*—naming Christians from the distinctive and continuous activity which makes them such (cf. v. 3, ii. 10, 13; Rom. iv. 11; 1 Cor. xiv. 22 &c.); οἱ πιστεύοντες = οἱ ἐκ πίστεως (Gal. iii. 7). Had the "imitators" of v. 6 been such in respect simply of their "*receiving* the word," they would have been a pattern not τοῖς πιστεύουσιν, but rather τοῖς πιστεύσασιν,—in respect of the initial act, not the continued life of faith: cf. τύπος γίνου τῶν πιστῶν in 1 Tim. iv. 12; also II. iii. 9, Phil. iii. 17, where μιμέομαι and τύπος are associated.

ἐν τῇ Μακεδονίᾳ καὶ ἐν τῇ Ἀχαίᾳ, the two European provinces now evangelized: see the *Map*, and *Introd.*, pp. xi., xv., xxxiii., xxxix. We know of Churches at Philippi and Berœa in Macedonia, while iv. 10 implies their existence in other parts of this province: "many of the Corinthians" by this time were baptized (Acts xviii. 8); and some of "the saints," outside of Corinth, "that were in the whole of Achaia" when 2 Cor. i. 1 was written, beside the handful of Athenian disciples (Acts xvii. 34), are doubtless included in this reference. 2 Cor. viii. 1–6, xi. 9, and 1 Cor. xvi. 5 f., illustrate the close connexion and Christian intercourse of the two regions.

Vv. **8–10** explain and re-affirm, with emphatic enlargement, the assertion of *v.* 7, which might otherwise appear to the readers over strong.

8. ἀφ' ὑμῶν γὰρ ἐξήχηται ὁ λόγος τοῦ κυρίου. *For from you hath rung out the word of the Lord:* ὥσπερ σάλπιγγος λαμπρὸν ἠχούσης ὁ πλησίον ἅπας πληροῦται τόπος (Chrysostom); *longe lateque sonitus* (Estius); *exsonuit, sive ebuccinatus est* (Erasmus). The verb ἐξηχέω —a *hap. legomenon* for N.T.—belongs to later Greek; used in Joel iii. 14 (LXX., in military context), Sirach xl. 13 (of *thunder*), it denotes a loud, resonant sound, like a trumpet-call. Ὁ λόγος τοῦ κυρίου, while redolent of O.T. associations (cf. Rom. x. 18; Ps. xviii. 5), denotes here, definitely, the message which "the Lord" Jesus (*v.* 6) speaks through His servants: cf. iv. 15, II. iii. 1; Col. iii. 16; Rom. i. 5. This reference is perfectly congruous with ii. 2, 13, for "the Lord" authoritatively brings word *from God* to men (Jo. xvii. 8, &c.); it accords with πίστις πρὸς τὸν θεόν in the sequel, for Christ's word brings men *to God* (cf. Eph. ii. 17 f.; Jo. xiv. 6, &c.). The *effect*, rather than the mere fact, of the conversion of the Thessalonians made the Good News "ring out from" them (*vv.* 3, 6; cf. iv. 10, II. i. 3 f.).

The range of this sound is widened from "the Macedonia and Achaia" of *v.* 7 (the provinces being here united, as one area, by the single ἐν τῇ)—οὐ μόνον ἐν τῇ Μακεδονίᾳ καὶ Ἀχαίᾳ, ἀλλ' ἐν παντὶ τόπῳ; and with this enlargement of the field in view the main assertion is restated—ἡ πίστις ὑμῶν ἡ πρὸς τὸν θεὸν ἐξελήλυθεν. This results in a curious anacoluthon, to which no exact parallel is forthcoming; it gives a sense natural and clear enough, as presented in the English Version. To this construction most interpreters, with Ellicott, Lightfoot, Schmiedel, WH, adhere. But Calvin, Hofmann Bornemann, and others, divide the verse by a colon at κυρίου: "For from you hath rung out the word of the Lord; not only in Macedonia and Achaia, but in every place your faith toward God hath gone abroad"—which makes an awkward asyndeton, out of keeping in a paragraph so smoothly continuous as this (see Note introd. to v. 3). Ἐξελήλυθεν is synonymous with ἐξήχηται (minus the *figure*), while ἡ πίστις κ.τ.λ. is practically equivalent to ὁ λόγος τοῦ κυρίου, since the Gospel has spread in this manner by the active faith of the readers (ἡ πίστις ὑμῶν); such faith is "the word of the Lord" in *effect*: cf. 2 Cor. iii. 3; Phil. ii. 15 f.; Matt. v. 14–16. What the Apostle affirms in this sense of the Thessalonians, he questions, in another sense, of the Corinthians: ἢ ἀφ' ὑμῶν ὁ λόγος τοῦ θεοῦ ἐξῆλθεν; (1 Cor. xiv. 36).

ἐν παντὶ τόπῳ signifies "in every place (that we visit or communicate with": see v. 9 a); cf. 1 Cor. i. 2; 2 Cor. ii. 14; 1 Tim. ii. 8. Aquila and his wife had just come from Rome (Acts xviii. 2), and may have brought word that the story was current there; the charge of treason against Cæsar (xvii. 7) would surely be reported at Rome. The three missionaries were, most likely, in correspondence with the Churches in Asia Minor, Antioch, and Jerusalem (cf. note on II. i. 4), and had received congratulations from those distant spots. The commercial connexions of Thessalonica (see *Introd.* p. xi.) facilitated the dissemination of news. The work of St Paul and his companions here had made a great sensation and given a wide advertisement to Christianity; cf. Rom. i. 8, xvi. 19.

ἡ πίστις ἡ πρὸς τὸν θεόν. A unique expression, indicating the changed direction and attitude on the part of the readers, which vv. 9, 10 set forth—*your faith, that is turned toward God*: cf. 2 Cor. iii. 4; Phm. 5; and see note on iii. 4, for the force of πρός.

ὥστε μὴ χρείαν ἔχειν ἡμᾶς λαλεῖν τι. This report preceded the missionaries in their travels; they even found themselves anticipated in sending the news to distant correspondents. Χρείαν ἔχω with dependent infinitive recurs twice in this Epistle (iv. 9, v. 1),—only here in St Paul; similarly in Matt. iii. 14, &c.; the phrase is complemented by the infinitive with τοῦ in Heb. v. 12; by ἵνα and subjunctive in Jo. ii. 25, &c. In Plato *Sympos.* 204 c it bears the opposite sense, *to be of service*; but see Aeschylus *Prom. V.* 169, ἐμοῦ...χρείαν ἕξει, for the use of this idiom in earlier Greek. Ὥστε μή and infinitive, of negative *result contemplated*; contrast ὥστε οὐ and indicative, of negative *consequence asserted*, in 1 Cor. iii. 7; Gal. iv. 7. Λαλεῖν τι, *loqui quidquam, to be saying anything—to open our mouths on the subject;* cf. note on λαλῆσαι, ii. 2.

The ὥστε-clause is supported by the reassertive and explanatory γάρ of *v.* 9, just as in the sequence of *vv.* 7, 8.

9. αὐτοὶ γὰρ περὶ ἡμῶν ἀπαγγέλλουσιν ὁποίαν, κ.τ.λ. *For of their own accord they* (the people we meet with in Macedonia or Achaia, or hear from "in every place") *report about us* (or *you*: see Textual Note). It must be remembered that these are the statements (*vv.* 7–9) not of St Paul alone, but of Silvanus and Timothy besides, who had newly joined the Apostle at Corinth after separately visiting Macedonia and traversing a wide extent of country.

ὁποίαν (the proper indirect interrog.: cf. note on οἷοι, *v.* 5) **εἴσοδον** —*qualem ingressum* (Calvin, Beza), rather than *introitum* (Vulg.)— *what sort of an entrance*, how happy and successful (*v.* 5; ii. 1 f., where εἴσοδος recurs; ii. 13: cf. also Heb. x. 19). The noun nowhere implies *reception*.

καὶ πῶς ἐπεστρέψατε πρὸς τὸν θεὸν ἀπὸ κ.τ.λ. completes the report of the success of the writers, just as *v.* 6 completed the description of the conversion of the readers given by *v.* 5. Πῶς— the direct for indirect interrogative (ὅπως in this sense only in Lk. xxiv. 20 in N.T.; otherwise *telic*)—implies the *manner* as well as the *fact* of conversion: see *v.* 6, ii. 13. Ἐπ- in the verb marks not regression (as in Gal. iv. 9, &c.), but *direction* (as in Acts ix. 40); πρός, as in 2 Cor. iii. 16, gives the object *toward* which "you turned," resuming the phrase of *v.* 8—oftener ἐπί in this connexion (as in Gal. iv. 9; Acts xiv. 15); εἰς, with characteristic difference, in Matt. xii. 44, Lk. ii. 39, &c.

The aforesaid report describes a conversion from Paganism to the service of "the (one, true) God"—πρὸς τὸν θεόν. The Thessalonian Christians had been mainly heathen, "not knowing God" (II. i. 8; Gal. iv. 8; cf. ii. 14 below); there was, however, a sprinkling of Jews among them, with "a great multitude" of proselytes more or less weaned previously from idolatry, according to Acts xvii. 4. "The God" whom they now "serve," is *a God living and real* (*vivo et vero*). This is the dialect of O.T. faith; so much might have been said of converts to Judaism.

ζῶντι καὶ ἀληθινῷ is categorically opposed to τῶν εἰδώλων: *Jahveh* (Jehovah), the *HE WILL BE*—(see Ex. iii. 13 f., for the Israelite reading of the ineffable Name; and cf. Isai. xlii. 8, xlv. 5 ff., 18, 21 ff., for its controversial use against heathenism), is by His very name "the true God and the living God" (Jer. x. 10); all other deities are therefore dead and unreal—mere λεγόμενοι θεοί (1 Cor. viii. 4 ff.). In this sense they are stigmatized as εἴδωλα, the Septuagint rendering of אֱלִילִים (*nothings*, Ps. xcvii. 7, &c.), or הֲבָלִים (*vapours, emptinesses*, Deut. xxxii. 21, &c.). Εἴδωλον denotes an *appearance*, an *image* or *phantom* without substance: the word was applied by Homer to the *phantasms* of distant persons imposed on men by the gods (*Iliad* v. 449; *Odyssey* IV. 796); cf. Bacon's *idola tribus, specus*, &c. In the *Theætetus* 150 A C E and 151 C, Plato identifies εἴδωλον with ψεῦδος (cf. Rom. i. 23, 25) and contrasts it with what is ἀληθινόν, γνήσιον, ἀληθές. Similarly, heathen gods and their rites are styled τὰ μάταια in Acts xiv. 15, as occasionally in the LXX. (cf. Rom. i. 21; Eph. iv. 17: for the O.T., see in illustration Ps. cxv. 4—8; Is. xliv. 9—20; Jer. x. 1—11). St Paul was powerfully impressed by observation with the hollowness of the Paganism of his time. Ἀληθινός, *verus*—to be distinguished from ἀληθής (cf. Rom. iii. 4), *verax*—denotes *truth of fact*, the correspondence of the reality to the conception or the name (see e.g. Jo. xv. 1, xvii. 3; 1 Jo. v. 20); θεὸς ἀληθινός is the "very God" of the Nicene Creed.

With **δουλεύειν**, *to serve as bondmen*, cf. St Paul's habitual designation of himself as δοῦλος Χριστοῦ, once δοῦλος θεοῦ (Tit. i. 1),—the O.T. עֶבֶד יהוה. Religious obligation was conceived under this usual form of personal service, which implied ownership on the master's and absolute dependence on the servant's part. Elsewhere St Paul corrects the term in contrasting Christian and pre-Christian service to God—"no longer a slave but a son": Gal. iv. 1—10; Rom. viii. 12—17; cf. Jo. viii. 31—36; 1 Jo. iii. 1 f.

10. **καὶ ἀναμένειν τὸν υἱὸν αὐτοῦ ἐκ τῶν οὐρανῶν.** (*You turned to God from idols, to serve...God*) *and to await His Son* (*coming*) *out of the heavens.* The emphasis laid on "hope" at the outset of the εὐχαριστία prepared us for this culmination. The mind both of writers and readers was full of the thought of Christ's glorious return (cf. iv. 13—v. 11; II. i. 7 ff., ii. 1—14; and see *Introd.* pp. xxvii. ff., lxiii. f.); St Paul's first preaching had given to Thessalonian faith this outlook. The farther we go back in the history of

the Apostolic Church, the more we find it intent upon the coming of its Lord. It held freshly in mind the promise of Acts i. 11, and set great store by such assurances as are recorded in Lk. xii. 36, xix. 12; Matt. xxvi. 64, &c. Cf. Acts iii. 21; 1 Cor. i. 7; Phil. iii. 20 f.; Col. iii. 1—4; Tit. ii. 13; 1 Pet. i. 7; Heb. ix. 27 f.; 1 Jo. ii. 28, iii. 3; Rev. i. 7, for the dominance in N.T. thought of this "blessed hope."

'Αναμένειν is a *hap. leg.* in the N.T.: ἀνα- implies *sustained* expectation; cf. ἀπεκδέχεσθαι in 1 Cor. i. 7; Phil. iii. 20. Τῶν οὐρανῶν, plural after שָׁמַיִם, heaven being conceived in Hebrew thought as multiple and various—rising tier above tier: cf. 2 Cor. xii. 2; Heb. iv. 14, &c.; also Eph. i. 3, &c.; and see the article "Heaven" in Hastings' *Dictionary of the Bible.*

Jewish hope was looking for a glorious descent from heaven of the Messiah, who was sometimes designated "the Son of God"; the added ὃν ἤγειρεν ἐκ τῶν νεκρῶν, Ἰησοῦν—*whom He (God) raised from the dead, even Jesus*—discloses the chasm parting the Church from the Synagogue: cf. the account given of St Paul's preaching to the Jews at Thessalonica in the *Introd.*, pp. xvii. f. The *resurrection of Jesus* was the critical fact in the controversy; the moment he was convinced of this fact, Saul of Tarsus became a Christian (see Gal. i. 1, 12, &c.; cf. Rom. x. 9; 1 Cor. xv. 3 ff.). God's raising of Him from the dead gave evidence that Jesus was "His Son" (cf. Rom. i 4), and Saviour and Lord of men (Rom. iv. 24 f., xiv. 9; 1 Cor. xv. 20 ff., &c.; also Acts ii. 32 ff., &c.). The resurrection, proving Jesus to be Lord and Son of God, preludes His return in glory; for such glory is promised and due to Him in this character (see Phil. ii. 9 ff.; Acts iii. 21, xvii. 31; Matt. xxvi. 63 f.; Lk. xxiv. 26 f.; Rev. v. 12). "Jesus" always stands with St Paul for the historical person: see iv. 14, and note.

The Thessalonians *await Jesus* as *our rescuer from the wrath that is coming*—τὸν ῥυόμενον ἡμᾶς ἐκ τῆς ὀργῆς τῆς ἐρχομένης. As the glorious return of Jesus filled the horizon of this Church, so the question of *final salvation or perdition* engrossed their thoughts respecting themselves and their fellows: see iv. 13, v. 3 ff.; II. i. 5 ff., ii. 12 ff. Accordingly, the Apostle dwells in these two Letters on the consummation of salvation, not its present experience as he did afterwards, e.g., in Rom. v. 1 ff.; Gal. iv. 6 f.; Eph. i. 4 ff., ii. 5 ff.; cf. v. 9 and note below, II. ii. 13—16. In the religion of the readers he emphasizes two things, serving the true God in place of idols and awaiting the return from heaven of the risen Jesus; but the doctrine of the forgiveness of sins, as that is expounded in the second group of the Epistles and hinted in v. 9 f. below, is really implied by the description of Jesus as the Deliverer from God's wrath; for that "wrath" is directed against human sin, and sin is only removed by forgiveness (justification): see iv. 6 ff.; II. i. 8 f.; cf. Rom. i. 18, ii. 5 ff., iv. 15, &c. The assurance of Rom. v. 9, σωθησόμεθα δι' αὐτοῦ [Χριστοῦ] ἀπὸ τῆς ὀργῆς, belongs to those δικαιωθέντες νῦν ἐν τῷ αἵματι αὐτοῦ. See on this point *Introd.*, Chap. III. (3).

The full manifestation of God's judicial anger is reserved for "the day of the Lord" (v. 2; see note), which the Apostle associates with the return of Jesus, who will bring at once punishment for the impenitent and deliverance for the faithful (II. i. 7—10: cf. 1 Cor. i. 7 ff., xv. 23 ff.; 2 Cor. v. 10; Acts xvii. 31; Jo. v. 27 ff.; Heb. ix. 27 f.). "The wrath" is described here not as "to come" (τῆς μελλούσης, Matt. iii. 7), as though referred to a future separated from the present, but as "coming" (so Eph. v. 6; Col. iii. 6: for the same participle, cf. Heb. x. 37; Rev. i. 4)—a future continuous with the present— since the conclusive punishment of sin is already in train: see Rom. i. 18 ff.; also ii. 16 below, and note. "The present ἔρχεσθαι is frequently used to denote the certainty, and possibly the nearness, of a future event, e.g. Matt. xvii. 11; Jo. iv. 21, xiv. 3" (Lightfoot).

Ὁ ῥυόμενος is a timeless present participle, equivalent to a noun (Winer-Moulton, p. 444), like ὁ καλῶν (v. 24; cf. Gal. i. 23; Eph. iv. 28); and ῥύομαι, as distinguished from ἐξαγοράζω (Gal. iii. 13) or λυτρόομαι (Tit. ii. 14), means deliverance by *power*, not *price*, indicating the greatness of the peril and the sympathy and might of the Redeemer: cf. the use of this verb in Rom. vii. 24; 2 Cor. i. 10; 2 Tim. iv. 17 f. The participle stands for הַגֹּאֵל, *the redeeming kinsman*, in Gen. xlviii. 16 (LXX.) and often in the Deutero-Isaiah; but such passages as Ps. vii. 1, lxxxvi. 13—where the Hebrew verb is הִצִּיל —represent the prevailing associations of the word. Under ἡμᾶς the writers include themselves with their readers, in the common experience of sin and salvation: cf. v. 8 ff., II. i. 7; Rom. v. 1—11.

CHAPTER II.

4. τῳ prefixed to θεῳ τῳ δοκιμαζοντι by ℵ^cAD^cGKL (Syrian witnesses), against ℵ*BCD*P 67** (Pre-Syrian): the first τῳ due to the presence of the second. Cf. *v.* 15 for anarthrous θεῳ in this connexion; also iv. 1, and Rom. viii. 8.

5. B precedes the later codd. in spelling κολακειας—its favourite itacism (-ει-). Etymologically -ει- is correct, the noun being derived from κολακευω: cf. βασιλευω, βασιλεια; see Winer-Schmiedel *Grammatik*, § v. 13 *c*, for this point of orthography.

The omission of εν before προφασει is based on Bℵ^c 17 39 47, against all other witnesses—an attestation scarcely decisive. The shorter reading might be preferred, intrinsically, as *the more difficult*; on the other hand, as Weiss observes, the familiarity of the bare (adverbial) dative προφασει (*pretendedly*: cf. Phil. i. 18) would tend to the dropping of the preposition.

7. Evidence for νηπιοι: ℵ*BC*D*G, some dozen minuscc., latt vg (*parvuli*) cop aeth, Clem Or Cyr. Origen, on Matt. xix. 14, writes: Παυλος ως επισταμενος το Των γαρ τοιουτων εστιν η βασιλεια των ουρανων, δυναμενος εν βαρει, κ.τ.λ., εγενετο νηπιος κ. παραπλησιος τροφῳ θαλπουσῃ το εαυτης παιδιον. To the like effect Augustine (*De catech. rudibus*, 15): "Factus est parvulus in medio nostrum tamquam nutrix fovens filios suos. Num enim delectat, nisi amor invitet, decurtata et mutilata verba inmurmurare?" For ηπιοι: Aℵ^cC^bD^cKLP, most minn., cat. txt, syrr sah basm, Clem Bas Chr. νηπιοι has by far the better attestation; yet it is rejected by most editors and commentators in favour of ηπιοι as alone fitting the context, since *gentleness* is the opposite of the arrogance disclaimed in *v.* 6, while in the next clause the writer describes himself as *a nurse*, not *a babe*: the mixture of metaphors involved in the reading of ℵB is violent, despite Origen's explanation. WH (with whom Lightfoot agrees), on the other hand, denounce ηπιοι as a "tame and facile adjective" characteristic of "the Syrian revisers" (*Appendix*, p. 128). In the continuous uncial writing N (after ετενηθημεν) might be insinuated or dropped with equal ease. The rarity of ηπιος (only 2 Tim. ii. 24 besides in N.T.), and the frequency of νηπιος (esp. in Paul), tell for the former in point of transcriptional probability. νηπιοι is clearly the older extant reading: we must either regard ηπιοι as a corruption, or a happy correction, of νηπιοι on the part of the Syrian revisers. On the latter view, νηπιοι must be attributed to a primitive and widely spread *dittography* of the final ν of εγενηθημεν, which however, as **A** and the Sahidic Version testify, was not universal. The confusion of these two words is rather common in the MSS.: see 2 Tim. ii. 24; Eph. iv. 14; Heb. v. 13.

8. ομειρομενοι, in all uncials and many minuscc. Theophylact writes, τινες δε ιμειρομενοι ανεγνωσαν, αντι του επιθυμουντες· ουκ εστι δε. WH (see *Appendix*, p. 144) give ομειρομενοι the smooth breathing; other editors have written it with the rough breathing, following the erroneous derivation from ομου and ειρομαι. In all likelihood, as WH suggest, this form was a local or vernacular variation of ιμειρομενοι, which later copyists substituted for the almost unexampled form in ο-. See Expository Note.

γεγενησθε (for εγενηθητε): **K**, and most minuscc.—a Syrian emendation, due seemingly to reading ευδοκουμεν as *present* instead of imperfect (see Expository Note); so the latter verb is rendered in deg, Ambrst (*cupimus*), Aug (*placet*). ηυδοκουμεν is actually read here in **B**; f vg give *volebamus*; cf. iii. 1, and note on ηυδοκησαμεν.

μαρτυρουμενοι (for -ομενοι): so T.R., after **D*G** 37 and other inferior minn. (but not in **HKL** Chr—*Syrian*); a bad Western corruption.

12. περιπατειν, in all pre-Syrian witnesses. The περιπατησαι of Eph. iv. 1, Col. i. 10, may have determined the Syrian reading here.

καλεσαντος: ℵA, six minuscc., f vg (*qui vocavit*) syrr cop sah go, Ambrst. καλουντος: **BDGHKLP**, &c., latt (generally) syr ʰᶜˡ ᵐᵍ. Both have good parallels in Paul. It is a question whether the *aorist* partic. should be explained as an Alexandrian corruption of the present, or the *present* as a Western corruption of the aorist.

13. αληθως εστιν, ℵᵃB cop (ℵ* omits αληθως, by *homœoteleuton* after καθως): all other codd. reverse the order; cf. Jo. iv. 42, vi. 14, vii. 40.

14. **A** and a few minn. write the Attic ταυτὰ for τα αυτα.

G reads απο twice, **D*** in the first instance, instead of υπο.

15. ἰδίους (before προφητας): a Syrian insertion.

16. BD* alone have preserved ἐφθακεν—the less obvious, but intrinsically better reading; cf. Eph. i. 20, ἐνηργηκεν (-σεν).

DG latt vg Ambrst, with Western license, gloss οργη by του θεου.

18. διοτι: so in all pre-Syrian uncials.

19. The T.R., following GL, most minn., and all versions except latt and vg (purer copies), adds Χριστου to Ιησου. Later MSS. habitually fill out the names of Christ.

---

§ 3. ii. 1—12. THE CONDUCT OF THE APOSTLES AT THESSALONICA.

The thanksgiving just offered to God for the conspicuous Christian worth of the Thessalonians reflects upon *the work of the writers* as the instruments of their conversion. The whole heart and interest of St Paul and his companions are bound up with the welfare of this Church (iii. 8); their thoughts in the previous paragraph (vv. 4—9) were constantly vibrating between "you" and "us," as in the ensuing paragraph between "us" and "you." This section is, in truth, an expansion of v. 5b in chap. i.: οἴδατε οἷοι ἐγενήθημεν [ἐν] ὑμῖν δι' ὑμᾶς. Starting from the εἴσοδος referred to in i. 9, the train of reflexion on the spirit and character of the past ministry of the writers amongst the Thessalonians, pursued through twelve verses with emphasis and relish, brings them back in v. 13 into the vein of thanksgiving from which they set out. The *Introd.*, pp. xxxiv. f., suggested some reasons for the writers' dwelling thus on themselves and their own behaviour. The section may be analysed as follows:— The mission of St Paul and his comrades at Thessalonica exhibited *the true power of the Gospel* (v. 1); which was manifest (1) by *the boldness* they showed on its behalf *in the face of persecution* (v. 2)— (2) the boldness of *religious sincerity untainted with personal ambition* (vv. 3—6), (3) united in their case with *a tender parental devotion* toward their charge (vv. 7—9), and with (4) *a solicitous fidelity to the high aims of the Christian calling* (vv. 11, 12). Four words resume the whole—*courage, purity, tenderness, fidelity*; cf. 2 Cor. v. 20— vi. 10.

1. Αὐτοὶ γὰρ οἴδατε, ἀδελφοί, τὴν εἴσοδον ἡμῶν τὴν πρὸς ὑμᾶς. *For yourselves know, brothers, that entrance of ours unto you*— resuming the thread of i. 9. This αὐτοὶ γάρ is antithetical to that of i. 9—"you know on your own part" what "they report upon theirs"; the indefinite εἴσοδον of the former sentence is now recalled to be defined, τὴν...τὴν πρὸς ὑμᾶς; and the historical (aorist) ἔσχομεν becomes the perfect γέγονεν, of the abiding effect. For the sense of εἴσοδος, see the previous note; for the *ordo verborum*, cf. τὴν πίστιν ὑμῶν τὴν πρὸς τὸν θεόν of i. 8. Here πρός has its primary local meaning; there it carried an ethical sense.

οἴδατε...τὴν εἴσοδον...ὅτι οὐ κενὴ γέγονεν. *You know...our entrance ...that it has proved no vain (entrance)*—i.e. *far from vain*. Οὐ negatives the whole predicate κενὴ γέγονεν, making it synonymous with ἐν δυνάμει ἐγενήθη (i. 5) or ἐνεργουμένη (-εῖται) of v. 13; cf. 1 Cor. xv. 10, 58; Phil. ii. 16. Κενός (*empty, hollow*) signifies in this context "void" of reality and power, as the entry of the Apostles would have proved had they "come in word" (i. 5), with hollow assumptions and κενοφωνία (1 Tim. vi. 20; 2 Tim. ii. 16), like "wind-bags" (cf. 1 Cor. ii. 1, 4, iv. 19 f.).

Οἴδατε claims beforehand the subject of γέγονεν for its object, according to the Greek idiom which extends to all dependent sentences, but prevails with verbs of *knowing*: see Winer-Moulton, p. 781, Rutherford's *Syntax*, § 244; and cf. II. ii. 4, ἀποδεικνύντα ἑαυτόν, κ.τ.λ.; 1 Cor. iii. 20; 2 Cor. xii. 3 f.; Lk. iv. 34.

2. οὐ κενὴ γέγονεν (v. 1), ἀλλά...ἐπαρρησιασάμεθα ἐν τῷ θεῷ ἡμῶν κ.τ.λ. The Apostles' παρρησία ἐν θεῷ excluded the thought of a κενὴ εἴσοδος: utterance so confident, and so charged with Divine energy, betokened a true mission from God. The aorists ἐπαρρησιασάμεθα... λαλῆσαι signify "We *took courage*...to speak," &c.—"waxed bold" (R.V.)—*fiduciam sumpsimus* (Calvin) rather than *habuimus* (Vulg.), *gewannen wir in unserm Gott den Muth* (Schmiedel); for in verbs of state, or *continuous action*, the aorist denotes *inception* (see Kühner's *Ausf. Grammatik*², II. § 386. 5; or Rutherford's *Syntax*, § 208), and the "entrance" of the missionaries is in question: contrast the imperfect as used in Acts xix. 8. Commonly St Paul grounds his "boldness" ἐν κυρίῳ, as in iv. 1; II. iii. 4; Phil. ii. 24, &c., or ἐν Χριστῷ, as in Phm. 8; here he is thinking much of his message as τὸ εὐαγγέλιον τοῦ θεοῦ—*in our God* the glad courage is grounded with which he speaks "the good news of God," who entrusted him therewith (v. 4); cf. ἐν θεῷ, i. 1; Col. iii. 3; ἐν δυνάμει θεοῦ, 2 Cor. vi. 4—7. Thus Jesus encouraged His disciples: "The Spirit of your Father speaketh in you....Fear not therefore" (Matt. x. 20 ff.). In this joyful mood, shortly before, Paul and Silas "at midnight sang praise to God" in the stocks at Philippi.

Παρρησιάζομαι occurs only here and Eph. vi. 20 in St Paul, in Acts frequently; the noun παρρησία (παν-ρησία) *passim*. Denoting first *unreserved speech*, it comes to mean *confident expression, freedom of bearing, frank and fearless assurance* (German *Freimuth*)—the tone and attitude suitable to Christ's servants (see 2 Cor. iii. 12 ff.; Lk. xii. 1 ff.); for the wider use of the term, cf. Phil. i. 20; Acts iv. 13; Heb. x. 35; 1 Jo. iii. 19—22, &c. Λαλῆσαι fills out the sense of ἐπαρρησιασάμεθα, as it denotes *utterance, form of speech*; while λέγειν (εἰπεῖν) would point to definite *content, matter of speech* (see iv. 15, v. 3, &c.).

λαλῆσαι is qualified by ἐν πολλῷ ἀγῶνι, *in much contention* : ἀγών —a term of the athletic arena (cf. 1 Cor. ix. 25; Heb. xii. 1)—may denote either external or (as in Col. ii. 1) internal conflict; cf. 1 Cor. xvi. 9, for the situation—ἀντικείμενοι πολλοί. The circumstances antecedent to their εἴσοδος, described in the introductory participial clause, προπαθόντες...ἐν Φιλίπποις, enhanced the courage shown by the missionaries in preaching at Thessalonica, making it the more evident that the power of God was with them. Their Philippian experience is graphically related in Acts xvi.; for the connexion of the two cities, see the *Map*, and *Introd*. pp. x., lxii. Προπάσχω, only here in the N.T.: for προ- of *time*, cf. iii. 4, iv. 6; for πάσχω in like connexion, *v*. 14, II. i. 5. ὑβρισθέντες shows the "suffering" to have taken the shape of *outrage, criminal violence*, as was the case in the imprisonment of Paul and Silas (Acts xvi. 37); ὕβρις denoted legally an actionable indignity to the person: the expression indicates "the *contumely* which hurt St Paul's feelings, arising from the strong sense of his Roman citizenship" (Lightfoot). What the Apostles suffered in Philippi was calculated to damage their character and arrest their work; their deliverance by so signal an interposition of Divine Providence emboldened them to proceed. καθὼς οἴδατε appeals to the familiarity of the readers with all that had transpired; cf. *v*. 1, and note on i. 5.

Vv. **3, 4** are attached by γάρ to the object of the sentence immediately foregoing, viz. τὸ εὐαγγέλιον τοῦ θεοῦ : the religious sincerity of the Apostles went to show that it was indeed "the gospel of God" that they brought, and that accordingly in their "entrance" there was no false pretence (*v*. 1). The note of contradiction, οὐκ...ἀλλά, is repeated from *vv*. 1, 2; and the main repudiation includes a minor, in *v*. 4 *b*.

3. ἡ γὰρ παράκλησις ἡμῶν οὐκ ἐκ πλάνης οὐδὲ ἐξ ἀκαθαρσίας οὐδὲ ἐν δόλῳ. *For our appeal (is) not of (does not proceed from) error, nor from impurity, nor (is it made) in guile*. Παράκλησις may denote any kind of *animating address* (see 1 Cor. xiv. 3; 1 Tim. iv. 13; Acts xiii. 15), then the *encouragement* which such address gives (II. ii. 16; 2 Cor. i. 3 ff., &c.); here it is not "exhortation" to those already

Christians, but "the appeal" of the Gospel to those who hear it; it includes the *totum præconium evangelii* (Bengel). It corresponds to διδαχή (Chrysostom's gloss, as in Rom. vi. 17, &c.) or διδασκαλία (2 Tim. iii. 10) on one side—"from both of which it is distinguished as being directed more to the feelings than the understanding" (Ellicott) —and on another side to κήρυγμα (2 Tim. iv. 17); it always contemplates the benefit of those addressed: cf. for παρακαλέω in like connexion, Acts ii. 40; Lk. iii. 18; and for other uses of the verb, *v.* 11 below, and II. ii. 17. The writers deny that they had been actuated by delusion or by impure motives (in other words, that they were either *deceived* or *deceivers*), or that they acted in crafty ways: ἐκ points to *source*, ἐν to *manner* of proceeding.

Πλάνη signifies (objective) *error*, as in II. ii. 11; Rom. i. 27, &c.,— the opposite of "the word of *the truth* of the gospel" (Col. i. 5; cf. 2 Cor. iv. 2, vi. 7; Eph. i. 13; 1 Jo. iv. 6; II. ii. 10—13 below); ἀκαθαρσία, (subjective) personal *uncleanness*. The latter expression commonly implies *bodily* defilement, as in Rom. i. 24, &c., and may have this reference here; but the term, on occasion, includes μολυσμὸς πνεύματος as well as σαρκός (2 Cor. vii. 1). There is no hint anywhere else in the Epistles that St Paul was taxed with *fleshly* impurity; and uncleanness *of spirit* (sordid and mercenary aims, the αἰσχροκερδία of 1 Tim. iii. 8, &c.) seems more to the point here. Against this reproach the Apostle jealously guarded himself (see 2 Cor. xi. 7—12, xii. 14—18); possibly he is taking the word ἀκαθαρσία in this passage from the mouths of his gainsayers. In classical Greek it denotes moral *foulness, dirty ways*, of any sort. Cf. note on iv. 7; also 1 Tim. vi. 5, where ἐξ ἀκαθαρσίας is recalled by διεφθαρμένων τὸν νοῦν, and ἐκ πλάνης by ἀπεστερημένων τῆς ἀληθείας. For ἐν δόλῳ, cf. 2 Cor. xii. 16; Mk xiv. 1; Jo. i. 47.

4. Base motives and methods were excluded, once for all, by the nature of the apostolic commission: ἀλλὰ καθὼς δεδοκιμάσμεθα ὑπὸ τοῦ θεοῦ πιστευθῆναι τὸ εὐαγγέλιον, κ.τ.λ. *But according as we have been approved by God to be put in trust with the Good News, we thus speak*—*quemadmodum probati fuimus a Deo, ut crederetur nobis Evangelium, sic loquimur* (Calvin). Δεδοκιμάσμεθα (in the perf. tense, of settled and resultful fact), which is echoed by δοκιμάζοντι τὰς καρδίας in the appended clause, is the decisive word: *God's approval,* shown by the conferment of this lofty commission, certifies the honesty of the Apostles and supplies its standard: cf., on this latter point, *v.* 12, εἰς τὸ περιπατεῖν...ἀξίως, κ.τ.λ.; and II. i. 11. There is a play on the double sense of δοκιμάζω (based on δόκιμος—see e.g. Rom. xvi. 10—*accepted, approved*, with its root in δέχομαι), which means first *to assay,*

put to proof, as one does metal, coin, &c. (see Jer. xi. 20, LXX, κύριε κρίνων δίκαια, δοκιμάζων νεφροὺς καὶ καρδίας: cf. Prov. xvii. 3; Zech. xiii. 9, &c.; also 1 Cor. iii. 13, and 1 Pet. i. 7, ii. 4), then *to approve on testing*, as in 1 Cor. xvi. 3: in the latter sense synon. with ἀξιόω, II. i. 11, in the former with πειράζω; see Trench's *Synon.* § 74. St Paul makes a similar appeal, in the face of disparagement, to the Divine judgement respecting himself in 1 Cor. iv. 1 ff.; and again in 2 Cor. i. 12, 17—23.

For πιστευθῆναι τὸ εὐαγγέλιον, cf., both as to sense and grammatical form, Gal. ii. 7; 1 Tim. i. 11 ff.: as to the *fact*, in St Paul's own case, see Gal. i. 12, 15 f., ii. 8 f.; Acts ix. 15 f., xxii. 14 f., xxvi. 16 ff.; Eph. iii. 2 ff.; 2 Tim. i. 11. Πιστεύομαι with nomin. of *person* (representing the *dative* after the active verb) and accus. of *thing* follows a sound Greek construction, occurring, for this particular verb, only in St Paul in the N.T.: add to the examples above given Rom. iii. 2, 1 Cor. ix. 17; consult Winer-Moulton, p. 326, Rutherford, *Syntax*, § 201, Goodwin's *Greek Grammar*, 1236. For λαλοῦμεν, see note to *v.* 2.

οὕτως λαλοῦμεν is defined a second time, by **οὐχ ὡς ἀνθρώποις ἀρέσκοντες ἀλλὰ θεῷ** κ.τ.λ., *not as (though we were) pleasing men, but (as pleasing) God who tries our hearts.* The sentence "doubles back on itself" in true Pauline fashion (cf. e.g. Col. i. 5 *b*, 6), the ὡς clause putting over again, in another light, what the καθώς clause had asserted. Those who serve human masters "speak" in a manner calculated to "please" them; the Apostles preach in a spirit accordant with their responsibility to God, whom they felt to be ever "trying" their "hearts." "'Αρέσκειν θεῷ can only be spoken *de conatu*, as in Gal. i. 10" (Schmiedel): for this idiom of the pres. and impf. tenses, see Kühner², II. § 382. 6, Rutherford, *Syntax*, § 210, Goodwin's *Greek Grammar*, 1255. For "pleasing God," cf. ii. 15, iv. 1; Rom. viii. 8; 1 Cor. vii. 32: for "men," Eph. vi. 6—in a good sense, 1 Cor. x. 33. On οὐ with partic., see Moulton, *Proleg. to Gram. of N.T. Greek*, p. 231.

For **δοκιμάζω**, see note on p. 37; the phrase comes from Jer. xi. 20. **τὰς καρδίας**, plural (cf. iii. 13; II. ii. 17, iii. 5), shows that St Paul carries his companions with him in all he writes (τὴν καρδίαν would have suited the conventional *pluralis auctoris*); see note on the Address (i. 1), and Lightfoot's note *ad hoc*. "The heart" in Scripture is not the seat of mere emotion, as when in modern usage it is opposed to "the head," but of "the inner man" comprehensively (see Eph. iii. 16 f.); it is the centre and meeting-point of the soul's movements. There the real self is found, which God sees (see Acts i. 24; 1 Sam. xvi. 7; Mk vii. 21, &c.)—hence contrasted with "the mouth" or "lips" or "body" (Rom. x. 10; Matt. xv. 8; Prov. xvi. 23; Heb. x. 22, &c.).

Vv. 5—8 contain a third apologetic denial, introduced by **γάρ**, and stated once more in the **οὐκ...ἀλλά** form of contradiction. The negative half consists of three members, as in *v.* 3, but is more extended; these are distinguished by **οὔτε**, not **οὐδέ** as before, since they are more closely kindred.

5. οὔτε γάρ ποτε ἐν λόγῳ κολακίας ἐγενήθημεν. *For neither at any time did we fall into the use of speech of flattery—sermone assentatorio usi sumus* (Beza); *were we found using* (*employed in*, Lightfoot) *words of flattery* (R.V.)—but "*found*" suggests *detection*, which is not in question. For γίνομαι ἐν, *versari in, to be engaged in*, see Liddell and Scott, s.v. II. 3 b; and cf. 1 Tim. ii. 14; Lk. xxii. 44. The aorist, pointed by ποτέ, implies *falling into* or *resorting to* the practice in question; cf. note on ἐπαρρησιασάμεθα, *v.* 2. Bornemann notices how the use of the paraphrastic γίνομαι, so frequent in this context, enables the writer to combine the grammatically heterogeneous predicates of *vv.* 5 and 6.

Κολακίας (classical spelling, κολακεία, from κολακεύω) is genitive of *content* rather than *characteristic*—" speech that flattered you" (cf. 1 Cor. xii. 8; 2 Cor. vi. 7, for similar genitives with λόγος). This term, *hap. leg.* in N.T., always implies sinister, self-interested compliment; Aristotle (*Eth. Nic.* IV. 12) defines the κόλαξ as ὁ ὅπως ὠφέλειά τις αὐτῷ γίγνηται εἰς χρήματα κ. ὅσα διὰ χρημάτων (sc. λέγων): accordingly the λόγος κολακίας would serve as a πρόφασις πλεονεξίας. The slander against the missionaries on this particular head is contradicted more distinctly in *vv.* 10—12.

οὔτε (ἐγενήθημεν ἐν) προφάσει πλεονεξίας, nor (*did we make use of*) *a cloak of covetousness*—i.e. any pretext, whether in the shape of flattering speech or otherwise, serving to hide a selfish purpose. "Πρόφασις (from προφαίνω) signifies generally the ostensible reason for which a thing is done; sometimes in a good sense (Thuc. I. 23, VI. 6, ἀληθεστάτη πρόφασις), but generally otherwise, the false or pretended reason as opposed to the true" (Lightfoot): hence in Phil. i. 18 προφάσει is contrasted with ἐν ἀληθείᾳ; cf. Lk. xx. 47. Πλεονεξία means *greed* of any kind—oftenest, but not always, *for money*; it is the spirit of *self-aggrandizement*, selfishness as a ruling motive: see Trench's *Synon.* § 24; and cf. Col. iii. 5; Eph. v. 3; 2 Cor. ix. 5; Lk. xii. 15; also πλεονεκτέω in iv. 6, and note; 2 Cor. xii. 17 f.

As to the λόγος κολακίας the readers were good judges (**καθὼς οἴδατε**: see note on i. 5); but "God" is cited as "witness" to the absence of πρόφ. πλεονεξίας, since this concerns "the hidden man of the heart" (see notes on *v.* 4): **θεὸς** (anarthrous) **μάρτυς,** (*there is*)

God (as) witness; cf. Rom. i. 9; Phil. i. 8. For the twofold sin repudiated, cf. Ps. xii. 2, "A flattering lip and a double heart."

6. οὔτε (ἐγενήθημεν) ζητοῦντες ἐξ ἀνθρώπων δόξαν. Along with *fawning lips* and *covert selfishness*, the writers disclaim *the pursuit of human reputation*; the three kinds of conduct are closely allied— flattery cloaking greed and ambition. The transition from the prepositional (*v*. 5) to the participial construction distinguishes the third vice as a *practice* rather than a disposition : *nor did we become seekers of* (or *fall into the pursuit of*) *glory from men*. To "men" God is tacitly opposed as the proper source of "glory": cf. *v*. 4, δεδοκιμάσμεθα ὑπὸ τοῦ θεοῦ...θεῷ ἀρέσκοντες ; also Jo. v. 41 ff., vii. 18; 1 Cor. iv. 3 ff.; Rom. ii. 7; and *v*. 19 f. below. That the Apostles have ἐξ ἀνθρώπων δόξαν, was stated in i. 9; but they never "seek" it.

οὔτε ἀφ' ὑμῶν οὔτε ἀπ' ἄλλων. The missionaries might conceivably have sought reputation either from their converts, or "from others" at a distance hearing about them (cf. i. 8 f.); but this object never influenced their work. If ἐξ and ἀπό may be distinguished here (this however is questioned), ἐξ points to the general source of such "glory" and indicates its nature, while ἀπό marks out the particular quarter from which it might be derived—*glory such as men could give, whether you or others supplied it*: cf. Rom. ii. 29 for ἐξ; for ἀπό in like connexion, Lk. xi. 50 f., xii. 20; also i. 8 above. As to the relations of ἀπό and ἐκ in N.T. Greek, see A. Buttmann's *N.T. Grammar*, p. 324.

δυνάμενοι ἐν βάρει εἶναι ὡς Χριστοῦ ἀπόστολοι is added to sustain the disavowal of ambition; accordingly βάρος signifies not so much the "weight" of *expense* that the "apostles of Christ" might have thrown on the Church for their maintenance (see 1 Cor. ix. 14, &c.), to which ἐπιβαρῆσαι refers a little later (*v*. 9, see note ; and cf. 2 Cor. xi. 9, ἀβαρῆ ἐμαυτὸν ἐποίησα), as the "weight" of authority and personal importance with which they might have imposed themselves on disciples—so Chrysostom paraphrases ἐν τιμῇ εἶναι, Erasmus *in dignitate*, Schmiedel *in Ansehen*, &c. The latter sense is borne out by the immediate context in *v*. 7. But the two meanings are compatible; for official importance was measured by *stipend*, by the demand made for personal support (cf. 2 Cor. xi. 7, ἐμαυτὸν ταπεινῶν ...ὅτι δωρεὰν...εὐηγγελισάμην, and the whole context); and it is just in St Paul's manner to play on the double sense of such a phrase: *when we might have sat heavily on you as Christ's apostles* reproduces, somewhat rudely, the *double entendre*; similarly Lightfoot *ad loc*. Polybius and other writers of the κοινή use βάρος in these two senses. With the locution ἐν βάρει εἶναι cf. ἐν ὑπεροχῇ ὄντων, 1 Tim. ii. 2; also γίνομαι ἐν, v. 5 above; see Liddell and Scott s. v. ἐν, II. 2. For the connexion of βάρος with δόξα, see 2 Cor. iv. 17; both ideas are contained in the Hebrew כָּבוֹד.

Silvanus and Timotheus are included in the plural Χριστοῦ ἀπόστολοι (not, however, as ἀπόστολοι Ἰησοῦ Χριστοῦ). The term ἀπόστολος, שָׁלִיחַ, was in current Jewish use (see Schürer's *History of the Jewish People in the Time of Christ*, II. ii. pp. 269, 290) as signifying *emissary, commissioner*; it was the title given to the delegates who conveyed to Jerusalem the contributions levied for sacred purposes from Jews of the Dispersion (cf. 2 Cor. viii. 23; Phil. ii. 25), but in all probability was not confined to this application. In Christian usage it took a narrower and a wider sense, as it denoted primarily "the Twelve," "*the* Apostles," commissioned in the first instance and from His own person by Jesus Christ, and as it was subsequently extended to others "sent out" from particular Churches,—either for general service in the Gospel or on some specific Christian errand. These were "apostles of the churches," but also, in a derivative sense, "apostles of Christ," since they belonged to Him and were despatched on His service: see further, for this larger use of the word in which it corresponds to our *missionary*, Acts xiv. 4, 14; Rom. xvi. 7; 2 Cor. xi. 13; Rev. ii. 2; also *Didaché*, xi. 2. Jo. xvii. 18 and xx. 21 give the fundamental Christian conception of the "apostle's" calling, and the basis of the wider application of the title. It appears always to imply a *travelling* commission, and an *authoritative* mandate. In later Epistles (2 Cor. i. 1; Col. i. 1) St Paul distinguishes himself as "the apostle" from "Timothy the brother," whose function was that of "an evangelist" (2 Tim. iv. 5; cf. Eph. iv. 11); he claimed the Apostleship in its higher and exclusive sense (see Gal. i. 1, 12, 17, ii. 6—8; Rom. i. 1—5; 1 Cor. ix. 1 ff., xv. 9—11; 2 Cor. xii. 11 ff., &c.). The Judaistic controversy that arose subsequently to the writing of the Thessalonian Epistles, compelled St Paul to assert his plenary authority and his place by the side of the Twelve; in this sense, he then became ἐν βάρει. But for the present, and at Thessalonica, there is no necessity for him to assume more than the common apostleship, nor to raise himself by way of prerogative above his companions. See the Excursus of Huxtable on *The name and office of an Apostle* (*Pulpit Commentary: Galatians*); Lightfoot, *Galatians*, pp. 92—101; Hort, *Ecclesia*, pp. 22 ff.; Weizsäcker's *History of the Apostolic Age*, Vol. II. pp. 293—296; also Smith's [2] and Hastings' *Dictionary of the Bible*, s. v. Apostle.

7. **ἀλλὰ ἐγενήθημεν νήπιοι ἐν μέσῳ ὑμῶν.** See Textual Note above. (*a*) According to the reading νήπιοι, the Apostles were simple, guileless, and unassuming (*vv*. 3—7) as " babes ": cf. ἀκέραιοι, τέκνα θεοῦ, in Phil. ii. 15; ἀκεραίους εἰς τὸ κακόν and τῇ κακίᾳ νηπιάζετε, Rom. xvi. 19 and 1 Cor. xiv. 20; also Matt. xviii. 4, and 2 Cor. xi. 7, 1 Pet. ii. 1 f., for the various Christian qualities represented by νηπιότης. This wider interpretation of νήπιοι is demanded by the contrast with *vv*. 5, 6; cf. that derived by Origen and Augustine from the clause which follows, given in the note below. (*b*) The reading ἤπιοι presents the apter contrast to *v*. 6; and it traverses the πλεονεξία, if not the κολακία, of *v*. 5. Ἐν μέσῳ ὑμῶν puts the ἐν ὑμῖν of i. 5 more vividly (cf. Matt. xviii. 2—4),—ὡς ἂν εἴποι τις Ὡς εἰς ἐξ ὑμῶν, οὐχὶ τὴν ἄνω λαβόντες τάξιν (Chrysostom); *non agebant quasi ex cathedra* (Bengel): cf. 1 Pet. v. 1; Rev. i. 9; Lk. xxii. 27; Heb. ii. 12, —the two latter passages relating to the Great Example.

νήπιοι (if this reading be genuine) **ἐν μέσῳ κ.τ.λ.** leads on to the comparison, **ὡς ἐὰν τροφὸς θάλπῃ τὰ ἑαυτῆς τέκνα**, *as haply a nurse might be cherishing her own children*; for the skill of a nurse lies in her coming down to the level of her babes,—as Origen puts it, λαλοῦσα λόγους ὡς παιδίον διὰ τὸ παιδίον; Augustine, *delectat...decurtata et mutilata verba inmurmurare*. But this is only a single trait of the picture: the nurse-*mother* (θάλπει τὰ ἑαυτῆς τέκνα) is child-like with her children,—as far from selfish craft as they, and filled besides with a care for them (see *v*. 8) which they cannot feel nor reciprocate toward her. Here St Paul paints himself as the mother τρέφουσα καὶ θάλπουσα, while in Gal. iv. 19 he is the mother ὠδίνουσα. Ὡς ἄν (later Gr. *ἐάν*), like other relative pronouns and adverbs with **ἄν** and subjunct., implies *a standing contingency*,—"as it may be (may be seen) at any time": cf. Gal. v. 17, Lk. ix. 57, &c., for the construction; the *temporal* ὡς ἄν of 1 Cor. xi. 34, &c., is different. Θάλπω, only here and in Eph. v. 29 (ἐκτρέφει καὶ θάλπει) in N.T.; in LXX, Deut. xxii. 6. Ἠπιότης however (if we prefer to read ἤπιοι) is a conspicuous trait of the τροφός with her τέκνα.

8. The figure of *v*. 7 *c*, while it looks back to νήπιοι (ἤπιοι), in its turn suggests another side of the relation of the Apostles to their converts: they had been as nursing mothers to their spiritual children not only in homely simplicity (or gentleness), but *in self-devotion*:—

ὡς...τροφὸς...οὕτως ὁμειρόμενοι ὑμῶν, (*like a nurse*)...*so tenderly yearning over you*. Ὁμείρομαι, a hap. leg. in Greek—except that it occurs as a *varia lectio* in Job iii. 21 (LXX) and in Ps. lxii. 2 (Symmachus)—is taken to be an obscure dialectic variation of ἱμείρομαι, a verb common in poetry from Homer downwards (not extant in Attic prose), which is spelt also by Nicander (c. 160 B.C.) μείρομαι. As a verb of *feeling*, it is construed with genitive of the object. 'Ἱμείρομαι describes in *Odyss.* I. 41 Odysseus' *yearning* for his native land; in classical Greek it implies *absence* of the beloved object, like ἐπιποθέω in iii. 6 below; otherwise here,—ἐνταῦθα τὴν φιλοστοργίαν δείκνυσι (Chrys.). On the *spiritus* (*asper* or *lenis?*), see Textual Note.

ηὐδοκοῦμεν μεταδοῦναι ὑμῖν κ.τ.λ. *We were well-pleased* (or *thought good*) *to impart to you not only the Good News of God, but also our own souls*. Ηὐδοκοῦμεν implies not something that the Apostles were *willing to do* (A.V.), or *would have done* if occasion had arisen—as though they had written ηὐδοκοῦμεν (or ηὐδοκήσαμεν) ἄν—but what they actually *did with hearty good-will*: so εὐδοκέω with the infinitive in iii. 1; cf. Rom. xv. 26; 1 Cor. i. 21; Gal. i. 15; Col. i. 19; Lk. xii. 32. The idea is not that the missionaries *were ready to lay down their lives for* their converts—as though the words were δοῦναι, or θεῖναι, ὑπὲρ ὑμῶν τὰς ψυχάς (cf. Mk x. 45; Gal. i. 4; 1 Jo. iii. 16)—but that they *gladly communicated* (μετα-δοῦναι; cf. Rom. i. 11) *their very selves to* them,—in other words, they gave with their message the best and utmost that was in them, *for the reason that* (διότι) the Thessalonians *had grown* (ἐγενήθητε) *dear* to them.

On ψυχή, see note to v. 23. It denotes the personality, the living self (hence plural, as including *the three*), and is synonymous with καρδία (*v.* 4, see note); καρδία is the inner man *by contrast with* the outer, while ψυχή is the man himself as *feeling and acting through* the outer organs, the soul within the body: cf. Col. iii. 23; Lk. xii. 19, 22 f.; 1 Pet. i. 22, ii. 11. St Paul and his fellows imparted themselves to this Church as the nursing-mother to her offspring (*v.* 7), with a tenderness in which one's very soul goes out to the beloved. Of this unstinting, uncalculating devotion (how opposite to all πρόφασις πλεονεξίας, *v.* 5) the κόπος κ. μόχθος of *v.* 9 gave evidence; the saying of 2 Cor. xii. 15, ἥδιστα ἐκδαπανηθήσομαι ὑπὲρ τῶν ψυχῶν ὑμῶν, is a striking parallel to ηὐδοκοῦμεν μεταδοῦναι τὰς ψυχὰς ἡμῶν. Bengel aptly paraphrases, "Anima nostra cupiebat quasi immeare in animam vestram"; and Calvin, more at length, "Mater in liberis suis educandis...nullis parcit laboribus ac molestiis, nullam solicitudinem refugit, nulla assiduitate fatigatur, suumque adeo sanguinem hilari animo sugendum praebet." The 3rd personal reflexive, ἑαυτῶν, is freely used in later Greek for all three persons in plural; see Winer-Moulton, pp. 187 f.

διότι (cf. *v.* 18, iv. 6) = διὰ τοῦτο ὅτι, a more distinct causal than ὅτι. **ἀγαπητοὶ ἡμῖν ἐγενήθητε,** *beloved to us,—in our eyes*. This adjective has in effect the force of a substantive (cf. *v.* 19 f.); elsewhere St Paul uses it of his people by way of endearing address, along with or in place of ἀδελφοί, or in describing their relation to God (Rom. i. 7; Eph. v. 1; cf. i. 4 above). Christ Himself is ὁ ἀγαπητός (Matt. iii. 17) or ὁ ἠγαπημένος (Eph. i. 6). **Ἐγενήθητε,** *you became* after your conversion and our acquaintance with you; cf. ὥστε γενέσθαι ὑμᾶς, i. 8.

9. μνημονεύετε γάρ, ἀδελφοί. *For you call to mind, brothers*: for μνημονεύω with accus., cf. 2 Tim. ii. 8; Matt. xvi. 9; Rev. xviii. 5; with the *genitive* it has a less active sense, as in i. 3 (see note). Referring to the same matter in II. iii. 7, the Apostles use the stronger expression, αὐτοὶ γὰρ οἴδατε, as in *v.* 1 above; here they speak as though the facts mentioned might not be at once present to the minds of the readers and would need to be recalled: cf. II. ii. 5.

On **κόπος,** see note to i. 3. **μόχθος** (kindred to μόγις, μόγος) implies outward difficulty, as κόπος personal strain,—"toil and moil" (Lightfoot); so μόχθος is used of the labours of Hercules in Sophocles, *Trach.* 1101, 1170. The combination recurs in II. iii. 8; 2 Cor. xi. 27.

νυκτὸς καὶ ἡμέρας ἐργαζόμενοι...ἐκηρύξαμεν κ.τ.λ., *by night and day working*, &c. : an explanatory sentence abruptly apposed to κόπον καὶ μόχθον, much as ὡς ἐὰν τροφός κ.τ.λ. to νήπιοι (ἤπιοι) in *v.* 7. The order "night and day" was common in Greek and Roman, as well as Jewish, usage (see Pliny, *Nat. Hist.* II. 77 [88]; Cicero, *De Finibus* I. 16. 51; Cæsar, *De Bell. Gall.* v. 38. 1); "day and night" is the order in Luke and John. Ἐργάζομαι bears the specific sense of *manual* labour also in classical Greek; so our "working man": cf. II. iii. 8; 1 Cor. ix. 6; Acts xviii. 3. The last of these parallels, which refers to St Paul's employment at this time, informs us of the nature of his handicraft; he was "a tentmaker by trade," σκηνοποιὸς τῇ τέχνῃ. Jewish fathers, even if well-to-do (as St Paul's family probably was, judging from the fact of his being sent to study at Jerusalem), had their sons taught some mechanical art as a remedy against poverty or idleness. St Paul had probably learnt at Tarsus the business of cutting out and stitching the coarse goats'-hair cloth (*cilicium*) used for making tents, also for shoes, mats, and other rough fabrics, which was a staple industry of Cilicia; and this skill proved a great resource to the wandering Apostle. An irksome labour it was, and ill-paid, most like the work of a shoemaker or carpet-sewer. "These hands," as the Apostle held them up to the view of the Ephesian

Elders (Acts xx. 34) hard and blackened with their daily task, told their tale of stern independence and exhausting toil. Silvanus and Timothy had probably other trades of their own. Yet the Apostle during his residence at Thessalonica more than once received help from his friends at Philippi, who would not be denied the privilege of relieving his wants: see Phil. iv. 10—16. This Church was composed mainly of working-class people (see iv. 11 f.), and demands soon began to be made by the Christian poor—in some cases, probably, deprived of their living by their change in religion—on the resources of its few wealthier members (including the γυναῖκες πρῶται of Acts xvii. 4); the Apostles acted therefore in the manner described πρὸς τὸ μὴ ἐπιβαρῆσαί τινα ὑμῶν, *so as to avoid laying a burden upon any of you*—words repeated in II. iii. 8, where *vv*. 9 f. add another reason for the mode of life pursued at Thessalonica: cf., to the like effect, 1 Cor. ix. 1—19; 2 Cor. xi. 7—12; Acts xx. 33 ff. This went to show not only the love of the Apostles toward their converts, but their disinterestedness, the absence in them of πλεονεξία in any shape (*vv*. 5 ff.: see note on ἐν βάρει). Ἐπιβαρέω has an ethical force in 2 Cor. ii. 5; the stronger καταβαρέω is used in the sense of this passage in 2 Cor. xii. 16.

ἐκηρύξαμεν εἰς ὑμᾶς τὸ εὐαγγέλιον τοῦ θεοῦ. *We brought to you as heralds the Good News of God*: cf. ὁ λόγος ἡμῶν ἐγενήθη εἰς ὑμᾶς, i. 5. Κηρύσσω εἰς (elsewhere with dative, Acts viii. 5; 1 Pet. iii. 19; and frequently with ἐν, as in 2 Cor. i. 19) implies *entrance* amongst those addressed (εἴσ-οδος, v. 1); cf. Mk i. 39; Lk. xxiv. 47, &c. Μεταδοῦναι τὸ εὐαγγ. (*v*. 8) indicates the charity of those who bring the Gospel, ἐκηρύξαμεν the dignity of their office. For the third time in this context (*vv*. 2, 8) the Gospel is called "the good news *of God*" (cf. i. 9); elsewhere only in Rom. i. 1, xv. 16. As God's heralds, bearing so lofty a commission and so welcome a message, the Apostles might have looked for some return in the supply of their bodily needs from those to whom they devoted themselves unsparingly (see 1 Cor. ix 7–14); but they forbore for the reason given. Jason's house, referred to in Acts xvii. 5 f., was probably the place of assembly for the Church; the Apostles, if they regularly lodged there, were not at Jason's charge for their maintenance.

10. ὑμεῖς μάρτυρες, καὶ ὁ θεός. In *v*. 5 the witness of men and that of God were separately invoked (see note); here jointly, for the writers' pastoral ministry, described in *vv*. 10—12, was the subject both of Divine and of human observation: cf. 1 Sam. xii. 3, 5.

ὡς ὁσίως κ. δικαίως κ. ἀμέμπτως ὑμῖν τοῖς πιστεύουσιν ἐγενήθημεν, *how religiously and righteously and in a manner beyond blame we devoted ourselves to* (or *bore ourselves toward*) *you that believe*. The construction of this clause is not quite obvious in point of grammar. (*a*) Ὑμῖν might be attached to ἐγενήθημεν, or to ἀμέμπτως singly, as a *dative of opinion* (see Winer-Moulton, p. 265): "how holily &c....we behaved, in the estimation of you that believe"—or "how holily..., and unblamably in the eyes of you that believe (*tametsi aliis non ita videretur*, Bengel), we bore ourselves": an interpretation condemned by Lightfoot as "inconceivably flat and unmeaning," after ὑμεῖς μάρτ. κ. ὁ θεός and in view of *vv.* 11, 12. (*b*) Or ὑμῖν is connected with ἐγενήθημεν as a *dativus commodi*: "how holily, &c.,...we behaved to you that believe." The adjectives ὅσιοι κ.τ.λ. would suit this sense better than the adverbs used. (*c*) Bornemann's explanation is perhaps the best. He combines ὑμῖν with ἐγενήθημεν as a *dative of close relationship*, or *of the* (ethical) *possessor*, making this dative convey the main assertion and reading the adverbs as qualifications of the whole predicate thus formed: "how holily &c....we made ourselves yours that believe." For this dative, somewhat rare with γίνομαι, cf. Rom. vii. 3, γενομένην ἀνδρί; and for the adverbs with γίνομαι, 1 Cor. xvi. 10. The interest of the paragraph centres in the close ties which bound the Apostles to the Thessalonians as Christian believers (see especially note on *v.* 7). To the fact that this relationship was contracted on the part of the Apostles in a godly, blameless fashion, the readers themselves, together with God, are summoned as witnesses.

Δίκαιος is distinguished from ὅσιος as when Marcus Aurelius (*Medit.* VII. 66) describes Socrates as δίκαιος τὰ πρὸς τοὺς ἀνθρώπους καὶ ὅσιος τὰ πρὸς τοὺς θεούς; similarly Plato writes in *Gorgias* 507 A, B; Polybius, *Hist.* XXIII. 10. 8, &c. In Deut. xxxii. 4, &c., Ps. cxlv. 17, Rev. xvi. 5, the double term is applied to *God*: see also Eph. iv. 24; Tit. i. 8; Lk. i. 75, for the combination. In distinction from ἅγιος, the characteristic N.T. word for 'holy,' ὅσιος signifies holy in disposition and attitude toward God,—*godly*; ἅγιος, holy in relationship and duty to God,—*consecrated* (see note on ἁγιάζω, v. 23). Ἄμεμπτος appears in iii. 13 and v. 23,—passages indicating that "blamelessness" is asserted before *God* (see θεὸς μάρτυς, *v.* 5, and note just above) as well as men, so that ἀμέμπτως is not to be limited by ὑμῖν.

11, 12. καθάπερ οἴδατε ὡς ἕνα ἕκαστον...παρακαλοῦντες κ.τ.λ. The ὡς...παρακαλοῦντες sentence is not completed, and ἕνα ἕκαστον remains in suspense, an object with no verb to govern it. The participial clause begins as if leading up to a finite verb, such as ἐνουθετοῦμεν (Acts xx. 31), or ἀνετρέφομεν (see τροφός, *v.* 7), or ἐπηρούμεν (v. 23); but the writer is carried away by the extension of his third participle, μαρτυρόμενοι, and in rounding off this clause forgets the missing verb, the sense of which is however practically supplied by the full import of the three participles. Similarly διὰ τοὺς παρεισάκ. ψευδαδέλφους is left suspended in Gal. ii. 4, and τὸ ἀδύνατον τοῦ νόμου in Rom. viii. 3; for a like participial anacoluthon, see 2 Cor. vii. 5 b. It is more natural, and much more after St Paul's manner, to admit such a lapse than to suppose that ἐγενήθημεν (v. 10) is resumed in thought across the intervening καθάπερ οἴδατε to support the participles, and that ἕνα ἕκαστον is conceived as object to παρακαλοῦντες κ.τ.λ., to be quickly followed by the pleonastic ὑμᾶς: see Ellicott ad loc.

Καθάπερ is more emphatic than καθὼς οἴδατε (v. 2, &c.),—" as verily," " even as "; cf. iii. 6, &c. Οἴδατε ὡς—for ὅτι, as often in classical Greek—implies the *manner* as well as the bare fact: " you know the way in which (we dealt with) each one "; cf. ἐπίστασθε πῶς, Acts xx. 18, and see note on οἷοι (ποῖοι), i. 5, for the difference between ὡς and πῶς. For ἕνα ἕκαστον, asserting the *individualizing* care of these true pastors, cf. Acts xx. 31; Jo. x. 3 b.

ὡς πατὴρ τέκνα ἑαυτοῦ adds the father's heedful oversight to the mother's tender self-devotion (v. 7; cf. τὰ ἑαυτῆς τέκνα): with every kind of solicitude the missionaries " imparted their souls " (v. 8) to this Church and made themselves over to it (ὑμῖν...ἐγενήθημεν, v. 10). St Paul calls the Corinthians also (I. iv. 14, II. vi. 13), and the Galatians (iv. 19), and Timothy (I. i. 2, &c.), his τέκνα; so in 1 John τεκνία, *passim*. 1 Cor. iv. 14—21 gives a different turn to the figure.

11. **παρακαλοῦντες ... παραμυθούμενοι ... μαρτυρόμενοι,** *exhorting ... encouraging ... testifying.* Παρακαλέω is the general term for animating address (cf. note on παράκλησις, v. 3, also iii. 2); παραμυθέομαι denotes exhortation on its soothing and consoling side (see v. 14; Jo. xi. 19), suitably to the afflicted state of the Thessalonians (i. 6): iv. 13 ff. and II. i. 5 ff. are specimens of Pauline παραμυθία (Lightfoot, however, in his note *ad loc.* questions this distinction). Hofmann thus defines the three terms: " παρακαλεῖν is speech that addresses itself to the will, παραμυθεῖσθαι to the sensibilities, while μαρτύρεσθαι signalizes the impressive seriousness with which the speaker personally vouches for what he says." For μαρτύρομαι, to *protest, give solemn witness,* cf. Eph. iv. 17; Gal. v. 3; Acts xx. 26, xxvi. 22: to be carefully distinguished from μαρτυρέω (-έομαι; see Rom. iii. 21). The Vulg. reads, " deprecantes vos, et consolantes, testificati sumus," turning the last participle into a finite verb to complete the

sentence, and confusing μαρτύρομαι with μαρτυρέω; Erasmus and Beza, more correctly, *obtestantes*; Estius, *contestantes*.

12. εἰς τὸ περιπατεῖν ὑμᾶς ἀξίως τοῦ θεοῦ. The sublime turn now taken by the participial clause carries the Apostle away from the scheme of sentence beginning at ὡς ἕνα ἕκαστον; he forgets what he and his comrades did, as he thinks of what God is doing for the readers: cf. 1 Cor. iii. 7. Εἰς τό with infin. is synonymous with πρὸς τό, v. 9; the former carries one on to the purpose (or sometimes result) aimed at ("in order to"), while πρός contemplates and points to it ("with a view to," "with reference to"): cf. iv. 9, II. i. 5. Περιπατεῖν, a familiar Hebraism (הִתְהַלֵּךְ) = ἀναστρέφεσθαι, 2 Cor. i. 12, &c.

That they should "behave worthily of God" is the proper aim of those who "have turned to God from idols" (i. 9), and the aim on their behalf of those who "were entrusted by God" with "the gospel of God" to convey to them (vv. 2, 4, 8 f.): ἀξίως has τοῦ θεοῦ for its fitting complement here (only in 3 Jo. 6 besides in N.T.),—τοῦ κυρίου in Col. i. 10, τοῦ εὐαγγελίου τοῦ χριστοῦ in Phil. i. 27, τῆς κλήσεως in Eph. iv. 1 (cf. II. i. 11 below). For other references to God as the standard of the religious life, see Eph. v. 1; 1 Pet. i. 15; Matt. v. 48; Lev. xix. 2; Gen. xvii. 1. For parallels to ἀξίως τοῦ θεοῦ, see Deissmann, *Bible Studies*, p. 248.

ἀξίως τοῦ θεοῦ τοῦ καλοῦντος ὑμᾶς κ.τ.λ., *worthily of the God who calls you*: for it is "*the* God (living and real," i. 9), whom the Thessalonians have come to know through His gracious "call" and "choice" (i. 4) of them for salvation, of whom they are urged to "walk worthily,"—i.e. in a manner befitting the relationship in which God places them to Himself and the glorious destiny to which He summons them. The present participle may intimate the continuousness of the call (cf. note on τὸν διδόντα, iv. 8); or rather—since God's call is commonly conceived as the single, initial manifestation of His grace to Christians (see iv. 7; 1 Cor. i. 9, &c.)—τοῦ καλοῦντος is substantival, like τὸν ῥυόμενον in i. 10 (see note): "God your caller" (similarly in v. 24); St Paul and the rest are only κήρυκες, bearers of the summons from Him.

εἰς τὴν ἑαυτοῦ βασιλείαν καὶ δόξαν, (*who calleth you*) *into* (i.e. *to enter*) *His own kingdom and glory*,—the kingdom of which God is the immediate Ruler, entering which men become His acknowledged and privileged servants. "Kingdom and glory" form one idea (observe the single article and preposition): "God's own kingdom" culminates in " His own glory,"—viz. the splendour of the revelation attending the return of Christ, which will exhibit God in the full glory of His accomplished purposes of salvation and of judgement (Jo. xvii. 1; 1 Cor. xv. 21—28; Ph. ii. 11); hence *kingdom* and *glory* match the *serving* and *waiting* of i. 9 f. The Christian's "hope of the glory of God" (Rom. v. 2) is one with his "hope in our Lord Jesus Christ" (i. 3), and is the crown of his service in God's kingdom.

The idea of *the kingdom of God* was developed in the teaching of Jesus, and lies at the basis of St Paul's doctrine. The announcement of it had been a leading feature of his preaching at Thessalonica (cf. II. i. 5; see *Introd.* pp. xviii. ff.); in his missionary work, like John the Baptist and Jesus Himself, the Apostle Paul "went about heralding the kingdom" (Acts xx. 25, xxviii. 31). He designates it sometimes "the kingdom of the Son" (Col. i. 13), "the kingdom of Christ and God" (Eph. v. 5; cf. Rev. xi. 15), since God rules in it through Christ; and, in 2 Tim. iv. 18, as "His (the Lord's) heavenly kingdom" (cf. Matt. iv. 17, vi. 10, xiii. 24, &c.). The Kingdom is represented as future and yet present, existing hidden as "the leaven in the meal," "the corn in the blade," ever struggling and growing towards its ripeness: see especially Lk. xvii. 21; Matt. v 3, 10, xiii. 31 ff., 38, &c., for our Lord's view of the Kingdom, which is indeed virtually comprised in the petitions of the Lord's Prayer, "Thy kingdom come, Thy will be done, as in heaven so on earth." The kingdom is realized in its essence and potency wherever there is "righteousness and peace and joy in the Holy Spirit" (Rom. xiv. 17); but whatever of it men now possess the Apostle regards as only the "earnest of our inheritance" (Eph. i. 13 f.; Rom. viii. 17; Tit. iii. 7). His appeals, consolations, and protestations to his Thessalonian converts point to the sublime issue of their admission into the perfected kingdom of God; he adjures them to be worthy both of the God who had set His love upon them and of the wondrous future assured to them as His sons in Christ.

§ 4. ii. 13—16. FELLOWSHIP IN PERSECUTION WITH THE JUDÆAN CHURCHES.

The rich fruits of the Gospel in the Thessalonian Church, for which the writers thank God (§ 2), led them to dwell, in the tone of self-defence, on their own signal and devoted work (§ 3), which had this happy result. (*a*) The recital brings them back, in renewed thanksgiving, to the thought of *the full acceptance* on the readers' part *of the message of God* (*v.* 13, resuming i. 2—10). (*b*) In this acceptance, the Epistle goes on to say, the Thessalonian believers *identify themselves with the mother Churches in Judæa* (*v.* 14 *a*). (*c*) This fact is evidenced by *the persecution* undergone *at the hands of their fellow-countrymen* (*v.* 14 *b*). (*d*) At this point the Letter breaks out into a stern denunciation of *the Jews*, who have been *persecutors of God's servants all along* (*v.* 15), (*e*) and by *obstructing the salvation of the Gentiles* have made themselves the objects of a settled wrath, that is bringing upon them a conclusive judgement (*v.* 16).

The passionate note of *vv.* 15, 16 is singular in St Paul's Letters; nowhere else does he assail the Jewish *nation* in this way (see the *Introd.* pp. xviii. f.). In Rom. ix. 1—5 the Apostle writes of his "kindred" in quite another mood. On this ground, and since *vv.* 15, 16 form a parenthesis and might be removed without injury to the context, Schmiedel, with a few other critics, regards the passage as an interpolation due to some anti-Jewish editor, dating from a time subsequent to the fall of Jerusalem, to which he supposes *v.* 16 *c* to refer as a *fait accompli* (see note below); A. Ritschl would excise the last clause only. It must be borne in mind, however, that St Paul was pursued from the beginning of his work in Thessalonica up to the time of writing with peculiar virulence by the Jews (Acts xvii., xviii.), that the troubles of the Thessalonian Christians had their origin in Jewish envy and intrigue (Acts xvii. 5), and that the slanderous insinuations brought against the missionaries at the present time in Thessalonica almost certainly proceeded from the same quarter; there was cause enough for severe resentment and condemnation. Moreover, Silvanus, who had a share in the Epistle (see note on i. 1), was a Judæan Christian; some recent news of persecution suffered by his brethren at home may have added fuel to the flame of righteous anger and awakened his prophetic spirit (Acts xv. 32).

13. **Καὶ διὰ τοῦτο καὶ ἡμεῖς εὐχαριστοῦμεν τῷ θεῷ ἀδιαλείπτως.** *And on this account we also give thanks to God unceasingly.* At the beginning of the Epistle the Apostles gave thanks to God in remembrance of the worth of their readers; they find a supplementary ground of thanksgiving in the fact that these had "received as God's word" "the word of hearing" coming from themselves: hence the emphatic ἡμεῖς καὶ εὐχαριστοῦμεν instead of the bare εὐχαριστοῦμεν of i. 1, and the peculiar phrase λόγον ἀκοῆς παρ' ἡμῶν τοῦ θεοῦ. Διὰ τοῦτο gathers its meaning from the previous paragraph: all the toil and sacrifice of the missionaries contributed to their satisfaction over

the result accomplished; their consuming devotion to the Thessalonians made the thanksgiving a thoroughly personal matter: see *vv*. 19 f., iii. 8 f.

Accordingly the clause ὅτι παραλαβόντες λόγον ἀκοῆς παρ' ἡμῶν τοῦ θεοῦ, κ.τ.λ., does not supply the correlative to διὰ τοῦτο (as if St Paul meant "on this account, viz. that," &c.); but it gives the subject-matter of εὐχαριστοῦμεν (cf. II. i. 3, ii. 13; 1 Cor. i. 4 f., &c.): *that* (or *in that*) *when you received the word of hearing from us—God's word —you accepted* (*in it*)...*a word of God*. Παραλαβόντες, denoting the objective fact of *receiving*—by way of information, tradition, or the like (cf. iv. 1; II. iii. 6; 1 Cor. xv. 1; Gal. i. 9, &c.)—leads up to ἐδέξασθε, which indicates subjective *acceptance* (see i. 6, and note; II. ii. 10; 1 Cor. ii. 14), the inner apprehension and appreciation of the message for what it truly is. The λόγος ἀκοῆς is the "word" as it came to the παραλαβόντες (cf. Ph. iv. 9, παρελάβετε κ. ἠκούσατε), and from the λαλοῦντες (*vv*. 2, 4) and κηρύσσοντες (*v*. 9),—the word of God *sounding in the ears* of the Thessalonians from the writers' lips; the phrase occurs again in Heb. iv. 2, "where, as here, it stands in contrast to the faithful *reception* of the Gospel" (Lightfoot). For ἀκοῆς (ἀκούω) παρά, implying a "word" lodged with the speakers (*v*. 3), cf. 2 Tim. i. 13, ii. 2; Acts x. 22, &c.; Jo. xv. 15. Others connect παρ' ἡμῶν with παραλαβόντες. In Rom. x. 17 it is said, ἡ πίστις ἐξ ἀκοῆς, where πίστις corresponds to δέχεσθαι in this passage; an ἀκοὴ ἀπιστίας is described in that context. Ἀκοῆς should probably be read, like its counterpart in Rom. x. 8—(τὸ ῥῆμα) τῆς πίστεως—as a lax *genitive of the possessor*, "the word which belongs to (or is for) hearing"; as ἀκοή is διὰ ῥήματος (Rom. x. 17), so λόγος is εἰς ἀκοήν. For ἀκοή, see further Gal. iii. 2; Jo. xii. 38; Isai. liii. 1 (LXX). Τοῦ θεοῦ is *genitive of subject* defining the noun-phrase λόγον ἀκοῆς and correcting παρ' ἡμῶν, —"*God's* word given you to hear from us"; cf. Col. i. 6 b, 7; 2 Cor. iii. 5 f., v. 19 f.; Eph. iii. 7 f.; Acts xv. 7: "the Apostle betrays a nervous apprehension that he may be unconsciously making claims for himself; the awkwardness of the position of the words τοῦ θεοῦ is the measure of the emphasis of his disclaimer" (Lightfoot).

ἐδέξασθε οὐ λόγον ἀνθρώπων ἀλλά, καθὼς ἀληθῶς ἐστίν, λόγον θεοῦ: *you accepted no word of men, but, as it truly is, God's word*. No need to understand ὡς before λόγον in either instance: the Thessalonians in point of fact did not accept a human but a Divine word; they were listening to Another behind Paul and Silas. Of the kind of hearing negatived St Paul's Athenian audience gave an example (Acts xvii. 18—21). With οὐ λόγον ἀνθρ. κ.τ.λ. cf. 1 Cor. iii. 5—9, οὔτε ὁ φυτεύων ἐστίν τι κ.τ.λ.; also 1 Cor. i. 12—17, 29—31. The phrase ἀληθῶς ἐστίν is *hap. leg.* in St Paul; rather frequent in St John.

ὃς καὶ ἐνεργεῖται ἐν ὑμῖν τοῖς πιστεύουσιν, *which (word) is also made operative* (or *is working effectually*) *in you that believe.* The active of ἐνεργέω has in St Paul a personal subject; the passive (or middle) voice is used of personal *powers, influences,* as in II. ii. 7; Gal. v. 6, &c. This relative clause carries the readers from past to present time: "God's word," which they had accepted as such at the mouth of His Apostles, from that time "also works on in" their hearts and lives. Ἐνεργεῖται recalls the ἔργον πίστεως (i. 1; see note), —the primary matter of thanks to God. This verb (= ἐνεργής εἰμι) signifies effective, fructifying operation (cf. Rom. vii. 5; Phil. ii. 13); see J. A. Robinson on *Ephesians*, pp. 241 ff., who gives reason for rendering ἐνεργέομαι as *passive* in the N.T. The "word is made to work in" those "that *believe*," since faith is the operative principle of the new life,—πίστις...ἐνεργουμένη (Gal. v. 6; cf. Jam. ii. 22; Heb. iv. 2). A second time ὑμῖν τοῖς πιστεύουσιν serves to designate the Christian readers (v. 10; see note); in i. 7 πᾶσιν τοῖς πιστεύουσιν denoted Christians at large.

14. The effective power of the readers' faith in God's word was shown in that which it enabled them to suffer (cf. Col. i. 11):—

ὑμεῖς γὰρ μιμηταὶ ἐγενήθητε, ἀδελφοί, τῶν ἐκκλησιῶν τοῦ θεοῦ κ.τ.λ. These "believers" had "become imitators" of the Apostles and their Lord through "receiving the word in much affliction with joy" (i. 6); they were thus identified with the original believers: *for you became imitators, brothers, of the churches of God that are in Judæa in Christ Jesus.* Silvanus belonged to the Jerusalem Church, of which he would be often thinking and speaking: this allusion may, possibly, be due to *him* (see *Introd.* to § 4 above). "The churches... in Judæa"—in the *plural*, as in Gal. i. 22, "the churches of Judæa that are in Christ": the Palestinian Christian communities, as we gather from the notices of the Acts, formed a unity under the direct oversight in the first instance of the Apostles. They are identified with the Thessalonian Christians (i. 1; see note) as "churches of God...*in Christ Jesus*"; this adjunct differentiates them from the Synagogue. A "church *of God*" is a sacred and august fellowship: cf. II. i. 4; 1 Cor. i. 1; Gal. i. 13. For the double ἐν, of *local* and *spiritual* sphere, both depending on τῶν οὐσῶν, cf. Phil. i. 1, 13; Col. i. 2, &c. In this connexion "Christ" or "Christ Jesus"—not "Jesus Christ"—is appropriate, pointing to the living Head of the Church; v. 18 (where the reading, however, is doubtful) supplies the only other example in these Epistles of the familiar Pauline combination "Christ Jesus."

ὅτι τὰ αὐτὰ ἐπάθετε καὶ ὑμεῖς ὑπό κ.τ.λ., *in that you also suffered the same things from your fellow-countrymen.* Ὅτι defines μιμηταί (cf. i. 5), showing in what specifically the resemblance lay,—it was a συμπάσχειν: cf. Phil. i. 29 f., τὸν αὐτὸν ἀγῶνα ἔχοντες; 2 Cor. i. 6 f.; 2 Tim. ii. 3; 1 Pet. v. 9, &c. **συμφυλέτης** (cf., for the form of compound, συμπολίτης, Eph. ii. 19), *contribulis* (Vulg.), *fellow-tribesman,* replaces the older φυλέτης (Plato, *Legg.* 955 D; Aristophanes, *Acharn.* 568); signifying properly a member of the same φυλή, *sept* or *clan,* it grew wider in use; *hap. leg.* for N.T. Greek. Πάσχειν ὑπό is the regular construction (so in Matt. xvii. 12; Mk v. 26), ἀπό in Matt. xvi. 21. Τῶν ἰδίων, antithetical to αὐτοί of the next clause.

καθὼς καὶ αὐτοὶ ὑπὸ τῶν Ἰουδαίων. The *doubled* καί in comparisons is an emphasizing idiom characteristic of St Paul: cf. Rom. i. 13; Col. iii. 13. Αὐτοί refers, by a *constructio ad sensum,* to the men of "the churches of God which are in Judæa." From Acts xvii. 5 ff. it appears that the native Thessalonian mob were the actual persecutors, and used a violence similar to that directed against the Judæan Christians at the time of Stephen (Acts vi.—viii.); but the Jews prompted the attack. Hence it is against their own συμφυλέται, not those of the readers, that the anger of the Apostles is directed. This is the earliest example, and the only instance in St Paul, of the designation "the Jews" applied in the sense made familiar afterwards by the Gospel of St John, as opposed to *Christians*—"the disciples," "the believers," &c.; in Gal. ii. 13—15, Rev. iii. 9, it has no such connotation. Τῶν Ἰουδαίων is qualified by the following participial clauses, showing how the nation is fixed in its hostility to God's purpose in the Gospel; vv. 15 f. justify the use of the phrase "the Jews" in its anti-Gentile and anti-Christian sense.

15. τῶν καὶ τὸν κύριον ἀποκτεινάντων Ἰησοῦν, *who both killed the Lord, even Jesus.* To have "slain *the Lord,*" who bears the title of God, "Him whom they were bound to serve" (Jowett)—the most appalling of crimes (cf. 1 Cor. ii. 8, τὸν κύριον τῆς δόξης ἐσταύρωσαν); that "Lord," moreover, *Jesus,* their Saviour (Matt. i. 21; Acts iv. 12), and such as "Jesus" was known to be. The emphasis thrown by the separation on the double name brings into striking relief the Divine glory and the human character of the Slain; cf. Acts ii. 36. These words echo those in which Jesus predicted His death in the Parable of Lk. xx. 9—18 and Mk xii. 1—11.

καὶ τοὺς προφήτας καὶ ἡμᾶς ἐκδιωξάντων. Jesus had represented

His murder as the culmination of that of "the prophets" (Lk. xi. 47—51, xiii. 33, xx. 9—16), a charge repeated by St Stephen in Saul's hearing (Acts vii. 52); cf. also Rom. xi. 3; 1 Kings xix. 10, 14; Jer. ii. 30; Neh. ix. 26: these parallels support the usual construction of the clause, *who both killed the Lord Jesus and the prophets, and drove us out.* But "the prophets" here *follow* "the Lord Jesus," making something of an anti-climax if governed by ἀποκτεινάντων. Grammatically this object may just as well be attached to ἐκδιωξάντων and coordinated to ἡμᾶς, with the comma placed after 'Ιησοῦν: *who both killed the Lord Jesus, and drove out (in persecution) the prophets and ourselves.* Our Lord identified His Apostles with the O. T. prophets in persecution (see Matt. v. 12); in the Parable of the Wicked Husbandmen (Matt. xxi. 33 ff.; cf. xxiii. 34), ἴt was "some" of the servants that "they slew," as they did "the Son" at last, while all were persecuted (cf. again Acts vii. 52). "The prophets" and the Apostles were alike bearers of "the word of God" (*v.* 13), and received the same treatment from His unworthy people. Ἐκ-διώκω, "to persecute out (of a place)," is the verb found in many ancient copies in Lk. xi. 49, with the same twofold object: "I will send to them prophets and apostles, and some of them they will kill and *will persecute*"; see also Ps. cxviii. 157, Sir. xxx. 19 (LXX). This is precisely what befell St Paul at Thessalonica and Berœa in turn.

καὶ θεῷ μὴ ἀρεσκόντων. To "please God," to "walk worthily of the Lord unto all pleasing," is a favourite Pauline definition of the true religious life (see *v.* 4, iv. 1; also Rom. viii. 8, xii. 1; 2 Cor. v. 9, &c., and Heb. xi. 5 f.),—to which the behaviour of "the Jews" stands in glaring contrast. A tragic *meiosis*,—to describe as "not pleasing" the conduct of those on whom God's heaviest "wrath" descends (*v.* 16). The participle after the article is regularly negatived by μή (see A. Buttmann, *N. T. Grammar*, p. 351), which tends to oust οὐ with all participles in later Greek; cf. τὰ μὴ εἰδότα, iv. 5. For the sentiment, cf. Isai. lxv. 5; Jer. xxxii. 30.

καὶ πᾶσιν ἀνθρώποις ἐναντίων, *and (are) to all men contrary.* So the terrible indictment of "the Jews" culminates. The two participles and the adjective ἐναντίων, under the regimen of the single article, form a continuous, closely linked statement. Tacitus and Juvenal, who knew the Jews at Rome, speak of their sullen inhumanity as a notorious fact, the former referring to their "adversus omnes alios hostile odium" (*Hist.* v. 5), and the latter to their rule, "Non monstrare vias eadem nisi sacra colenti, Quæsitum ad fontem solos deducere verpos" (*Sat.* xiv. 103 f.). Testimonies to the like effect may be gathered from Philostratus, *Vita Apoll. Tyan.* v. 33; Diodorus Siculus xxxiv. 1; Josephus, *contra Apion.* II. 10, 14. The offer of "the good news" of Christ to the heathen provoked Jewish jealousy and contempt to fury: when the Gentiles flocked to St Paul's preaching in the synagogue of Pisidian Antioch, the Jews present ἰδόντες τοὺς ὄχλους ἐπλήσθησαν ζήλου (Acts xiii. 45); when the Apostle in his speech of defence at Jerusalem appealed to the Lord's command, "Go, for I will send thee far hence *unto the Gentiles*," hearing him ἄχρι τούτου τοῦ λόγου, they burst out, Αἶρε ἀπὸ τῆς γῆς τὸν τοιοῦτον (Acts xxii. 22). These were incidents in a constant experience.

There is a connexion in the nature of things between the two last clauses. The sense of God's displeasure sours a man's temper toward his fellows; unbelief breeds cynicism. The *Judenhasse* of modern times is a lamentable result of the ancient feud of Jew and Gentile, of which the figure of Shylock and his part in Shakespeare's *Merchant of Venice* afford a classical illustration.

16. κωλυόντων ἡμᾶς τοῖς ἔθνεσιν λαλῆσαι ἵνα σωθῶσιν, *forbidding us to speak to the Gentiles in order that they may be saved.* As much as to say, "These Jews would stop our mouths if they could, and prevent us uttering a single word to you about the Gospel; they would gladly see all the Gentiles perish." While many individual Jews were of a humaner spirit, this was the dominant feeling and the cause of the murderous enmity that pursued the Apostle Paul, bringing about his long imprisonment and finally his death. Here he exposes the motives of his traducers: they poisoned the minds of the Thessalonians against *him* to rob *them* of the Gospel of salvation; cf. the denunciation of Jewish Christian proselytizers in Gal. vi. 12 f.

Κωλυόντων, anarthrous participle, in explanatory apposition to the last clause (or, perhaps, to the two last clauses, θεῷ...ἐναντίων). This verb in pres. and impf. is regularly *tentative*: "being fain to forbid." Ἵνα is so weakened in later Greek, that λαλῆσαι ἵνα κ.τ.λ. might mean "to tell the Gentiles to be saved—to bid them be saved": "a periphrasis for εὐαγγελίζεσθαι τοῖς ἔθνεσιν" (Ellicott). This usage is clear in the case of the verb εἰπεῖν in Lk. iv. 3, x. 40; but it does not occur elsewhere with λαλεῖν, the force of which here lies in its connexion with τοῖς ἔθνεσιν (cf. v. 2; also Acts iv. 17, xi. 19 f., Jo. iv. 27, 1 Cor. iii. 1, for the stress on the *person* addressed in construction with λαλεῖν; and Eph. iii. 8, for τοῖς ἔθνεσιν in like emphasis): the Jews would not have a word said *to the Gentiles* "with a view to effect" their salvation. For ἵνα σωθῶσιν, cf. 1 Cor. x. 33; 2 Tim. ii. 10.

εἰς τὸ ἀναπληρῶσαι αὐτῶν τὰς ἁμαρτίας πάντοτε states the issue for the Jews of their sustained and violent resistance to the word of God, now consummated by their rancorous opposition to the Gentiles' receiving it. On εἰς τό, see note on v. 12; the preposition may signify *consequence* here, as in 2 Cor. viii. 5 f., Heb. xi. 3, but with a meaning *akin to purpose* (*a blind aim*),—"to the effect that," "in a manner calculated to"—whereas ὥστε (i. 8, &c.) expresses bare consequence ("so that," "so as to"). Ellicott and Bornemann may be right, however, in seeing here *the purpose of God*, "which unfolds itself in this wilful and at last judicial blindness on the part of His chosen people": cf. Rom. i. 24, διὸ παρέδωκεν αὐτοὺς ὁ θεός…εἰς ἀκαθαρσίαν, where sin is declared to be punished by further and more flagrant sin. The phrase "fill up their sins" recalls Gen. xv. 16, οὔπω ἀναπεπλήρωνται αἱ ἁμαρτίαι τῶν Ἀμορραίων—an ominous and humiliating parallel for Israelites; cf. also Dan. viii. 23. Still more distinctly the words of Jesus are echoed (Matt. xxiii. 31 f.): υἱοί ἐστε τῶν φονευσάντων τοὺς προφήτας· καὶ ὑμεῖς πληρώσατε τὸ μέτρον τῶν πατέρων ὑμῶν. Ἀνα-πληρόω, "to fill up (to the brim)," implies a measure quite complete: cf. II. ii. 6—8; Rom. ii. 5 f. Πάντοτε covers the whole ground of v. 15, indicating a course of misdoing repeated at every turn. On ἵνα and εἰς τό, see Moulton's *Prolegomena*, pp. 218—20.

That *God's* purpose was at work in the above ἀναπληρῶσαι is shown by the last clause, ἔφθασεν δὲ ἐπ᾽ αὐτοὺς ἡ ὀργὴ εἰς τέλος, *but the* (*Divine*) *wrath has hastened* (*to come*) *upon them, to* (*make*) *an end*. Whose wrath goes without saying; cf. ἡ ὀργή in i. 10, and Rom. v. 9. In i. 10 "the wrath" was contemplated in its approaching manifestation to the world; here in its imminence upon the Jewish people: there it is "coming" (ἐρχομένη); here it "has arrived." Φθάνω—construed with εἰς in Rom. ix. 31, Phil. iii. 16; with ἐπί in Matt. xii. 28, &c. —signifies *reaching* the object aimed at, with the associated idea of *speed* or *surprise*; with a direct object, it means to *overtake*, *anticipate* (see iv. 15). For the element of unexpectedness in the judgement, cf. v. 2 f., and Matt. xxiv. 50, Lk. xxi. 34 f., &c., in our Lord's prophecies; this sense of φθάνω is unmistakable in Matt. xii. 28, and accords with the emphatic position of the verb here. The sentence is prophetic, resembling in its aorist (or perfect: see Textual Note) the Hebrew *perfect of prediction* (where the certain future is realized in thought); the Apostles infer this from the facts before their eyes. "The Jews" have rejected the Name in which alone there is salvation (Acts iii. 19 ff., iv. 12); by their crime in killing the Lord Jesus, and by forbidding His Gospel to the world, they have sealed their doom. The tragedy of Israel's fate hurries visibly to its pre-determined close.

And this calamity will be *final*—ἔφθασεν (or ἔφθακεν)...εἰς τέλος. In former threatenings God had said, "Yet will I not make a full end" (Jer. iv. 27, &c.); this time He does make an end—of the Old Covenant and of national Israel. Still Rom. xi. opens out a new prospect for the Jewish race; after all it is εἰς τέλος, not εἰς τὸ τέλος, that is written. For St Paul's use of τέλος as implying the goal and terminus of some Divine dispensation, cf. Rom. x. 4; 1 Cor. x. 11, xv. 24; also Lk. xxii. 37. In Lk. xviii. 5, Jo. xiii. 1, εἰς τέλος has much the same force as here, meaning not *at last*, but *finally* (so as to reach an end), *by way of crown and finish* to the matter in hand.

Within twenty years of the writing of this Letter Jerusalem fell, after the most dreadful and calamitous siege known in history; and the Jewish people ever since have wandered without a home and without an altar. "Tristis exitus," writes Bengel: "urgebat miseros ira Dei, et εἰς τέλος urbem cum templo delevit."

§ 5. ii. 17—iii. 5. THE SEPARATION OF THE APOSTLES FROM THEIR CONVERTS.

After the pause for thanksgiving to God, which in its turn led up to the stern denunciation of Jewish persecutors in *vv.* 15 f., the Letter resumes the strain of *v.* 13. The happy intercourse between the Apostles and their newly-won converts (*vv.* 10—12) had been broken off by the assault just alluded to; the missionaries had left Thessalonica prematurely and in grief, planning a speedy return (*v.* 17). St Paul in particular had twice resolved on this, but in vain (*v.* 18). For the Thessalonian Church gave its ministers the greatest joy and hope (*v.* 19 f.). Failing to return themselves, the other two had sent Timothy, to cheer the Thessalonians and sustain their faith under present trials, of which indeed they had been forewarned (iii. 1—4); especially on St Paul's motion had Timothy gone, to enquire how the Church fared under this prolonged and anxious trial (*v.* 5).

17. Ἡμεῖς δέ, ἀδελφοί, ἀπορφανισθέντες ἀφ' ὑμῶν. *But we on our part, brothers, torn from you in bereavement—desolati a vobis* (Vulg.), *orbati vobis* (Calvin, &c.)—"sicut parentes filiis absentibus" (Bengel). Ἀπ-ορφανίζομαι (*hap. leg.* in N. T., only found besides in Æschylus, *Choeph.* 246) is derived from ὀρφανός (*orphan*, Lat. *orbus*; cf. Jo. xiv. 18; Jam. i. 27), a term applying to the loss of any near relation or friend; it describes here the severing of new-found and tenderly attached "brothers," or of parents from children (*v.* 11): similarly in Pindar, ὀρφανὸς ἑταίρων (*Isthm.* 7. 16), as well as ὀρφανοὶ

γενεᾶς (Ol. 9. 92); Hesychius defines ὀρφανός as ὁ γονέων ἐστερημένος καὶ τέκνων. The doubled ἀπο- emphasizes the separation. Ἡμεῖς δέ, in contrast with ὑμεῖς γάρ, v. 14 : the last paragraph has thrown into relief the worth of the Thessalonians as ἀδελφοί.

πρὸς καιρὸν ὥρας, προσώπῳ οὐ καρδίᾳ. Mitigating circumstances of the bereavement (cf. Jo. xiv. 18 ff., xvi. 16 ff., &c.): the parting was expected to be *brief*; while it lasted, there would be *no severance of heart*. Πρὸς καιρὸν ὥρας, ad momentum horæ (Beza); cf. Horace, Sat. I. i. 7 f.: πρὸς καιρόν occurs in 1 Cor. vii. 5, Lk viii. 13; πρὸς ὥραν in 2 Cor. vii. 8, Gal. ii. 5, Phm. 15, Jo. v. 35—the former implying *a passing crisis*, the latter *a brief interval*; the combination is unique; see however κατὰ καιροὺς ὡρῶν in Exod. xiii. 10. The antithesis πρόσωπον...καρδία is found in 2 Cor. v. 12; it contrasts the apparent and real in the case, the outer aspect with the inner mind of those concerned—*aspectu non corde* (Vulg.): cf., for a like antithesis in πρόσωπον, Matt. vi. 16 ff.; in καρδία, Rom. ii. 28 f.

περισσοτέρως ἐσπουδάσαμεν τὸ πρόσωπον ὑμῶν ἰδεῖν ἐν πολλῇ ἐπιθυμίᾳ, *made more earnest endeavours to see your face in great longing*. The comparative adverb, according to its use elsewhere (2 Cor. i. 12; Gal. i. 14, &c.), signifies not "*the* more abundantly" (because of our strong affection, because of the anxious circumstances, or the like), but "more abundantly" (than otherwise, than in ordinary circumstances)—"in no small degree"; it is explained by ἐν πολλῇ ἐπιθυμίᾳ: the "abundant desire" filling the souls of the Apostles stirred them to an uncommon zeal in the attempt to get back to Thessalonica. Parted from their brethren "in face not in heart," the writers longed and strove "to see" their "face." Ἐπιθυμία denotes *intent* desire, and most often *bad* desire, *lust*: cf. for its good sense, Phil. i. 23; Lk. xxii. 15; and for the verb ἐπιθυμέω, Gal. v. 17; 1 Tim. iii. 1; Matt. xiii. 17, &c.

18. διότι ἠθελήσαμεν ἐλθεῖν πρὸς ὑμᾶς, *because we had resolved to come to you*: place a colon only at the end of v. 17. The A. V.— "Wherefore we would have come"—confounds διότι with διό (cf. iii. 1, &c.): for διότι, which regularly introduces an antecedent ground, not a consequence, see v. 8, iv. 6, Rom. i. 19, 1 Cor. xv. 9, &c.; it is an emphasized causal ὅτι. The R.V. also fails to do justice to θέλω here, which signifies *will* rather than *wish* (see Buttmann's *Lexilogus*, Lidd. and Scott's *Lexicon*, Tittmann's *Synonyms*, *sub voce*: Grimm in his *Lexicon* seems to be at fault); had St Paul meant " we would fain have come " (R.V.), or " were fain to come," he would presumably have written ἐβουλόμεθα, as in 2 Cor. i. 15 or Phm. 13. This rendering,

moreover, makes ἠθελήσαμεν but a weakened repetition of ἐσπουδάσαμεν...ἐν πολλῇ ἐπιθυμίᾳ. The Apostles had "*made up their minds to come*"—they were resolved and bent upon it; hence their strenuous effort (v. 17). Θέλω (ἐθέλω), with θέλημα, in the N.T. as in classical Greek, always implies, more or less distinctly, *active volition*,—even in Matt. i. 19; " auf das entschiedene Wollen, den festen, bestimmten Vorsatz und Entschluss geht " (Bornemann *ad loc.*).

ἐγὼ μὲν Παῦλος καὶ ἅπαξ καὶ δίς. *I, Paul, indeed both once and twice.* The plural of vv. 17, 18 a shows that the three writers—at any rate more than one of them (see iii. 1)—shared in this strong desire and determined attempt; St Paul, on his part, had "twice" definitely "resolved to come." Perhaps the former of these plans to revisit Thessalonica was formed at Berœa, while Paul and Silas were together (Acts xvii. 10—14); and the second at Athens, which Paul reached alone (v. 15), or on the way from Berœa to Athens. The phrase καὶ ἅπαξ καὶ δίς is found in Phil. iv. 16, where it is rendered as here, "once and again (you sent to relieve my need)": cf. Neh. xiii. 20, 1 Macc. iii. 30 (LXX), where ἅπαξ κ. δίς, like our "once or twice," means "several times" indefinitely; but the definite numerical sense is appropriate here and in Phil., and with repeated καί—"not once only, but twice," "as often as twice." For the double καί, cf. Matt. x. 28; 1 Cor. x. 32. The μέν *solitarium* connotes a tacit contrast, *scil.* "but the others once"; see Blass' *Grammar of N.T. Greek*, p. 267.

καὶ ἐνέκοψεν ἡμᾶς ὁ Σατανᾶς. This clause coordinates itself by καί (not δέ) quite appropriately to v. 17, v. 18 a being subordinate and parenthetical; the entire sentence reads thus: "But we, brothers,... made extraordinary efforts to see your face, in our great longing (for we had set our minds on coming to you,—I Paul, for my own part, not once but twice); and Satan hindered us." The "hindering" did not obstruct the "willing" (ἠθελήσαμεν, v. 18 a), but the "endeavouring" (ἐσπουδάσαμεν, v. 17). If this interpretation be right (see Bornemann at length *ad loc.*), the punctuation both of A.V. and R.V. is misleading; cf. the two foregoing notes.

Ἐνκόπτω (see Gal. v. 7, and Lightfoot's note; Rom. xv. 22) is a military term of later Greek, signifying "to make a break in (the enemy's way)," to "cut up (the road)." Ὁ Σατανᾶς (Heb. הַשָּׂטָן, Aramaic סָטָנָא), "the Adversary," is the Captain of the powers of evil,—undoubtedly a personality, not a personification, to St Paul; the same as ὁ πειράζων of iii. 5, ὁ πονηρός of II. iii. 3. This O.T. name recurs in II. ii. 9 (see note); it is frequent in St Paul, along with ὁ διάβολος, and is used by most N.T. writers as the proper name of the great spiritual Enemy of God and man. What form the hindrance took is not stated; Jewish malice probably supplied a chief element in it (see v. 16, κωλυόντων ἡμᾶς κ.τ.λ.); most likely an order had been procured from the magistrates of Thessalonica forbidding the return of the missionaries. For similar references by Paul to the personal hostility of Satan, see 2 Cor. ii. 11, xii. 7.

Vv. 19, 20 go to explain the great eagerness of St Paul and his companions, and the repeated attempt of the former, to get back to Thessalonica.

V. 19 is best punctuated—after WH, Lightfoot, Nestle, and others—by reading ἢ οὐχὶ καὶ ὑμεῖς; as a parenthesis: *For what is our hope or joy or glorying's crown (or is it not you indeed?) before our Lord Jesus in His coming?*" as much as to say, "What else than you?" Not that other Churches fail to afford such hope; "alios non excludit, hos maxime numerat" (Bengel): cf. Phil. ii. 16, iv. 1; Jo. xv. 11, xvii. 10; 3 Jo. 4. The Apostles' "hope," like that of their readers (i. 4, 10, iii. 13), is fixed on the glorious return of the Lord Jesus; then their work will be appraised (see 1 Cor. iv. 1—5; 2 Cor. v. 9 f.), and "joy" or "grief" (Heb. xiii. 17), "glorying" or shame, will be theirs, as the objects of their care prove worthy or unworthy (cf. II. i. 11 f.). Hence all their prayers and efforts look to this end, as in iii. 13, v. 23 f.; Col. i. 28—ii. 2; 2 Cor. xi. 2. At Christ's coming St Paul expects his "crown" (2 Tim. iv. 8; cf. 1 Cor. ix. 25; Jam. i. 12; 1 Pet. v. 4, &c.).

στέφανος καυχήσεως—*corona gloriationis* (Calvin, Bengel), not *gloriæ* (Vulg.)—renders תִּפְאֶרֶת עֲטֶרֶת in Isai. lxii. 3; Ezek. xvi. 12, xxiii. 42; Prov. xvi. 31—the crown which a king or hero wears on some day of festal triumph; cf. Sophocles, *Ajax* 465. St Paul anticipates a consummation of the καύχησις which he already enjoys: see II. i. 4; Rom. xv. 17; 1 Cor. xv. 31; 2 Cor. vii. 4, &c. The appealing interrogative (ἢ οὐχὶ καὶ ὑμεῖς;) is characteristic: cf. Rom. ix. 21; 1 Cor. vi. 2, 19, &c.

Note the first appearance here of the word παρουσία, which plays so large a part in the two Epistles: see iii. 13, iv. 15, v. 23; II. ii. 1, 8, 9; once besides, in 1 Cor. xv. 23; also in 1 Jo. ii. 28. It stood for the "coming," or "presence," of the expected (Jewish) Messiah, His advent and accession to power and glory. Since Jesus had claimed to be this Messiah, but had not in the first instance "come in power" or "in His kingdom" or "in the glory of His Father"

(Matt. xvi. 28, xxiv. 30; Mk viii. 38, ix. 1, &c.), this remained to be realized at His future παρουσία, to which the term thus came to be specifically applied (Matt. xxiv. 3, &c.); it is synonymous in this sense with ἐπιφάνεια (1 Tim. vi. 14, &c.), and ἀποκάλυψις (1 Cor. i. 7).

20. ὑμεῖς γάρ ἐστε ἡ δόξα ἡμῶν καὶ ἡ χαρά. *Yes, truly, you are our glory and our joy.* In this reply to the rhetorical question of *v.* 19, δόξα covers ἐλπίς and στέφανος καυχήσεως, while χαρά is repeated. The emphasis on ὑμεῖς, and the close correspondence of *vv.* 19 and 20, scarcely admit of our reading ἐστέ as a distinctive *present*—as though the sentence meant, "You are now, as you will be then, our glory." The δόξα, like the στέφανος of Christians, belongs to the future (see Rom. xiii. 18, &c.); and yet, like their καύχησις (see note above), it is begun already (see Rom. viii. 30).

The division of Chapters is misjudged here; *v.* 17 above supplies a much better break.

CHAPTER III.

1. For **διο** B has the impossible διοτι, probably through transcriptional assimilation to μηκετι.

ηυδοκησαμεν, in ℵBP. Cf. ηυδοκουμεν, the reading of B in ii. 8; also Rom. xv. 26, 27, 1 Cor. x. 5, where WH adopt ηυδ- from ℵB*, ℵA, and **AB*C** respectively; and 1 Cor. i. 21, where these editors retain ευδ., **C** alone of the uncials having ηυδ.; in Gal. i. 15, **A** alone has ηυδ. Outside of Paul, the augment in this verb is ill-attested.

2. The verse presents a complicated and difficult problem:

(a) **τον αδελφον ημων και διακονον του θεου** is the reading of ℵAP 67** 71 and several other minn., vg cop basm syr[hcl txt], Bas Euthal Pelag; the sah and the Harleian* copy of the vg omit *dei*.

(b) *τον αδελφον ημων κ. συνεργον του θεου*: so **D*d e**, Ambrst—clearly the Western reading. **B** gives, barely, **τον αδελφον ημων κ. συνεργον** (minus *του θεου*). **C** is wanting here.

(c) **G** contains a conflate text: *τον αδελφον ημων κ. διακονον κ. συνεργον του θεου*; while the T.R. (Syrian) furnishes another combination, *τον αδελφον ημων κ. διακονον του θεου κ. συνεργον ημων*—so in **D**[c]**KL**, most minn., syrr, Chr Thdrt, &c.

Manifestly (a) and (b) are the parents of the two forms of (c). Which of the former is the original, it is hard to say. The substitution of συνεργον for the smooth and unexceptionable διακονον in conjunction with του θεου is not transcriptionally likely; and ℵAP (ℵBP in Tischendorf[8] is a misprint), with the cop, have the look of an Alexandrian group. 1 Cor. iii. 9 may have suggested the added genitive, *του θεου* after *συνεργον* (as in **D**), which is less relevant here (see Expository Note); and the Syrian reading points to an earlier συνεργον unqualified by *του θεου*; observe also the absence of *dei* in sah and harl*, under (a) above. It is noticeable that in the other ten Pauline instances of συνεργος, the συν- refers to *the writer himself* (see the Concordance); cf. also 1 Cor. xvi. 16, συνεργουντι. The history of the text may thus be construed: **B** preserves the original reading, that intrinsically probable here, viz. Τιμοθεον τον αδελφον ημων κ. συνεργον. The Western scribe, or editor, added του θεου, recalling 1 Cor. iii. 9. The Alexandrian editor, reasonably stumbling at this, smoothed down συνεργον του θεου into διακονον του θεου. The copyist of G combined the 3rd and 2nd, the Syrian editors the 3rd and 1st of the above readings. See on this passage B. Weiss, *Textkritik der Paulinischen Briefe*, p. 13.

3. **το (σαινεσθαι)** in all uncials. G has the Latinism ινα; latt vg, *ut nemo moveatur*.

5. **την υμων πιστιν** (WH, *margin*), B 37 73 116: this (for Paul) unusual order (cf. e.g. vv. 2, 6) may be original. On the other hand, v. 7 may have deflected the reading of B here.

7. **αναγκη και θλιψει** (in this order): all uncials except KL, and the best minn. and versions. Θλιψις is much the more familiar word of the two; see v. 3, i. 6.

8. **στηκετε**, rather than -ητε: all uncials except ℵ*D, and many good minn. See Expository Note.

9. **τω κυριω**, instead of **τω θεω**, ℵ* (also εμπροσθεν του κυριου later) D*G (the Gothic Version has *domino deo*, by conflation): an aberrant Western reading—perhaps determined by εν κυριω at the end of v. 8.

B reads **περι ημων**, for **περι υμων**.

11. **χριστος** supplements **ο κυριος ημων Ιησους** in D^cGKL: a characteristic Western and Syrian addition; see note on ii. 19 above.

13. **αμεμπ**-τως, for -**τους**, BL: perhaps due to ii. 10, v. 23. See Expository Note.

αγιοσυνῃ: this unusual spelling in B*DG—a frequent itacism (ο for ω). So DG in 2 Cor. vii. 1.

The closing **αμην** (WH, *margin*) is found in ℵ*AD 37 43 d e vg cop: a strong combination of evidence; and transcriptional probability tells in support of the reading, for the "Amen" would seem premature in the middle of the Epistle. "Videtur αμην hoc loco offendisse" (Tisch.). BG and the Syrian witnesses, with some Latins, omit.

(§ 5, *continued*.)

1. **Διὸ μηκέτι στέγοντες.** *Wherefore no longer bearing (it)*—viz. the pain of bereavement, the hindering of their return (ii. 17 f.), and the concern the Apostles felt for their converts left under a storm of persecution (v. 3) and with a still imperfect faith (vv. 2, 10). Διό

has a like comprehensive reference in v. 11. On μή with participles, see Lightfoot *ad loc.*; the clause does not state a bare fact, as οὐκέτι στέγοντες would have done, but the fact which motived the action taken; cf. Winer-Moulton, pp. 606 ff. On στέγω, repeated in *v.* 5, see Lightfoot again. Kindred to Latin *tego, to cover,* the verb means both *to hold in* one's feelings (Plato *Gorgias* 493 c), and to *hold out against* the pressure of circumstances: either sense is appropriate here; the latter accords with 1 Cor. ix. 12, xiii. 7—the other N.T. exx.—and with later Greek usage, exemplified by Philo *in Flaccum* 974 c (§ 9), μηκέτι στέγειν δυνάμενοι τὰς ἐνδείας.

ηὐδοκήσαμεν καταλειφθῆναι ἐν Ἀθήναις μόνοι, *we thought good* (or *determined*) *to be left behind in Athens alone*: *censuimus ut* (Calvin), or *optimum duximus ut* (Estius) *Athenis soli relinqueremur.* For the force of the plural *we,* and for the movements of the missionary party at this time, see *Introd.*, pp. xx. f. Εὐδοκέω implies not the bare determination (ἔδοξεν ἡμῖν), but a conclusion come to heartily and with goodwill (cf. ii. 8; 2 Cor. v. 8, &c.)—often used of God's " good pleasure " in His saving acts and choices (Lk. xii. 32, &c.). Κατα- adds intensity to λείπω; the simple verb however only occurs intransitively in the N.T. Μόνοι indicates that Timothy was *missed*; Paul and Silas were "lonely" without him: cf. Phil. ii. 20; 1 Tim. i. 2; 2 Tim. i. 2 ff., iv. 9 ff., indicating the value set upon Timothy's company. To give up Timothy, their ὑπηρέτης (cf. Acts xiii. 5), was a sacrifice; both the older men, probably, found a comfort in his presence which they could not in the same way give to each other. Timothy, as well as Silas, must previously have rejoined St Paul at Athens, according to the instructions of Acts xvii. 15.

2. καὶ ἐπέμψαμεν Τιμόθεον, τὸν ἀδελφὸν ἡμῶν κ. διάκονον τοῦ θεοῦ. For the name Τιμόθεος, see note on i. 1. This description of Timothy—*our brother, and God's minister* (or *fellow-worker,* συνεργόν)—raises the question whether he had been at Thessalonica; for it looks as though he were being *introduced* to the readers, and only Paul and Silas are actually named in St Luke's account of the mission at Thessalonica in Acts xvii. 1—10, Timothy appearing on the scene at Berœa just when Paul is departing for Athens (*vv.* 14 f.). On the other hand, Timothy shares in the greeting, from which point the Epistle proceeds in the 1st pers. plural; and there is no hint of his exclusion from the reminiscences of chaps. i. and ii. The sending of this young and somewhat timid helper probably dictates the commendation, designed to obviate any disparagement of Timothy on the part of the Church: cf. 1 Cor. xvi. 10; 1 Tim. iv. 12. It

seems that in Thessalonica, as previously in Philippi, Timothy had not been marked out for attack in the same way as his leaders; he could return when they could not. Cf. the eulogy upon Epaphroditus (Phil. ii. 25), who is going back to Philippi; also 2 Cor. viii. 23, referring to Titus, who was already well known to the Corinthian Church. The surpassingly high epithet συνεργὸν τοῦ θεοῦ (cf. 2 Cor. vi. 1) was calculated (if this reading be genuine: see the Textual Note) to exalt Timothy in the eyes of the readers and to silence complaint about *his* being sent. But the adjunct ἐν τῷ εὐαγγελίῳ τοῦ χριστοῦ hardly suits συνεργὸν τοῦ θεοῦ, since *God's* part has been emphatically contrasted with that of His servants "in the good news of the Christ" (see ii. 4; 1 Cor. xii. 6): the reading διάκονον τοῦ θεοῦ ἐν τῷ εὐαγγ. is preferable, assuming τοῦ θεοῦ authentic; cf. Rom. i. 9; Phil. ii. 22; Phm. 13. For the bare συνεργόν (without τοῦ θεοῦ), see 2 Cor. viii. 23; in 1 Cor. iii. 9 συν- probably conjoins *Paul and Apollos*, and θεοῦ is genitive of possession. For διάκ. τοῦ θεοῦ, cf. 1 Cor. iii. 5; 2 Cor. vi. 4. As distinguished from δοῦλος, expressing the *personal relation* binding the "slave" to his master, διάκονος connotes the *help* or *service* rendered.

Τὸ εὐαγγέλιον τοῦ χριστοῦ, "the good news about the Christ," who is the object of the Divine proclamation (see Rom. i. 3; 1 Cor. i. 23; &c.); previously τὸ εὐαγγέλιον τοῦ θεοῦ in this Epistle (ii. 2, &c.; see note), with the subjective genitive. The phrase "servant of God," or " our fellow-worker," requires the definition ἐν τῷ εὐαγγ. (see Rom. i. 1 f., 9, xv. 16, 19; and Ph. ii. 22, iv. 3), which reminds the Thessalonians of their indebtedness to Timothy.

The elder missionaries had sent Timothy **εἰς τὸ στηρίξαι ὑμᾶς καὶ παρακαλέσαι ὑπὲρ τῆς πίστεως ὑμῶν,** *in order to establish you and encourage (you) in furtherance of your faith.* The two infinitives (στηρίξαι κ. παρακαλέσαι), with a single article, form one idea, the latter being the means to the former: they are coupled in the reverse order in II. ii. 17; cf. also *v.* 13 below. On παρακαλέω, see notes to ii. 12, and παράκλησις, ii. 3. Timothy's presence and exhortations, it was expected, would steady and strengthen the buffeted faith of the Thessalonians. In its primary meaning (cf. Lk. xvi. 26), στηρίζω goes back to Homer; its ethical use belongs to later Greek, occurring e.g. in Epictetus, *Gnomologium Stobæi,* 39 (ed. Schenkl), τοὺς ἐνοικοῦντας εὐνοίᾳ κ. πίστει κ. φιλίᾳ στήριζε. For εἰς τό with infin., see note on ii. 12. Ὑπέρ signifies more than *about* (περί, as in i. 9, iii. 9, &c.), rather *on behalf of, in the interest of* (cf. II. i. 5, ii. 1); somewhat differently used in II. i. 4.

3. τὸ μηδένα σαίνεσθαι ἐν ταῖς θλίψεσιν ταύταις. *To wit, that no one be shaken in mind* (or *befooled*) *amid these afflictions.* "These" are the θλίψεις of i. 6 and ii. 2, 14 (cf. II. i. 4 ff.), from which Timothy would find the Thessalonians still suffering. Σαίνω is a N.T. hap. leg.; its sense is doubtful. It does not seem to be cognate with σείω, *to shake, disturb*, as commonly supposed, but signifies *to move quickly, to swish* or *wag* (as the dog his tail: so in Homer and Hesiod); then, in the Attic poets, *to fawn upon, wheedle, greet pleasingly*, and so *to befool, cozen.* The latter meaning is put upon the word here by Hofmann, Lightfoot, Schmiedel, after Beza (*adblandiri*), supposing that St Paul regards the persecuted Thessalonians as in danger of *seduction* by the arts of the enemies of the Gospel, who would know how to flatter the Apostle's converts (cf. Gal. iv. 17), while they vilified himself (see ii. 3—12; *Introd.* pp. xxxiv. f.). But the verb is read by the Greek interpreters as synonymous with σαλεύω or ταράττω; cf. Diogenes Laertius, VIII. 41, οἱ δὲ σαινόμενοι τοῖς λεγομένοις ἐδάκρυόν τε καὶ ᾤμωζον, where σαινόμενοι signifies "moved" in feeling, "affected" in mind; also παιδός με σαίνει φθόγγος, Sophocles, *Antig.* 1214. Thus σαίνεσθαι is in contrast with στηρίξαι, v. 2, and with ἐὰν στήκετε ἐν κυρίῳ, v. 8: cf. 1 Cor. xv. 58; Col. i. 23; Eph. vi. 11 ff., &c.

The phrase τὸ...σαίνεσθαι, of which τῷ σαίνεσθαι (T.R.) is a clumsy emendation, stands in the accus. case, in loose explanatory apposition to εἰς τὸ στηρίξαι κ.τ.λ., as though St Paul had written τουτέστι τὸ μηδένα κ.τ.λ.; similarly τὸ μὴ ὑπερβαίνειν in iv. 6 (see note). Some commentators suppose εἰς to be repeated in thought—an unlikely ellipsis; others (Ellicott, Hofmann, A. Buttmann) regard the clause as an accus. of the object (content) to παρακαλέσαι—a forced construction.

αὐτοὶ γὰρ οἴδατε. Almost a formula of this Epistle: see note on ii. 1.

ὅτι εἰς τοῦτο κείμεθα, *that we are set* (*appointed, destined*) *for this:* εἰς τοῦτο, scil. εἰς τὸ θλίβεσθαι. "We" includes readers with writers; the θλίψεις of the latter were alluded to in ii. 2, again in II. iii. 2. For St Paul's *destination* in this respect, see Acts ix. 16, and 2 Cor. xi. 23—33: and for Christians generally, Acts xiv. 22 (where the characteristic expressions of this passage—στηρίζω, παρακαλέω, πίστις, θλίψεις—appear: St Luke was recalling the actual words of the Apostle); Jo. xvi. 1 ff., 33, &c.; 1 Pet. ii. 21 (εἰς τοῦτο ἐκλήθητε). Κεῖμαι is a virtual passive to τίθημι, *to set*, or to τίθεμαι (middle), *to appoint* (see v. 9); for κεῖμαι εἰς, cf. Phil. i. 16, Lk. ii. 34. To "know" that one's sufferings belong to the Divine order of things and are proper to the Christian calling, is to be assured not only of their necessity but of their beneficial purpose and joyful issue: see the Beatitudes in Matt. v.; also Rom. viii. 17 f.; 2 Tim. ii. 11 f.; 1 Pet. iv. 12 ff.

4. καὶ γὰρ ὅτε πρὸς ὑμᾶς ἦμεν, προελέγομεν κ.τ.λ. In support of the rule just stated, the Apostles recall their own definite and repeated warnings. For εἰμὶ πρός—the "with" of personal converse—cf. II. ii. 5, iii. 1, 10; also Gal. i. 18; Jo. i. 1. The impf. προελέγομεν, like ἐλέγομεν in II. ii. 5, supposes reiterated warning; the language of the sequel, μέλλομεν κ.τ.λ., sustains the sense "fore-tell" for this verb—otherwise it might be rendered, "we told you *openly* (or *plainly*)," as in R.V. margin; cf. πρόκειμαι in 2 Cor. viii. 12. The same ambiguity attaches to προ-λέγω in 2 Cor. xiii. 2; Gal. v. 21.

ὅτι μέλλομεν θλίβεσθαι, *that we are to be afflicted* (writers and readers; see note on κείμεθα, v. 3). The persecution of the missionaries and their converts sprang from the same source (see ii. 14 f.; Acts xvii. 5), the malignity and persistence of which were patent from the first in Thessalonica.

Ὅτι μέλλομεν, not μέλλοιμεν: the moods of *oratio recta* are almost always in N.T. Greek taken over unchanged in the subordinate clause, whether the *verbum dicendi* be primary or historical in tense; see Winer-Moulton, p. 376.

καθὼς καὶ ἐγένετο καὶ οἴδατε, *as indeed it proved, and you know*: an appeal to the *facts* of the case and the *experience* of the readers. On the latter point, and the recurrence of this appeal (cf. v. 3), see notes to i. 5 and ii. 1. The reminder should help to prevent the Thessalonian believers from being "shaken amid these afflictions": what had happened was natural and expected; it is "no strange thing" (1 Pet. iv. 12).

5. διὰ τοῦτο κἀγὼ μηκέτι στέγων ἔπεμψα κ.τ.λ. *On this account I myself also, no longer bearing (it), sent,* &c.: a re-assertion, in the singular number, of what *v.* 1 related in the plural, with an additional reason brought into view—διὰ τοῦτο, *scil.* εἰς τὸ γνῶναι κ.τ.λ. Some suppose (*a*) that the plur. and sing. of *vv.* 1 and 5 are used indifferently, that indeed the 1st plur. throughout the Epistle is a conventional *pluralis auctoris*; but this is improbable, on general grounds (see *Introd.* pp. xxxix. f.). (*b*) Hofmann and Spitta (*Urchristenthum*, Band I., pp. 121 f.) draw quite another inference from the discrepancy of number; they conclude that St Paul in his impatience sent a *second* messenger, on his own account, with the enquiry stated in this verse, after Timothy had been despatched by himself and Silas (*v.* 1). But the words of *v.* 1 are deliberately resumed, as if expressly to identify the two (quite congruous) purposes stated in *vv.* 2 and 5; moreover it is Timothy (*v.* 6) who returns with the report that allayed St Paul's anxiety. (*c*) Assuming, then, that *vv.* 1 and 5 refer to one and the same visit, and that the distinction of number in the double grammatical subject is not otiose, we must understand that, while the two chiefs concurred in sending Timothy to Thessalonica from Athens, the action was St Paul's principally; and that, while both the senders were wishful to strengthen the faith of the Thessalonians, St Paul attributes to himself, rather than to Silas, the apprehension that this faith might have given way. In ii. 18 St Paul distinguished himself as having made a *second*, unshared, attempt to get back to Thessalonica; and here, as being actuated by a *second* motive, that was perhaps not at the time so explicit, in directing Timothy's errand. If διὰ τοῦτο be prospective to εἰς τὸ γνῶναι, the construction resembles that of 1 Tim. i. 16, 2 Tim. ii. 10, Phm. 15; but the above interpretation is consistent with the more usual retrospective reference of the prepositional phrase—*scil.* to προελέγομεν κ.τ.λ.—the purpose of Timothy's visit being understood as growing out of the prevision expressed in *v.* 4: "expecting this continued trial for you, I sent, in some apprehension, to see how you were bearing it."

εἰς τὸ γνῶναι τὴν πίστιν ὑμῶν. (*On this account I indeed sent Timothy*), *so that I might ascertain your faith*: to learn its condition— whether, and how, you are maintaining it. Γινώσκω, in distinction from οἶδα, *to be aware of, acquainted with* (*v.* 4, &c.), means *to get to know, perceive, recognize*: cf. Col. iv. 8, and the two verbs as associated in Eph. v. 5; also 2 Cor. ii. 9. "The brevity of the expression shows how entirely ἡ πίστις forms the all-comprising and fundamental concept for the whole life of Christianity as it is called into existence by the Gospel" (Bornemann).

μή πως ἐπείρασεν ὑμᾶς ὁ πειράζων καὶ εἰς κενὸν γένηται ὁ κόπος ἡμῶν, *lest* (*fearing that*) *somehow the Tempter had tempted you, and our toil should prove in vain*. Upon this, the generally accepted, construction, the μή *of apprehension* is followed by the aorist indicative in the first clause inasmuch as the πειράζειν belongs to the sphere of historical facts, while the εἰς κενὸν γενέσθαι was matter of eventual contingency (aor. subjunctive): see Winer-Moulton, pp. 633 f., Blass, *Grammar*, p. 213, Ellicott *ad loc.*: the opposite transition—from subjunctive to indicative, after μήπως—is observed in Gal. ii. 2 (see

Lightfoot *ad loc.*). It is possible, however, both in this passage and in Gal. ii. 2, to read μήπως as the indirect interrogative, in which case γένηται (subj.) implies contingency in the matter of enquiry (see Winer-Moulton, pp. 373 f.; and the exx. in Liddell and Scott, s.v. μή, C.II. 1): (*enquiring*), *Had the Tempter anyhow tempted you, and would our toil prove in vain?* *ut cognoscerem...num forte tentator vos tentaverit, adeo ut labor meus* (rather *noster*) *irritus fieri possit* (Schott). See Grimm-Thayer, *Lexicon*, s.v. μήπως; also Hofmann's, Bornemann's, or Lünemann's (Meyer's *Commentary*) note *ad loc.* Ἔπεμψα εἰς τὸ γνῶναι describes an act of virtual interrogation; in the two members of the question united by καί, upon this construction, ἐπείρασεν relates to (presumable) fact, and the dubitative γένηται to the possible consequence thereof. Eph. vi. 21 (ἵνα εἰδῆτε τὰ κατ' ἐμέ, τί πράσσω) and Acts xv. 36 (ἐπισκεψώμεθα τοὺς ἀδελφοὺς..., πῶς ἔχουσιν) afford similar instances of the indirect question attached to the accusative after a *verbum cognoscendi*. Only one other instance is quoted of *interrogative* μήπως, viz. *Iliad* x. 101, while μήπως *of apprehension* is frequent in St Paul (1 Cor. viii. 9, ix. 27; 2 Cor. ix. 4, xi. 3, xii. 20, &c.); but there is nothing in the added πως inconsistent with interrog. μή: cf. εἴπως in Rom. i. 10, xi. 14, Acts xxvii. 12. The difference between the constructions is small; cf. Moulton's *Prolegomena*, pp. 192, 3.

Ὁ πειράζων (for the substantival participle see note on ὁ ῥυόμενος, i. 10) is ὁ Σατανᾶς of ii. 18, in his characteristic activity: cf. Matt. iv. 3, vi. 13; Mk i. 13; 1 Cor. vii. 5. *God* is ὁ δοκιμάζων (ii. 4), "the Prover (of hearts)": the difference of the verbs lies in the bad or good intent of the trial; see Trench's *Synon.* § 74. The repetition of the verb in subject and predicate almost assumes the fact of temptation; the stress of the apprehension (or interrogation: see previous note) rests on the second half of the sentence. For εἰς κενόν (*to a void issue*), cf. note on κενή, ii. 1; also 2 Cor. vi. 1; Gal. ii. 2; Phil. ii. 16; in the LXX, Isai. lxv. 23, Jer. xxviii. (Heb. or Eng. li.) 58, Mic. i. 14. For κόπος, see note on i. 3. Ὁ κόπος ἡμῶν closes the question with emphasis: that "our toil"—such labour as i. 9—ii. 12 described, and attended with such success—"should prove abortive," was a fear that wrung St Paul's soul.

§ 6. iii. 6—13. THE GOOD NEWS BROUGHT BY TIMOTHY.

Timothy has just returned from Thessalonica; and his report is entirely reassuring (*v.* 6), so that it gives new life to Paul and Silas (*vv.* 7, 8). They know not how to be thankful enough to God for the joy with which their breasts are filled by this good news

(vv. 9, 10), which revives their yearning for the sight of Thessalonian faces. They offer now a solemn prayer that the way may be opened for this journey (v. 11); and that meanwhile the readers may grow in love and be made blameless in holiness, gaining thus a steadfast heart in view of the Lord's expected coming (vv. 12, 13).

6. Ἄρτι δὲ ἐλθόντος Τιμοθέου πρὸς ἡμᾶς ἀφ' ὑμῶν. *But now that Timothy, at this moment, has come to us from you.* From Acts xviii. 5 it would appear that Timothy had joined Silas before arriving at Corinth, where the two found St Paul (see *Introd.* p. xxi.). Ἄρτι (√αρ-, as in ἀραρίσκω, *to fit* or *join*) means *just now* or *then, at this,* or *that, juncture*; cf. II. ii. 7; 1 Cor. xiii. 12, xvi. 7; Gal. iv. 20, &c. The temporal adjunct qualifies the two participles jointly, ἐλθόντος...καὶ εὐαγγελισαμένου; it is needless and awkward to carry it past them to παρεκλήθημεν: Timothy had come with his tidings *at the nick* of *time*, just when such refreshment was needed; see note on *v*. 7, and the *Introd.*, pp. xxxiii., lxiii. Ἀφ' ὑμῶν bears emphasis; it was news "from *you*" that St Paul was pining for; cf. *v*. 8, and ii. 19 f.

ἐλθόντος...καὶ εὐαγγελισαμένου ἡμῖν τὴν πίστιν καὶ τὴν ἀγάπην ὑμῶν, *has come...and brought us the good news of your faith and love*. Nowhere else in the N.T. is εὐαγγελίζομαι (εὐαγγέλιον) used of any other but "*the* good news"; see, however, in the O.T. (LXX) 1 Ki. xxxi. 9; 2 Ki. i. 20; 1 Paral. x. 9. There is a fine play upon the word: Timothy's report was, in effect, *gospel* news, as it witnessed to the power of God's message (λόγος θεοῦ ὃς ἐνεργεῖται ἐν ὑμῖν, ii. 13); and it was the best of news to Paul and Silas—a very "gospel" coming to them in return for the Gospel they had brought to the readers (i. 5, ii. 2, &c.). For πίστις καὶ ἀγάπη, comprising together the whole Christian life, cf. i. 3 (and note), II. i. 3; Eph. i. 15; Phm. 5—7; 1 Jo. iii. 23, &c.

καὶ ὅτι ἔχετε μνείαν ἡμῶν ἀγαθὴν πάντοτε, *and (reporting) that you keep a good remembrance of us at all times*: this was reciprocal (cf. i. 2 f.). "A *good*" is a well-disposed, kindly "remembrance" (cf. notes on ἀγαθός, v. 15; II. ii. 16); and ἔχειν μνείαν (cf. 2 Tim. i. 3) is "*to hold, maintain* a recollection"—so of other faculties or exercises of mind (iv. 13; Phil. i. 23; Col. iii. 13; 1 Tim. i. 19, &c.); μνείαν ποιοῦμαι, "*to express* the recollection" (*scil.* in word), i. 2. Bound up with the concern of the Apostles for the faith of the persecuted Thessalonians was the fear, dictating the self-defence of ii. 1—12 and the explanations of ii. 17—iii. 5, lest the attachment of the latter to their fathers in Christ should have been weakened through absence and by the detractions of the enemies of the Gospel (see *Introd.* pp. xxxiv. f.). It was a great relief to find that this goodwill had never wavered. The ὅτι clause is co-ordinate with τὴν πίστιν κ. τὴν ἀγάπην ὑμῶν, and serves to expand τὴν ἀγαθὴν περὶ ἡμῶν μνείαν ὑμῶν. This "good remembrance" the Thessalonians cherish, ἐπιποθοῦντες ἡμᾶς ἰδεῖν καθάπερ κ.τ.λ.—*while you long to see us, just as we indeed (to see) you*; cf. ii. 17 f., for this latter longing. Ἐπιποθέω (cf. Rom. i. 11; Phil. i. 8, ii. 26; 2 Tim. i. 4; only in Jam. iv. 5, 1 Pet. ii. 2, in the N.T. outside St Paul) denotes a tender yearning towards an absent beloved. The affection as well as the esteem of their disciples remained with the Apostles; the longing for reunion was equal on both sides. For καθάπερ, see ii. 12; and for the antithetic ἡμεῖς ὑμᾶς (thrice in this verse), cf. i. 6, ii. 17—20.

7. **διὰ τοῦτο παρεκλήθημεν, ἀδελφοί, ἐφ' ὑμῖν ἐπὶ πάσῃ τῇ ἀνάγκῃ** κ.τ.λ. *On this account we were encouraged, brothers, over you in all our necessity and affliction.* Διὰ τοῦτο is resumptive, as commonly. For παρακαλέω, a characteristic word of the Thessalonian Epistles, see note on ii. 11. Cf. with this occasion that of 2 Cor. vii. 6 f., when Titus' return to the Apostle Paul relieved his fears for the loyalty of the Corinthian Church. Ἐπί with dative follows verbs, and verbal nouns, of *emotion*, giving the occasion "at" or "over" which the feeling arises; cf. *v.* 9; 2 Cor. i. 4, vii. 4, 7; Rom. vi. 21, &c.: here a double ἐπί, since there were coincident occasions (see note on ἄρτι, *v.* 6) of comfort—in the perilous condition of the Thessalonians (*vv.* 3—5), and in the troubles surrounding the missionaries at Corinth. Encouragement on the former account (ἐφ' ὑμῖν) heartened the Apostles to encounter the latter (ἐπὶ πάσῃ τῇ ἀνάγκῃ κ.τ.λ.); this happy effect appears to be hinted at by St Luke in Acts xviii. 5.

Ἀνάγκη signifies *outward constraint*, whether of circumstances or duty (1 Cor. vii. 26, ix. 16, &c.); θλίψις, *trouble from men* (i. 6, iii. 3 f., &c.). For similar combinations, see 2 Cor. vi. 4, xii. 10—bearing on St Paul's hardships at *Corinth*, where he is now writing; 1 Cor. iv. 11, ix. 12, and 2 Cor. xi. 6 (ὑστερηθείς), show that there St Paul was in pecuniary straits: ἀνάγκη includes this, and more.

(**παρεκλήθημεν**)...**διὰ τῆς ὑμῶν πίστεως**. "Your faith" conveyed the needed solace: here lay the critical point (*vv.* 2, 5; cf. Lk. xxii. 32); for the readers' "faith" the writers first gave thanks (i. 3; see note; also on *v.* 5 above). In the conception of πίστις the thought of *fidelity* often blends with that of *belief* and *trust*.

8. **ὅτι νῦν ζῶμεν ἐὰν ὑμεῖς στήκετε ἐν κυρίῳ.** *For now we live, if*

you are standing fast in the Lord. Νῦν is temporal (cf. note on ἄρτι, *v.* 6)—*under these circumstances.* Ζῶμεν, " we live indeed!"—in the full sense of the word ; " vivimus, hoc est recte valemus " (Calvin); "vivere mihi videor et salvus esse, si res vestræ salvæ sunt " (Estius): cf. 2 Cor. vi. 9, for this rhetorical usage (ἡ ὄντως ζωή in 1 Tim. vi. 19 is quite different); also Ps. lxx. 20, cxviii. 77, &c., cxxxviii. 7. But St Paul is thinking of something beyond his own revived energy; the persistence of Thessalonian faith reveals the vitality of the Gospel itself, the λόγος ἐνεργούμενος ἐν...τοῖς πιστεύουσιν (ii. 13) ministered by Christ's servants. They " live " to purpose, in so far as their message lives on in others. 2 Cor. iv. 7—16 supplies a commentary upon this text : ὁ θάνατος ἐν ἡμῖν ἐνεργεῖται, ἡ δὲ ζωὴ ἐν ὑμῖν...διὸ οὐκ ἐγκακοῦμεν ; cf. also Phil. i. 21—26 ; Jo. iv. 31—34. St Paul felt as though the defection of the Thessalonians would have killed him. Ὑμεῖς is emphatic—"if *you* are standing fast"— since the cause of the Gospel depends in a peculiar sense upon the Thessalonian Church, the *point d'appui* of the present mission (i. 8). Ἐὰν στήκετε has grammatical parallels in ἐὰν οἴδαμεν (1 Jo. v. 15), ὅταν στήκετε (Mk xi. 25) &c. ; classical sequence in the use of ἐάν (as of εἰ) was not strictly maintained in N.T. Greek ; this is true of later Greek generally (Winer-Moulton, p. 369). The indicative (for subjunctive : if -ετε be not an itacistic writing) states the hypothesis more assertively ; and ἐὰν στήκετε is a virtual appeal : "You must show that my misgiving was needless; you will go on to justify my confidence." For ἐν in this connexion, cf. i. 1, iv. 1, v. 12 ; and for στήκω (a late verb based on ἕστηκα), cf. Phil. iv. 1 ; 1 Cor. xvi. 13. To " stand fast *in the Lord*" implies an obediently steadfast faith.

9. τίνα γὰρ εὐχαριστίαν δυνάμεθα τῷ θεῷ ἀνταποδοῦναι περὶ ὑμῶν... ; *For what due thanksgiving can we render to God for you...* ? Ἀντί in ἀνταποδοῦναι implies *correspondence* between the boon and its acknowledgement (cf. II. i. 6 ; Lk. xiv. 14 ; Col. iii. 24, &c.); ἀποδοῦναι, *to give back, repay,* appears in v. 15, Rom. ii. 6, xiii. 7, Lk. xx. 25, &c. For εὐχαριστία, see note on -τέω, i. 2. Γάρ, of explanation, naturally introduces this question : the fact that the writers cannot thank God enough for " the joy" given to them by Timothy's report, shows how greatly they were encouraged by it (*v.* 7), and how vital to them is the fidelity of this Church (*v.* 8). This inexpressible thanks is due *to God,* who upholds the readers under the storm of persecution : see ii. 12, v. 24 ; II. iii. 3; and cf. Jo. x. 29, xvii. 11, &c.

ἐπὶ πάσῃ τῇ χαρᾷ ᾗ χαίρομεν δι' ὑμᾶς ἔμπροσθεν τοῦ θεοῦ ἡμῶν, *for all the joy with which we rejoice because of you before our God.* For ἐπί in this connexion, see note on v. 7. Πᾶσα ἡ χαρά is "the *sum* of joy" collectively: cf. v. 7; 1 Cor. xiii. 2; Phil. i. 3. Ἥ, perhaps by attraction for the cognate accus. ἥν, as in Matt. ii. 10; yet χαρᾷ χαίρειν in Jo. iii. 29 (cf. 1 Pet. i. 8): Hebraistic feeling favoured such emphatic assonant combinations (see e.g. Isai. xxxv. 2, lxvi. 10), but they were idiomatic in Greek poetry. Χαίρειν διά, as in Jo. iii. 29, xi. 15; while the ordinary ἐπί (as with παρακαλοῦμαι, εὐχαριστία above) would give the *occasion* of χαίρειν, and ἐν the *ground* (Phil. i. 18, iii. 1, &c.), διά introduces the *reason* of joy, that to which it is referred on reflexion: when the Apostles consider what this news from Thessalonica means and all it implies in their converts (cf. i. 4), their hearts overflow with gladness before God. For the ἔμπροσθεν clause, cf. i. 3; since "our God"—the God of the Christian faith and revelation—sent His servants on the errand of the Gospel (ii. 2, 4, &c.), "to" Him "thanks" are "rendered back," and "before" Him "the joy" is testified which its assured success awakens. *Ten times*, with an emphasis of affection, is the pronoun ὑμεῖς repeated in vv. 6—10.

10. **νυκτὸς καὶ ἡμέρας ὑπερεκπερισσοῦ δεόμενοι εἰς τὸ ἰδεῖν ὑμῶν τὸ πρόσωπον**, *by night and day making supplication in exceeding abundant measure, to the end that we may see your face.* On the temporal expression, see note to ii. 9; it repeats more graphically the ἀδιαλείπτως of i. 3 (or 2), ii. 13: "night and day" the Apostles are "working" and "praying" at once; they could pray while occupied with manual labour. For the union of *thanksgiving* and *prayer*, cf. i. 2, v. 17 f. Ὑπερ-εκ-περισσοῦ (cf. v. 13, -ως; Eph. iii. 20) is an almost extravagant intensive, *plusquam abunde*, found outside St Paul (who affects ὑπερ- compounds) only in Dan. iii. 22 (Theodotion), and in Clemens Rom. *ad Corinth.* xx. 11; it surpasses περισσοτέρως (ii. 17): cf. 2 Cor. i. 8 *b*; Eph. iii. 8; 1 Cor. iv. 13, xv. 8, for like ardours of hyperbole. Δέομαι is *to beg*, as for some personal boon, something that one "wants for oneself"; cf. Rom. i. 10; Lk. ix. 38, xxii. 32, &c. Εἰς τὸ ἰδεῖν κ.τ.λ. expresses *the ulterior aim* of these importunate supplications: cf. Phil. i. 23, τὴν ἐπιθυμίαν ἔχων εἰς τὸ ἀναλῦσαι); the writer's prayers touched on intervening objects—the removal of hindrances (ii. 18), the progress of the work in hand (II. iii. 1 f.)—but this longing always animated them: cf. for εἰς τό with infin. ii. 12, 16, and notes. For ἰδεῖν τὸ πρόσωπον ὑμῶν, see ii. 17.

The aim of the above δεῖσθαι is twofold: "to see the face" of their beloved Thessalonians would be an extreme gratification to the writers;

and this satisfaction is identified, by the vinculum of a single article, with the blessing thus brought to their readers,—εἰς τὸ...καὶ καταρτίσαι τὰ ὑστερήματα τῆς πίστεως ὑμῶν, *in order to* (*see your face*) *and make good the deficiencies of your faith:* "ut suppleamus" (not "compleamus," as in Vulg.) "quæ vestræ fidei desunt" (Calvin), "ut sarciamus, &c." (Beza). Ἡ πίστις ὑμῶν, just as in *vv.* 2, 5 (see notes), stands for the whole Christianity of the Thessalonians. Τὰ ὑστερήματα points to what was lacking not *in* but *to* "the faith" of the readers. Strong and steadfast in itself (see i. 3, 8, ii. 13, iii. 6—8; II. i. 3), that faith required more *knowledge* (see e.g. iv. 13), more *moral discipline and sanctity of life* (iv. 1—12) and *practice in the ways of piety* (v. 12—22), more *sobriety of temper*, more *steadiness and self-possession* (v. 1—8; II. ii. 1 ff.). For the objective genitive to ὑστέρημα, cf. Col. i. 24; 2 Cor. viii. 13 f.; also Mk x. 21, ἕν σε ὑστερεῖ. Καταρτίζω means *to set right, correct*—not *to complete* something defective in itself, but *to make good and fit out* that which lacks the resources or conditions necessary to its proper action or destination: cf. Rom. ix. 22; Heb. xiii. 21; Matt. iv. 21,—"repairing their nets"; and see Lightfoot's note *ad loc.*

Verses **11—13** breathe out the prayer which the writers, as they have just said, are continually making, *v.* 11 corresponding to εἰς τὸ ἰδεῖν κ.τ.λ., and *vv.* 12 f. to the καταρτίσαι τὰ ὑστερήματα of *v.* 10.

11. **Αὐτὸς δὲ ὁ θεὸς καὶ πατὴρ ἡμῶν καὶ ὁ κύριος ἡμῶν Ἰησοῦς κατευθύναι τὴν ὁδὸν ἡμῶν** κ.τ.λ. *Now may our God and Father Himself, and our Lord Jesus, direct our way unto you.* The Apostles appeal to "God *Himself* and Christ" to clear their way to Thessalonica, hitherto obstructed by Satan (ii. 18; cf. II. iii. 3, 5). So many prayers, however, in these two Epistles begin with the formula Αὐτὸς δὲ ὁ θεός or ὁ κύριος, which is peculiar to them (v. 23; II. ii. 16, iii. 16), that one hesitates to lay stress on the αὐτός here: this may mean only, as Lightfoot puts it, that "After all said and done, it is for God Himself to direct our path." From "our God and Father" (see i. 3, and note) the Apostles crave the help which, in this sovereign and gracious character, He is surely bound to give (cf. II. ii. 16; Matt. vi. 8 f.; Lk. xi. 13; Jo. xvii. 11). Κατευθύνω, *to make straight*—a classical verb, found only here and in II. iii. 5, Lk. i. 79, in the N.T.; a common O.T. word (see e.g. Ps. **v.** 9, cxviii. 5, LXX): it is the opposite of ἐνκόπτω, ii. 18 (see note).

The association of "our Lord Jesus" with "God the Father" in acts of prayer and thanksgiving is a very noticeable feature of these two Letters; it affords impressive evidence, coming from the oldest N.T. writings, of the deity of Jesus Christ as this was conceived by the first Christians; the two are so identified that they count as one (cf. the words of Jesus in Jo. x. 30, ἐγὼ καὶ ὁ πατὴρ ἕν ἐσμεν), blending in the singular optative predicate, κατευθύναι: see also II. ii. 16 f., and note. The petition of *v.* 12 is addressed to "the Lord" solely.

12. ὑμᾶς δὲ ὁ κύριος πλεονάσαι καὶ περισσεύσαι τῇ ἀγάπῃ εἰς ἀλλήλους καὶ εἰς πάντας. *But you may the Lord make to increase and overflow in your love toward one another and toward all.* Verse 12 passes from writers to readers with the contrastive δέ. "The Lord," in St Paul's general usage—above all, where it directly follows ὁ κύριος ἡμῶν 'I. X.—means Jesus Christ, not the Father: cf. *v.* 8, i. 6, iv. 15 ff., v. 27, and the ἡμῖν...εἰς κύριος of 1 Cor. viii. 6; Eph. iv. 5. In II. iii. 5 and 16 "the Lord" is again addressed, quite unreservedly, in prayer: cf. 2 Cor. xii. 8; 2 Tim. i. 16, 18; Acts i. 24, vii. 59 f. The Lord Jesus is asked, in effect, to aid the fulfilment of His own command of love (Jo. xiii. 34, &c.) and to perfect in His disciples the grace of which He is the example and channel (see Gal. ii. 20; Eph. v. 2, &c.).

Περισσεῦσαι (*make abundant*) caps πλεονάσαι (*make more*): cf. the variation in Rom. v. 20; 2 Cor. iv. 15. Elsewhere in the N.T. the latter verb is always, the former usually, intransitive—the original usage in each case; πλεονάζω (הִרְבָּה) has the active sense in Num. xxvi. 54; Ps. lxx. 21; 1 Macc. iv. 35: cf. the double usage of the Eng. *increase, multiply.* In iv. 10 the wish is expressed that the Thessalonians may "abound (still) more in love"; in II. i. 3 thanks are given because their "love multiplies." The passages just referred to speak of ἀγάπη εἰς ἀλλήλους, iv. 10 embracing "all the brethren in all Macedonia"; but here, as in v. 15, καὶ εἰς πάντας is added: cf. Rom. xii. 16, 18; Gal. vi. 10; 1 Tim. ii. 1; 1 Pet. ii. 17. For the cruelly persecuted Thessalonians this wider love was peculiarly difficult—and necessary; it meant loving their *enemies,* according to Christ's command (Matt. v. 44).

καθάπερ καὶ ἡμεῖς εἰς ὑμᾶς, *as verily we also (do) towards you—* i.e. "as we increase and abound in love toward you"; for the Apostles' love to their flock was not stationary, nor limited; the εὐαγγέλιον of *v.* 6 gives it a new impulse. This clause (repeated from *v.* 6) rests naturally upon the foregoing verbs, mentally resumed in their intransitive sense; or, after Theodoret, we may supply διετέθημεν, *affecti sumus erga vos* (Calvin); see also Lightfoot *ad loc.* In support of this claim of the writers, cf. the statement of i. 5 *b,* and the language of ii. 7—12, 17—20: for similar references on St Paul's part, see II. iii. 7—9; Phil. iii. 17, iv. 9; 1 Cor. iv. 16, xi. 1; Acts xx. 35; cf. also the appeal of Jesus in Jo. xiii. 15, 34, &c.

13. εἰς τὸ στηρίξαι ὑμῶν τὰς καρδίας ἀμέμπτους ἐν ἁγιωσύνῃ κ.τ.λ., *to the end He may establish your hearts, (made) unblamable in holiness*, &c.: the ultimate end (see note on εἰς τό with infin. v. 10) of the prayer for increased love in v. 12; such love will lead to confidence of heart in view of the coming of Christ in judgement. A like connexion of thought appears in 1 Jo. iii. 18—21 and iv. 16 f.: " Herein is love made perfect with us, that we may have boldness in the day of judgement....Perfect love casts out fear." The prayer for improved *faith* (v. 10) led to prayer for increased *love* (v. 12), and now for assured *hope* (cf. i. 3). "Love" prepares for judgement, as it imparts "holiness"; in this Christian perfection lies (see v. 23). *Love* and *holiness* are associated in the apostolic prayer, as (with reversed order) in the apostolic homily of iv. 1—12. Ἀμέμπτους is attached, proleptically, as an objective complement to στηρίξαι τὰς καρδίας ὑμῶν, "found unblamable": cf. for the construction, 1 Cor. i. 8; Phil. iii. 21 (σύμμορφον). Clearly some of those addressed in the exhortations immediately following (iv. 1—8) were not yet ἄμεμπτοι ἐν ἁγιωσύνῃ, as they must be ἐν τῇ παρουσίᾳ.

ἀμέμπτους...ἔμπροσθεν τοῦ θεοῦ καὶ πατρὸς ἡμῶν imports freedom from blame *in God's eyes*, before whom believers in Christ will be presented at His coming: see Col. i. 22, 28; 1 Cor. xv. 24; and cf. Phil. ii. 15; Eph. i. 4; 1 Cor. i. 8; 2 Pet. iii. 14. "Our God and Father" listens to the Apostles' prayers for the welfare of His chosen (v. 11; i. 4), and will delight hereafter to recognize them as His holy children. While ἁγιότης (2 Cor. i. 12; Heb. xii. 10) denotes the *abstract quality* of "holiness," ἁγιασμός the *process*, and then the *result*, of "making holy" (iv. 3; frequent in St Paul), ἁγιωσύνη is the *state* or *condition* of the ἅγιος (see note on this word below): cf. Rom. i. 4; 2 Cor. vii. 1. This holy state is that toward which the love now vigorously active in the Thessalonians must grow and tend, so that their holiness may at Christ's coming win God's approval, the anticipation of which will give them a calm strength of heart in prospect of that tremendous advent (cf. i. 10; II. i. 7 ff.).

On στηρίζω, see note to v. 2. The phrase στηρίζειν καρδίαν is found in Jam. v. 8, and in the O.T. (LXX) in Ps. ciii. 15; Sirach vi. 37: it means not the *strengthening of character*, but the *giving of conscious security*, of *a steady, settled assurance*—the opposite of the condition deprecated in *v.* 3, or in II. ii. 2. On καρδία, see note to ii. 17.

The last clause, ἐν τῇ παρουσίᾳ κ.τ.λ., might be attached grammatically to στηρίξαι, as by Bornemann, the whole sentence being thus rendered : "so as to give you steadfast hearts—hearts unblamable in holiness before our God and Father—in the coming of our Lord Jesus Christ with all His saints"; the words implying that the desired assurance is to be realized at the hour of the Lord's appearing. But this is somewhat forced in construction; and the στηρίζειν thought of in *v.* 2, as in II. ii. 17, relates to no future and prospective assurance of heart, but to that which is needed *now*, in the midst of present trials and alarms (*vv.* 3 ff.; II. ii. 2, &c.). "The coming" of the Judge will *reveal* the blamelessness in question—ἀμέμπτους...ἐν τῇ παρουσίᾳ (cf. Rom. viii. 18 f.; 1 Cor. iii. 13, iv. 5; 2 Cor. v. 10; Col. iii. 4), *unblamable...in the appearing*, &c.; but the holy character then disclosed exists already in the saints, who thus prepared joyfully await their Lord's return (see Lk. xii. 35—46). St Paul was sensible of such readiness in his own case (2 Cor. i. 12; Phil. i. 19—21; 2 Tim. iv. 7 f.; cf. 2 Pet. iii. 14). The παρουσία is the goal of all Christian expectation in the N.T.—the crisis at which character is assayed, and destiny decided; see, in particular, II. i. 5—12, ii. 13 f.; and our Lord's parables of the Wedding Feast and Robe, and of the Lighted or Unlit Lamps (Matt. xxii. 11—13, xxv. 1—13).

That "our Lord Jesus comes (*attended*) *with all His saints*"—μετὰ πάντων τῶν ἁγίων αὐτοῦ—is explained in iv. 14—16. These are not the "angels" of II. i. 7 (see note); οἱ ἅγιοι denotes always with St Paul *holy men* (II. i. 10, and *passim*): here *the holy dead*, who will "rise first" and whom "God will bring with Him"—with Jesus —when He returns to His people upon earth. To be fit for this meeting (ἡμῶν ἐπισυναγωγή, II. ii. 1), Christians must be "blameless in holiness"; only the holy can join the holy. Hofmann, and a few others, connect μετὰ τῶν ἁγίων with ἀμέμπτους ἐν ἁγιωσύνῃ instead of παρουσίᾳ—"blameless in holiness...along with His holy ones"; but this construction appears artificial, and misses the thought developed in iv. 13—18, which is already in the writer's mind, viz. that Christ will be attended in His παρουσία by the sainted Christian dead. For the word παρουσία, see note on ii. 19; and for the name "Lord Jesus," see ii. 15 and 19.

CHAPTER IV.

1. ουν (WH, *margin*)—wanting in B, some dozen minn., syr[pesh] cop, Chr—may easily have slipped out, after the *-ον* of λοιπον. The combination λοιπον ουν occurs nowhere else in the N.T.

ινα καθως παρελαβετε...—ινα περισσευητε: BD*G* 17 37 73, latt vg cop syr[pesh]. The first of the two *ινα*'s is omitted as superfluous by ℵA (an example of Alexandrian editing) and the Syrians. The clause **καθως και περιπατειτε** is wanting in D[c]KL and most minn., followed by the Greek commentators, and T. R. This looks like a deliberate erasure on the part of the Syrian editors, attempting to rectify the sentence. When the former *ινα* had been struck out—as appears in ℵA—the true construction of the sentence was lost, and the second καθως clause became intolerably awkward.

6. κυριος, anarthrous, ℵ*ABD*H 17; *ο* is a Syrian addition.

-ειπαμεν becomes *-ειπομεν passim* in the T. R. These 1st, for 2nd, aorist endings, in certain verbs of common occurrence, were characteristic of the vernacular; they occur to a limited extent in the literary κοινή, and prevail in contemporary Papyri.

7. ημας is υμας in several minn., as in cop syr[pesh]; but in no uncial.

8. διδοντα: ℵ*BDG, Or Ath Did. δοντα: AKL, &c., latt vg (*qui dedit*); the aorist in this connexion in 2 Cor. i. 22, v. 5; Acts xv. 8. See Expository Note.

και (before the partic.) wanting in ABD[b, c] 17 73 cat[txt], cop syr[pesh] go, Or[cat] Ath, &c.; found in ℵ*D*GKL, most minn., vg syr[hcl], Clem. Evidence fairly divided: the conjunction seems to be either a Western wordy insertion, or an Alexandrian severe omission. The motive for insertion is not obvious, and *κ* before ΔΙΔΟΝΤΑ might easily have been overlooked: transcriptional probability favours retention.

υμας is ημας in A and many minn., two good copies of vg, syr[hcl txt], and later Fathers.

9. εχομεν (for εχετε) in א°D*G 67**, latt vg syr^hcl, Chr Ambrst; while B, am, Pelag read ειχομεν—probably a Western emendation, pointing to an older εχομεν. Weiss, however, and Tregelles^mg prefer ειχομεν as the hardest reading, regarding εχετε as conformed to v. 1; see Expository Note. εχετε, in א*AD^cHKL, &c., cop syr^pesh aeth. The 1st plural looks like a stylistic assimilation to παρακαλουμεν δε, v. 10.

10. τους (before εν ολη) wanting in א*AD*G, and presumably in codd. followed by latt vg, Ambrst. On the one hand, the article may have been lost by homœoteleuton after αδελφους; or on the other, supplied (as in BHKL) by way of grammatical improvement.

11. ιδιαις is supplied by א*AD^cKL, &c.—an Alexandrian emendation (? harmonistic: see 1 Cor. iv. 12; Eph. iv. 28), adopted by the Syrians. WH relegate the adjective to the mg in Eph. iv. 28, where it is attested by the same chief uncials as here, with the additional support of the versions.

13. θελομεν in all uncials, latt vg; θελω in many minn., syrr cop.

κοιμωμενων, אAB 67** and other minn., latt vg (*dormientibus*) syrr. κεκοιμημενων is a patent Western and Syrian emendation, conformed to 1 Cor. xv. 20; it is found in DGKL, &c. See Expository Note.

λυπεισθε, AD*GL, and many minn.: itacistic.

15. For (την παρουσιαν) του κυριου B has του Ιησου (? taken up from v. 14); Marcion (apud Tert^5, 15), *Christi.*

16. πρωτον: D*G and many Fathers, πρωτοι; latt. vg, *primi.*

17. For απαντησιν, υπ- in D*G. For του κυριου D^b, latt vg, most Lat Fathers, read τῳ κυριῳ (*obviam domino*); D*G, with some Latins, τῳ χριστῳ. The dative may be a Latinism; but cf. Acts xxviii. 15.

Instead of συν B reads εν κυριῳ: "ganz gedankenlos" (Weiss).

---

§ 7. iv. 1—12. A Lesson in Christian Morals.

We pass from the first to the second half of the Letter, from *narration* to *exhortation*. Chh. i.—iii. are complete in themselves, setting forth the relations between the writers and the readers since their first acquaintance, and explaining the failure of the former to return to Thessalonica as they had promised. The Thanksgiving and Prayer of the last section would have fittingly closed the Epistle, had no admonition been necessary. But *v.* 10 of ch. iii. indicated certain ὑστερήματα πίστεως in this Church (see note *ad loc.*), which Timothy had reported to his leaders, having found himself unable to supply them from his own resources, especially in so short a visit. These defects must be remedied by letter. Hence the addition of chh. iv. and v., which attach themselves by λοιπόν to the main portion of the Epistle. The ὑστερήματα were chiefly twofold—lying (*a*) in a defective Christian morality (iv. 1—12), and (*b*) in mistaken and unsettling notions about the Lord's advent (iv. 13—v. 11). (*c*) Brief and pungent exhortations are further appended, of a more general scope, bearing on Church life and personal character (v. 12—22). Exhortation (*a*) covers three topics: (1) *social purity* (*vv.* 3—8); (2) *brotherly love* (*vv.* 9 f.); (3) *diligence in secular work* (*vv.* 11 f.).

1. The adverbial λοιπόν, or τὸ λοιπόν, *for the rest* and so *finally* (*de cætero*, Vulg.; or *quod superest*), is similarly used, to attach an addendum, in 2 Thess. iii. 1; 1 Cor. i. 16; 2 Cor. xiii. 11; Ph. iii. 1, iv. 8: this verse covers all the writers have further to say.

ἐρωτῶμεν ὑμᾶς καὶ παρακαλοῦμεν ἐν κυρίῳ Ἰησοῦ. *We ask you and exhort (you) in the Lord Jesus.* Ἐρωτάω, in classical Greek used only of *questions* (*interrogo*), in later Greek is extended to *requests* (*rogo*), like the Eng. *ask* and Heb. שָׁאַל—e. g. in v. 12, II. ii. 1—a usage frequent in St John. Ἐρωτάω conceives the request in a question-form ("Will you do so and so?")—in Lk. xiv. 18 f., Jo. xix. 31, 38, e.g., the interrogative note is quite audible—and thus gives a personal urgency to it, challenging the answer as αἰτέω does not (cf. the Note under αἰτέω in Grimm-Thayer's *Lexicon*, correcting the distinction laid down in Trench's *Syn.*, § 40). Παρακαλέω (see note on ii. 12 above) connotes possible slackness or indifference in the party addressed.

Ἐν κυρίῳ Ἰησοῦ belongs to the latter verb (cf. *v.* 2; II. iii. 12; 1 Cor. i. 10, v. 4; Rom. xii. 1; Eph. iv. 17; Ph. ii. 1; Phm. 8, &c.); for it is on the Divine authority of Jesus, recognized by the readers, that the apostolic παράκλησις rests (ii. 3 f.; 1 Cor. ix. 1; 2 Cor. x. 8, xiii. 3: cf. note on ἐκκλησία...ἐν κυρίῳ Ἰησοῦ, i. 1; and for the title "Lord Jesus," ii. 15, 19): as much as to say, "We appeal to you, servants of Christ, in His name and as men bearing His commission." The exhortation is urgent (ἐρωτῶμεν), rousing (παρακαλοῦμεν), and solemnly authoritative (ἐν κυρίῳ Ἰησοῦ). Its general matter is stated in the remainder of the verse:—

ἵνα καθὼς παρελάβετε παρ' ἡμῶν τὸ πῶς κ.τ.λ....ἵνα περισσεύητε μᾶλλον, *that, according as you received from us how you ought to walk...that you abound (therein) more (than you already do), or more* and more (R. V.). The first ἵνα—which is dropped in the T.R. along with the second καθώς clause of the verse—is naturally repeated on resuming the thread of the protracted sentence after the parenthesis. The parenthetical **καθὼς καὶ περιπατεῖτε** (see Textual Note; cf. v. 10, v. 11, II. iii. 4, for the commendation), *as indeed you do walk*, gives a new turn to the principal verb, which is accordingly qualified by μᾶλλον, whereas the first καθώς clause suggests ἐν τούτῳ or οὕτως for complement (cf. ii. 4); so περισσεύειν μᾶλλον follows καὶ γὰρ ποιεῖτε αὐτό in *v*. 10. On παραλαμβάνω, see ii. 13: in that passage it relates to the primary message of the Gospel (λόγον ἀκοῆς); here it includes the precepts of life based thereon (τὸ πῶς δεῖ περιπατεῖν). For the use of περισσεύω, see note on iii. 12. For the sub-final use of ἵνα after ἐρωτῶμεν κ.τ.λ.—the *content* of the request or appeal stated in the form of *purpose*—cf. II. iii. 12, 1 Cor. i. 10, Col. i. 9, &c.,—also note on εἰς τό with infinitive, ii. 12: on this idiom of N.T. Greek, see Winer-Moulton, p. 420, or A. Buttmann, *N.T. Grammar*, pp. 236 f. That the readers had "received παρ' ἡμῶν " the instructions recalled, gives the Apostles the right to "ask and exhort" respecting them.

τὸ πῶς δεῖ ὑμᾶς περιπατεῖν καὶ ἀρέσκειν θεῷ, *how you ought to walk and please God.* Τό grasps the interrogative clause and presents it as a single definite object to παρελάβετε, giving it "precision and unity" (Lightfoot); for τό before the dependent sentence in such construction, cf. Rom. viii. 26, xiii. 9; Gal. v. 14; Lk. i. 62; Acts iv. 21: see Winer-Moulton, pp. 135, 644, Goodwin, *Greek Grammar*, 955. The Apostles had instructed their disciples in Christian practice as well as belief, the ἔργον πίστεως (i. 3) consequent on πίστις. Δεῖ denotes *moral necessity*, lying in the relationship presupposed (cf. II. iii. 7; Rom. i. 27; 2 Cor. v. 10; 1 Tim. iii. 15, &c.). "To walk and please God" is not a hendiadys for "to walk so as to please God": the Christian *walk* (moral behaviour) was first described and inculcated, then the obligation *to please God* by such a walk was enforced; contrast ii. 15, also the subsequent warning of *vv*. 6—8. Ἀρέσκειν θεῷ, a leading Pauline, and Biblical, conception of the true life for man (ii. 4; Rom. ii. 29, viii. 8; 1 Cor. iv. 5, vii. 32 ff.; Gal. i. 10; 2 Tim. ii. 4; Heb. xi. 5 f.; also Jo. viii. 29; 1 Jo. iii. 22), combining religion and morals as they spring from the personal relations of the believer to God. This representation is parallel to that of ii. 12, τὸ περιπατεῖν ἀξίως τοῦ θεοῦ; cf. Col. i. 10, περιπατ. ἀξίως...εἰς ἀρεσκίαν.

2. **οἴδατε γὰρ τίνας παραγγελίας ἐδώκαμεν ὑμῖν.** *For you know what charges we gave you.* See notes on this characteristic οἴδατε, i. 5, ii. 1, above. Οἴδατε τὰς παραγγελίας ἅς κ.τ.λ. (cf. ii. 1; 2 Tim. i. 12,

iii. 15; 2 Cor. ix. 2) would have meant, "You are acquainted with the charges we gave you"—you could describe them; but οἴδατε τίνας παραγγ. (with dependent *interrogative*; cf. 2 Tim. iii. 14, εἰδὼς παρὰ τίνων ἔμαθες) is, "You know what the charges are"—you could define them &c.; cf. note on οἴδατε οἷοι, i. 5. The παραγγελίαι originally given by the Apostles (cf. II. iii. 4, 6, 10; Eph. iv. 20—v. 2; Tit. ii. 11—14) were not bare rules of conduct (ἐντολαί), but injunctions drawn from the nature of the Gospel and urged affectionately and solemnly, doctrine and precepts forming one παράκλησις (ii. 3) or παραγγελία (1 Tim. i. 5). In classical Greek παραγγέλλω, παραγγελία, are used of commands or watchwords transmitted along (παρά) a line of troops (see Xenophon, *Anab.* I. 8. 3; *Cyrop.* II. 4. 2), then of military orders in general, of pedagogic precepts, &c.; in distinction from κελεύω (which St Paul never uses), παραγγέλλω connotes moral authority and earnestness in the command,—a "charge" not a mere "order," "præcepta" (Vulg.) rather than "mandata" (Beza). The 1st plur. ἐδώκαμεν is rare, but not unknown, in Attic Greek; see Winer-Moulton, p. 102.

The defining διὰ τοῦ κυρίου Ἰησοῦ recalls ἐν κυρίῳ Ἰησοῦ of v. 1 (see note): διά points to the name and authority of "the Lord Jesus" as the sanction "through" which the "charges" were enforced (scarcely "*prompted by* the Lord Jesus," as Lightfoot puts it), while ἐν κ. Ἰ. implied that the apostolic precepts moved "in the sphere of" His rule: cf., not overlooking the difference of title, διὰ τοῦ χριστοῦ in 2 Cor. i. 5, and Rom. i. 8, v. 11; somewhat similarly, διὰ θεοῦ in 1 Cor. i. 9, Gal. iv. 7, &c.; and παρακαλεῖν διά, Rom. xii. 1, xv. 30, 1 Cor. i. 10, 2 Cor. x. 1.

3. Τοῦτο γάρ ἐστιν θέλημα τοῦ θεοῦ, ὁ ἁγιασμὸς ὑμῶν, ἀπέχεσθαι κ.τ.λ. *For this is God's will—(it is) your sanctification—that you abstain* &c. The usual construction which makes ὁ ἁγιασμὸς ὑμῶν, anticipated by τοῦτο, subject of ἐστὶν θέλημα τοῦ θεοῦ, is not satisfactory: to say that "the sanctification" of Christians "is God's will," is almost tautological (to be sanctified is to be subject to God's will, which the readers already are: cf. Heb. x. 10); while, on the other side, to identify ἁγιασμός with ἀπέχεσθαι κ.τ.λ. is to narrow and lower the idea of Sanctification. What these Greek Christians do not sufficiently realize is that the "will of God," having already taken effect in their "sanctification" (see II. ii. 13; cf. 1 Cor. i. 2, 30, vi. 11, &c., and v. 7 below), requires in them a perfect chastity. *This* was the specific matter of the apostolic παραγγελία; τοῦτο points on, not to ὁ ἁγιασμὸς ὑμῶν (which is assumed by the way), but to the infinitives ἀπέχεσθαι, εἰδέναι, κ.τ.λ.,—as much as to say, "This is

God's will for you, on this your sanctification turns, viz. that you keep clear of fornication, &c." Θέλημα τοῦ θεοῦ and ὁ ἁγιασμὸς ὑμῶν constitute a double predicate, setting forth the objective and subjective ground respectively, of the pure family and social life inculcated; the apostolic "charges" enforced clean living as being "God's will" for His chosen (i. 4; cf. v. 8 below; 1 Pet. i. 14 ff.), and accordingly a condition essential to personal holiness (καθὼς πρέπει ἁγίοις, Eph. v. 3; Col. iii. 9, 12).

The anticipation of the anarthrous infinitives by τοῦτο has a parallel in 1 Pet. ii. 15 (οὕτως); similarly in Jam. i. 27; see the examples in Krüger, *Griech. Sprachlehre*, I. § 51. 7. 4. Θέλημα, anarthrous, since "God's will" is the general conception under which these παραγγελίαι fall (cf. v. 18; 1 Pet. iv. 2); ὁ ἁγιασμὸς ὑμῶν, because chaste living is *the* critical factor in Thessalonian sanctification.

Since ἁγιασμός attaches to the body along with the spirit (v. 23), πορνεία directly nullifies it: see 1 Cor. vi. 15—20. So prevalent was this vice in the Pagan cities (cf. διὰ τὰς πορνείας, 1 Cor. vii. 2), so little condemned by public opinion—it was even fostered by some forms of religion as a sort of consecration—that abstention became a sign of devotion to a holy God, of possession by His Holy Spirit (v. 8). The temptations to licentiousness, arising from former habits and from the state of society, were fearfully strong in the case of the first Christian converts from heathenism; all the Epistles contain warnings on this subject: see e.g. 1 Pet. iv. 1—4, and the relapses at Corinth (1 Cor. v. 1; 2 Cor. xii. 21, &c.); also Acts xv. 29. The very sense of pudicity had in many instances to be re-created. The Christian doctrine of Holiness is the surest prophylactic against social evils; in the maintenance of personal purity it is our best support to know that God calls us to holiness of living and that His almighty will is pledged to help our weak resolves.

Ἁγιασμός (from ἁγιάζω) denotes *the act* or *process of making holy*, then the resulting *state*, as in II. ii. 13; Rom. vi. 22; Heb. xii. 14, &c. Ἅγιος (קָדוֹשׁ) is the word which in Scripture denotes *the character of God* as He is made known by revelation, in its moral transcendence, infinitely remote from all that is sensuous and sinful (see 1 Sam. ii. 2; Ps. xcix., cxi. 9; Isai. vi. 3, 5, lvii. 15, &c.). Now it is the revealed character of God, "the Holy One of Israel," that constitutes His claim to human devotion; our "sanctification" is the acknowledgement of God's claim on us as the Holy One who made us, whom Christ reveals as our Father looking for His image to be reproduced in us: see Matt. v. 48; 1 Pet. i. 14 ff. In God, first the character disclosed, then the claim enforced; in us, first the claim acknowledged, then the character impressed. See, further, notes on v. 7 and v. 23; also on ii. 10, for the synonyms of ἅγιος.

4. εἰδέναι ἕκαστον ὑμῶν τὸ ἑαυτοῦ σκεῦος κτᾶσθαι ἐν ἁγιασμῷ καὶ τιμῇ—the positive παραγγελία completing the negative (ἀπέχεσθαι... πορνείας)—*that each of you know how to win his own vessel in sanctification and honour.* Κτᾶσθαι always signifies *to acquire, get possession of* (see Lk. xviii. 12, xxi. 19, &c.),—the perfect κεκτῆσθαι, *to hold possession of* (not occurring in N.T.); and οἶδα with the infin. signifies not only a fact (*to know that*; as in 1 Pet. v. 9), but more frequently a possibility (*to know how to, to have skill, aptitude* to do something: cf. Ph. iv. 12; Matt. vii. 11; Jam. iv. 17). The difficulty of the passage lies in τὸ ἑαυτοῦ σκεῦος, which (*a*) the Greek interpreters (except Theodore of Mopsuestia), as also Tertullian, Calvin, Beza, Bengel, Meyer (on Rom. i. 24; cf. *Camb. Bible for Schools* on this verse), refer to *the body of the man* as "the vessel of himself,"—that in which his personality is lodged: 2 Cor. iv. 7 ("this treasure ἐν ὀστρακίνοις σκεύεσιν"; cf. 2 Cor. v. 1—4) and Rom. i. 24 (where "the body" is the subject of "dishonour" through sexual vice; cf. ἐν τιμῇ below, also Col. ii. 23) are passages which afford an approximate parallel to this reading of the sense. The comparison of the human body to a vessel (σκεῦος, ἀγγεῖον, *vas*—of the soul, spirit, *ego*) was common enough in Greek writers; it occurs also in Philo Judæus, and in Barnabas (*Ep.* vii. 3, xi. 9), and Hermas (*Mand.* v. 2). 1 Pet. iii. 7 may be fairly claimed as supporting this view rather than (*b*); for St Peter does not call the wife a σκεῦος in virtue of her sex, but he regards man and wife alike as σκεύη of the Divine Spirit, the latter being the ἀσθενέστερον of the two. The idea of this interpretation is certainly Pauline, viz. that mastery of bodily passion is a point of "honour" and of "holiness" with the Christian (see 1 Cor. vi. 15—20). Nor is the verb κτάομαι incongruous with σκεῦος in this sense, if "winning a vessel" can be understood to mean "gaining" the object in question for this purpose,—in other words, getting possession of one's body in such a way that it becomes one's instrument for God's service; thus interpreted, κτᾶσθαι τὸ σκεῦος is nearly synonymous with δουλαγωγεῖν τὸ σῶμα, 1 Cor. ix. 27; similarly κτᾶσθαι in Lk. xxi. 19 is synonymous with περιποιεῖσθαι τὴν ψυχήν of xvii. 33. Chrysostom writes, Ἡμεῖς αὐτὸ (*scil.* τὸ σῶμα) κτώμεθα ὅταν μένῃ καθαρὸν καί ἐστιν ἐν ἁγιασμῷ, ὅταν δὲ ἀκάθαρτον, ἁμαρτία· εἰκότως, οὐ γὰρ ἃ βουλόμεθα πράττει λοιπόν, ἀλλ' ἃ ἐκείνη ἐπιτάττει. No other example, however, is forthcoming of κτᾶσθαι in the signification required ("to gain the mastery of"); and it must be admitted that

ἑαυτοῦ σκεῦος would be an awkward and obscure expression for the body as the vessel of the man's true life. But the decisive objection against (a) lies in the pointed contrast in which κτᾶσθαι τὸ ἑαυτοῦ σκεῦος is placed to πορνεία. This forces upon us (b) the alternative explanation of σκεῦος, expounded by Augustine and Theodore and adopted by most modern interpreters,— viz. that "his own vessel," to be "won" by "each" man, means *his own wife*: cf. the parallel παραγγελία of 1 Cor. vii. 2, διὰ τὰς πορνείας ἕκαστος τὴν ἑαυτοῦ γυναῖκα ἐχέτω. For Christian wedlock as being ἐν ἁγιασμῷ, see 1 Cor. vii. 14; and ἐν τιμῇ, Heb. xiii. 4 (τίμιος ὁ γάμος ἐν πᾶσιν). Κτᾶσθαι, however, seems to describe *courtship and the contracting of marriage*, rather than the married state: the position supposed is that of a man at the outset of life deciding whether he shall yield himself to a course of license or engage in an honourable marriage; this was the choice lying before the readers. To say that ἕκαστον upon this view precludes the celibate state commended by St Paul in 1 Cor. vii., is an insufficient objection; for *v*. 2 of that chapter recognizes celibacy as being practically out of the question, though preferable on some religious grounds. The verb κτάομαι is appropriate to the winning of a bride (see Ruth iv. 10; Sirach xxxvi. 29, in LXX; also Xenophon, *Symp.* ii. 10). Rabbinical writers afford instances of the wife described as a "vessel" (see Schöttgen, *Horæ Hebraicæ*, I. 827; also Bornemann or Lightfoot *ad loc.*, for full examples); the last-named cites Shakespeare's *Othello*, IV. 2, l. 83, "to preserve this vessel for my lord" (Desdemona). The figure indicates the wedded partner as *instrumental* to the sacred purposes of marriage, whereas fornication is the debasement of sexual affection severed from its appointed ends.

The above κτᾶσθαι τὸ σκεῦος is ἐν ἁγιασμῷ, as it is conducted by the ἡγιασμένος under the sense of his devotion to God, and of the sanctity of his body (see note on ἁγιασμός, *v*. 3: cf. 1 Cor. vi. 15—20; also Gen. ii. 21—24; Eph. v. 28—31). It is accordingly ἐν...τιμῇ (note the single preposition), since the "honour" of the human person has a religious basis in the devotion of the body and its functions to God (cf. 1 Cor. xii. 23 f.). Perhaps the thought of "holiness" attaches rather to the wooer in his Christian self-respect, while the "honour" is paid to the object of his courtship (1 Pet. iii. 7).

5. **μὴ ἐν πάθει ἐπιθυμίας καθάπερ καὶ τὰ ἔθνη τὰ μὴ εἰδότα τὸν θεόν,** *not (to do this) in passion of lust, even as the Gentiles also (do), who know not God.* Ἐν πάθει ἐπιθυμίας, "in a state of lustful passion": where the man's action is dominated by animal desire, there is

no sanctity nor honour in the union; even a lawful marriage so effected is a πορνεία in spirit. Πάθος is synonymous with ἀκαθαρσία and ἐπιθυμία κακή in Col. iii. 5, and is qualified by ἀτιμίας (see ἐν τιμῇ above) in Rom. i. 26; the παθήματα of Rom. vii. 5, Gal. v. 24, are particular forms or kinds of πάθος. This word signifies not, like Eng. "passion," a violent feeling, but an overmastering feeling, in which the man is borne along by evil as though its passive instrument; in this sense Rom. vii. 20 interprets the παθήματα of vii. 5. For ἐπιθυμία, cf. ii. 17; this sinister sense of ἐπιθυμέω (-ία) prevails.

For καθάπερ, cf. ii. 11, iii. 6, 12; used freely by St Paul in the two first groups of his Epistles, but not later. "The Gentiles that know not God," is an O.T. designation for the heathen, whose irreligion accounts for their depravity (Ps. lxxix. 6; Jer. x. 25); it recurs in II. i. 8 (see note), Gal. iv. 8. Unchastity, often in abominable forms, was a prominent feature of Gentile life at this time; honourable courtship and fidelity in wedlock were comparatively rare. In Rom. i. 24 ff. St Paul points to this sexual corruption, by which in fact the classical civilization was destroying itself, as a punishment inflicted upon the heathen world for its idolatry and wilful ignorance of God, and a terrible evidence of His anger on this account. Man first denies his Maker, and then degrades himself. The God, whom these lustful "Gentiles know not," is "the living and true God" to whom Thessalonian believers had "turned from their idols" (i. 9). Obeying the call of His gospel, they had consecrated themselves to His service (ἐν ἁγιασμῷ), and so they were redeemed from shame; their affections were hallowed, and their homes founded in the sanctities of an honourable love.

To "know God" is more than an intellectual act; it implies acknowledgement and due regard,—the esteeming Him for what He is (see e.g. Jer. ix. 23 f.; Tit. i. 16). Γινώσκειν is the commoner verb in affirmative statements with *God* for object (Jo. xvii. 3; Gal. iv. 9, &c.), as it implies tentative, progressive knowledge; cf., for εἰδέναι, v. 12 below.

Bornemann proposes a new interpretation of the whole passage, vv. 3—6, placing a comma at σκεῦος, thus made the object of εἰδέναι, and reading κτᾶσθαι in the absolute sense, "to make gain," with τὸ μὴ ὑπερβαίνειν κ.τ.λ. placed in apposition to the latter. So he arrives at the following rendering: "that you abstain from fornication, that each of you know his own vessel (i.e. acknowledge, appreciate and hold to, his own wife: cf. 1 Pet. iii. 7), seek gain in sanctification and honour, not in the passion of covetousness as the Gentiles &c., that he do not overreach and take advantage of his brother in business." But εἰδέναι τὸ ἑαυτοῦ σκεῦος, thus taken by itself, forms a very obscure clause, and an inadequate complement to ἀπέχεσθαι...πορνείας; nor is the use of κτᾶσθαι without an object sufficiently supported by the parallels drawn from Ezek. vii. 12 f. (LXX) and Thucyd. I. 70. 4. Moreover the transition to the new topic of *fairness in business dealings* would be abrupt and unprepared for, if made by κτᾶσθαι without a mediating conjunction; while ἐν πάθει ἐπιθυμίας is an expression decidedly suggesting lust and not avarice. This construction introduces more difficulties than it removes.

V. 6 appears to stand in apposition to *vv*. 3—5, ἀπέχεσθαι...εἰδέναι κ.τ.λ. Τὸ πρᾶγμα, on this interpretation, is the matter of the marriage relationship expressly violated by πορνεία (*v.* 3), which must be guarded from every kind of wrong (*v.* 6). In acts of impurity men sin against society; while defiling themselves, they trick and defraud others in what is dearest. To this aspect of "the matter" τὸ μὴ ὑπερβαίνειν κ.τ.λ. seems to point. For the use of τὸ πρᾶγμα as relating to "the matter" in hand, cf. 2 Cor. vii. 11. ἐν τῷ πράγματι gives a wide extension, under this veiled form of reference, to the field of injury. No wrongs excite deadlier resentment and are more ruinous to social concord than violations of womanly purity; none more justly call forth the punitive anger of Almighty God (see the next clause).

On the above view, the article in τὸ μὴ ὑπερβαίνειν καὶ πλεονεκτεῖν has an emphatic resumptive force, as in τὸ μηδένα σαίνεσθαι (iii. 3; see note): (*I say*, or *I mean*) *that none* (understand τινά, in view of the following αὐτοῦ, rather than ἕκαστον as carried over from *v.* 4) *transgress (exceed the limit), and take advantage of his brother in the matter.* The verbs ὑπερβαίνειν and πλεονεκτεῖν are quite as appropriate to adulterers, and the like, as to perpetrators of commercial fraud; πλεονεξία includes sins of lust as well as greed (Eph. iv. 19). Ὑπερβαίνειν, "to step over"—a good classical compound, *hap. leg.* in N.T.—governs, in this sense, an object of the *thing* (law, limit, &c.), not the *person*; it is probably intransitive here. Πλεονεκτεῖν in earlier Greek took a genitive of comparison, "to have advantage over"; in the κοινή it adopted an accusative,—"to take advantage of" any one. Τὸν ἀδελφόν appears to denote the wronged person not specifically as a Christian brother, but in his human claim to sympathy and respect: cf. Matt. v. 23 f., vii. 3 ff.; 1 Jo. ii. 9 ff.; also v. 15 below.

The interpretation just given is that of the Greek Fathers, followed by Jerome; and of many moderns, including Estius, Bengel, Alford, Ellicott, Lightfoot, Schmiedel. Most of the Latin interpreters (Vulg.

in negotio), with Erasmus, Calvin, Beza, Grotius, Winer, de Wette, Hofmann, Lünemann, Bornemann, understand *covetousness* to be denounced in these words. They take ἐν τῷ πράγματι to signify "in business" generally, like the plural τὰ πράγματα; or "the (particular) business" in hand, each matter of business as it arises—cf. ἐν τῷ ἀνθρώπῳ in Jo. ii. 25 (τῷ cannot be read as τῳ=τινί—so in A.V.; this usage is foreign to N.T. Greek). But there is no example of πρᾶγμα (singular) used in the sense supposed; and in view of the strong emphasis thrown on the question of sexual morals in *vv.* 4 f., the transition to another subject should have been clearly marked. Besides, ἀκαθαρσία (*v.* 7) is applied elsewhere to *sins of the flesh* (with the possible exception of ii. 3 above), and this topic covers the whole ground of the preceding *vv.* 3—6.

διότι ἔκδικος Κύριος περὶ πάντων τούτων, *because the Lord is an avenger respecting all these things*—everything that concerns the honour of the human person and the sacredness of wedded life; cf. Heb. xiii. 4, πόρνους κ. μοιχοὺς κρινεῖ ὁ θεός. For ἔκδικος, see Rom. xiii. 4; Wisd. xii. 12; Sir. xxx. 6; in earlier Greek the adjective signified *unjust (exlex)*. For the maxim, cf. Rom. xii. 19; Gal. v. 21; Eph. v. 5 f.; Col. iii. 6; and in the O.T., Deut. xxxii. 35 (Heb.),— the original of St Paul's allusions. "All these things" lie within the scope of that vengeance of God which pursues. the wrongs of men toward each other; cf., in this connexion, Prov. v. 21 f., vi. 32 ff., vii. 22—27. For διότι, see note on ii. 18. There is no reason to suppose that Κύριος means any other than "the Lord Jesus Christ," through whom God judges the world at the Last Day: cf. II. i. 7—9; Acts xvii. 31, &c.

καθὼς καὶ προείπαμεν ὑμῖν καὶ διεμαρτυράμεθα, *as indeed we foretold you and solemnly protested.* As to the indispensableness of chastity to the Christian life and the fearful consequences of transgression against its laws, the Thessalonians had been plainly and impressively instructed in the first lessons of the Gospel. For προείπαμεν—in the 1st aorist form, which many familiar 2nd aorists assumed in the κοινή (see Winer-Moulton, pp. 86 f., Blass, *Grammar of N.T. Greek*, p. 45)—cf. προλέγω, iii. 4 and Gal. v. 21; προ-, "before" the event. The μαρτύρομαι of ii. 12 (see note) is strengthened by διά, which implies the presence of *God*, or *the Lord*, "through" whom—*scil.* in whose name—this warning is given; cf. διὰ τοῦ κυρίου Ἰησοῦ, *v.* 2, and the references there supplied.

7. **οὐ γὰρ ἐκάλεσεν ἡμᾶς ὁ θεὸς ἐπὶ ἀκαθαρσίᾳ ἀλλ' ἐν ἁγιασμῷ.** *For God did not call us for (with a view to) uncleanness, but in*

sanctification. A further reason (γάρ), put by way of explanation at the close, for chastity amongst Christians. That purity of life was God's purpose for us in sending the Gospel-message, explains in part the peculiar anger with which a departure from it will be visited. The A.V. misrenders both ἐπί and ἐν here. 'Eπί with dative may signify either *on terms of* or *with a view to*, according as the reference is subjective or objective—i.e. as the intention implied was in the mind of the called themselves, or of God who called them; the latter rendering is preferable in this connexion (cf. Gal. v. 13; Eph. ii. 10). 'Eν ἁγιασμῷ, as in v. 4 and II. ii. 13, marks out "sanctification" not as the ultimate aim, nor as a gradual attainment, of the Christian life, but as its basis and ruling condition, the assumption on which God's dealings with Christian men rest,—viz. that they are ἅγιοι, consecrated persons; cf. note on ὁ ἁγιασμὸς ὑμῶν, v. 3. Accordingly ἐκάλεσεν bears the emphasis of the sentence (cf. ii. 12, and note; also i. 4 and II. ii. 13). God's call in the Gospel, from which the Christian status of the readers took its rise, would be frustrated by any relapse into the filthiness of heathen life.

V. 8 concludes the rehearsal of the apostolic παραγγελία on this subject by an appeal to God, such as διεμαρτυράμεθα in v. 6 already implied (see note above) :—

τοιγαροῦν ὁ ἀθετῶν οὐκ ἄνθρωπον ἀθετεῖ ἀλλὰ τὸν θεόν. *Wherefore then the rejecter is not rejecting a man, but God.* The compound particle τοι-γαρ-οῦν, "collective and retrospective" (Ellicott), "introduces its conclusion with some specific emphasis or formality" (Grimm, in *Lexicon*), in a style suitable to the solemn language of *vv.* 6 *b*, 7: Heb. xii. 1 supplies the only other example of this conjunction in the N.T.; it is common in Epictetus. 'Αθετέω (α- privative, and √ θε- of τίθημι, through ἄθετος) means *to set out of position, to make void* (a promise, law, or the like; see Gal. iii. 15; Heb. x. 28), *to set aside, deny*, in his authority or rights, a person (Mk vi. 26; Lk. x. 16; Jude 8). For the antithesis of *man and God*, cf. ii. 13 *b*; Gal. i. 10; Acts v. 4. While ἄνθρωπος is anarthrous (indefinite) in the negative clause, the articular ὁ θεός signifies *the* (*one, actual*) *God;* cf. Gal. iv. 31, for the article.

Romanist divines (e.g. Estius), following the received Latin reading of the two last words of the verse (*in nobis*), quote this text in proof of the Divine sanction of ecclesiastical authority. The Apostles, however, are insisting not on their own commandment as Divine, but on *God's* commandment as distinct from and immeasurably above theirs. That the "charge" of *vv.* 3—6 comes from God is evidenced

(1) by the nature of the injunction itself, (2) by the moral purpose of the Gospel (*v.* 7), and (3) by the witness of the Holy Spirit given to the readers (*v.* 8 *b*):—

τὸν διδόντα τὸ πνεῦμα αὐτοῦ τὸ ἅγιον εἰς ὑμᾶς, (*God*) *who gives His Spirit, the Holy* (*Spirit*), *to be within you.* Even if εἰς ἡμᾶς were the true reading (see Textual Note, and last paragraph), this would refer not to the writers specifically or officially, but to writers and readers communicatively; cf. the 1st plural in the same connexion in Rom. viii. 15 f., Gal. iv. 6. Lightfoot sees in the participle διδόντα an indication of "ever fresh accessions of the Holy Spirit" (cf. Gal. iii. 5; 1 Cor. xii. 11); it is, perhaps, better conceived as a substantival present, like τὸν ῥυόμενον in i. 10 or τῷ δοκιμάζοντι in ii. 4—"the giver of His Holy Spirit"; for this bestowment is God's prerogative, and sets Him in an abiding relation of inward guidance and command toward believers: cf. Lk. xi. 13; Jo. iii. 34, vii. 38 f.; 2 Cor. i. 22, v. 5; Rom. viii. 9, 14 f.; Gal. iii. 2, iv. 6, v. 25; 2 Tim. i. 7; 1 Jo. iii. 24, iv. 13. The epithet ἅγιον is emphasized by its position, in accordance with the stress thrown on holiness throughout (*vv.* 3, 4, 7). (Τὸν διδόντα) εἰς ὑμᾶς means not "to you" (ὑμῖν) but "into you," so as to enter your hearts and dwell within you: Ezek. xxxvii. 6 (δώσω πνεῦμά μου εἰς ὑμᾶς, נָתַתִּי בָכֶם רוּחַ) probably suggested the phrase; cf. δίδωμι εἰς in Acts xix. 31; Heb. viii. 10; also εἰς in Eph. iii. 16; Mk ii. 1, &c. That God who called us to a pure life, *puts His Spirit in* us, is a consideration heightening the fear of Divine vengeance upon sins of inchastity; for they affront God's indwelling Presence and defile "God's temple": cf. 1 Cor. iii. 16 f., vi. 19; Eph. iv. 30. Seen in this light, uncleanness is profanity.

9. Περὶ δὲ τῆς φιλαδελφίας οὐ χρείαν ἔχετε γράφειν ὑμῖν. *About love of the brethren, however, you have no need that one* (or *that we*) *write to you.* There *was* need (note the contrastive δέ) to write on the former subject. The introduction of a fresh topic by περὶ δέ, as in v. 1 below, prevails in 1 Corinthians (περὶ μέν, 2 Cor. ix. 1), and then drops out of use in the Epistles.

Φιλαδελφία is enjoined, as a distinctive Christian virtue arising out of the relation of believers to each other in "the household of faith," in Rom. xii. 10, Heb. xiii. 1 (see also 1 Pet. i. 22, and Hort's Note). It is distinguished from ἀγάπη, the general principle of spiritual love, in 2 Pet. i. 7 : cf. iii. 12 ; II. i. 3; Gal. v. 13 ff.; Phil. ii. 1 ff.; also Jo. xiii. 34 f., xv. 17; 1 Jo. ii. 9 ff., iii. 14 ff., 23, iv. 11. In 1 Jo. iv. 19—v. 2 love to God in Christ, and love to the children of God, are shown to be an identical affection devoted to kindred objects.

In common Greek the word φιλάδελφος, -ία, did not go beyond the literal sense. There is a slight laxity of expression in the words οὐ χρείαν ἔχετε γράφειν: either ἔχομεν...γράφειν (cf. i. 8; also Acts xxv. 26; 2 Jo. 12), or ἔχετε...γράφεσθαι (v. 1), would have been more exact. On the constructions of χρείαν ἔχειν, see note to i. 8. Cf. περισσόν μοί ἐστιν τὸ γράφειν, 2 Cor. ix. 1.

αὐτοὶ γὰρ ὑμεῖς θεοδίδακτοί ἐστε εἰς τὸ ἀγαπᾶν ἀλλήλους, *for of yourselves you are God-taught, to the end you should love one another.* Not simply "taught to love," as though this were the one lesson of God's grace, "but taught of God that you may love," this being τὸ τέλος τῆς παραγγελίας (1 Tim. i. 5); "doctrinæ divinæ vis confluit in amorem" (Bengel): cf. οὐ...ἐκάλεσεν.. ἐπὶ ἀκαθαρσίᾳ, v. 7. God's own teaching (*scil.* through His Spirit, v. 8, and His word) had been received by the readers so abundantly and directly, that further advice on this subject seems superfluous. Αὐτοί...ὑμεῖς presents a tacit contrast to ἡμεῖς, much as in i. 8 f., ii. 1. For the idiomatic use of εἰς τό with infinitives, see notes on ii. 12, 16.

Θεο-δίδακτος is a *hapax leg.* in Scripture (cf. θεο-στυγής, probably passive, in Rom. i. 30; θεό-πνευστος in 2 Tim. iii. 16); its elements are found in Jo. vi. 45, which rests upon Isai. liv. 13, Jer. xxxi. 33 f.,— passages probably in the Apostle's mind here: cf. Psalms of Solomon xvii. 35; and Matt. xxiii. 8. The phrase διδακτοῖς πνεύματος in 1 Cor. ii. 13 is very similar. The compound word was naturalized in the Greek Fathers.

V. 10 proves that the Thessalonian Christians are "God-taught" to the above effect: *for indeed you are doing that* (showing mutual love) *toward all the brethren in the whole of Macedonia.*

ποιεῖτε αὐτό is a chief instance of the καθώς...περιπατεῖτε credited to the readers in v. 1; this agrees with the testimony of i. 3, 7 ff., II. i. 3, iii. 4. εἰς πάντας τοὺς ἀδελφοὺς τοὺς ἐν ὅλῃ τῇ Μακεδονίᾳ extends the ἀλλήλους of v. 9 beyond the bounds of Thessalonica; a close intercourse and friendship linked the Macedonian Christians, including those of Philippi (see Ph. iv. 16) and Berœa along with other Christian communities that had by this time sprung from these,—or the writers could hardly have said, "in *the whole* of Macedonia"; see *Introd.* pp. xv. f., lxii. Εἰς signifies *direction* of effort (cf. Eph. i. 15: Phm. 5 f.). If the second τούς be inauthentic (see Textual Note), ἐν ὅλῃ κ.τ.λ. must be attached to ποιεῖτε as denoting the region "in" which the readers display their "love of the brethren." Thessalonica, being the capital and commercial centre of Macedonia, was a place of constant resort; and the Christians there had frequent opportunities of giving hospitality to those of other towns; this was a chief form of brotherly love in the primitive Church (see Rom. xii. 13; 1 Tim. iii. 2; Tit. i. 8; Heb. xiii. 1; 1 Pet. iv. 9). Ποιεῖτε conveys a slight contrast to -δίδακτοι of the last clause: "you are not only *taught*, for indeed you *do* it": cf. v. 24; 2 Cor. viii. 10 f.; Matt. vii. 21, 24; Jam. i. 23 ff., for similar antitheses to ποιεῖν.

As ποιεῖτε αὐτό repeats the καθὼς περιπατεῖτε of v. 1, so παρακαλοῦμεν...περισσεύειν μᾶλλον resumes the παρακαλοῦμεν...ἵνα περισσεύητε μᾶλλον of that context: see notes above. In ἀγάπη there is always room for increase and growth: cf. Eph. iii. 19; Rom. xiii. 8 (a debt never quite discharged). II. i. 3 shows that the present exhortation was acted upon. The infinitive is the more regular construction after παρακαλέω; ἵνα in v. 1 (see note).

11. (παρακαλοῦμεν δὲ ὑμᾶς)...καὶ φιλοτιμεῖσθαι ἡσυχάζειν καὶ πράσσειν τὰ ἴδια, *and to be ambitious to keep quiet and to attend to your own business*. This somewhat surprising turn to the παραγγελία was due to an element of restlessness in the Thessalonian Church, of which the 2nd Epistle, in ch. iii. 6—16, will give emphatic evidence; the symptoms indicated in *vv*. 12 ff. below may be traced to the same cause; see *Introd.* pp. xxxvi., xliii. f. The association of this appeal with the topic of φιλαδελφία suggests that the disorder hinted at disturbed the harmony of the Church.

Φιλοτιμεῖσθαι (*ut operam detis*, Vulg.; better, *ut contendatis*, Beza) is *to act as a* φιλό-τιμος, a "lover of honour,"—which signifies in common Greek a man *ambitious*, whether in a good or bad sense (oftener the latter), *of public distinction*; in later Greek the word became synonymous with ζηλωτής or πρόθυμος, denoting a man eager and restless in any pursuit; but there clings to it the connotation of some *desire to shine* or *pursuit of eminence*: see Rom. xv. 20, 2 Cor. v. 9, for the only other N.T. examples. In the combination φιλοτιμ. ἡσυχάζειν there is an oxymoron, a touch of Pauline irony, as though it were said, "Make it your ambition to have no ambition; be eminent in unobtrusiveness!" The love of distinction was universal and potent for mischief in Greek city life, and the Thessalonians betray something of the uneasy, emulous spirit which gave the Apostle subsequently so much trouble at Corinth: cf. also Gal. v. 26; Ph. ii. 3. For τὰ ἴδια, "one's own (private or home) affairs," cf. Lk. xviii. 28; Jo. xix. 27, &c. Lightfoot refers in illustration to Plato's *Repub.* 496 D, describing the philosopher who escapes from the turmoil and degradation of political affairs, as ἐν ἡσυχίᾳ ἄγων καὶ τὰ αὑτοῦ πράττων; similarly Dio Cassius LX. 27.

The closing admonition, **καὶ ἐργάζεσθαι ταῖς χερσὶν ὑμῶν** (cf. II. iii. 8—12; Eph. iv. 28), implies that some of those reproved forsook their daily work in pushing themselves into public activity and notoriety. Most of the Thessalonian Christians practised some handicraft; they belonged to the lower walks of social life (cf. 1 Cor. i. 26 ff.). Ἡσυχάζειν...καὶ ἐργάζεσθαι κ.τ.λ. are combined in the μετὰ ἡσυχίας ἐργαζόμενοι of II. iii. 12; cf. also 1 Tim. ii. 2, 11 f.; 1 Pet. iii. 4. For the use of ἐργάζεσθαι, see note on ii. 9. Christianity through such precepts as these, and through the example of Jesus and the Apostles, has given a new dignity to manual labour, ennobling the life of the great bulk of mankind in a manner very contrary to the sentiments of classical culture and philosophy.

To "work with your hands" had been matter of a special "charge" on the part of the missionaries—**καθὼς ὑμῖν παρηγγείλαμεν**—a παραγγελία supported by the example of the παραγγέλλοντες: see II. iii. 8—12; cf. Eph. iv. 28 f.; Acts xx. 34 f.

12. It is especially to the last particular of the lengthened παραγγελία that the final clause, **ἵνα περιπατῆτε εὐσχημόνως κ.τ.λ.**, applies: *that you may walk honourably* (*honeste*, Vulg.; Old Eng. *honestly*) *toward those without, and have need of nothing.* Εὐσχημόνως (cf. Rom. xiii. 13; 1 Cor. vii. 35) means *in decent, comely fashion*, in such manner as to "adorn the doctrine of our Saviour God" (Tit. ii. 10) and to win respect for the faith from those who had not embraced it. For such regard shown by St Paul to οἱ ἔξω (Heb. הַחִיצוֹנִים), "the outsiders," cf. Col. iv. 5 (identical with this, except that ἐν σοφίᾳ replaces εὐσχημόνως), 1 Tim. iii. 7, Tit. ii. 8; and for the phrase οἱ ἔξω elsewhere, 1 Cor. v. 12 f., Mk iv. 11. On its distinction from οἱ λοιποί, see note to v. 13 below. For περιπατεῖν, see note on ii. 12. Πρός, "in your *attitude towards, converse with* the outsiders"; cf. note on πρὸς ὑμᾶς ἦμεν, iii. 3. In a thriving commercial city like Thessalonica, indolence or pauperism, and unfitness for the common work of life, would bring peculiar disgrace on the new society.

μηδενός is ambiguous in gender; some interpreters render it, "may have need *of no one*": the fact that χρείαν ἔχειν is frequently used with a genitive of *the thing* (e.g. in Matt. vi. 8, Lk. x. 42, Heb. v. 12; 1 Cor. xii. 21 is not really different) "turns the scale in favour of the neuter" (Lightfoot); the context (ἐργάζεσθαι κ.τ.λ.) suggests "need" of *sustenance*,—ἄρτος (II. iii. 8, 12; cf. 1 Jo. iii. 17; Jam. ii. 15). The repetition of χρείαν ἔχειν (*v*. 9) is accidental. The sense of honourable independence, which was so strong in the Apostle (see ii. 6, 9, &c.), he desires his converts to cultivate. The Church was from the first in danger of having its charities abused by the idle.

§ 8. iv. 13—18. CONCERNING THEM THAT FALL ASLEEP.

Thessalonian faith had its "deficiencies" on the doctrinal as well as the practical side (see note introductory to last section). In regard to the coming of the Lord Jesus, which filled a large place in the missionary preaching of the Apostles and in the thoughts and hopes of their converts (see i. 3, 10, ii. 12, iii. 13; Acts xvii. 30 f.), there was misgiving and questioning upon two points; and about these the Thessalonians appear to have sent enquiries to St Paul (see *Introd.* p. xxxvi.) : (*a*) as to *the lot of those dying before the Lord's return*—would they miss the occasion and be shut out of His kingdom? (iv. 13 ff.); (*b*) as to *the time* when the advent might be expected (v. 1—11). The two subjects are abruptly introduced in turn by περί, as matters in the minds of the readers; they are treated in an identical method. With the former of these questions, made acute by the strokes of bereavement falling on the Church since St Paul's departure, the Letter proceeds to deal. The readers (1) are assured that their departed fellow-believers are safe with Jesus, and will return along with Him (*vv*. 13 f.); (2) they are informed, by express revelation, that these instead of being excluded will have the first place in the assembling of the saints at Christ's return (*vv*. 15—17); (3) they are bidden to cheer one another with this hope (*v*. 18). Lightfoot quotes from the *Clementine Recognitions*, i. 52, the question, "Si Christi regno fruentur hi quos justos invenerit ejus adventus, ergo qui ante adventum ejus defuncti sunt, regno penitus carebunt?" showing that the difficulty raised by the Thessalonians was felt elsewhere in the Early Church. This passage stands by itself in Scripture, containing a distinct λόγος κυρίου (*v*. 15), in the disclosure it makes respecting the circumstances of the Second Advent; it is on this account the most interesting passage in the Epistle. The discussion of the subject (iv. 13—v. 11) reflects with a directness unusual in the Apostle the personal teaching of Jesus, and wears the colours of Jewish eschatology. See Milligan's Commentary *ad loc.*

13. Οὐ θέλομεν δὲ ὑμᾶς ἀγνοεῖν, ἀδελφοί. *But we would not have you to be ignorant, brothers.* The impressive phrase οὐ θέλω...ἀγνοεῖν (cf. Rom. i. 13, xi. 25; 1 Cor. x. 1; 2 Cor. i. 8) calls attention to a new statement which St Paul is anxious that his readers should well understand; it disappears after the second group of the Epistles: cf. the similar expressions of 1 Cor. xii. 3; Ph. i. 12; Col. ii. 1. Such formulæ are common in the Epistolary style of the period. Δέ follows οὐ θέλομεν, which form practically one word, *Nolumus* (Vulg.).

περὶ τῶν κοιμωμένων, *concerning them that are falling asleep*; "are asleep" (A.V.) represents the faulty reading of the T. R., κεκοιμημένων. The present participle denotes what is going on. This trouble had now arisen for the first time; see *Introd.* p. xliv. So vivid was the anticipation of the Parousia conveyed to the minds of St Paul's converts, that the thought of *death* intervening to blot out the prospect had scarcely occurred to them. Now that some of their number have died, or are dying,—*what about these?* have they lost their part in the approaching ἀποκάλυψις τοῦ κυρίου Ἰησοῦ (1 Cor. i. 7)? There entered, further, into the sorrow of the bereaved some doubt as to the future resurrection and eternal blessedness of those prematurely snatched away; for the sentence continues, *in order that you may not sorrow* (λυπῆσθε, continue in sorrow: pres. subjunctive) *as the rest (of men) who are without hope.* The grief of some of the readers bordered on extreme despair (cf. 1 Cor. xv. 18); yet they had been taught from the first the Christian hope of the resurrection (see i. 10; Acts xvii. 18, &c.). We must allow for the short time that the Thessalonians had been under instruction and the many new truths they had to master, for the stupefying influence of grief, and for the power with which at such an hour, and amid the lamentations of unbelieving kindred, the darkest fears of their pre-Christian state would re-assert themselves. This dread was vaguely felt by the mourners; what they distinctly apprehended was that those dying beforehand could not witness the return of the Lord Jesus to His people "living" on the earth (vv. 15, 17). This implied a materialistic conception of the Parousia—almost inevitable in the first instance —which is tacitly corrected in v. 17, and more fully rectified in the later teaching of 1 Cor. xv. 42—55: "Flesh and blood cannot inherit the kingdom of God"; "we shall be changed." Sorrow over the departed is not forbidden, but the dark sorrow **of** οἱ λοιποί: "Permittantur itaque pia corda de carorum suorum mortibus contristari dolore sanabili, et consolabiles lacrimas fundant, quas cito reprimat fidei gaudium" (Augustine).

Κοιμᾶσθαι (the synon. καθεύδειν in v. 10, see note; Matt. ix. 24, and parallels) represents death as *sleep*, **after** the style of Jesus (see Jo. xi.

11 f.; 1 Cor. vii. 39, &c.), the term indicating the *restful* (and perhaps *restorative*) effect of death to the child of God, and at the same time its *temporary nature*,—"I go," said Jesus of Lazarus, "that I may awake him from sleep." So the early Christians called their burial-places κοιμητήρια, *cemeteries*, or *dormitories*. In the O.T. (Isai. xiv. 18, xliii. 17; 1 Ki. ii. 10, xi. 43), and occasionally in classical Greek, the same expression is found, but by way of euphemism or poetical figure; its use in 2 Macc. xii. 44f., however, clearly implies a doctrine of the resurrection. This truth is assumed, to begin with, by the expression περὶ τῶν κοιμωμένων in reproof of despondent mourning. One does not grieve over "the sleeping."

οἱ λοιποί, *the rest, the lave*—as in Eph. ii. 3—synon. with οἱ ἔξω of *v.* 12: that expression implies *exclusion*, this implies *deprivation*. οἱ μὴ ἔχοντες ἐλπίδα are the same as τὰ ἔθνη τὰ μὴ εἰδότα τὸν θεόν, *v.* 5; Eph. ii. 12 identifies Gentile hopelessness **and** godlessness. Despair of any future beyond death was a conspicuous feature of contemporary civilization. The more enlightened a Greek or Roman might be, the less belief he commonly held in the old gods of his country and in the fables of a life beyond the grave: see the speeches of Cato and of Caesar in the *Catiline* of Sallust, and the quotations given by Lightfoot or Bornemann *ad loc.* from ancient elegiac poetry and sepulchral inscriptions. The loss of Christian faith in modern times brings back the Pagan despair,—"the shadow of a starless night." Against this deep sorrow of the world the word *sleep*, four times applied in this context to the Christian's death, is an abiding protest. *Vv.* 14—17 will give the reasons why **the** Thessalonians should not sorrow over their dead, as they are tempted to do.

14. εἰ γὰρ πιστεύομεν ὅτι ʼΙησοῦς ἀπέθανεν καὶ ἀνέστη. *For if we believe that Jesus died and rose again*: the faith of a Christian in its briefest statement (cf. 1 Cor. xv. 3 f.); the form of supposition, εἰ with pres. indicative, assumes the fact,—for writers and readers alike (*we believe*: cf. 1 Cor. xv. 11). In Rom. x. 9 St Paul declares the faith that "saves" to be the heart-belief that "God raised Jesus our Lord from the dead"; in 1 Cor. xv. 13—19 he argues that "if Christ hath not been raised" the whole Gospel is **false**, affording no salvation from sin, and no assurance that dying Christians do not perish in the grave. Granted this one certainty, and these consequences are reversed. See 1 Cor. vi. 14, xv. at large; 2 Cor. iv. 14; Rom. iv. 24, v. 10, viii. 11, xiv. 7—9; Ph. iii. 10 f., for other teaching of St Paul bearing on the momentous and manifold effects of the resurrection of Jesus. In this connexion the Redeemer is "Jesus," being thought of in His human person and in the analogy of His experience to our own; hence οὕτως καί in the apodosis. What we believe of this "firstborn amongst many brethren, firstborn out of the dead" (Rom. viii. 29; Col. i. 18), we trust to see fulfilled in His brethren: ἀπαρχὴ Χριστός, ἔπειτα οἱ τοῦ χριστοῦ ἐν τῇ παρουσίᾳ αὐτοῦ (1 Cor. xv. 20—23).

οὕτως καὶ ὁ θεὸς τοὺς κοιμηθέντας διὰ τοῦ Ἰησοῦ ἄξει σὺν αὐτῷ. *So also will God, (in the case of) those who fell asleep through Jesus, bring (them) along with Him:* this awkward rendering reproduces the order of the Greek words, which throw emphasis on the action of *God,* who is conceived as the Raiser-up of the Lord Jesus, and associate Christ's people *with Him* in this restoration (cf. i. 10; 1 Cor. vi. 14; 2 Cor. iv. 14; Gal. i. 1; Eph. i. 19 f.). The aorist participle, τοὺς κοιμηθέντας, looks back to the "falling asleep" from the standpoint of the Parousia (ἄξει σὺν αὐτῷ).

The διά clause may belong grammatically either to the participle or to the principal verb ἄξει (note the article, τοῦ Ἰησοῦ, "*the* Jesus" who "died and rose again," &c.) : two considerations make for its association with κοιμηθέντας—the occurrence of the like combination in *v.* 16, οἱ νεκροὶ ἐν Χριστῷ; and the fitness of the adjunct as an explanation of the emphatically reaffirmed κοιμᾶσθαι. "Through Jesus" (*per Jesum,* Vulg.; not *in Jesu,* as in Beza) the Thessalonian Christians had "fallen asleep": death in their case was robbed of its terrors, as the survivors would remember, and transformed into sleep; clinging to the name of Jesus, they defied death (cf. Rom. viii. 38 f.). Such faith in Him whom He raised from the dead, God will not disown; He "will bring them (back from the unseen world) with Him."

"*Jesus!* my only hope Thou art,
Strength of my failing flesh and heart!"
(Charles Wesley's *Dying Hymn.*)

The argument of this verse is elliptical, its compression being due to the vivacity and eagerness of the Apostle's mind, especially manifest under strong emotion. More completely expressed, his syllogism would read thus : " If we believe that Jesus died and rose again on our behalf, we are bound to believe that He will raise up those who fell asleep in death trusting in Him, and will restore them to us at His return." St Paul leaps over two steps in drawing out his conclusion : (1) he argues from *belief in the fact* in his protasis to *the fact itself* in the apodosis ; (2) he tacitly assumes *the immediate consequence,* viz. the resurrection of the κοιμηθέντες guaranteed by the resurrection of Jesus, in his haste to anticipate *the ultimate consequence,* their return along with Jesus; for it was about the share of their beloved dead in the Advent that the readers were anxious. Underlying this assurance we trace St Paul's deep and characteristic doctrine of the union between Christ and Christians. This unity becomes clearer as we proceed: see *vv.* 16 f. (οἱ νεκροὶ ἐν Χριστῷ, πάντοτε σὺν κυρίῳ ἐσόμεθα); v. 10; II. i. 12, ii. 14; cf. 1 Cor. xv. 23; 2 Cor. iv. 10; Rom. vi. 5; Col. iii. 1—4; 2 Tim. ii. 11, &c. The nerve of the Apostle's reasoning lies in the connexion of the words "*died and rose* again": Jesus has made a pathway through the grave; by this passage His faithful, fallen asleep but still one with Him, are conducted to appear with Him at His return. Ἄξει, "*ducet,* suave verbum: dicitur de viventibus*"* (Bengel). Cf. Heb. ii. 10, πολλοὺς υἱοὺς εἰς δόξαν ἀγαγόντα; but the thought here is that of reunion with the living saints, rather than of guidance to heavenly glory (see II. ii. 1).

15. Τοῦτο γὰρ ὑμῖν λέγομεν ἐν λόγῳ κυρίου. *For this we say to you, in a word of the Lord,*—i.e. in the character of a message coming from "the mouth of the Lord": cf. 1 Cor. vii. 10, "I give charge,— not I, but the Lord"; also *v.* 8 and ii. 13 above;= יהוה בִּדְבַר, 1 Ki. xiii. 17 f., xx. 35, &c.; "quasi Eo ipso loquente" (Beza). St Paul reports an express communication from Christ on the question: while the language of *v.* 16, ὅτι αὐτὸς...οὐρανοῦ, reflects the predictions of Jesus reported in Matt. xxiv., ⁻xxv., &c., there is nothing in the record of the Gospels which covers the important statement made in this verse. The Apostles are either quoting some ἄγραφον of Jesus, known through tradition, like the memorable dictum of Acts xx. 35; or they are disclosing a new revelation made to themselves—either to St Paul (cf. Acts xviii. 9 f., xxvii. 23; 2 Cor. xii. 1 ff.; Gal. ii. 2), or to Silas (see Acts xv. 32), or to some other Christian prophet of their acquaintance (cf. Acts xx. 23, xxi. 10 f.). The brief, authoritative form of statement leads us to suppose that the writers are speaking out of their own inspiration; they seem to be giving a message from the Lord received at the time and to meet this specific case.

ὅτι ἡμεῖς οἱ ζῶντες οἱ περιλειπόμενοι εἰς τὴν παρουσίαν τοῦ κυρίου, *that we who are alive, who survive until the coming of the Lord.* The second designation, carefully repeated in *v.* 17, qualifies and guards the first—"we the living,—those (I mean) who remain, &c." St Paul did not count on a very near approach of the Second Advent (cf. II. ii. 1 f.); but his language implies the possibility of the event taking place within his lifetime or that of the present generation (this is obviously a comprehensive "we"). Christ had left this an open question, or rather a matter on which questioning was forbidden (Acts i. 7; Matt. xxiv. 36); cf. v. 1 ff. below. The Apostles "knew in part" and "prophesied in part," by piecemeal (ἐκ μέρους), about the mysteries of the Last Things; until further light came, it was inevitable that the Church, with its ardent longing to see its Lord, should speak and think as St Paul does here. The same expectant "we" is found in this connexion in 1 Cor. xv. 51; cf. Jam. v. 8 f.; 1 Pet. iv. 5 f. But from the time of the crisis in his life alluded to in 2 Cor. i. 8 f., the prospect of death occupied the foreground in St Paul's anticipations of his own future; he never afterwards writes "we that remain." Bengel minimizes the significance of the plural when he writes: "Sic τὸ nos hic ponitur, ut alias nomina Gajus et Titius"; more justly he continues, "idque eo commodius quia fidelibus illius ætatis amplum temporis spatium ad finem mundi nondum scire licuit." Περιλείπεσθαι, here and in v. 17 only in N.T.; a classical word. For παρουσία, see note on iii. 13.

οὐ μὴ φθάσωμεν τοὺς κοιμηθέντας, *shall by no means precede* (or *anticipate*) *those that fell asleep,*—"that had fallen asleep" before the Coming. The shadow cast over the fate of the sleeping Thessalonian Christians is imaginary. Instead of their having no place, these will have, it is now revealed, a *foremost* place in the Lord's triumphant return. Though dead, they are "the dead in Christ" (v. 16); they departed to "be with the Lord" (v. 17, v. 10)—"absent from the body," but "at home with the Lord," as St Paul subsequently expressed it (2 Cor. v. 6 ff.; Phil. i. 23). If so, it is impossible that those remaining in the flesh when Christ returns should be beforehand with them. "God will bring them with Jesus," for they are with Him already—the tacit link of thought connecting vv. 14 and 15.

Οὐ μή with aorist subj. appears in its well-known use as an *intensive negative*; see Moulton's *Prolegom.*, pp. 187 ff.; Goodwin, *Gr. Grammar*, 1360. For φθάνω, cf. ii. 16; this transitive force of the verb is as old as Homer,—*Iliad* xi. 451, xxi. 262.

That the sleeping saints will be found already "with the Lord," when He returns to "those living" on earth, is shown by the description of the Advent in vv. 16 f. (note the order πρῶτον, ἔπειτα):—

16. ὅτι αὐτὸς ὁ κύριος ἐν κελεύσματι, ἐν φωνῇ ἀρχαγγέλου καὶ ἐν σάλπιγγι θεοῦ, καταβήσεται ἀπ' οὐρανοῦ. *For the Lord Himself with a shout-of-command, with the archangel's voice and with the trumpet of God, will come down from heaven;* cf. i. 10 (and note); Acts i. 11. Αὐτὸς ὁ κύριος: "in His personal august presence" (Ellicott); cf. iii. 11, v. 23; II. ii. 16, iii. 16, for this kind of emphasis,—particularly frequent in these Epistles. In each context the "grandis sermo" (Bengel) indicates the majesty with which "the Lord," or "God," rises above human doings and desires.

The three prepositional adjuncts prefixed to καταβήσεται depict the Lord's descent from heaven under the sense of its Divine grandeur. In this κατάβασις the κοιμώμενοι are to participate: how glorious, then, how far from sorrowful their lot! 'Εν is the preposition of "attendant circumstance" (Lightf.); cf. II. i. 8, ii. 9 f. (see notes): its repetition adds vividness and rhetorical force; the second and third particulars, apparently, explicate the first. We must not look for literal exactness where realities are described beyond the reach of sense. The three phrases may express a single idea, that of "the voice of the Son of God" by which the dead will be called forth (see Jo. v. 25—29), His "command" being expressed by an "archangel's voice," and that again constituting the "trumpet of God." Christ predicted His return attended by "angels" (Matt. xxv. 31; cf. II. i. 7); and the Divine "voices" of the Apocalypse are constantly uttered by "an angel," or "mighty angel" (Rev. v. 2, vii. 2, &c.). In the same Book, *voice* and *trumpet* are identified in the description of the glorified Son of Man: "I heard behind me a great voice, as of a trumpet talking with me" (Rev. i. 10, 12, iv. 1); cf. Matt. xxiv. 31, "He shall send forth His angels with a trumpet of great voice." In 1 Cor. xv. 52 the whole accompaniment is gathered into one word, σαλπίσει (impersonal). This vein of description, in its vocabulary and colouring, is derived from the Theophanies and Apocalyptic of the Old Testament: see Exod. xix. 11, 13, 16 ff.; Deut. xxxiii. 2; Joel ii. 1; Mic. i. 3; Zech. ix. 14; Isai. xxvii. 13; Ps. xviii. 9—11, xlvii. 5.

Κέλευσμα (*hap. leg.* in 'N.T.; Prov. xxiv. 62 [xxx. 27], LXX; see Lightfoot's illustrations from classical Greek) is the "word of command" or "signal"—the shout with which an officer gives the order to his troops or a captain to his crew. Such "command" he might utter either by "voice"—his own or another's—or through a "trumpet"; the "archangel" in this imagery stands by the Lord's side as the σαλπιγκτής beside his general, to transmit His κέλευσμα. The σάλπιγξ is the *military* trumpet of the Lord of Hosts, mustering His array; cf. v. 8, with its "breastplate" and "helmet" (see note). "As a commander rouses his sleeping soldiers, so the Lord calls up His dead, and bids them shake off the fetters of the grave and rise anew to waking life" (Hofmann); cf. with this, in view of the words ἄξει σὺν αὐτῷ of v. 14, the scene imagined in Rev. xix. 14 and its context.

Φωνῇ ἀρχαγγέλου (not τῇ φωνῇ τοῦ ἀρχαγγ., as though some known angelic chief were intended) is added in explanation of ἐν κελεύσματι, and to indicate the majesty and power of the summons. This is the earliest example of the title ἀρχάγγελος. In Jude 9 we read of "*Michael* the archangel"—an expression probably based on the Greek of Dan. xii. 1, Μιχαὴλ ὁ ἄγγελος (ἄρχων) ὁ μέγας ; cf. Rev. xii. 7. Ranked with Michael was *Gabriel*, the angel of comfort and good tidings in Dan. viii. 16, ix. 21, and Lk. i. 19, 26. The military tenor of this context suggests *Michael*. Next to these two, amongst the seven chief angels recognized in Jewish teaching, stood *Raphael*, "the affable archangel" (Milton) ; cf. Tobit xii. 15. St Paul doubtless ranked the ἀρχάγγελοι amongst his heavenly ἀρχαί : cf. Rom. viii. 38 ; Eph. i. 21, iii. 10 ; Col. i. 16, ii. 10, 15. See the articles on *Angel* in Hastings' *Dict. of the Bible* and Smith's *Dict. of Christian Antiquities*.

καὶ οἱ νεκροὶ ἐν Χριστῷ ἀναστήσονται πρῶτον, *and the dead in Christ will rise first*. Οἱ νεκροὶ ἐν Χριστῷ are οἱ κοιμηθέντες διὰ τοῦ Ἰησοῦ of *v.* 14 (see note)—this phrase defining their present situation as "the dead," that their past experience in dying. Being "in Christ" (cf. notes on the ἐν of i. 1 and iv. 1 ; and see Winer-Moulton, p. 486, note 3), nothing can part them from Him,—death no more than life (Rom. viii. 38 f.). Οἱ νεκροὶ ἐν Χριστῷ forms a single idea in this context ; hence οἱ is not repeated : see Winer-Moulton, p. 169. "Will rise *first* "—not before the other dead rise, as though theirs were a select and separate resurrection of the *élite* (cf. Jo. v. 28 f.), but before "the living" saints are "caught up to meet the Lord" (*v.* 17) : πρῶτον is antithetical to ἔπειτα ἡμεῖς οἱ ζῶντες.

V. 17 resumes in its subject, under the aforesaid antithesis, the ἡμεῖς οἱ ζῶντες οἱ περιλειπόμενοι of *v.* 15 (see notes above). For πρῶτον— ἔπειτα, apposing things consecutive either in time or in importance, cf. 1 Cor. xii. 28, xv. 46 ; 1 Tim. iii. 10 ; Mk iv. 28 ; Jam. iii. 17.

ἅμα σὺν αὐτοῖς ἁρπαγησόμεθα ἐν νεφέλαις, *together with them will be caught up in* (*the*) *clouds*. Ἅμα σὺν αὐτοῖς bears the stress of the sentence, explaining definitely the οὐ μὴ φθάσωμεν of *v.* 15, which formed the central word of the λόγος κυρίου ; cf. ἐπισυναγωγή, II. ii. 1 (see note). The combination ἅμα σύν, denoting full association (*una cum* ; rather than *simul cum*, Vulg.), recurs in v. 10, where, as here, the temporal sense of ἅμα is inappropriate ; cf. Rom. iii. 12, 1 Tim. v. 13, Acts xxiv. 26, in which passages ἅμα signifies not *simultaneity* but *conjunction* : "we the living shall join their company, who are already with the Lord."

Ἁρπάζω implies a sudden, irresistible force : "we shall be seized, snatched up...into the air"; cf. 2 Cor. xii. 2, 4 (of St Paul's *rapture* into the third heaven); Matt. xi. 12, xiii. 19; Acts viii. 39; Rev. xii. 5. Ἐν νεφέλαις, not "into" but "amid clouds,"—surrounding and upbearing the rapt "like a triumphal chariot" (Grotius). Christ Himself, and the angels at His ascension, spoke of His coming thus attended (Matt. xxiv. 30, xxvi. 64; Acts i. 9 ff.; cf. Rev. i. 7, x. 1, xi. 12, xiv. 14 ff.). The Transfiguration gave an earnest of Christ's heavenly glory, when "a bright cloud overshadowed" those who were with Him, and "a voice" spake "out of the cloud" (Matt. xvii. 5). There is something wonderful and mystical about the clouds,—half of heaven and half of earth; their ethereal drapery supplies the curtain and canopy of this glorious meeting.

The raising of the living bodies of the saints along with the risen dead implies a physical transformation of the former; this the Apostle sets forth later in 1 Cor. xv. 50 ff.: "We shall not all sleep, but we shall all be changed," &c. (cf. 2 Cor. v. 1—4; Phil. iii. 21). Some mysterious change came upon the sacred body of Jesus at His resurrection, for it was emancipated from the ordinary laws of matter. Such a metamorphosis St Paul seems to have conceived as possible without dissolution.

Ἀρπαγησόμεθα is qualified further by two εἰς- clauses of direction: **εἰς ἀπάντησιν τοῦ κυρίου, εἰς ἀέρα,** *to meet the Lord, into (the) air.* "The air," like the "clouds," belongs to the interspace between the heaven from which Christ comes and the earth which He visits. He is represented as *met by* His Church, which does not wait till He sets foot on earth, but ascends to greet Him. The somewhat rare (Hebraistic?) idiom εἰς ἀπάντησιν (cf. לִקְרַאת הָאֱלֹהִים, Exod. xix. 17) is found in Matt. xxv. 1 (ὑπάντησιν), 6, with reference to the Virgins of Christ's parable, "going forth *to meet* the Bridegroom"; our Lord's words are running in the writer's mind. This prepositional phrase occurs with the dative in Acts xxviii. 15. Chrysostom finely says: καὶ γὰρ βασιλέως εἰς πόλιν εἰσελαύνοντος, οἱ μὲν ἔντιμοι πρὸς ἀπάντησιν ἐξίασιν· καὶ πατρὸς φιλοστόργου παραγινομένου, οἱ μὲν παῖδες καὶ ἄξιοι παῖδες εἶναι ἐπ' ὀχήματος ἐξάγονται, ὥστε ἰδεῖν καὶ καταφιλῆσαι...ἐπὶ τοῦ ὀχήματος τοῦ πατρὸς φερόμεθα...ἐν νεφέλαις ἁρπαγησόμεθα· ὁρᾷς τὴν τιμὴν ὅσην καὶ τὴν ἀπάντησιν καταβαίνοντι ποιούμεθα· καὶ τὸ πάντων μακαριώτερον, οὕτω σὺν αὐτῷ ἐσόμεθα. Whether St Paul imagined that after this meeting Christ and His people would return to earth, or move upwards to heaven, he does not indicate.

καὶ οὕτως πάντοτε σὺν κυρίῳ ἐσόμεθα, *and so we shall be always with the Lord.* This last word of consolation addressed to the sorrowing bereaved of Thessalonica, includes their sleeping beloved with themselves. Toward this conception of future happiness St Paul's mind gravitates, rising clear of all images of place and circumstance in its view of the state of the departed and the glory of the redeemed: cf., to the like effect, v. 10; II. ii. 1; Rom. viii. 17, 39; 2 Cor. v. 8; Eph. ii. 6; Col. iii. 1—4; Phil. i. 23; 2 Tim. iv. 18; also Jo. xii. 26, xiv. 3, xvii. 24; Acts vii. 59; 1 Jo. iii. 2; Rev. xxii. 4. "The entire content and worth of heaven, the entire blessedness of life eternal, is for Paul embraced in the one thought of being united with Jesus, his Saviour and Lord" (Bornemann).

18. **Ὥστε παρακαλεῖτε ἀλλήλους ἐν τοῖς λόγοις τούτοις.** *Therefore cheer one another in these words,*—the λόγος κυρίου which *vv.* 15—17 have communicated, and the other apostolic words accompanying it. Ὥστε with imperative, or cohortative subjunctive, is an idiom St Paul often uses at the point where argument or explanation passes into appeal; cf. 1 Cor. iii. 21, iv. 5, v. 8, &c.: the *present* imperative enjoins habitual comforting. For παρακαλέω, in its varied uses, see note on ii. 12; here synonymous with παραμυθέομαι, as it stands opposed to λυπεῖσθαι (*v.* 13). Ἐν τοῖς λόγοις τούτοις, "in (the use of) these words,"—at their public reading in the Church assembly (cf. v. 27; see note); then, presumably, in the repetition of their teaching by Thessalonians to each other when need occurred. Ἐν is perhaps *instrumental* (see Ellicott *ad loc.*)—"with these words": later Greek tended to prefix ἐν to the bare dative thus. To this message of their Letter the Apostles attach great weight; they expect it to be distinctly remembered and often recalled: cf. v. 11, 14, and notes. See, for the Jewish allusions and linguistic expressions of the above section, and for similar matter throughout the Epp., Milligan's very valuable *Commentary*.

CHAPTER V.

1. For εχετε, εχομεν in Aug^ep 199 : "*non opus habemus vobis scribere, vel sicut alii codices habent, non opus habetis vobis scribi.*" The same variation in iv. 9 (see note above); other latt *non est necesse vobis scribere* (Tert *non est necessitas scribendi vobis*), vg *non indigetis ut scribamus vobis*. The Greek idiom makes ungrammatical Latin.

2. **AKL** introduce η before ημερα κυριου: cf. *v.* 4; II. ii. 2, &c.

3. (*a*) οταν alone : ℵ*AG, 17, 47, latt syr^pesh, Tert Cyp Or^int.

   (*b*) οταν δε, ℵ^cBD, cop syr^hcl.

   (*c*) οταν γαρ, **KLP**, &c., vg, Dam Ambrst.

This grouping of witnesses is peculiar. (*c*) may be ruled out as a Syrian emendation; cf. 1 Cor. xi. 31. (*b*) makes a rather difficult sense (see Expos. Note); and with cop and Harclean syr testifying in its favour, and **G** and the latt against it, the δε can hardly be a Western addition. Moreover λε before λεγωcιN might easily escape the eye of the copyist; cf. δε δοκιμαζετε, *v.* 21, and note.

For αιφνιδιος **AD*G** read, itacistically, εφνιδιος.

επισταται in ℵB 17 37, against the εφισταται of **DKP**, &c.; see Expository Note.

4. υμας η ημερα (in this order), **ADG** latt vg Ambrst; a Western deviation.

The case of (*a*) κλεπτας in **AB** cop, *versus* (*b*) κλεπτης in **ℵDGKLP** and every other witness, is one of crucial difficulty. Is -ης a conformation to *v.* 2, or -ας to the foregoing υμας (cf. τυπους, for -ον, i. 7)? The change of metaphor involved in (*a*) is so oddly abrupt as to amount to almost a levity of style; nor is there anything in the context to bear out the idea of Christians being, conceivably, in the position of *thieves*; intrinsic probability speaks strongly for (*b*). Yet the external attestation of (*a*) is weighty; the group **AB** cop bears a high character. κλεπτας, if not the original, is a very ancient reading.

5. (παντες) γαρ in all uncials except (probably) K, and all versions. υιοι ημερας : several latt read *filii dei*, instead of *diei*,—a slip easily made in Latin.

D*G and latt read εστε (bis) for εσμεν.

6. ως without και, ℵ*AB 17, cop syr^{pesh}: και belongs to the Western and Syrian witnesses; cf. iv. 13, Eph. ii. 3.

9. ο θεος ημας (in this order) B 37, 116; similarly in ii. 16 B distinguishes itself by the order εφθακεν η οργη επ' αυτους.

B aeth omit χριστου: the general probability of the insertion of χριστος by copyists where it was previously absent, must be weighed against the special probability of its omission *in this Epistle* where the combination ο κυριος Ιησους prevails.

10. περι in ℵ*B 17, against all other codd., which have υπερ: cf. the variants in 1 Cor. i. 13, Gal. i. 4; and see Expository Note.

12. προιστανομενους in ℵA (?Alexandrian); cf. Rom. xii. 8, and 1 Tim. iii. 4, for the reading of ℵ.

13. For ηγεισθαι, B cop go syr^{hcl} aeth have ηγεισθε —an error partly of itacistic confusion, and partly of misinterpretation. B shows the same trick in II. ii. 2, θροεισθε (-αι); cf. the double alternative of imperative or infinitive in II. iii. 14.

υπερεκπερισσως: so in BD*G (WH *margin*). -σσου in the rest may be due to iii. 10 and Eph. iii. 20; cf. Mk xiv. 31 (εκπερισσως).

(*a*) (ειρηνευετε εν) αυτοις, ℵD*GP, some minn., f vg *cum eis*; probably Western : (*b*) εαυτοις, ABD^cKL. The harshness of (*a*) appears in the rendering of εν by *cum* in the vg : the reading αυτοις has been "mechanically conformed to αυτους and αυτων" in the same verse (Weiss).

15. For αποδῳ, αποδοι in ℵ*D^bG; in D*, αποδοιη: these latter are not optatives, but subjunctives of the κοινή; see Winer-Moulton's *Grammar*, p. 95, note ³.

και before εις αλληλους given by Bℵ^cKLP, &c. (so WH *margin*): omitted in ℵ*ADG, 17, 37, 67**; iii. 12 may have prompted the omission.

18. D*G and several minn. insert εστιν in 2nd clause (τουτο γαρ εστιν)—an example of seeming Latinisms in the Western text; cf. note on iv. 17 above. Or is εστιν due to the parallel in iv. 3?

ℵ*A, του θεου for θεου.

19. ζβεννυτε: so spelt in B*D*G. See WH *Appendix*, p. 148.

21. δε in the first clause is omitted by ℵ*A and many minn., cop syr^pesh, Or Bas Chr Tert Ambrst, probably through confusion with the following syllable in the continuous uncial script: πλΝΤΑΔΕΔΟ-ΚΙΜΑΖΕΤΕ; cf. note on disputed δε. in v. 3. Intrinsic probability speaks for the antithetic conjunction: the sense seems to be, "Do not despise...*but test*..." (see Expository Note). K, followed by many minn. and several Fathers, after dropping the δε alters δοκιμαζετε to δοκιμαζοντες—a change due, perhaps, to loose quotation; Dam gives δοκιμασαντες. The participle employed in Eph. v. 10 may have furthered this corruption.

25. BD*, and some good minn., insert και after προσευχεσθε.

27. ενορκιζω, as against ορκιζω, is preserved in ABD* 17: a *hapax legomenon* for the N.T., and rare in Greek; see Grimm-Thayer, *Lexicon* s.v.

αγιοις, before αδελφοις, in Aℵ^cKLP &c., cop syrr vg go, wanting in ℵ*BDG latt. The only parallel to αγιοι αδελφοι *in Paul* is αγιοις αποστολοις of Eph. iii. 5 (see Expository Note; cf. Heb. iii. 1); the copyists were more likely to add αγιοις to the text than to cancel it. Weiss suggests that it was lost in ℵB through homœoteleuton.

28. αμην wanting in BD*G 17 67** latt; stands in AD^b,c KLP &c. Is this a Western omission, or Alexandrian supplement to the text? Cf. iii. 13, and note above: the case for retention is stronger there than here.

In the SUBSCRIPTION: ℵB* read προς Θεσσαλονικεις ᾱ (B -νεικεις).

§ 9. v. 1—11. THE COMING OF THE DAY.

The second misgiving of the Thessalonians respecting the παρουσία (see *Introd.* to § 8, and general *Introd.* p. xxxvi.) was closely connected with the first (iv. 13 ff.). If only "the living, οἱ περιλειπόμενοι," might count on witnessing the παρουσία, then any uncertainty about its date throws a cloud upon the prospects of all believers; if the season was delayed, any of those living might be cut off before the time and no one could count on seeing the wished-for day! This apprehension made the desire of the Church to know περὶ τῶν χρόνων κ.τ.λ. painfully keen; no mere curiosity prompted the question, but a practical motive, a natural fear arising from the very loyalty of the Thessalonians to Christ and the "love" of "His appearing" which the Gospel awakened in them. The Epistle has allayed the main cause of disquiet by showing that there will be no essential difference in the lot of those found "sleeping" and those "waking" at the Lord's return (cf. *v.* 10 below); it goes on to remind the readers of what they had been taught already, viz., that "the day of the Lord" is to come by way of *surprise* to the wicked, for which reason its date must be hidden (*vv.* 2 f.). The "sons of light and of day" will be ready for "the day" whenever it dawns (*vv.* 4 f.). Their duty and safety is to be wakeful and sober, arming themselves with faith and hope (*vv.* 6—8)—a hope grounded on God's purpose of salvation revealed in the Gospel, which assures to them through Christ's death a life of union with Him remaining unchanged in life and death (*vv.* 9 f.), and secure whether His coming be earlier or later.

1. **Περὶ δὲ τῶν χρόνων καὶ τῶν καιρῶν, ἀδελφοί.** *But about the times and the seasons, brothers.*

Χρόνος signifies time as *duration*, καιρός as a specific *point, occasion*: asking περὶ τῶν χρόνων, one wants to know the length of *the periods* that may elapse before the Advent; asking περὶ τῶν καιρῶν, the number and nature of *the critical events* that must intervene and lead up to it; *de temporibus et momentis* (Vulg.). Ὁ μὲν καιρὸς δηλοῖ ποιότητα, χρόνος δὲ ποσότητα (Ammonius). For the association of these terms, cf. Tit. i. 2 f.; Acts i. 7, iii. 20 f.; also Dan. ii. 21, vii. 12; Eccles. iii. 1; Wisd. viii. 8: for καιρός further, ii. 17 above; II. ii. 6; Rom. iii. 26; Gal. vi. 9 f.; Lk. xxi. 8, &c. Ἀδελφοί is repeated in *v.* 4, as though the Apostles instinctively drew their friends near to themselves under the shadow of the solemn future; cf. ἡμῶν ἐπισυναγωγῆς, II. ii. 1. Chrysostom attributes the inquisitiveness περὶ τῶν χρόνων κ.τ.λ. to an idle, restless disposition (cf. iv. 11; II. iii. 11): πολλὰ ἐπείγεται μανθάνειν ἤδη καὶ καταλαμβάνειν ἡμῶν ἡ διάνοια ὡς περίεργος καὶ λίχνος πρὸς τὴν τῶν ἀφανῶν καὶ κεκαλυμμένων μάθησιν· τοῦτο δὲ σημαίνει ἀπὸ τοῦ θρύπτεσθαι καὶ ἀπὸ τοῦ μηδὲν ἔχειν ποιεῖν.

On οὐ χρείαν κ.τ.λ., see note to iv. 9.

2. **αὐτοὶ γὰρ ἀκριβῶς οἴδατε.** *For of yourselves you know precisely.* On αὐτοὶ οἴδατε, see ii. 1; and cf. again iv. 9. The readers "know," because they have been already told (cf. iii. 4; II. ii. 5); their question was needless, if they reflected on what they had previously learned respecting "the day of the Lord." The allusions in the sequel to our Lord's discourse on the Judgement imply that the Apostles had quoted His sayings on this mysterious theme. While in regard to the matter of § 8 a new revelation was required (iv. 15), on this question the Lord's own well-remembered words were sufficient.

The word ἀκριβῶς is puzzling here: "perfectly" (A.V., R.V.) is not a strict equivalent; in Matt. ii. 8 it is rendered "carefully," in Lk. i. 3 "accurately," and so on; the Vulg. turns it into *diligenter*; Erasmus and Estius, better, *exacte*. The adverb seems out of place, until one remembers that the Apostles are replying to enquiries from their readers, and that in such correspondence St Paul is fond of retorting words addressed to him (see J. Rendel Harris in the *Expositor*, V. VIII. 161—180; also W. Lock in *Expositor*, V. VI. 65 ff.). Probably the Thessalonians in sending their query had used this very word: "We should like to know *more precisely* about the times and seasons, and when the day of the Lord will be." The Apostle replies, with a touch of irony (cf. note on iv. 11): "You already know precisely that nothing precise on the subject can be known—the Great Day will steal on the world like a thief in the night!" II. ii. 1—3 shows that even after this caution the Church continued to entertain speculations about the details of the Advent.

ὅτι ἡμέρα Κυρίου ὡς κλέπτης ἐν νυκτὶ οὕτως ἔρχεται, *that the day of the Lord, as a thief in the night, so is coming*. Ἡμέρα Κυρίου—anarthrous (cf. Ph. i. 6, 10, ii. 16), as a sort of proper noun—the well-known prophetic "Day of the Lord" (יוֹם יהוה). It "is coming," —is on the way (cf. notes on i. 10, ii. 16; also Eph. v. 6; Rom. i. 18; 2 Pet. ii. 3, &c.). Even in the act of departing Jesus said repeatedly, "I come," "I am coming to you" (John xiv. 3, 18, 28, &c.). Lightfoot, Winer-Moulton (pp. 331 f.), and others, read this as a prophetic present: "cometh" = "will surely come." The event is certain and in preparation; *when* it will arrive none can tell.

The figure of the κλέπτης ἐν νυκτί points (v. 3) to the unhappy surprise that "the day" brings to the wicked. This simile of Jesus (cf. Matt. xxiv. 43; Lk. xii. 39 f.; see note above, on αὐτοὶ οἴδατε) recurs in 2 Pet. iii. 10; Rev. iii. 3, xvi. 15. It gave rise to the tradition that the Advent would take place on the night before the Passover, through which therefore vigil was wont to be kept (see Jerome on Matt. xxv. 6; Lactantius *Instit.* VII. 19). The metaphor possibly implies, beside the *unexpectedness*, the *bereaving effect* of the Coming: that Day will *rob* the wicked of ease and wealth (cf. Lk. xii. 20, 33). There is a certain incongruity in the representation of a "*day* coming" (breaking in upon evildoers) "as a thief *in the night*"; but it is the Lord Himself who "comes" on this great day of His (II. i. 7 ff.; cf. Rev. iii. 3, &c.).

The doctrine of "the day of Jehovah" may be traced through the O.T., in Joel i. 15, ii. 1 ff., &c., iii. 14; Am. v. 18 ff.; Isai. ii. 11 ff.,

xiii. 6, &c., xix. 16—25, xxvi. 1, xxvii. 1 ff.; Zeph. i. 7 ff., &c.; Jer. xxxi. 31 ff., xlvi. 10; Ezek. xiii. 5, xxxix. 8, &c.; Mal. iii. 2, &c. It denotes the great epoch of judgement impending over Israel and the surrounding nations, which dominated the prophetic horizon; it had a further outlook, however, of blessing and restoration for God's people (see Zech. xiv. 7 ff.). The judicial aspect of the Day of the Lord in the O.T. was carried over into the New, *mutatis mutandis*. The Judgement now assumes a more spiritual and supernatural character; it is individualized, bearing no longer on nations and their destiny, but on *men* universally—on personal character and relations to God; it follows upon the resurrection of the dead; and, above all, Jesus Christ is disclosed as the Judge of "that Day": see, amongst many other passages, Matt. xxv. 31—46; Jo. v. 21—29, vi. 39 f.; Lk. xvii. 24, 26, 30; Acts xvii. 31; Rom. ii. 16; 1 Cor. iv. 3 ff.; 2 Cor. v. 10, &c. Hence this Day of the Lord is called by the Apostle "the day of Jesus Christ" (Phil. i. 6, &c.); sometimes "that day" (2 Tim. i. 12, &c.), since it is the *finale* to which all Christianity points. St Paul loves to regard it on its brighter side, as the time when Christ's glory will be revealed in His saints (iii. 13; II. i. 10; Phil. ii. 16; Rom. viii. 19, &c.). Now the world has its day; "this is your hour," said Jesus to the Jewish officers, "and the power of darkness" (Lk. xxii. 53): then comes *the Lord's* day, when He will be vindicated both in salvation and in judgement, when "the glory of the Lord shall be revealed, and all flesh shall see it together" (Isai. xl. 5). At a later period the weekly day of Christ's resurrection received this name (see Rev. i. 10; cf. 1 Cor. xvi. 2)—this is also a day of Divine vindication, and thus a pledge and anticipation of the great Day; cf. the connexion between the resurrection of Jesus and the Last Judgement indicated in i. 10, Acts xvii. 31.

3. ὅταν λέγωσιν Εἰρήνη καὶ ἀσφάλεια. *When they are saying, (There is) peace and safety (security)*. This verse stands in abrupt (asyndetic) explanatory relation to ὅτι...ἔρχεται (*v.* 2). Once more the prophetic language of the O.T. is drawn upon: see Mic. iii. 5 f.; Jer. vi. 14 f., viii. 11; Ezek. xiii. 10—where the false assurances of lying prophets are denounced. "It seems not unlikely that this sentence," continuing as it does verse 2 without a break, "is a direct quotation from our Lord's words" unrecorded elsewhere (Lightfoot): cf. notes above on αὐτοὶ...οἴδατε and ὡς κλέπτης ἐν νυκτί; also note below on τότε αἰφνίδιος κ.τ.λ. The subject of λέγωσιν is given by the context, viz., the men "of night" and "of darkness." Εἰρήνη κ.τ.λ. forms an elliptical clause—the utterance of those cherishing a false

security. At the very moment when men of the world are wrapped in ease and are assuring each other that all is well, the ruin breaks upon them,—e.g. in the case of the πλούσιος ἄφρων of Lk. xii. 16 ff. Periods of self-complacent prosperity are pregnant with calamity; they prelude some awful "Day of the Lord."

τότε αἰφνίδιος αὐτοῖς ἐπίσταται ὄλεθρος: *then suddenly over them stands destruction*. *Tunc repentinus eis superveniet interitus* (Vulg.), *imminet excidium* (Beza)—not seen approaching, but first visible as it presses close upon the doomed transgressors and is on the point of overwhelming them. The words of Jesus reported in Lk. xxi. 34 are distinctly echoed, not in thought only but in phraseology: προσέχετε ἑαυτοῖς μή ποτε βαρηθῶσιν αἱ καρδίαι ὑμῶν ἐν κραιπάλῃ καὶ μέθῃ (cf. *v.* 7 below) καὶ μερίμναις βιωτικαῖς, καὶ ἐπιστῇ ἐφ' ὑμᾶς **αἰφνίδιος** (in these two places only in N.T.) ἡ ἡμέρα ἐκείνη ὡς παγίς; cf., besides Matt. xxiv. 38 ff., Lk. xvii. 26 ff. "One out of several special points of coincidence between St Paul's Epistles and the Third Gospel, where it diverges from the others" (Lightfoot); cf. 1 Cor. xi. 23—26, xv. 5, 1 Tim. v. 18. Αἰφνίδιος bears emphasis by its place at the beginning, and ὄλεθρος at the end of the sentence; being a secondary adjectival predicate, the former is best rendered by the English *adverb*. For ὄλεθρος, see note to II. i. 9.

Ἐπίσταται stands for ἐφίσταται in the best MSS. (see Textual Note above). The earlier Greek Codices show considerable variation and uncertainty in regard to the aspirate: "the *spiritus asper* tended gradually to disappear" (Winer-Schmiedel, *Grammatik*, p. 38). Here the form of the cognate verb ἐπίσταμαι probably reacted on the middle voice of ἐφίστημι; "aspiration is" almost "universal in the other 14 examples of compounds of ἵστημι with a preposition capable of showing aspiration" (WH). The same double spelling appears in the MSS. of Wisdom vi. 8 (9); and D makes the opposite confusion, ἐφ- (for ἐπ-)ίστασθε, in Acts x. 28.

ὥσπερ ἡ ὠδὶν τῇ ἐν γαστρὶ ἐχούσῃ, *as the birth-pang (comes on) her that is with child*: another O.T. simile (Isai. xiii. 6—8, xxxvii. 3; Hos. xiii. 13; Mic. iv. 9 f.; thrice in Jeremiah); used by Jesus, on the happier side of its application, in Jo. xvi. 21; also in Gal. iv. 19. Ἐν γαστρὶ ἔχειν, or φέρειν, is an established Greek locution for pregnancy. There lie in this comparison the three points of *inevitable certainty, suddenness*, and *intense pain*. Hence the added clause, **καὶ οὐ μὴ ἐκφύγωσιν**, *and they shall in no wise escape*: a further reminiscence of the warning of Lk. xxi.—ἵνα κατισχύσητε ἐκφυγεῖν ταῦτα πάντα (*v.* 36); for ἐκφεύγειν in similar threatenings, cf. Rom. ii. 3; Heb. ii. 3, xii. 25.

Verses 4—6 contrast the outlook of the readers, in view of the dread "day"—so certain in itself, so uncertain in its date—with that of the careless world around them.

4. ὑμεῖς δέ, ἀδελφοί, οὐκ ἐστὲ ἐν σκότει, ἵνα ἡ ἡμέρα κ.τ.λ. *But you, brothers, are not in darkness, that the day should overtake you as thieves* (or *as a thief*). With the opening ὑμεῖς δὲ οὐκ cf. Eph. iv. 20; and for ἐν σκότει, see 2 Cor. vi. 14; Eph. v. 8; Col. i. 12 f. In the last of the above passages also "darkness" and "light" are conceived as two opposite regions or realms, dividing men between them; cf. Jo. iii. 19 ff.; 1 Jo. i. 5 ff. "In darkness" one may be "surprised"— one is sure to be so if asleep, or ἐν μέθῃ (*v.* 7)—by the breaking in of "the day." Ἡ ἡμέρα is "the day" whose coming was described in *v.* 2; for this emphatic breviloquence, cf. Rom. xiii. 12, 1 Cor. iii. 13, Heb. x. 25; similarly "the wrath" in i. 10 above.

We have preferred in the Textual Note the Received reading κλέπτης to κλέπτας, which is adopted by WH and Lightfoot. The inversion involved in κλέπτας, transforming the "thief" from the *cause* of the surprise (*v.* 2) into its *object*, abrupt as it is, one might admit as possible in St Paul; but it seems incongruous here, and such incongruity is un-Pauline: the subsequent context describes the "sons of night" as *sleeping* or *drunken*, quite otherwise than as thieves, who are alert and careful. Moreover, **καταλάβῃ** bears a stress which should have fallen upon ὡς κλέπτας in the *ordo verborum*, if the metaphor had been turned about and a new bearing unexpectedly given to it. It is a *thief-like surprise* that "the day" brings with it; not such a surprise *as falls upon thieves* at their night's work. For καταλαμβάνω in this *hostile* sense, cf. Jo. xii. 35, Mk ix. 18; in its *good* sense, Phil. iii. 12. With the reading ὡς κλέπτας, the verb would have a shade of *detection* in it; cf. [Jo.] viii. 3.

The strict telic force of ἵνα might be maintained by conceiving the clause as a statement of God's purpose "in His merciful dispensation implied in οὐκ ἐστὲ ἐν σκότει" (Ellicott); or better, according to Bornemann, as the purpose of God for the opposite class of men who are ἐν σκότει, as though the Apostle meant, "You are not in darkness,—not so placed that the day may surprise you." "But the word is better taken here as simply expressing the result or consequence [of being in darkness], a meaning which, in the decline of the Greek language, gradually displaced the original signification of ἵνα" (Lightfoot); cf. Gal. v. 17. This conjunction in the κοινή was slipping down from the final (telic), through the eventual (ecbatic), sense into the use assigned to it in Byzantine and Modern Greek, where, in the form νά, it serves as a bare infinitive particle. See Winer-Moulton, pp. 572 ff.; A. Buttmann, pp. 235 ff. The ἵνα after παρακαλοῦμεν (iv. 1) is somewhat different (see note). See also Moulton's *Prolegomena*, pp. 206—9.

5. πάντες γὰρ ὑμεῖς υἱοὶ φωτός ἐστε καὶ υἱοὶ ἡμέρας: *for you are all sons of light and sons of day.* More than a denial of ἐστὲ ἐν σκότει: the "son of light" is not merely "*in* the light," he is "*of* the light," possessed by it and of its nature; he "*is* light in the Lord" (Eph. v. 8: cf. Eph. ii. 2 f.; Rom. xiii. 11 ff.; Lk. xvi. 8; Jo. xii. 36; 1 Pet. i. 14; 2 Pet. i. 19). In Hebrew idiom, one is "a son" of anything that determines or distinguishes his character; cf. "sons of Belial," "sons of the resurrection," &c. "Light" is the pervading element of the Christian's life; "day" is the sphere in which the light-possessed men move; it culminates in "the day of the Lord." This figure is even more familiar with St John than with St Paul. Christ applies it to His own person as well as His doctrine (Jo. viii. 12, ix. 5; cf. Ps. xxxvi. 9). The metaphor signifies (1) *moral purity* (see *vv.* 7 f.), (2) *saving effect* (see Ps. xxvii. 1; Isai. lx. 1 ff.; Jo. viii. 12, xi. 9; 2 Cor. iv. 6, &c.), (3) *mental enlightenment* (Eph. i. 17 f. &c.).

Πάντες...ὑμεῖς (cf. *v.* 27): the Apostles know of no exception; there are weak and faulty individuals in this Church (see *v.* 14), but *all* are claimed as true Christians and counted upon for the maintenance of the watchful hope which becomes the sons of light and day. Note the sustained emphasis on ὑμεῖς, ὑμᾶς, ὑμεῖς in *vv.* 4 f., by contrast to αὐτοῖς of *v.* 3.

Οὐκ ἐσμὲν νυκτὸς οὐδὲ σκότους. *We are not of night nor of darkness.* This sentence forms the negative counterpart of the last, and translates its Hebrew idiom ("sons of light," &c.) into the Greek genitive of *characteristic*. At the same time it looks forward, and belongs strictly to *v.* 6 instead of *v.* 5. It exchanges the 2nd person of the previous context for the 1st, in which the exhortation continues through *vv.* 6—10. This transition is a feature of St Paul's hortatory manner: he identifies his readers with himself as he proceeds, drawing them along with him into the trials and hopes common to the Christian life (cf. ii. 14). The same silent and almost unconscious change of grammatical person is observed in i. 9 f., iii. 2 f., iv. 6 f., 13 f.

Night, in contrast with *day*, is the period, and the state, of ignorance and estrangement from God (cf. iv. 5; Rom. xiii. 12 f.); while "darkness" is the element or empire of "night," the evil condition in which "the rest" (*v.* 6) live and act, and find their doom (cf. Eph. iv. 18, v. 8; Col. i. 13; 2 Cor. iv. 4; Jo. xii. 35; Matt. xxv. 30).

5 6] NOTES. 113

6. ἄρα οὖν μὴ καθεύδωμεν ὡς οἱ λοιποί, ἀλλὰ γρηγορῶμεν καὶ νήφωμεν: *accordingly then let us not sleep on like the rest, but let us be wakeful and sober.* This consequential clause should be separated from the last (v. 5 b) by a colon only, while the full-stop is placed in the middle of v. 5: "We are not of night, &c....; so then let us not sleep" (see the last note). "*Ἄρα* in classical usage never commences an independent sentence. But in later Greek it assumes a more strictly argumentative sense than in the earlier language, and so frequently occupies the first place" (Lightfoot). The combination ἄρα οὖν is peculiar to St Paul (the interrogative ἆρα οὖν...; occasionally in classical authors), occurring eight times in Romans, and once each in Galatians, Ephesians, 1 and 2 Thessalonians (also in Ignatius *ad Trall.* x.); it brings in the conclusion with a full and round emphasis, as though enforcing what reason and duty both demand. Ἄρα connotes a logical inference, a conformity of thought: οὖν draws the practical consequence, and is as freely used in exhortations as in statements; cf. τοιγαροῦν in iv. 8.

"Sleep" is natural to those who are "of the night" (cf. Eph. v. 11 ff.); it symbolizes the moral insensibility and helpless exposure to peril resulting from sin: cf. Rom. xiii. 11 f., "The night is far spent...it is high time to awake out of sleep," &c.; also Ps. xiii. 3. For καθεύδω in this ethical sense, cf. Eph. v. 14, Mk xiii. 36; distinguish the verb from κοιμάομαι, iv. 13, &c. (see note above). On οἱ λοιποί, see iv. 13.

Γρηγορέω, the antithesis of καθεύδω, is a verb of later Greek, a new present formed from ἐγρήγορα, the perf. of ἐγείρω. The word occurs many times in the warnings of Jesus—Matt. xxiv.—xxvi., Mk xiii. f., and Lk. xii.; in Acts xx. 31; thrice in Revelation; twice besides in Paul; and once in Peter (I. v. 8) coupled, as here, with νήφω. It enjoins the continued *wakeful activity* of a mind given to Christ's service and occupied with the thought of His coming. The Lord's return is the chief object of this "watching" (v. 2; 1 Cor. i. 7; 2 Pet. iii. 12; Lk. xii. 37); *prayer* is specified as its accompaniment in Col. iv. 2, Mk xiv. 38, &c. Watching protects against the "thief" (vv. 2 f.; Lk. xii. 39): thus Chrysostom, Ἐπὶ γὰρ τῶν ἐγρηγορότων καὶ ἐν φωτὶ ὄντων, κἂν γένηταί τις εἴσοδος λῃστοῦ, οὐδὲν λυμανεῖσθαι δυνήσεται.

Νήφωμεν prescribes the moral, as γρηγορῶμεν the mental, side of the attitude and temper befitting the "sons of day." In νήφειν the literal and ethical senses are combined; the word excludes, with actual drunkenness (cf. v. 7; Lk. xii. 45 f., xxi. 34; Rom. xiii. 12, &c.), all immoderation and self-indulgence (cf. 1 Pet. iv. 7, σωφρονήσατε καὶ νήψατε εἰς προσευχάς; νηφάλιος, 1 Tim. iii. 2, Tit. ii. 2, &c.). In this connexion, the term deprecates excitability and credulity about the Parousia (cf. II. ii. 1 ff.). Καὶ γὰρ ἐν ἡμέρᾳ, ἂν γρηγορῇ μέν τις μὴ νήφῃ δέ, μυρίοις περιπεσεῖται δεινοῖς, ὥστε ἐγρηγόρσεως ἐπίτασις ἡ νῆψίς ἐστιν (Chrysostom).

7. The υἱοὶ ἡμέρας must be γρηγοροῦντες and νήφοντες, for the opposite conditions belong to the σκότος and are proper to its children: οἱ γὰρ καθεύδοντες νυκτὸς καθεύδουσιν, καὶ οἱ μεθυσκόμενοι νυκτὸς μεθύουσιν, *for those that sleep, sleep by night, and those who get drunk are drunken by night*,—day is no time for such indulgences. To be drunk by day was a monstrous, unheard-of thing (Acts ii. 15). "Μεθύσκομαι notat actum, μεθύω statum vel habitum" (Bengel); for the former—"to make oneself drunk," *sich betrinken*—cf. Lk. xii. 45, Eph. v. 18; for the latter, Acts ii. 15, Rev. xvii. 6. The *genitive* of time is partitive, signifying a whole within which something happens or is done: νυκτός, *by night*; but νυκτί, *at night*; νύκτα, *through the night, all night* (Lk. xxi. 37; Acts xxvi. 7). The verse is an adage, adduced in its literal sense.

8. ἡμεῖς δὲ ἡμέρας ὄντες νήφωμεν : *but let us, since we are of the day* (not *qui diei sumus*, Vulg., &c., as if οἱ...ὄντες; but *quum diei simus*), *be sober*. The νήφω of verse 6 is resumed, with the added force gathered from verse 7, and to be supported by the participial clauses that follow. "As the metaphor of sleep is applied to the careless and indifferent, so that of *drunkenness* to the reckless and profligate. The one is to the other as positive to negative sin" (Lightfoot): νήφωμεν forbids everything wild or unbridled (cf. ἐκνήψατε in 1 Cor. xv. 34). The simile of the sequel identifies the Christian's "soberness" with that of the soldier under arms and on guard, in whom drunkenness, or sleep, would be a crime. The same association of thought appears in Rom. xiii. 12, and again in 1 Pet. i. 13,—ἀναζωσάμενοι...νήφοντες τελείως ἐλπίσατε κ.τ.λ.

ἐνδυσάμενοι θώρακα πίστεως καὶ ἀγάπης, καὶ περικεφαλαίαν ἐλπίδα σωτηρίας : *putting on the breastplate of faith and love, and (by way of) helmet the hope of salvation*. The aorist partic. attached to the cohortative present specifies an act that forms a part of the exhortation : νήφωμεν enjoins a state; ἐνδυσάμενοι an act belonging to the state, and that goes to determine and characterize it. The daylight rouses the soldier : if he has slept, with the dawn he is awake and alert ; if he has spent the night in carousals, he is instantly sobered ; at the bugle-call he dons his armour, and steps out to his post vigilant and steady. In Rom. xiii. 12 f. the same figure is still more graphically applied. Cf., for the *military* style of the passage, iv. 16 and notes. The θώραξ κ.τ.λ. form the *day-dress* of the Christian warrior. Πίστεως καὶ ἀγάπης, genitives of *apposition*. "Veluti ad arma conclamat, ut ostendat non esse dormiendi tempus. Belli quidem nomen subticet; verum dum nos armat thorace et galea, proeliandum esse admonet" (Calvin). The armour-simile (cf. 2 Cor. vi. 7, x. 4 ff.; Rom. vi. 13, xiii. 12; Eph. vi. 11 ff.) is not original in St Paul, but only its application and working out. Its use is based, doubtless, on Isai. lix. 17 (LXX): ἐνεδύσατο δικαιοσύνην ὡς θώρακα, καὶ περιέθετο περικεφαλαίαν σωτηρίου ἐπὶ τῆς κεφαλῆς; cf. also Wisd. v. 19; Baruch v. 2. In Isaiah *God* is the warrior, girding Himself to fight for the salvation of His people.

St Paul developes the above image with greater completeness, and somewhat differently, in a much later passage, Eph. vi. 13—17. He thinks here only of *defensive* weapons—breastplate and helmet—since the soldier is guarding himself against surprise. "The breastplate of faith and love" protects the heart, the centre of life and spring of the vital forces; to this quarter Faith and Love are assigned. These virtues are divided in Ephesians between "shield" and "breastplate." The "helmet" is alike in both passages—there styled "salvation," here the "hope of salvation," Hope being a key-note of this Epistle. For this last defence the next two verses supply the ground. The correspondence of "hope" with the "helmet" lies in the place of the helmet as the crown of the soldier's armour, its brightest and most conspicuous piece, covering the *head* which invites attack; cf. ii. 19, where ἐλπίς is associated with στέφανος καυχήσεως; also Rom. v. 2; Heb. iii. 6. Hope is held high, and shines out.

Σωτηρία (cf. σώζω, ii. 16) embraces, in St Paul and the N.T., the entire well-being that the Gospel brings (II. ii. 13 f.; Eph. i. 13), both to the individual man and to the world. It is identified specifically with its two essential elements or moments—of ἄφεσις ἁμαρτιῶν (Lk. i. 77, &c.), and of deliverance from the grave and from the condemnation of the Last Day (Ph. i. 19; 2 Tim. ii. 10; 1 Pet. i. 5, &c.): in the synonymous ἀπολύτρωσις this double reference is conspicuous; see Eph. i. 7, 14. Σωτηρία here stands opposed to ὀργή, as in Rom. i. 16—18, v. 9, since the present salvation from sin effected in believers by God's "grace," and realized in "forgiveness" (Eph. i. 7, 13, iii. 1—8), gives assurance of eventual salvation from sin's future penalties and fatal consequences in another world (Rom. v. 9 f., vi. 22 f., &c.).

Faith, love, hope—the Apostle's triad of graces; see notes on i. 3. "Faith" is directed especially toward God and Christ (i. 9, iv. 14;

1 Jo. v. 4 f., &c.), "love" toward one's neighbour (iv. 9 f.; II. i. 3, &c.); "hope" concerns oneself. Ἐλπίς seems here to be the μείζων τούτων (cf. 1 Cor. xiii. 13).

9. ὅτι οὐκ ἔθετο ἡμᾶς ὁ Θεὸς εἰς ὀργὴν ἀλλὰ εἰς περιποίησιν σωτηρίας κ.τ.λ., *because God did not appoint us unto wrath, but to (the) securing of salvation through our Lord Jesus Christ*. Ὅτι is read by Hofmann as *explicative* not *causative*, as stating the content of ἐλπὶς σωτηρίας (v. 8) rather than the reason for it—"a hope *that God did not appoint us*," &c.; cf. 2 Cor. v. 11, where ἐλπίζομεν is complemented by a perfect infinitive. But the common interpretation is more natural. Ἔθετο εἰς has "a partially Hebraistic tinge" (Ellicott); the idiom is parallel to לְ שׂוּם, לְ שִׁית, לְ נָתַן; but this is not incorrect Greek: see 1 Tim. i. 12; 2 Tim. i. 11; Acts xiii. 47; 1 Pet. ii. 8—the last the only precise parallel; and cf. Jer. ii. 7, xxv. 12, &c. (LXX). Cf. with εἰς ὀργὴν θέσθαι Rom. ix. 22, σκεύη ὀργῆς κατηρτισμένα εἰς ἀπώλειαν: in the (hypothetical) event of "appointing unto wrath" the Divine foreordination supposes foresight, and takes into account all the moral conditions of the case; see Rom. viii. 29, for the opposite case of predestination to life. That God cherishes no angry purpose toward the Thessalonians, that there is no θησαυρὸς ὀργῆς (Rom. ii. 5) laid up for them in His plans but an opposite destiny (i. 4; II. ii. 13 f.); of this the writers are assured by all that they know of them (see i. 5 ff., &c.). *On this ground* (ὅτι κ.τ.λ.) the readers may with a joyful confidence "put on" the "helmet of ἐλπὶς σωτηρίας": cf. Rom. v. 2—11; 2 Cor. i. 7, 21 f., iv. 16 ff., &c. Rom. viii. 31—39 is a virtual commentary on this passage. Ἔθετο...εἰς περιποίησιν σωτηρίας reminds us of ἐκλογή (i. 4); the verb implies the *authority* with which God "called" the Thessalonians (ii. 12), and His gracious *intentions* towards them: cf. iii. 3; also 1 Tim. i. 12, θέμενος εἰς διακονίαν.

Περιποίησις (from περιποιέομαι, *to make* (to remain) *over for oneself*) signifies in its primary active sense *obtaining permanently, making secure* some desired object (in the O. T. frequently, *preserving alive*)—so here "in acquisitionem salutis" (Vulg.), "ad salutem obtinendam" (Beza); see II. ii. 14; Heb. x. 39; 2 Paral. xiv. 13; for the verb, 1 Tim. iii. 13; Lk. xvii. 33; Acts xx. 28; Isai. xliii. 21; 1 Macc. vi. 44: this usage is also classical. The noun acquired a further passive meaning, and represents in Mal. iii. 17 (LXX) סְגֻלָּה, *peculium, a treasure, prize*—ἔσονταί μοι...εἰς περιποίησιν; hence λαὸς εἰς περιποίησιν, in 1 Pet. ii. 9 (= λαόν μου ὃν περιεποιησάμην, Isai. xliii. 21); the like signification is found in Eph. i. 14, εἰς ἀπολύτρωσιν τῆς περιποιήσεως (see J. A. Robinson's *Commentary*). Lightfoot regards the περιποίησις as *God's* act, and so renders, after the Old Latin, "for the adoption of (consisting in) salvation," thus making περιποίησις synonymous with ἐκλογή (i. 4); as though the Apostle's thought were that God has destined the Thessalonians not to be objects of His anger but of His appropriative and saving grace. The parallel passage in Ep. II. does not seem, however, to admit of this interpretation of περιποίησις, and it is far from obvious here; *vv*. 6—8 incite the readers to a wakeful, soldierlike activity, such as will be crowned by the "*winning* of salvation," the glorious end for which "God destined" them when He first "called them to His own kingdom and glory" (ii. 12),—the soldier's prize; cf. 1 Tim. vi. 12, ἀγωνίζου τὸν καλὸν ἀγῶνα...ἐπιλαβοῦ τῆς αἰωνίου ζωῆς. This final attainment of salvation, like its beginning (Rom. v. 2 ; cf. v. 9—11), comes *through Christ*: see II. i. 7 ff.; 2 Tim. iv. 18 ; 1 Cor. xv. 57. For "the Lord Jesus Christ" is the Mediator of salvation, from the first step to the last. The whole basis of redemption, the ground of the believer's hope of its accomplishment, is laid down in the next verse:—

10. **τοῦ ἀποθανόντος περὶ ἡμῶν, ἵνα...ἅμα σὺν αὐτῷ ζήσωμεν**, *who died for us, that...together with Him we might live*. Περὶ ἡμῶν specifies "us" as the objects of the Saviour's death, those "*about*" whom He was concerned in dying; the reading ὑπὲρ ἡμῶν might signify those "for the good of" whom He died—but "this distinction is growing dull" in the κοινή (Moulton); ἀντί would have been required to signalize the vicarious nature of the death, as in 1 Tim. ii. 6, Matt. xx. 28.

The main point is that *His death* secures *our life*; thus it gives a sure warrant for the cherished ἐλπὶς σωτηρίας (*v*. 8). Further, the "life" which Christ's death secures for those resolved to "win" it (*v*. 9), is a *life associated*, indeed *identified, with His* (ἅμα σὺν αὐτῷ: cf. for the phrase, iv. 17); He died for the very end that we might partake of His deathless life: cf. Jo. vi. 51, x. 10 f., 18 ; also Rom. v. 10, vi. 4 ff. ; 2 Cor. iv. 10 ff., v. 14 ff. ; Rev. i. 5 f., 18, &c. In His "dying that we might live *along with Him*," Christ's own resurrection is taken for granted (cf. iv. 14). The principle which connects the Saviour's death with the life, present and ultimate, of His people is assumed, but not drawn out, in this passage; it was present to the mind of the readers, or these words would have been meaningless. The propitiatory atonement which Christ made upon the cross for the sins of mankind, constitutes the indispensable link; this clause involves the teaching about redemption by the death and resurrection of Jesus, which is distinctive of the second group of the

Pauline Epp.: see Rom. iii. 21—26, iv. 25—v. 11, vi. 1—11, viii. 1—4; Gal. ii. 10—21, iii. 9—14; 2 Cor. v. 14—vi. 2. The whole theology of the Cross is latent here. In writing to the Corinthians and referring to his preaching at the very time when the Thessalonian letters were penned, St Paul calls his doctrine simply " the word of the cross" (1 Cor. i. 17 f., 23, ii. 2); cf., for an earlier period, Acts xiii. 38 f., Gal. iii. 1, vi. 14. "In his earliest writings this doctrine was present to St Paul's mind, though he has busied himself generally in these Epistles with other matters. It was not, therefore, as has been maintained, an aftergrowth of his maturer reflexions" (Lightfoot). See further the *Introd.* pp. xxv ff., and Milligan's *Commentary*.

In ἅμα σὺν αὐτῷ lies St Paul's other fundamental doctrine of the believer's *union with Christ in His heavenly life*, which is the complement of his doctrine of *union with Christ in His sacrificial death for sin*: see, on this correspondence, 2 Cor. v. 15, 21; Rom. vi. 5—11; Gal. ii. 19 f.; Rom. xiv. 8 f. Risen from the grave, our Saviour "lives" evermore "to God"; "death no longer lords it over Him." And those who are Christ's, being "cemented to the Lord in one Spirit" (1 Cor. vi. 17), share the life which flows from the Head through all His earthly members. This "life hid with Christ in God" (Col. iii. 3) is, in St Paul's view, "life indeed" (1 Tim. vi. 19); ζήσωμεν is emphatic: "that...together with Him we might *live*,"— not dying even though we "sleep"; cf. Jo. vi. 50 f., xi. 25 f.

The parenthetical clause, εἴτε γρηγορῶμεν εἴτε καθεύδωμεν, takes up into this sentence the comfort the Apostles had given their readers in § 8. The life of union with Christ which He died to procure for men, is untouched by mortality: He "died for us, in order that, *whether we be waking or sleeping*, together with Him we should live." Just as our natural life holds its course unbroken through waking or sleeping hours, so our spiritual life in Christ continues whether we are awake to this world or the body lies asleep in the grave (cf. Matt. xxii. 32); the Christian dead are οἱ νεκροὶ ἐν Χριστῷ, iv. 16, and return to us σὺν αὐτῷ, when "God shall bring" Jesus back to the world He left (iv. 14; see notes). Hence we gather that "the sleeping" are living somewhere with and in Christ; their "sleep" makes no vital difference: cf. Rom. viii. 38 f.; Jo. xiv. 19 b.

The verbs γρηγορέω and καθεύδω, understood ethically in *vv.* 6 f., by a change of metaphor become synonyms for natural life and death; see note on κοιμάομαι, iv. 13. This figurative use of καθεύδω (=κοιμάομαι) is a Biblical *hap. legomenon* (cf. καλὸς νέκυς, οἷα καθεύδων, Bion I. 71); it is suggested by the context (*vv.* 6 ff.), and γρηγορέω matches it in meaning. See Rom. xiv. 7 ff., where Christ's lordship over His people is declared to extend to the world beyond death: ἐάν τε ζῶμεν ἐάν τε ἀποθνήσκωμεν, τοῦ κυρίου ἐσμέν· εἰς τοῦτο γὰρ Χριστὸς ἀπέθανεν καὶ ἀνέστη, ἵνα καὶ νεκρῶν καὶ ζώντων κυριεύσῃ; cf., in this light, Eph. iv. 9 f. and Rev. i. 18 with the passage before us. The subjunctive after εἴτε, in place of indic., occurs also in 1 Cor. xiv. 5, Phil. iii. 11, and might be justified by later Greek usage; but here it appears to be due to the influence of ἵνα just preceding, the subordinate conditional clause being let into the final clause; see Winer-Moulton, p. 368. The aorist ζήσωμεν is antithetical to ἀποθανόντος, denoting the "life" which "Christ died" to procure "for us," not as a continued state but as a single fact, a definite attainment won for us by Christ's death and holding good alike in our "waking" or "sleeping." For the *aorist* of ζάω, cf. Lk. xv. 24; Rom. vii. 9 (contrast ἔζων with ἀνέζησεν), xiv. 9; Gal. ii. 19; Tit. ii. 12; 1 Jo. iv. 9; Rev. ii. 8, xx. 4 f.: the *present*, on the other hand, in iii. 8, iv. 15 above; Rom. xiv. 8; 2 Cor. v. 15, &c.

11. **Διὸ παρακαλεῖτε ἀλλήλους**, a repetition of iv. 18, showing that the matter of this section is closely bound up with that of the last; their misgiving about the lot of Christians dying prematurely before the Lord's return, and their uncertainty about the precise time of the return, were troubling the Thessalonian believers in the same way. Διό however (cf. iii. 1) replaces ὥστε: the former throws the reader back upon the ground of encouragement just given (*vv.* 9 f.); the latter particle carried him onward to the encouragement to be gathered from the previous words.

καὶ οἰκοδομεῖτε εἰς τὸν ἕνα, *and edify each the other*—lit. "one the one." Εἰς τὸν ἕνα (= ἀλλήλους) is "a rather late, though not unclassical expression": so Lightfoot, who finds the idiom in Theocritus xxii. 65, εἰς ἐνὶ χεῖρας ἄειρον; 1 Cor. iv. 6 affords the only N.T. parallel, where, however, the addition of κατὰ τοῦ ἑτέρου makes the phrase εἷς ὑπὲρ τοῦ ἑνός run more smoothly. In later Epp. ἑαυτούς serves as the variant for ἀλλήλους: see Col. iii. 13; Eph. iv. 31 f.; Phil. ii. 3; cf. *v.* 13 below. There is no occasion to refer the repetition of the numeral to Syriac (Aramaic) idiom; still less to turn εἷς into εἰς τὴν ἕνα, making the prepositional phrase equal to ἕως ἑνός, Rom. iii. 12 ("to the last man") —a harsh and unsuitable expression here), or rendering, as in Eph. ii. 15, "into the one" (the new Christian man, in whom all differences are reconciled)—which again is incongruous and far-fetched.

This is the first appearance of the Christian figure οἰκοδομέω (οἰκοδομή), which plays so large a part in St Paul's writings (cf. however Matt. vii. 24 ff.), and contains implicitly his great conception of the

Church as the οἶκος or ναὸς θεοῦ : see 1 Cor. iii. 9—17 ; 2 Cor. vi. 16; Eph. ii. 20 ff. ; 1 Tim. iii. 15 ; 2 Tim. ii. 19 ff. καθὼς καὶ ποιεῖτε. Cf. iv. 1, 9 f., and notes ; also II. iii. 4; and similar expressions in Rom. xv. 14, 1 Cor. xi. 2, 2 Pet. i. 12.

§ 10. v. 12—15. The Church's Internal Discipline.

The specific ὑστερήματα of this Church's faith (iii. 10) are now made good, in ch. iv. 1—v. 11, so far as they can be by Apostolic admonition and comfort. On the basis of the instruction thus given, the readers were urged to "encourage" and to "edify one another " (iv. 18, v. 11). But (δέ, v. 12) the office of exhortation, while devolving on any Christian brother who can speak a word of comfort to the sorrowing or of help to the feeble and timid, falls chiefly on the leaders of the community (οἱ προϊστάμενοι, v. 12). Thus the writers, in drawing their Letter to a close, find occasion to speak of these, (a) bidding the Church recognize their position and lovingly appreciate their work (vv. 12 f.). Having commended to the goodwill of the Church its officers, the Apostles (b) turn to the latter and charge them, on their side, to be faithful, helpful, and patient toward the more troublesome or weak members of Christ's flock, to prevent the retaliation of evil and to promote every kind of well-doing, both within and without the Christian fellowship (vv. 14 f.). The distinction just drawn between (a) and (b), which is insisted on by the Greek interpreters and recognized by the paragraph-division of WH, is indeed doubtful; but the varied expression, ἐρωτῶμεν δὲ ὑμᾶς and παρακαλοῦμεν δὲ ὑμᾶς, of vv. 12 and 14 is best explained by supposing that the writers appeal, with conversational freedom, first to the Church at large respecting its προϊστάμενοι, and then to the latter respecting the difficult part of their duties to the former. This tacit distinction between the ὑμᾶς of v. 14 and that of v. 12 accounts for the formal repetition of phrase with which the two short sections are introduced; the νουθετεῖν, moreover, required in v. 14, should, in consistency, be expected from the νουθετοῦντες of v. 12. The four hortatory offices prescribed in v. 14 would, in the nature of the case, devolve chiefly, though not exclusively, on the προϊστάμενοι. In v. 15 the exhortation reverts without formal transition to the body of the Church addressed throughout the Letter. At the same time, the whole of vv. 14 f. might be addressed suitably to "the brethren" at large; in favour of this construction the repeated, and unqualified, ἀδελφοί of vv. 12 and 14 seems to speak. Upon this view of the connexion—preferred by recent interpreters— v. 14 resumes, after the introductory reference to the Church-officers in vv. 12 f., and particularizes the παρακαλεῖτε κ. οἰκοδομεῖτε of v. 11, as though the Apostles wrote : "Now while we bid you respect your Church leaders, &c., we urge you on your own part to admonish the disorderly and console the sad, &c., amongst yourselves"; but would not αὐτοί, or the like, have been attached to νουθετεῖτε (by way of distinction from νουθετοῦντας, v. 13) in this case? See the discussion of Bornemann on the connexion of thought, in pp. 228—231 of Meyer's *Kommentar*[6]. On this section see Hort's *Christian Ecclesia*, pp. 125 ff.

12. Ἐρωτῶμεν δὲ ὑμᾶς, ἀδελφοί, εἰδέναι τοὺς κοπιῶντας ἐν ὑμῖν κ.τ.λ. But we ask you, brothers, to know those that toil among you, &c. For the ἐρωτᾶν of *request*, and its difference from παρακαλεῖν (v. 14), see note on iv. 1. The note of personal urgency in this word indicates some difficulty existing at Thessalonica on the point in question; certain members of the Church lightly regarded the προϊστάμενοι,— *scil.* "the disorderly" (v. 14 ; cf. iv. 11 f.; II. iii. 11 ff.), men disposed to resent admonition.

Εἰδέναι bears a pregnant force in this connexion—"*to know* those that toil, &c., *as such, to know* them *for what they are*" (cf. 1 Cor. xvi. 15); or, more generally, "*to know* them *properly*, *to know what you possess* in them," much as in 1 Cor. ii. 2, 12, Jo. vii. 28 f., viii. 19, 55. There is no need to import the looser Hebraistic use of οἶδα, and its synonyms, from the LXX rendering of יָדַע.

(τοὺς κοπιῶντας ἐν ὑμῖν) καὶ προϊσταμένους ὑμῶν ἐν κυρίῳ καὶ νουθετοῦντας ὑμᾶς, (*those that toil amongst you*) *and preside over you in the Lord and admonish you*. The three participles, bound by the vinculum of the single article, describe one and the same set of persons,—probably the πρεσβύτεροι who figure in the earliest Church organization carried over from the Judæan to the Pauline Christian communities : see Acts xi. 30, xiv. 23, xx. 17 ; Tit. i. 5 ; 1 Tim. v. 1, &c.; Jam. v. 14 ; 1 Pet. v. 1. These are included in the ἡγούμενοι of Heb. xiii. 7, 17, 24. Approved "elders" are described in 1 Tim. v. 17 as οἱ καλῶς προεστῶτες πρεσβύτεροι (amongst whom "those who labour in word, &c." are "especially" distinguished), their function being compared to that of a good father "*presiding* well over his own house" (1 Tim. iii. 4 f., 12). Like ἡγούμενος, however, προϊστάμενος is not a technical term of office implying stated presidency in Church meetings; it is "a word usually applied to informal leaderships and managements of all kinds" (Hort), as in Rom. xii. 8, xvi. 2 (προστάτις ; cf. Tit. iii. 8, 14). The existence at Thessalonica, so early, of distinct Church-officers may be probably, but not certainly, inferred from this passage ; these προϊστάμενοι, like the family of Stephanas in Corinth

(1 Cor. xvi. 15 ff.), may have "presided" only in the sense that they took spontaneously a leading part in Church business and discipline (but see note on ἐν κυρίῳ below): this appeal is parallel to 1 Cor. xvi. 15 f., and has the words εἰδέναι and κοπιᾶν in common with that passage. St Paul emphasizes the *service* done to the community by these leaders—οἱ κοπιῶντες...διὰ τὸ ἔργον αὐτῶν—not their authority. For κοπιᾶν, see note to κόπος, ii. 9. Ἐν ὑμῖν might signify "on," rather than "among you" (so Winer-Moulton, p. 483), as denoting the *matter*, *substratum*, of the labour, but less suitably here; the toil exercised *amongst* the Thessalonians (cf. i. 5, ii. 7) should be "known" to them. For ἐν κυρίῳ, see note, iv. 1: this adjunct attaches to the position of the προϊστάμενοι a more weighty and solemn character; it appears to connote *authority* upon their part, since it bases their relation to the Church upon the connexion of both parties with "the Lord": His Lordship underlies their leadership.

In the third place, the Church-leaders are commended to esteem as νουθετοῦντες ὑμᾶς. Νουθεσία is the primary duty enjoined upon them in *v.* 14 (supposing these to be specifically addressed there); it comes last here, being that in which the offence of their service lay. So Theodore paraphrases εἰδέναι...τοὺς νουθ. κ.τ.λ., "non resultantes illis, quando vos corripere volunt." Νουθετέω (= ἐν τῷ νῷ τίθημι) means "to put one in mind of " (*ans Herz legen*) that one has forgotten or might forget; it bears an ethical, sometimes a disciplinary, sense (cf. νουθετεῖν πληγαῖς, in Aristophanes); hence its application to "the unruly" in *v.* 14 and II. iii. 15 (cf. 1 Cor. iv. 14); it implies kindly, hopeful "admonition." The word is confined to St Paul (including Acts xx. 31) in the N.T. Νουθετεῖν is distinguished from διδάσκειν in Col. i. 28, iii. 16, the latter appealing to the understanding, the former to the conscience and will; it is the function of the ποιμήν as distinguished from the διδάσκαλος of Eph. iv. 11.

13. καὶ ἡγεῖσθαι αὐτοὺς ὑπερεκπερισσοῦ ἐν ἀγάπῃ διὰ τὸ ἔργον αὐτῶν, *and to regard them in love in the most supereminent degree because of their work.* The words ἡγεῖσθαι...ἐν ἀγάπῃ (put last for emphasis) may be read as one complete expression—so Chrysostom and Theodore, the Vulgate (*habeatis ..in charitate*), Beza (*charos ducatis*), Hofmann, Ellicott, Lünemann, Schmiedel; most other interpreters, with the Eng. Ver., treat ἐν ἀγάπῃ as a detached adjunct to ἡγεῖσθαι. The verb by itself hardly bears the sense of "esteem" (Lightfoot thinks that the adverb ὑπερεκπ. supplies this connotation); it can be read *in malam* or *in bonam partem* according to the definition: hence ὡς ἐχθρὸν ἡγεῖσθαι in II. iii. 15; cf. Phil. ii. 6, iii. 8, 1 Tim. i. 12, Heb. x. 29, xi. 11, &c.

For ἡγεῖσθε...ἐν ἀγάπῃ, cf. Jo. xv. 9 f. ; Jud. 21: the construction of Phil. ii. 29, ἐντίμους (=ἐν τιμῇ) ἔχετε, and Phm. 17, resembles that here employed; so Rom. i. 28 (ἔχειν ἐν ἐπιγνώσει); and Thuc. II. 18. 3, 21. 3, &c. (ἔχειν ἐν ὀργῇ, &c.). Schmiedel supplies the parallels ποιεῖσθαι ἐν ὀλιγωρίᾳ from Thuc. IV. 5, VII. 3. 2; λαμβάνειν ἐν πόθῳ, from Sophocles *Oed. Col.* 1679; see also Liddell and Scott on ποιεῖσθαι ἐν (s.v. ποιεῖσθαι, A. v.), the classical equivalent of ἡγεῖσθαι ἐν. Ἐν ἀγάπῃ =the predicate ἠγαπημένους (cf. Rom. ix. 25), and something more: the προϊστάμενοι are to be "held dear" in that sphere and upon that ground of love wherein the Church has its being: cf. iii. 12; 1 Cor. xvi. 14.

Ἡγεῖσθαι...ἐν ἀγάπῃ is qualified by the triple Pauline intensive ὑπερ-εκ-περισσῶς, "beyond-exceeding-abundantly" (cf. note on ὑπερεκπερισσοῦ, iii. 10—this precise form is *hap. leg.*; also περισσοτέρως, ii. 17) ; and by διὰ τὸ ἔργον αὐτῶν, stating the special reason for the extraordinary regard of love due to the Thessalonian leaders, in accordance with the character given to them as κοπιῶντες in *v.* 12. In "work" this Church excelled, and work it knew how to appreciate; see note on τοῦ ἔργου κ.τ.λ., i. 3.

This clause has given occasion to some caustic observations, such as that of Erasmus *ad loc.*: " Hunc locum oportet annotare diligenter episcopos...Paulus jubet eos haberi in honore propter opus, non propter inanem titulum"; and Calvin, still more sharply, "Unde sequitur e numero Pastorum excludi omnes otiosos ventres." Wyclif inferred from the text that tithes might be refused to idle or incompetent priests,—an inference which the Roman Catholic Estius earnestly contests.

εἰρηνεύετε ἐν ἑαυτοῖς, *be at peace amongst yourselves*; cf. Mk ix. 50. Supposing ἑαυτοῖς (or αὐτοῖς) to be genuine (see Textual Note), then the general "peace" is to be kept through affectionate loyalty to the approved leaders; it was disturbed by the ἄτακτοι, whom the Church-officers had to "admonish" (*vv.* 12, 14). A sense not dissimilar is given by the harder reading ἐν αὐτοῖς, if this be understood, with Bornemann (who cites 1 Cor. vi. 2, xiv. 21, Mt. ix. 34, in illustration), as signifying "through them,"—on the basis of their leadership—"find your peace in them"; on this application of ἐν, see Winer-Moulton, pp. 485 f. The common rendering of ἐν αὐτοῖς by *cum eis* (Vulg.)—as though equivalent to μετ᾽ αὐτῶν (see Rom. xii. 18)—or *in eos* (toward them), is ungrammatical and inappropriate; the "ministry" exists to bind together the whole body of Christ, πρὸς τὸν καταρτισμὸν τῶν ἁγίων (Eph. iv. 12 ; cf. *v.* 16). The present imperative enjoins not the *making* of peace, like the aorist in 1 Macc. vi. 60, but the *maintaining* of it.

14. Παρακαλοῦμεν δὲ ὑμᾶς, ἀδελφοί. *But we exhort you, brothers.* Upon the analysis suggested at the head of the section, ὑμᾶς is distinctive: the writers now *speak to those spoken of* in vv. 12 f., viz. the Church-officers; ἐνταῦθα πρὸς τοὺς ἄρχοντας διαλέγεται (Chrysostom). They need to be "encouraged" (see notes on παρακαλέω, ii. 12, iv. 1, and παράκλησις, ii. 3) to the duties imposed on them, while the Church is "asked" (see note, v. 12) to pay them deference. Παρακαλέω is not often complemented by a sentence in direct narration; 1 Cor. iv. 16 and Acts ix. 38 give instances of this.

Three classes needing special pastoral care at Thessalonica—or, on the other view of the connexion, a specially interested attention on the part of the Church—are οἱ ἄτακτοι, οἱ ὀλιγόψυχοι, and οἱ ἀσθενεῖς—*the unruly, the pusillanimous,* and *the weak.* The first category the brethren are to *admonish,* the second to *comfort,* the third to *hold to* or *help.*

The attitude and disposition of the ἄτακτοι in this Church come to light in II. iii. 6 ff.—on which passage see the notes; see also *Introd.* pp. xxxi., xxxviii.; ch. iv. 11 f. already gave some hint of trouble of this sort. For νουθετεῖτε, see note to v. 12: the recurrence of this verb suggests that οἱ νουθετοῦντες of the former verse are the persons addressed in this; the disorder described in Ep. II. is of such a kind that those directing the business of the Church were bound to come into conflict with it. Ὀλιγόψυχος is a LXX word, used to render several Hebrew phrases denoting "broken in spirit" and the like (Isai. liv. 6, lvii. 15, &c.). St Paul's ὀλιγόψυχος is not therefore the μικρόψυχος of Aristotle (*Nic. Eth.* IV. 7—9), the opposite of the latter's μεγαλόψυχος—"the magnanimous, high-spirited man" so much commended by the philosophers; not generosity nor self-respect, but *courage, confidence* are wanting to him; ch. iv. 13 ff. illustrate this condition, and again II. ii. 2. On παραμυθέομαι, see note to ii. 11 above. Ἀντέχεσθαι uniformly means elsewhere "to hold by," "cleave to" a person or thing (Matt. vi. 24; Luke xvi. 13; Tit. i. 9), and bears this sense here: "the feeble" are apt to be neglected, or even cast off, through contempt and impatience of the trouble they give; *attaching oneself* to them is the way to help them and give them strength; cf. the synon. ἀντιλαμβάνεσθαι, e.g. in Acts xx. 35, ἐπιλαμβάνεσθαι in Heb. ii. 16. These ἀσθενεῖς are men "weak in faith" (Rom. xiv. 1), not "the sick" (as in 1 Cor. xi. 30) or "weak" in worldly resources (Acts xx. 35).

The ὀλιγόψυχοι and ἀσθενεῖς stand contrasted with the ἄτακτοι. The latter are overbold, and need to be checked; the former are despondent, and need stimulus and help. "Fainthearted" men think themselves "weak" when they are not so; encouragement may make them bold.

If the instructions of this verse apply to the προϊστάμενοι (see note on Παρακαλοῦμεν δὲ ὑμᾶς above), μακροθυμεῖτε πρὸς πάντας refers consequently to the body of the Church, in contrast with the three faulty classes already noticed; whereas εἰς πάντας in the next verse, contrasted with εἰς ἀλλήλους, looks to the world outside. The duties of Church office require in him who exercises them good temper and patience *all round* (πρὸς πάντας), even where infirmity or disorder is not in question. The μακρόθυμος, *longanimis*, is the opposite of the ὀξύθυμος (short-tempered): μακροθυμία implies *personal* relationship—patience (on the part of God or man) toward the troubles and provocations arising in human intercourse; whereas ὑπομονή (i. 3, &c.) is a brave endurance of the ills of life generally, of *trying things*; see Trench's *Syn.* § 53.

15. ὁρᾶτε μή τις κακὸν ἀντὶ κακοῦ τινὶ ἀποδῷ. *See (to it) that none pay back evil in return for evil to any one.* This further direction seems to be addressed, in keeping with the last, to the προϊστάμενοι: it is their duty to check and prevent every act of retaliation; they are responsible for the conduct of their brethren. On the other hand, the wide bearing of the antithetical (ἀλλά) clause which follows suggests the same comprehensive reference here. Had the writers, however, intended to warn individual members of the Church about their own conduct, they would, presumably, have used the 2nd person, ὁρᾶτε μὴ ἀποδῶτε (cf. Matt. viii. 4, xviii. 10, xxiv. 6; Matt. ix. 30 resembles this passage), or written τις ὑμῶν instead of the bare τις. For κακόν, see note on πονηρόν, *v.* 22. The same command, in general terms, is given in Rom. xii. 17 and 1 Pet. iii. 9; it echoes the teaching of our Lord in Matt. v. 43 ff.

ἀλλὰ πάντοτε τὸ ἀγαθὸν διώκετε [καὶ] εἰς ἀλλήλους καὶ εἰς πάντας, *but always pursue that which is good, [both] toward one another and toward all men.* This last injunction is not, by its nature, specific to Church-officers: if the five previous imperatives have been addressed to these, we must suppose the writers to turn here by a kind of mental gesture, dispensing with any particle of transition, to their readers at large, who were virtually (if not directly) admonished in μή τις κακὸν ...ἀποδῷ. For διώκειν in the sense of *practising, pursuing a line of conduct,* cf. Rom. xii. 13, xiv. 19; 1 Cor. xiv. 1; 1 Tim. vi. 11; 2 Tim. ii. 22: it implies *persistence* in good—not only in the way of reciprocity (by antithesis to κακὸν ἀντὶ κακοῦ), but in all other respects and contingencies. Τὸ ἀγαθόν is "the beneficial"; while denoting the morally good in chief, the term is not limited to this: cf. Rom. ii. 10, xiii. 3 f.; Gal. vi. 10; Eph. iv. 28; Phm. 14; Lk. vi. 35, ἀγαθοποιεῖτε καὶ δανίζετε. For εἰς ἀλλήλους κ.τ.λ., see iii. 12 and note; also note on πρὸς πάντας, v. 14.

Πάντοτε—occurring six times in this Letter, oftener than anywhere else in St Paul—means "on every occasion" (cf. i. 2); while ἀεί means "perpetually" (2 Cor. vi. 10): ἀδιαλείπτως in v. 17, i. 3, &c., is the negative equivalent of either.

§ 11. v. 16—24. DIRECTIONS FOR HOLY LIVING.

In § 7 (iv. 1—12) *the saintship* of the Thessalonians supplied the basis and the nerve of the Apostles' charge. The virtues of chastity, brotherly affection, and diligence in labour were enforced on the readers under the sense of their consecration to God; the indwelling of the Holy Spirit supplied the most powerful motive for the leading of a pure life (see iv. 3, 7 f.). The closing exhortations of the Epistle rest on the same principle. The appeal to "quench not the Spirit" forms their centre; and this leads up to an impressive prayer for the complete sanctification of those addressed (*vv.* 23 f.).

The last section was occupied with *social* and comparatively *external duties*; this deals with *personal obligations* and exercises of *internal piety*, which may be distinguished, (1) as they are of a general religious character (*vv.* 16—18), and (2) as they arise specifically from the new endowments of the Spirit enjoyed by the Church (*vv.* 19—22). In Rom. xiii. 6—21 there is found a similar but much longer train of hortatory epigrams.

16—18. Πάντοτε χαίρετε, ἀδιαλείπτως προσεύχεσθε, ἐν παντὶ εὐχαριστεῖτε. *Always rejoice; unceasingly pray; in everything give thanks.* The adverbs, emphatically prefixed to the three imperatives, continue the strain of *v.* 15 in its wide inclusiveness; see the note there on πάντοτε. The command to "rejoice always" is notable in a Letter addressed to a suffering people (see i. 6, ii. 14, iii. 2—4); it must have struck the readers as a paradox. St Paul had learnt the secret, which he thus virtually teaches—as he does expressly in Rom. v. 3—5—that sorrow endured for Christ's sake opens a new spring of joy: cf. 2 Cor. xii. 10; Col. i. 24; 1 Pet. iv. 12—14; also the Beatitudes of Matt. v. 10—12. St Paul's subsequent Letter, dated from prison, to the neighbouring Philippian Church (see Phil. iv. 4 f., also i. 29) is a descant on this theme.

The Christian's constant joy puts him in the mood to "pray without ceasing." Twice the Apostles have used the adverb ἀδιαλείπτως concerning their own grateful remembrance of their readers before God (i. 3, ii. 13): a crowd of other objects occupied their minds through the hours of each day; they could not be continuously thinking of this one Church, nor presenting it distinctly to God in every act of devotion, but they felt that it was never out of remembrance; thankfulness on its account mingled with and coloured all their thoughts at this time. In like manner Prayer is the accompaniment of the whole life of Christians—a stream always flowing, whether sensibly or in the background of consciousness; it forms the undercurrent of thought, which imparts its direction and tone to everything upon the surface. This unbroken course of prayer belongs to the "life hid with Christ in God" (Col. iii. 3).

18. ἐν παντὶ εὐχαριστεῖτε contains the same paradox, for the Thessalonians, as πάντοτε χαίρετε (see note above). "In everything,"— even in persecution and shame; cf. again Ph. i. 29, 2 Cor. xii. 9 f., &c. This too St Paul taught by example: see i. 2, iii. 9 f.; Acts xvi. 25. Ἐν παντί differs from περὶ παντός (i. 2, &c.) as denoting the *circumstances*, not the object, nor the occasion (ἐπί), of thanksgiving. For the phrase ἐν παντί (not to be limited by καιρῷ), cf. 2 Cor. vii. 5, 11, 16; Ph. iv. 6, 12. On εὐχαριστέω, see note to i. 2. Chrysostom's comment, τὸ ἀεὶ δηλονότι εὐχαριστεῖν, τοῦτο φιλοσόφου ψυχῆς, is very characteristic; to the Greek Christian, an intelligent piety was the true φιλοσοφία.

Prayer and Thanksgiving are companions in the language of Scripture and counterparts, as the two wings of the soul by which it rises toward God. The latter, however, may be tacitly included in προσεύχομαι,—a comprehensive term for devout address to God: see Ph. iv. 6, "In everything by prayer and by supplication, along with thanksgiving, let your requests be made known to God," where δέησις (cf. δέομαι, iii. 10 above) is distinguished from προσευχή as the "petition" for some specific boon, while "thanksgiving" for past blessings and for promised good accompanies both.

τοῦτο γὰρ θέλημα θεοῦ ἐν Χριστῷ Ἰησοῦ εἰς ὑμᾶς, *for this is God's will in Christ Jesus with regard to you.* The three foregoing precepts are thus linked together; they constitute one habit and temper, the spirit of a true devotion to God, so that τοῦτο includes them collectively. Τοῦτο γὰρ θέλημα κ.τ.λ. adduces not so much a reason for obedience to Divine commands, as an assurance of their practicability; the argument is not, "You *must* do it, for God so wills," but "Knowing that it is God's will, you *can* do it": cf. v. 24

below; also iv. 3 (see note), of which this sentence is a repetition; and Ph. ii. 13; 2 Cor. iii. 5, &c. As though the Apostles said: "You Thessalonian believers, so greatly afflicted and tempted to murmuring and despondence, are the objects of a special and gracious purpose on God's part. God intends your life to be one of constant prayer, constant joy and thanksgiving; and this is made possible for you in Christ." *In Christ Jesus* (the living, reigning Saviour: cf. note on this locution in ii. 14) the basis is laid and the sphere is found of all saving purpose and action on God's side (see e.g. 2 Cor. v. 19; 1 Cor. i. 30), and of all experience and attainment of Divine grace on man's side (Gal. iii. 14; Eph. ii. 13, &c.). This θέλημα is not a mere "resolve of God" made known through Christ, but a "volition" operative and effective "in" Him, like "all the promises of God" (2 Cor. i. 20). Εἰς ὑμᾶς, "(going out) unto you," "(directed) towards you": for εἰς denoting the *direction* of mind or moral activity, cf. *v.* 15, II. i. 11, Ph. i. 23, Acts xxvi. 6, &c.; and see Winer-Moulton, p. 495.

19, 20. τὸ πνεῦμα μὴ σβέννυτε, προφητείας μὴ ἐξουθενεῖτε. *The Spirit do not quench; prophesyings do not despise.* From *joy, prayer,* and *thanksgiving* it is a natural transition to *the Spirit* and *prophesying* (see i. 6; also Rom. viii. 26; Eph. vi. 18; Jud. 20). "Praying" and "prophesying" are kindred exercises (1 Cor. xi. 4). The R.V. reduces the stop between these injunctions to a semi-colon: they are parallel, the second explaining the first. Possibly, as Lightfoot says, "there was the same tendency amongst the Thessalonians to underrate prophecy in comparison with other more striking gifts of the Spirit, which St Paul condemns in writing to the Corinthians"; see 1 Cor. xiv. 1, ζηλοῦτε τὰ πνευματικά, μᾶλλον δὲ ἵνα προφητεύητε, and the discussion which follows. But the warning against *quenching* the Spirit is directed, surely, against rationalism rather than fanaticism, against the chill distrust of the more fervid spiritual manifestations which was excited in sober minds at Thessalonica by the extravagance, or insincerity, of such πνευματικοί as e.g. those "prophets" who are virtually censured in the warning of II. ii. 2, μήτε διὰ πνεύματος. The agitation and morbid anxiety respecting the Parousia, which both Epistles seek to allay, was fed by "prophesyings" upon this subject; in such prophesyings Millenarianism has at all times abounded. The scepticism thus awakened tended to discredit prophecy generally in this Church, and with it the whole supernatural agency of the Spirit. That this counsel has in view the reflective and critical part of the Church, is strongly suggested by the δοκιμάζετε of the next exhortation. But this caution is one which St Paul's general observation of the Greek temper might suggest, without any local occasion. For προφητεία, cf. Rom. xii. 6; 1 Cor. xiii. 2, xiv. 6: it comes by ἀποκάλυψις, as διδαχή by γνῶσις. Prediction is only one branch of "prophecy," which means etymologically the *forth-speaking* of that which was hidden in the mind of God and which comes to the προφήτης, for communication to others, through the specific inspiration of His Spirit; see Lightfoot's note *ad loc.*, and Cremer's *Lexicon* s.v. προφήτης. As to the dependence of προφητεία on τὸ πνεῦμα, see further Joel ii. 28 f. (iii. 1 f., in Hebrew text); Acts ii. 17, xix. 6, xxviii. 25; Lk. i. 67; Rev. i. 2 and 10, &c. Σβέννυτε is a N.T. *hap. legomenon*: since the Holy Spirit is a "fire" (Acts ii. 3; cf. Rom. xii. 11; Acts xviii. 25; Lk. xii. 49), the arrest of His action is described as a "quenching." As "resisting the Holy Spirit," in Acts vii. 51 (Isai. lxiii. 10), describes a perverse unbelief, so "quenching the Holy Spirit" describes a cold scepticism. Prophecy exhibited His working in its vehemence and ardour.

Ἐξουθεν-έω (also in the forms ἐξουδενέω, -όω), a word of the κοινή, "to make utterly nothing of," "reduce to nought," is frequent in St Paul (see 1 Cor. i. 28, 2 Cor. x. 10, &c.). This verb denotes contempt *objectively*, as it bears on the person or thing despised; while καταφρονέω (1 Cor. xi. 22) describes contempt *subjectively*, as it is in the mind of the despiser.

21. πάντα [δὲ] δοκιμάζετε, τὸ καλὸν κατέχετε: [but] *everything put to proof; the good hold fast*,—pres. imperative of settled rule and practice. Mark off this verse, again, from the foregoing by a colon or semi-colon: while "prophesyings" are not to be "despised," neither are they to be accepted wholesale and because of their pretensions. The chaff must be sifted out from the wheat. Prophecy is brought under a universal Christian rule laid down in πάντα δοκιμάζετε, which vindicates "private judgement" in religion, vv. 19, 20 having warned us beforehand against its *sceptical* or *prejudiced* use. For the purpose of discriminating true and false inspiration, the faculty of διάκρισις πνευμάτων (1 Cor. xii. 10) had been given by "the one and self-same Spirit," side by side with προφητεία. In 1 Cor. xii. 3 St Paul supplies a criterion for exercising this διάκρισις or δοκιμασία; 1 Cor. xiv. 29 exhibits this very faculty in exercise,— προφῆται δύο ἢ τρεῖς λαλείτωσαν, καὶ οἱ ἄλλοι διακρινέτωσαν. Similarly St John bids his readers μὴ παντὶ πνεύματι πιστεύειν ἀλλὰ δοκιμάζειν τὰ πνεύματα in his First Epistle, iv. 1, furnishing his test of "the spirits" in the context. Claims to inspiration, supernatural pheno-

mena, are therefore chiefly, though not exclusively, aimed at in πάντα δοκιμάζετε. For the meaning of δοκιμάζειν, see note on ii. 4. For the reading πάντα δέ—on the whole the more likely—see Textual Note.

Cyril of Alexandria quotes this passage several times, combining with it the famous apophthegm, γίνεσθε δόκιμοι τραπεζῖται, "Be ye approved money-changers" (testers of current coin), credited by other Fathers to our Lord, which is now generally ascribed to Him as a traditional ἄγραφον. Possibly, this saying of Jesus was in the writers' mind; if so, the allusion helps to elucidate the next clause (see note following). See Lightfoot's note *ad loc.*

Tὸ καλόν signifies what is *good* or *fine in quality*, and is so contrasted with τὸ κακόν, the *base*, in Rom. vii. 21; Heb. v. 14 (see also 2 Cor. xiii. 7; Gal. vi. 9), while ἀγαθός (see note on *v.* 15) is opposed to πονηρός, and to φαῦλος besides. For κατέχω in its other (adverse) sense, see II. ii. 6; in this sense, 1 Cor. xi. 2, xv. 2.

Verse 22 completes negatively the exhortation of *v.* 21: *testing* results in *holding fast* or *abstaining from* (κατέχειν or ἀπέχεσθαι ἀπό) the *good* or *evil* offered for choice. From the antithesis thus presented, in view of the application of δοκιμάζειν to the *testing of coin* (see note to ii. 4, and foregoing note on *v.* 21), it has been argued that ἀπὸ παντὸς εἴδους πονηροῦ signifies "from all bad *coinage*," as though εἶδος were synonymous with νόμισμα (cf. *specie*, from Latin *species*),— prevalent doctrines or moral practices being thus represented, it is supposed, under the figure of *currency*. But lexical evidence is wanting for such a use of εἶδος. This word denotes (*a*) *visible form, appearance* (as in Lk. iii. 22, ix. 29, &c.); or (*b*) *sight, appearance* in the abstract, as contrasted with *faith* (2 Cor. v. 7); or (*c*) *show, appearance*, in contrast with reality (like εἴδωλον, i. 9, e.g.)—the rendering of the A.V., which, beside its lack of parallels, gives a sense intrinsically weak, as it would recommend the studying of appearances (see, against this, Matt. xxiii. 5); (*d*) *kind, sort*, the most obvious rendering—a sense perfectly familiar in the κοινή though *hap. leg.* in Biblical Greek, and derived originally from philosophical usage. Our choice lies between (*a*) and (*d*). The former appears to be intended in the *ab omni specie mala* of the Vulgate, as though the Apostles meant: "Keep away from every evil sight," or "show," from all that is evil in the aspect of things about you, from the fleeting shows of the world. A better turn is given to the *species mala* by understanding it to mean that which *appears evil* in the eyes of others and would cause needless offence (cf. 1 Cor. viii. 13, x. 32 f.). The common rendering (as in R.V.), on which we must fall back, failing (a)—*from every kind of evil*—is open to the objection that πονηροῦ, thus rendered as a neuter (abstract) substantive, requires the article (like τὸ καλόν; cf. Rom. xii. 9). But this is not an invariable rule; "in Plato the anarthrous neuter singular for abstract ideas frequently occurs" (Kühner's *Grammatik*², II. § 462 *l*): see e.g. εἶδος ἀγαθοῦ in Plato *Repub*. 357 c. Thus πονηρόν stands for "evil" collectively, evil *quâ* evil: cf. πρὸς διάκρισιν καλοῦ τε καὶ κακοῦ in Heb. v. 14; also, for the use of εἶδος, Josephus *Ant*. VII. 4. 2, x. 3. 1, εἶδος μέλους, πονηρίας.

Τὸ καλόν is opposed by πονηρόν, as κακόν in *v*. 15 by τὸ ἀγαθόν. The phrasing was perhaps suggested by Job i. 1, 8, ii. 10,—ἀπεχόμενος ἀπὸ παντὸς πονηροῦ (κακοῦ) πράγματος; widening the prohibition to include the manifold πονηρά enticing their readers, the Apostles insert εἴδους into their sentence. For ἀπέχομαι ἀπό, see note on iv. 3,—a passage perhaps intentionally recalled in this dehortation; certainly πορνεία was one εἶδος πονηροῦ to be shunned at Thessalonica. The notion of πονηρός is that of "irredeemable badness," "intrinsic absolute badness" (see F. H. Chase: Essay on *The Lord's Prayer in the Early Church*, pp. 89 ff.); while κακός (*v*. 15) signifies *base, malicious, cowardly* (bad in quality and disposition).

23. **Αὐτὸς δὲ ὁ Θεὸς τῆς εἰρήνης—.** *But may the God of peace Himself...*: cf. iii. 11 (see note), and II. ii. 16, where a like contrast seems to be implied, under Αὐτὸς δέ, between human wish or effort and Divine power. Ph. ii. 12 f. ("Work out your own salvation, for God it is that worketh in you") illustrates the connexion between *vv*. 22 and 23: "Keep yourselves from...evil. But may God...sanctify you." Ὁ Θεὸς τῆς εἰρήνης, a favourite designation with St Paul in pious wishes (see II. iii. 16; Rom. xvi. 20, &c.), found also in Heb. xiii. 20. For εἰρήνη, see note on i. 1: God's distinguishing gift in the Gospel, that by which he signalizes His grace in the hearts of men; as the Christian God is ὁ Θεὸς τῆς εἰρήνης, so the Christian peace is ἡ εἰρήνη τοῦ Θεοῦ (Ph. iv. 7). The epithet recalls *v*. 13, εἰρηνεύετε ἐν ἑαυτοῖς; the directions of the previous context, from *v*. 12 onwards, are τὰ τῆς εἰρήνης κ. τὰ τῆς οἰκοδομῆς (Rom. xiv. 19); when the Church is at peace, the work of sanctification goes on. As from this gift of Peace, so God is specifically named from other of His χαρίσματα in Rom. xv. 5, 13, 2 Cor. xiii. 11, 1 Pet. v. 10; in each place suitably to the wish expressed. The prayer for Sanctification in iii. 11—13 above had *love* for its basis; this prayer rests on the thought of *peace*.

ἁγιάσαι ὑμᾶς ὁλοτελεῖς, *sanctify you to full completeness*,—*per omnia* (Vulg.), *ganz und gar* (de Wette), *nach eurer ganzen Person* (Schmiedel). Ὁλοτελής, *hap. leg.* in N.T., is a coinage of late Greek, found occasionally in Plutarch, and in Aquila's rendering of Deut. xiii. 17 (for כָּלִיל). It does not appear to be qualitative, as though denoting the completeness of sanctification by way of degree, but quantitative as signifying its range and unlimited comprehension; ὁλοτελεῖς is expounded by ὁλόκληρον...τὸ πνεῦμα καὶ ἡ ψυχὴ κ.τ.λ. in the sequel; thus Œcumenius, ὁλοτελεῖς· τοῦτ᾽ ἔστι σώματι κ. ψυχῇ. Ὁλοτελής and ὁλόκληρος are closely synonymous, both insisting on the *wholeness* of the process: the former is collective, the latter distributive—the one implying a totality from which no part is excluded, the other an integrity in which each part has its due place and proportion (*vollständig* and *vollkommen* respectively, Hofmann); for ὁλόκληρος, see Trench's *Syn.* § 22, and cf. Jam. i. 4, Acts iii. 16. In the LXX and in Philo, ὁλόκληρος (rendering the Hebrew שָׁלֵם) is regularly used of the sacrificial victims, which were required to be *sound* and *perfect* in every part, ὁλόκληρος κ. τέλειος or παντελής. The doubling of ὁλο- sustains the rhetorical effect of the seven times repeated παν- of vv. 14—22.

For ἁγιάζω, cf. notes on ἁγιωσύνη, iii. 13, and ἁγιασμός, iv. 3. The readers are already, by their calling and relations to God as believers in Christ, ἅγιοι, ἡγιασμένοι; what the Apostles ask in this closing prayer, up to which all the exhortations and warnings of the Epistle, and especially those of the last eleven verses, lead, is a sanctity impressed on the readers by God Himself, of such thoroughness moreover that it shall embrace and gather up into the integrity of a complete manhood every element and function of their nature, in which, that is to say, the soul and body shall participate no less than the spirit.

So the parallel clause, carrying forward the *sanctification* into *preservation* (note the reverse order in the prayer of Jo. xvii. 11—19), runs καὶ ὁλόκληρον ὑμῶν τὸ πνεῦμα καὶ ἡ ψυχὴ καὶ τὸ σῶμα...τηρηθείη, *and in full integrity may your spirit and your soul and your body...be preserved!* Ὑμῶν, standing in the Greek at the head of the triple subject and belonging to each member of it, we represent by the repeated "your," in order to bring out the distinctness, marked by the tripled article, with which the three several subjects are stated. The verb at the end is singular, in consonance with ὁλόκληρον at the beginning; there is one "keeping," embracing the totality of the man, but a keeping in which each of the three constituents has its place and share.

Over this passage the Trichotomists and Dichotomists wage war, who maintain respectively that Scripture distributes man's nature into three or two elements—*spirit, soul, and body*, or *spirit and flesh* (body). For the former theory, see Heard's *Tripartite Nature of Man*; Ellicott's *The Destiny of the Creature*, &c., and the note in his *Commentary* on this passage; or Delitzsch's *Biblical Psychology*: for the latter, Laidlaw's *Bible Doctrine of Man*, or Beck's *Biblical Psychology*; also the art. *Psychology* in Hastings' *Dict. of the Bible*, and Cremer's *Biblico-Theological Lexicon* s. vv. The nature of this passage forbids our finding a logical analysis in the three terms; they serve to make the wish exhaustive in its completeness.

The Apostles begin with the inmost—τὸ πνεῦμα, nearest to God who "is spirit" (Jo. iv. 24); for with man's spirit the Holy Spirit directly associates Himself (Rom. viii. 16, &c.), and it is the primary object of Divine salvation (cf. II. ii. 13; also 1 Cor. v. 5, xv. 45). They end with "the body," the vessel and envelope of the spirit (see 2 Cor. iv. 7, v. 1, &c.; if not iv. 4 above), the man's outer part, through which he belongs to the κόσμος and communicates with it. "The soul," poised between these two, is the individual self, the living personality in which flesh and spirit, common to each man with his fellows, meet and are actualized in *him*. When St Paul in 2 Cor. vii. 1 bids his readers "cleanse" themselves "from all defilement *of flesh and spirit*," that phrase covers the same ground as this, but contrasts the man's inner and outer relations; while the expression of 1 Pet. i. 22, "having purified *your souls*," fastens upon the individual man and his personality in its distinctive impulses and habits; here the entire man is surveyed, with his whole nature in its manifold aspects and functions, as the subject of sanctifying grace. The πνεῦμα is "kept," when no evil reaches the inner depths of our nature or disturbs our relations to God and eternity; the ψυχή, when the world of self is guarded and every personal motive and activity is holy; and the σῶμα, when our outward life and participation in the material world are sacred. The connexion between *sanctity* and *safety* lies in the fact that what is sanctified is given over to God, to be "kept" by Him for His own uses. The thought that Christ's disciples, οἱ ἐν Χριστῷ as St Paul would say, belong to God the Father and are therefore cast upon His almighty protection, is at the basis of our Lord's parting prayer in Jo. xvii. (see also Jo. vi. 37—45, x. 26—30); it comes out in the πιστὸς ὁ καλῶν of the next verse: cf. i. 4; II. ii. 13; Eph. i. 18 *b*; 2 Tim. i. 12, also Ps. cxxi.; Isai. xxvii. 3; "He will keep the feet of His saints," 1 Sam. ii. 9.

Between subject (τὸ πνεῦμα κ.τ.λ.) and verb (τηρηθείη) comes in the adverbial adjunct, **ἀμέμπτως ἐν τῇ παρουσίᾳ τοῦ κυρίου ἡμῶν Ἰησοῦ Χριστοῦ**: (*may your spirit*, &c., *be preserved*) *without blame in the appearing of our Lord Jesus Christ.* Ἐν τῇ παρουσίᾳ qualifies ἀμέμπτως: the blamelessness ("in holiness," iii. 13; see ἁγιάσαι ὑμᾶς above) is to be manifest "in," certified at, "the παρουσία" (cf. iii. 13, also ii. 19 and parallels); "the day will disclose it," 1 Cor. iii. 13. For παρουσία, see notes on ii. 19, &c.; and for τοῦ κυρ. Ἰ. Χ., i. 1, 3, &c. The grammatical attachment of ἀμέμπτως is not so obvious. The Apostles do not write ἄμεμπτον, which would give the "*preserved blameless*" of the A.V., as though they were defining the state in which the readers should be kept "*unto the coming*" (a gross misrendering of ἐν), but ἀμέμπτως, "blamelessly," using the adverb of manner. Now this qualification can hardly apply to τηρηθείη by itself (for the writers could not think of *blame* as attaching, conceivably, to God's keeping of His saints); it defines the foregoing ὁλόκληρον, which is grammatically dependent on τηρηθείη as its secondary predicate, but logically dominates the sentence. The interjected adverbial adjunct indicates the manner in which the desired integrity of sanctification, for whose maintenance prayer is made, is to be realized at last. We may render the whole sentence thus: "In full integrity may your spirit and your soul and your body be preserved,—found blamelessly so at the coming of our Lord Jesus Christ." From iv. 13—18 it might be inferred, as 1 Cor. xv. abundantly shows, that in St Paul's teaching the body, along with the spirit, of the saints participates in the glory of the Parousia; see Ph. iii. 20 f.

24. **πιστὸς ὁ καλῶν ὑμᾶς, ὃς καὶ ποιήσει.** *Faithful is He that calls you, who also will do* (*it*). The Thessalonians are conscious that God is calling them to a life of consecration to Himself, to be crowned by heavenly glory (see ii. 12, iv. 3, v. 18, and notes); He speaks in the Gospel as ὁ καλῶν: the "call" proves the possibility of the complete sanctification prayed for, since it pledges God's all-sufficing aid to this effect. See 1 Cor. i. 9; Ph. i. 6; Rom. xi. 29; 2 Tim. ii. 13; Ps. lvii. 2, cxxxviii. 8, for similar assumptions and tacit arguments. Elsewhere the Apostle points to the σφραγίς, or the ἀρραβών, or the ἀπαρχή, "of the Spirit" as warranting the same certainty: see 2 Cor. i. 22; Eph. i. 13 f., iv. 30; Rom. viii. 14—17, 23. Under the formula πιστὸς ὁ θεός (or κύριος) St Paul appeals to God's fidelity, in various ways: see II. iii. 3; 1 Cor. i. 9, x. 13; 2 Cor. i. 18; 2 Tim. ii. 13; cf. Deut. vii. 9, Isai. xlix. 7, &c. For the timeless present, ὁ καλῶν, see note on ii. 12: it implies God's abiding character.

Ποιήσει is elliptical and without expressed object: the verbs are apposed in their bare idea—"Your Caller will *do* "; God will put His summons into execution, He will not let it remain futile nor leave its fulfilment to man's weakness. "Hath He *said*, and shall He not *do*?" Num. xxiii. 19; cf. Ps. xxii. 31; Isai. xliv. 23, lv. 11; Lk. i. 37, &c.

§ 12. v. 25—28. THE CONCLUSION.

The conclusion of the Epistle is very brief. It makes no reference to the autograph signature, which the Apostle Paul in II. iii. 17, and in subsequent letters, is careful to notify. The request "that the Epistle be read to all the brethren" (*v.* 27), is its notable feature.

25. Ἀδελφοί, προσεύχεσθε [καὶ] περὶ ἡμῶν. *Brothers, pray* [*also*] *for us.* The καί of the R.V. margin (see Textual Note) is appropriate; since the Apostles have just prayed for their readers (*v.* 23), *their* prayers for the writers are due in turn; for similar reciprocity indicated by καί, see iii. 6 *b* above and Col. i. 8. The absence of καί in the parallel II. iii. 1 and Heb. xiii. 18 (where it is not required) might occasion its omission by copyists here. For the general wish, beside II. iii. 1 f. where it is expanded, cf. Eph. vi. 19; Col. iv. 3 f.; Ph. i. 19; Rom. xv. 30—"that you strive together with me in your prayers to God for me." St Paul, in all the strength of his gifts and office, felt his dependence on the prayers of the Church, and realized through this means his fellowship with distant brethren in Christ.

26. Ἀσπάσασθε τοὺς ἀδελφοὺς πάντας ἐν φιλήματι ἁγίῳ. *Salute the brothers all in a holy kiss.* In 1 Pet. v. 14 the kiss is defined, by its quality, φίλημα ἀγάπης: *love* and *holiness* were identified in the prayer of iii. 12 f. above (see notes); the injunction of the φίλημα is followed by words upon love, and of love, in 1 Cor. xvi. 20—24; cf. also 2 Cor. xiii. 11—13. Such love was implied in the fellowship of prayer expressed in the verses just preceding. The "kiss" is ἅγιον as the token of love amongst the ἅγιοι (iii. 13, iv. 7 f.); it is called in the *Apost. Constitt.*, ii. 57, τὸ ἐν Κυρίῳ φίλημα, and by Tertullian, for the Latin Church, *osculum pacis*, by St Augustine *osculum sanctum.* The Apostles wish the φίλημα to be given in conveying their "greeting," and by way of signifying their love to "all" the Thessalonian believers; its communication in this form pre-supposes, and simultaneously expresses, the mutual love reigning in the Church (i. 3; II. i. 3). The direction is presumably given, as Lightfoot and Bornemann point out, to the primary receivers of the Letter—probably the προϊστάμενοι, *scil.* Elders, spoken of in *v.* 12 above and addressed in *vv.* 14 f. (see notes) ; these are to give the kiss in the name of the writers to the Church at large. Such a salutation they were probably accustomed to bestow at Church gatherings ; on the occasion of reading this Letter, it is to be given and received *as from Paul and his companions.*

The kiss, as the natural sign of affection amongst kindred and near friends in meeting or parting, was common in the primitive Christian assemblies, with their strong sense of fraternity. It is still a usage of the Greek and Oriental Churches at Holy Communion ; but the ceremony died out in the West during the Middle Ages, being less suitable to the colder manners of the Germanic races. The custom fell into suspicion as the simplicity of Christian feeling declined ; it was the subject of numerous regulations in early Councils. See the article *Kiss* in the *Dict. of Christian Antiquities,* and φίλημα in Suicer's *Thesaurus* ; also "Salutations" in *Encycl. Biblica.*

27. **Ἐνορκίζω ὑμᾶς τὸν κύριον ἀναγνωσθῆναι τὴν ἐπιστολήν,** κ.τ.λ. *I adjure you by the Lord that the letter be read to all the brothers.* Observe the 1st person *singular,* previously occurring only in ii. 18 and iii. 5, which gives to the wish, on St Paul's part, an emphatic personal note ; cf. the concluding note on *v.* 28. This appeal unmistakably implies, as probably does the direction of *v.* 26 (see note above), certain responsible persons to whose address the Epistle was sent and who had it in charge for the Church. That the request should take the form of a solemn *adjuration,* is surprising. The tenor of the Epistle (see *Introd.* pp. xxxiii., lxii.) indicates no contention or jealousy that might occasion the withholding of the Letter from one party by another. It must be remembered (1) that this is the earliest Apostolic Letter extant, and that the custom of reading such Epistles had yet to be established. The appeal gives expression to the authority of the communication, and the importance attaching to it in the writers' minds (cf. iv. 1, 15). (2) The desire felt for St Paul's presence and the disappointment of the Church at his failure to return (iii. 6), to which he addressed himself in chaps. ii. and iii., might lead some to say, "O, it is *only a letter* from him ! we do not want that ! " (3) Further, amongst the bereaved members of the Church whom the writers are wishful to console (iv. 13 ff.), some in consequence of their recent and deep sorrow might be absent when the Epistle was read ; the Apostles will make sure that these shall not lose its benefit. Lightfoot suggests (4) that St Paul had "a sort of presentiment or suspicion that a wrong use might be made

of his name and authority" in some quarters in regard to the matters agitated touching the Parousia—as appears, from the subsequent allusion of II. ii. 2, to have proved the case; and that he therefore takes care that no one shall misunderstand his meaning from merely hearing it at second-hand and by report. Or, finally, (5) the ἄτακτοι (v. 14) might escape hearing the Letter, unless they were sought out and had it brought to their knowledge. A somewhat similar injunction is found in Col. iv. 16.

ἐνορκίζω—"probably stronger than ὁρκίζω, I bind you by an oath" (Lightfoot)—appears to be found otherwise only on one or two Inscriptions, and probably (by emendation) in Josephus Antiq. VIII. 15. 4; ὁρκίζω in Mk v. 7; Acts xix. 13. Like verbs of its class, it takes two accusatives. Ὁρκόω is the correct Attic form. Τὴν ἐπιστολήν refers to the Letter now complete. The benediction μακάριος ὁ ἀναγινώσκων κ. οἱ ἀκούοντες, of Rev. i. 3, says much the same thing as this verse in another way. Bengel remarks, in regard to the reading of Scripture on the part of the laity: "Quod Paulus cum adjuratione jubet, id Roma sub anathemate prohibet."

28. Ἡ χάρις τοῦ κυρίου ἡμῶν Ἰησοῦ Χριστοῦ μεθ' ὑμῶν. *The grace of our Lord Jesus Christ (be) with you.* St Paul's customary form of final benediction, which he expands later into the full Trinitarian blessing of 2 Cor. xiii. 13, or shortens into the brief ἡ χάρις μεθ' ὑμῶν of Col. iv. 18; cf. 1 and 2 Tim. and Titus besides. It contains all good that Christians can wish each other; see notes on χάρις, i. 1, and II. i. 12. "Grace" is "with" us, when it constantly attends us, when it forms the atmosphere we breathe, the guiding and sustaining influence of life.

From II. iii. 17 f. we learn that the Apostle Paul, using an amanuensis, was accustomed to write the benediction with his own hand as a characteristic token—perhaps in this case the whole postscript (vv. 26–28: the sing. ἐνορκίζω—see note above—speaks for this inclusion); cf. Gal. vi. 11–18. This formula "was adopted after him by those especially who were his companions or disciples, as by the inspired writer of the Epistle to the Hebrews (xiii. 25), and by Clement in his Epistle to the Romans. Compare likewise the conclusion of the Epistle of Barnabas, ὁ κύριος τῆς δόξης καὶ πάσης χάριτος μετὰ τοῦ πνεύματος ὑμῶν. Afterwards it became the common salutation or benediction of the Church in her liturgies" (Lightfoot).

2 THESSALONIANS.

CHAPTER I.

On the TITLE, see note to Epistle I.
1. Σιλουανος is spelt Σιλβανος in DG^{gr} 67**; cf. note on I. i. 1. The Latin *v* is ambiguous in its Greek transliteration.
2. This whole verse is omitted by 177 and Damasus, probably through homœoteleuton with *v*. 1.

ℵAGKL &c., vg cop syrr, Or (expressly), add ημων to πατρος; BDP 17, Thphyl Pelag, dispense with the pronoun. The latter group outweigh the former; the addition is suggested by *v*. 1 and by Pauline usage in such formulæ: 2 Tim. i. 2, Tit. i. 4, Eph. vi. 23 afford exceptions parallel to the shorter reading here.

3. Minuscule 17 and vg (in good copies), with Aug, omit παντων, while ℵ* omits third ημων: in either case probably through homœoteleuton, the duplicate final -ων misleading the copyist's eye.

4. αυτους ημας (in this order), ℵBP 17 73 syr^{hcl}; ημας αυτους, in ADGKL &c.—a Western emendation, followed by the Syrians.

ενκαυχασθαι, in ℵABP 17 Chr Euthal (P 17 adopt the classical spelling εγ-). καυχασθαι is read by DKL, &c. (G, καυχησασθαι), discarding the exceptional compound, or omitting the initial εν- through confusion with the final -ιν of the foregoing υμιν.

ενεχεσθε is found in B alone—hence rejected by all the editors except WH (*margin*): a not improbable reading, since it yields a forcible and fitting sense, and constitutes a solitary usage in this connexion; whereas the smooth and obvious ανεχεσθε is common in St Paul, and is exchangeable with ενεχεσθε by an easy itacism. See Expository Note.

7. εν φλογι πυρος is the reading of BDG 47 71, vg cop syr^{pesh, hcl txt}, Tert; it appears to be a conformation to Isai. lxvi. 15, Ex. iii. 2 (*Hebrew*): so Acts vii. 30, with a *varia lectio*; Heb. i. 7; Rev. i. 14, &c. Weiss, on the other hand, supposes εν πυρι φλογος (given by ℵAKLP

&c., and adopted by other critics) to be due to assimilation of ἐν φλογὶ πυρὸς to the LXX text of Ex. iii. 2.

8. **διδούς**, for **διδόντος, D*G** latt.: a *false concord*; cf. Rev. *passim*, and Papyri.

Χριστοῦ added to Ιησοῦ by ℵAG &c.; see note on I. ii. 19.

10. **τοῖς πιστεύσασιν** in all uncials. The Received πιστεύουσιν rests on the testimony of a handful of minuscules.

For **ἐπιστεύθη**, two minn.—31 and 112, of no special value—furnish, whether through accident or design, the reading ἐπιστώθη desiderated by Hort. The rendering of Ambrst, *fidem habuit*, may have been based on ἐπιστώθη. See Expository Note.

12. **AGP 17 &c.**, add Χριστοῦ to the first Ιησοῦ. Cf. *v.* 8 above.

§ 1. **i. 1—4. Salutation and Thanksgiving.**

1. This ADDRESS differs from that of Epistle I. (see notes *in extenso*) only in the addition of ἡμῶν to πατρί : " in God *our* Father and the Lord Jesus Christ "—*Father of us*, whom He loves and calls into His own family: cf. ii. 16 ; I. i. 4 ; Rom. i. 7, viii. 15, 29 ; Gal. iv. 4—7 ; Eph. i. 5 ; Lk. xii. 32, &c. This appropriative ἡμῶν is usual in later epistolary formulæ ; cf. *vv.* 11 and 12, and notes.

2. The GREETING is more considerably enlarged. The reference of χάρις ὑμῖν καὶ εἰρήνη (see notes to I. i. 1) to their double source— ἀπὸ θεοῦ πατρὸς καὶ κυρίου Ἰησοῦ Χριστοῦ—unauthentic in the T.R. of Epistle I., is amply attested here, and prevails in subsequent Epistles. " God the Father " is the ultimate spring, " the Lord Jesus Christ " the mediating channel of " grace and peace "; cf. 1 Cor. i. 30, ἐξ αὐτοῦ (i.e. τοῦ θεοῦ) ὑμεῖς ἐστε ἐν Χριστῷ Ἰησοῦ.

Vv. 3 f. The THANKSGIVING, resembling that of Epistle I., has at the same time a stamp of its own. The Apostles dwell (*a*) on *the extraordinary growth* of the Thessalonian Church in faith and love, *v.* 3 ; (*b*) on *their own boasting* over their stedfastness in other Churches ; (*c*) on *the token* given by this fidelity *of God's righteous judgement* as between the persecuted Church and its oppressors, which will take effect, with glorious results for the former, at the approaching παρουσία, *vv.* 5—12. On this third, ulterior motive for thankfulness the writers dilate in such a way that it detaches itself from the εὐχαριστία and becomes an integral and prominent topic of the Epistle. We therefore treat it separately in the following section.

3. Εὐχαριστεῖν ὀφείλομεν τῷ θεῷ πάντοτε περὶ ὑμῶν, ἀδελφοί, καθὼς ἄξιόν ἐστιν. *We ought to give thanks to God always for you, brothers, as it is befitting.* For εὐχαριστεῖν, see note on parallel in Ep. I. Ὀφείλομεν is repeated in this connexion in ii. 13—nowhere else in St Paul. As I. iii. 6—9, ii. 18 f., show, the writers felt themselves under a peculiar *debt* of gratitude on their readers' account— hence this turn of expression. For ὀφείλω in matters of affection, see Rom. xiii. 8, xv. 1, 27; Jo. xiii. 14; and of debt *to God*, Matt. vi. 12, xxiii. 16, 18. Καθὼς ἄξιόν ἐστιν, "ut par est" (Erasmus, Beza), adds the *human* side of this claim; "it is also merited by your conduct" (Lightfoot): cf., for the use of the adjective, Lk. xxiii. 41, ἄξια ὧν ἐπράξαμεν, "the due reward of our deeds"; and Ph. i. 7, καθώς ἐστιν δίκαιον κ.τ.λ., for the Pauline sentiment. Ἄξιος recurs twice in the sequel, referring to the Thessalonians, in καταξιόω and ἀξιόω, vv. 5, 11. There is nothing pleonastic, and nothing constrained or formal, here; St Paul was under abiding and warmly felt bonds of gratitude for the timely comfort administered by this Church, which had given "life" to his ministry at Corinth; see note on I. iii. 8. Bengel's question is apposite: "Tuine Christianismi specimina digna sunt, quorum nomine gratias Deo agant, qui te norunt?"

ὅτι ὑπεραυξάνει ἡ πίστις ὑμῶν. The ground and subject-matter of thanksgiving: *in that your faith grows mightily* (or *more and more*)—*vehementer augescit* (Calvin, Beza). Earlier, St Paul had been anxious "about the faith" of his Thessalonian converts (I. ii. 2, 5); he had written the former Letter partly to remedy their ὑστερήματα τῆς πίστεως (iii. 10). Since that time it has *grown* in a degree beyond his hopes; this is his first ground of thankfulness. Timothy's report had been reassuring on this vital point (iii. 6); subsequent tidings had arrived to the same effect (see *Introd.* p. xxxvii.). The compound ὑπερ-αυξάνω is *hap. leg.*; St Paul is fond of the prefix ὑπερ- (cf. ii. 4; I. iii. 10, v. 13).

καὶ πλεονάζει ἡ ἀγάπη ἑνὸς ἑκάστου πάντων ὑμῶν εἰς ἀλλήλους, *and the love of each single one of you all to one another multiplies.* This the First Epistle marked as the shining excellence of the Thessalonian Church (iv. 9 f.); for its increase the Apostles had prayed (iii. 12): this prayer is fulfilled, and thanksgiving is therefore *due.* Πλεονάζω, an active verb in I. iii. 12 (see note), is neuter here. Ἑνὸς ἑκάστου (also in I. ii. 11), *uniuscujusque* (Vulg.), pointedly individualizes the statement, which πάντων ὑμῶν extends to the entire community. To the Thessalonian faith and love *hope* was added, completing the matter of thanksgiving, in I. i. 3; hope is implied here by ὑπὲρ τῆς ὑπομονῆς ὑμῶν below.

4. ὥστε αὐτοὺς ἡμᾶς ἐν ὑμῖν ἐνκαυχᾶσθαι ἐν ταῖς ἐκκλησίαις τοῦ θεοῦ. *So that we on our own part are boasting in you in the Churches of God,*—*scil.* in Corinth and the neighbouring Achaian Churches springing up round that city (see 2 Cor. i. 1, ix. 2; Rom. xv. 26, xvi. 5); and in other Churches with which the Apostles were in communication at the time (Paul e.g. with Antioch, &c., Silvanus with Jerusalem, Timothy with S. Galatia). 2 Cor. viii. 1—6 affords an example at a later date of St Paul's boasting over the Macedonians to their neighbours.

The emphatic *αὐτούς* marks this "boasting" as unusual on the writers' part—perhaps in view of their known reluctance (cf. I. ii. 6 f.) to dwell on anything redounding to their own credit (cf. Gal. vi. 14 ; 2 Cor. xii. 1—6 ; yet see Rom. xv. 18 f., 1 Cor. xv. 10, showing how St Paul would sometimes "glory" in his work), despite which they are bound to make God's grace in this instance, and at this stage, known throughout the Christian brotherhood. From I. i. 8 f. it appears that up to a certain point the Apostles refrained from speaking publicly of the success of their mission to Thessalonica, which had advertized itself in the best possible way ; but now, out of gratitude to God, and from the sense of what is due to their Thessalonian brethren, they can no longer refrain : " while others have been telling about our work, we *ourselves* are now constrained to glory in it." Ἐνκαυχάομαι, another N.T. *hap. leg.*; but this compound is used in the LXX. Ἐνκαυχᾶσθαι ἐν, of the *general ground* of boast (cf. Rom. ii. 17; Gal. vi. 13, &c.); ὑπέρ, of its *specific subject-matter* (2 Cor. xii. 5), or that *in the interest of* which one boasts— see παρακαλέσαι ὑπέρ, I. iii. 2 ; ἐρωτῶμεν ὑπέρ, ii. 1 below. But ἐνκαυχᾶσθαι ἐν may be Hebraistic (ἐν = בְּ); see Ps. li. 3, cv. 47 (LXX). On " churches of God," see I. ii. 14.

ὑπὲρ τῆς ὑπομονῆς ὑμῶν καὶ πίστεως, *over your endurance and faith.* For ὑπομονή, see note to I. i. 3. Since πίστις follows ὑπομονή here, and under the vinculum of the single article, it might appear to denote the moral virtue of *faithfulness* to the Christian cause, rather than the religious principle of *faith* out of which the Christian life springs (v. 3); so Bengel, Lünemann, and Bornemann interpret the word. But it is arbitrary to give it, with no mark of distinction, this double sense in two consecutive clauses; indeed it is questionable whether πίστις anywhere in Paul—even in Gal. v. 22 or Rom. iii. 3 —means *fidelity* in distinction from *faith*. The prepositional adjunct attached to πίστις gives appropriateness and force to the repetition of this fundamental word: the Apostles "glory," in the case of the

Thessalonians, "over" their "endurance and *faith* (*maintained*) *in all*" their "*persecutions and afflictions*"; so that πίστεως ἐν πᾶσιν τοῖς διωγμοῖς ὑμῶν κ.τ.λ. is explicative of ὑπομονῆς and forms one idea therewith; cf. Acts xiv. 22. The maintenance of *faith amid affliction* was the crucial trial of this Church (see I. iii. 2—5); and the trial was endured unflinchingly. Well might the missionaries be proud of such converts! For the anarthrous prepositional adjunct, cf. ἐν θεῷ, I. i. 1, ἐν Χριστῷ, I. iv. 16, and notes.

Διωγμοῖς (cf. ἐκ-διωξάντων, in connexion with τὰ αὐτὰ ἐπάθετε, I. ii. 13 f.; and the combination in Rom. viii. 35, &c.) refers to the specific attacks made on the Christians in Thessalonica, commencing with the assault on the Apostles related in Acts xvii.; θλίψεσιν, comprehensively, to the various injuries and vexations attending the persecution; on the latter word, see note to I. i. 6.

αἷς ἀνέχεσθε affords a unique example of relative attraction, supposing ἀνέχομαι to govern *the genitive*, as uniformly in the N.T. (see 2 Cor. xi. 1, &c.); classical rule limits such attraction to *the accusative*, the case governed by this verb sometimes in older Greek—a regimen conceivably occurring here for once in the N.T. (so Winer-Moulton, p. 204; and Ellicott *in loc.*). Since, however, the reverse attraction, *from dative to genitive*, occurs elsewhere, one does not see any objection of principle to the attraction here supposed upon the usual construction of ἀνέχομαι with genitive (so A. Buttmann, *N.T. Grammar*, and others). Probably vernacular idiom was not over nice in points like these. The grammatical anomaly may have occasioned the variant reading of **B**, αἷς ἐνέχεσθε (cf. Gal. v. 1), *in which you are involved* (see Textual Note). But this gives after all a very suitable sense; and the dative would then be regularly governed by ἐν-. The present tense shows the persecution to be going on; it seems to have been continuous from the foundation of this Church.

§ 2. i. 5—12. THE APPROACHING JUDGEMENT.

The thought of the recompense awaiting the persecuted Thessalonian Church and its persecutors, respectively, swells the opening thanksgiving of the Epistle, and leads up to its introductory prayer (*vv.* 11 f.). The writers enlarge, however, upon this δικαία κρίσις in a sense that exceeds the bounds of the εὐχαριστία, and constitutes this section a distinct item in the teaching of the Epistle, a new and express assurance conveyed to the readers. The doctrine it contains is continuous with that of I. v. 1—11, as it describes *the issue of Christ's parousia*, the time and circumstances of which were there referred to;

in so doing it supplies a starting-point for the further discussion about the *parousia* arising in the next section. At *v.* 6, where the Apocalyptic description begins, the composition assumes a Hebraistic style and rises into a kind of chant, as is frequently the case with St Paul's loftier contemplative passages; at the same point O.T. allusions and snatches of prophecy crowd into the page. So marked is the liturgical rhythm of *vv.* 6—10, that Bornemann conjectures this passage to be borrowed from some primitive Christian psalm or hymn: cf. Eph. v. 14; 1 Tim. iii. 16; Rev. i. 5 ff., iv. 8, 11, &c., for passages of a similar complexion.

ANALYSIS: The brave endurance of persecution by the readers affords a token (enhancing thankfulness on their behalf) of retribution awaiting them, and in justice awaiting their persecutors on the contrary part, at the advent of the Lord Jesus. In the view presented of this judgement we observe—(1) its *essential righteousness, vv.* 5 f.; (2) its *dependence upon Christ's promised advent, vv.* 7, 9 f.; (3) that *the vindication of Christ's faithful people* forms the proper purpose of the advent—to this the vengeance visiting their oppressors is incidental, *vv.* 6, 8, 10; and (4) that *the personal glory of the Redeemer* is its supreme and most desired outcome, *vv.* 7, 10, 12.

5. ἔνδειγμα τῆς δικαίας κρίσεως τοῦ θεοῦ, *a plain token of the righteous judgement of God.* Ἔνδειγμα, not *exemplum*, as in the Vulg.— this renders παράδειγμα; but *indicium* (Beza), or better still, *argumentum et indicium* (Estius). The sufferings of the righteous afflicted do not "exemplify" Divine justice; they seem to contradict it. They do not exhibit, but "point to" a future readjustment. In what sense? (*a*) By way of *moral argument*, on the principle of Lk. xvi. 25; thus many interpreters, with Calvin, e.g.: "Nam si justus est mundi judex Deus, restitui oportet quæ nunc sunt confusa." But this cannot be got out of the word ἔνδειγμα, which implies *evidence* to the point in question lying in the facts stated (*vv.* 3 f.), not argument upon them; the affliction taken in itself affords no proof of retributive justice—rather an occasion for it. (*b*) The true answer is supplied by the parallel in Phil. i. 28: μὴ πτυρόμενοι ἐν μηδενί...ἥτις ἐστὶν αὐτοῖς ἔνδειξις ἀπωλείας, ὑμῶν δὲ σωτηρίας. The heroic faith of the Thessalonians *shows that God is on their side*, since He manifestly inspires it (cf. I. i. 6); so it gives token of His final judgement in their case and is a kind of ἀπαρχή thereof (cf. Rom. viii. 15—23). This prophetic sign, joyously evident to the Apostles, ought even to impress the persecutors at Thessalonica; perhaps St Paul remembered some misgivings due to the like cause in *Saul* **the** persecutor! The

joy of St Stephen before the Jewish Council (Acts vi. 15), the triumph of Paul and Silas singing in the Philippian prison, the rapture of later Christian martyrs and the impression often made by it, are instances of such ἔνδειξις. Ἔνδειγμα then refers neither to the subject, nor even to the object of the verb ἀνέχεσθε—as though one should render, "which you endure by way of token (*in exemplum*, Vulg.) of God's righteous judgement"; but to the main purport of *v.* 4, viz. the ὑπομονὴ κ. πίστις ἐν τοῖς διωγμοῖς of the readers. The noun may be construed as *accusative of apposition* to the previous sentence (cf. Rom. xii. 1 : so Lightfoot; A. Buttmann, p. 153), or, better, as *an elliptical nominative*, for ὅ ἐστιν ἔνδειγμα, which in full expression would be awkward after αἷς ἀνέχεσθε (cf. Phil. i. 28; Eph. iii. 13: so Winer-Moulton, p. 669, Schmiedel, Blass, Bornemann). The verb ἐνδείκνυμαι (middle) signifies *to point out* (something) *in oneself*, to give ostensible evidence (see Rom. ii. 15; 2 Cor. viii. 24). Ἔνδειξις (Phil. i. 28; Rom. iii. 25) is the evidencing action, ἔνδειγμα the evidence in act. There may be in the term a lingering, to the persecutors an ominous, suggestion of its Attic legal sense of *incriminating statement* (see Lidd. and Scott, s.v. ἔνδειξις); the constancy of the Christians was, virtually, an indictment of their injurers before the Great Judge.

εἰς τὸ καταξιωθῆναι ὑμᾶς τῆς βασιλείας τοῦ θεοῦ, *so that you may be accounted worthy of the kingdom of God*. For εἰς τό with infin., see note to I. ii. 12. Here again the construction is somewhat loose. The adjunct, expressing half purpose and half result, belongs to κρίσεως—God's "righteous judgement" aiming at the admission to His "kingdom" of its destined heirs (cf. Matt. xxv. 34), who are now giving "token" of "worthiness" by their faithful "suffering on" its "account." The construction of ἔνδειγμα above adopted forbids our attaching this clause to ἀνέχεσθε, as though it expressed *the aim of the sufferers* (which would, moreover, render ὑπὲρ ἧς κ.τ.λ. superfluous). And to make the clause depend on ἔνδειγμα itself is to treat it as synonymous with τῆς δικαίας κρίσεως (" God's righteous judgement...viz. that you be counted," &c.), an apposition of which εἰς τό does not admit. See Moulton's *Prolegomena*, pp. 218—20.

Κατ-αξιόω (cf. *v.* 11; the intensive compound also in Lk. xx. 35; Acts v. 41) is a judicial term, like the Pauline δικαιόω, specifying a kind of κρίσις, and denotes "to reckon (not *to make*) worthy"; so in Lk. vii. 7; 1 Tim. v. 17, &c. There must be apparent a fitness of character in those admitted to God's heavenly kingdom, if His judgement in their favour is to be recognized as "righteous"; see the opposite case in Matt. xxii. 8, and the warning of Rev. xxii. 10—15. God is "calling" the Thessalonians now to "His kingdom and glory"; they are "walking worthily" in the courage and patience of faith (cf. I. ii. 12); on such conditions, He cannot fail to "account" them "worthy" at the last. Acting otherwise, He would repudiate His own call (cf. I. v. 24), and would be no longer a righteous God (cf. 1 Cor. i. 9; Heb. vi. 10). "The kingdom of God" includes the "kingdom and glory" of I. ii. 12; His kingdom, already present in its spiritual principles and hidden operation (Rom. xiv. 17; Lk. xvii. 20 f.), is "coming" to its fulfilment and manifestation (Matt. vi. 10; Lk. xiii. 29; 1 Cor. xv. 24 f.).

In ὑπὲρ ἧς καὶ πάσχετε—*for which sake indeed you are suffering*— πάσχετε resumes τῆς ὑπομονῆς κ.τ.λ. of *v*. 4, while ὑπὲρ ἧς indicates the *motive* of the Church's endurance,—a further reason for the aforesaid κρίσεως : such suffering loyally endured out of faith in God's kingdom, it is but just that God should approve and crown at last (*v*. 6); cf. I. iii. 4; 2 Tim. ii. 12 ; Acts xiv. 22.

6. εἴπερ δίκαιόν ἐστιν παρὰ θεῷ, *if to be sure it is righteous with God*. Εἴπερ is *siquidem* (Ambrose, &c.), not *si tamen* (Vulg.); cf. Rom. iii. 30, viii. 9, 17 ; 1 Cor. viii. 5 : the particle states rhetorically, in the form of hypothesis, a recognized fact ; so Theodoret, οὐκ ἐπὶ ἀμφιβολίας τέθεικεν ἀλλ' ἐπὶ βεβαιώσεως ; "veluti verum inferens de quo nefas sit dubitare" (Erasmus). Δίκαιόν κ.τ.λ. repeats the δικαίας κρίσεως of *v*. 5 ; *justice* one certainly expects from God (Rom. iii. 5 f., 26, ix. 14) : "a token," I say, " of God's *righteous* judgement...for *righteous* it is with Him to pay back the afflicters with affliction, &c." Παρὰ θεῷ, *apud Deum, in His sight*, or *estimate, at His tribunal;* cf. Rom. ii. 11, 13 ; Lk. i. 30, &c.

ἀνταποδοῦναι τοῖς θλίβουσιν ὑμᾶς θλίψιν, *to recompense to those that afflict you affliction*. For θλίβω, θλίψις, see notes to *v*. 4 and I. i. 6 ; and for ἀνταποδίδωμι, on I. iii. 9. Τοῖς θλίβουσιν...θλίψιν follows the *jus talionis*, an axiom of justice inculcated by the Law of Moses in Lev. xxiv. 20, and generalized by St Paul in Col. iii. 25 as the principle of God's future retributions ; our Lord pictures its application in the story of Dives and Lazarus (Lk. xvi. 25); see also Matt. xxvi. 52 ; Rev. xiii. 10. Θλίψις is used once besides of the future pains of the wicked, in Rom. ii. 9 : θλίψις κ. στενοχωρία ἐπὶ πᾶσαν ψυχὴν ἀνθρώπου τοῦ κατεργαζομένου τὸ κακόν ; it represents their anguish as *a personal infliction*, that which God Himself lays upon them.

Ἀνταποδίδωμι (or ἀποδίδωμι), with its derivatives, is found in a series of O.T. sayings relating to God's vengeance on the enemies of Israel, or upon His enemies within Israel (the *idea* pervades prophecy): see Is. lxvi. 4 ff., 14 ff., lxiii. 4, 7, xxxiv. 8, xxxv. 4, lix. 18; Jer. xxviii. (LXX) 6, 24, 56; Thren. iii. 63; Obad. 15; Sirach xxxii. (xxxv.) 13, 23 ff. (LXX). The first of the above passages is evidently before the writers' mind; the context supplies other parallels to it, in the κρίσεως (κριθήσονται) of the last verse, the ἐν πυρὶ φλογός, ἐκδίκησιν, and τοῖς μὴ ὑπακούουσιν (οὐχ ὑπήκουσαν, τοῖς ἀπειθοῦσιν) of v. 8. The whole Isaianic passage should be read in the LXX, also Ps. lxxviii. 6, and Jer. x. 25, xxv. 12 (εἰς ἀφανισμὸν αἰώνιον), along with Is. lxi. 2, in order to realize how St Paul's conception and imagery of the future judgement are steeped in the O.T. Apocalyptic. Other parallels will appear when we come to *vv.* 9 ff.; cf. *Introd.* pp. lx. f.

7. **καὶ ὑμῖν τοῖς θλιβομένοις ἄνεσιν μεθ' ἡμῶν,** *and to you that are being afflicted rest with us*: the other and principal side of the coming reversal. Ἄνεσις, here opposed to θλίψις (*pressura*), is commonly the antonym of ἐπίτασις (*tension, strain*); it signifies *relaxation, relief,* as of a tightly strung bow, or of the paroxysms of fever; cf. 2 Cor. ii. 13, vii. 5, viii. 13. The synonymous ἀνάψυξις (Acts iii. 19; 2 Tim. i. 16) is *refreshment* as from a cooling wind, a breath of fresh air; while ἀνάπαυσις (Matt. xi. 29, &c.) is *cessation,* the *stopping* of labour or pain. Job iii. 17, "There the wicked cease from troubling; and there the weary are at rest," resembles this text in the Hebrew, but is discrepant in the Greek: that passage relates, as this does not, to *rest in death.* St Paul says "with *us,*" for his life was full of harassing fatigue—a sigh on his own account! cf. Gal. vi. 17; 2 Cor. v. 2; 1 Cor. iv. 9 ff. In the Apostle's visions of glory and reward his children in Christ were always present to his mind; cf. "with you," 2 Cor. iv. 14: also 2 Cor. i. 7, 2 Tim. iv. 8.

ἐν τῇ ἀποκαλύψει τοῦ κυρίου Ἰησοῦ ἀπ' οὐρανοῦ μετ' ἀγγέλων δυνάμεως αὐτοῦ, *in the revelation of the Lord Jesus from heaven (attended) with angels of His power.* This means more than "*at* the revelation"; the retribution just spoken of is a part of the Lord's "revelation," it belongs to the programme of the ἀποκάλυψις. It suits the O.T. imagery, in which the thought of the Epistle here moves, that the coming of the Lord is styled ἀποκάλυψις, not παρουσία as heretofore (I. iii. 13, &c.) and afterwards in ii. 1: see also 1 Cor. i. 7; Lk. xvii. 30; 1 Pet. i. 7, 13, iv. 13. Ἐπιφάνεια is its synonym in the Pastoral Epistles (cf. ii. 8). St Paul uses ἀποκάλυψις (-πτω) of the **extraordinary manifestation of Jesus Christ to** himself at his conversion (Gal. i. 12, 16); this Biblical term implies always a supernatural disclosure, whether inward or outward in its sphere; cf., further, note on ii. 6. On ἀπ' οὐρανοῦ, cf. I. i. 10, and note. This "unveiling from heaven" affords a complete contrast to the lowly and obscure first coming of the Redeemer; see His own words in Matt. xxvi. 64. For the office of the " angels " at the Advent, see note on I. iv. 16. These beings attend the judicial Theophanies of the O.T., as contributors to God's glory and ministers of His power: see Ps. lxviii. 17, ciii. 20; Deut. xxxiii. 2. It is significant that " in some cases the very expressions used in the Hebrew prophets of God have been adopted by St Paul in speaking of Christ " (Lightfoot).

Αὐτοῦ, qualifying δυνάμεως, forbids our reading the latter in the abstract, as a mere (Hebraistic) epithet of ἀγγέλων; so the A.V., "mighty angels," and Beza, "potentibus." The δύναμις of this sentence and the ἰσχύς of v. 9 form a part of the consolation: now "power" belongs to the wrongdoers (cf. Lk. iv. 5 f., xxii. 53; Eph. vi. 12, &c.); with this attribute, on "the day of the Lord," His "angels" will be clothed.

ἐν πυρὶ φλογός has been wrongly carried over to v. 8; the clause qualifies ἀποκαλύψει (v. 7), and completes the foregoing description given in terms of local movement (ἀπό), personal accompaniment (μετά), and material surrounding (ἐν). *Fire of flame* is Christ's awful robe: cf. Rev. i. 13—16; Is. lxvi. 15. Πῦρ φλογός (or φλὸξ πυρός) was a recognized sign of miraculous, especially judicial, theophanies; it attends angelic mediations, in such a way that the "angel" and the "flame" are more or less identified: see on the latter point, Ps. civ. 4 (as read in Heb. i. 7); Is. vi. 2, 4; and, generally, Ex. iii. 2—6; Is. iv. 4 f., xxx. 27, 30, lxiv. 1 f.; Dan. vii. 9 f.; also reff. under v. 7 (*angels*). This "fire of flame" surrounding the returning Jesus may have been associated in St Paul's mind with the "light from heaven surpassing the brightness of the sun," which flashed on him in the "revelation of Jesus Christ" that brought about his conversion (Acts xxvi. 13); that first appearance to himself unmistakably colours his prediction of the final ἐπιφάνεια in Phil. iii. 20 f. "Fire" symbolizes Divine anger and majesty; "flame" is fire in motion, leaping and blazing. In 2 Pet. iii. 7, 10, "fire" is the predicted means of destruction for the material world at the Day of the Lord (a *conflagratio mundi* was anticipated by Stoic philosophy); St Paul in 1 Cor. iii. 13 ff. makes this fire, symbolically, the means of final judgement.

8. διδόντος ἐκδίκησιν τοῖς μὴ εἰδόσι θεόν, *rendering vengeance to those that know not God*: see the reff. under v. 7. Ἐκ-δίκη-σις, derived from ἔκδικος (I. iv. 6; see note) through ἐκδικέω, carries no thought

of vindictive passion; it is the inflicting of *full justice* on the criminal (echoing δικαίας κρίσεως, δίκαιον, vv. 5 f.; and echoed by δίκην in v. 9) —nothing more, nothing less: cf. for the noun, frequent in the O.T., Rom. xii. 19, 2 Cor. vii. 11, Lk. xviii. 3, 7; add to the O.T. parallels above, Is. lxvi. 15 (ἀποδοῦναι...ἐκδίκησιν αὐτοῦ), Ezek. xxv. 14. Δίδωμι ἐκδίκησιν is Hebraistic (= נָקָם נָתַן). Διδόντος transfers to the Lord Jesus the dread prerogative reserved in the O.T. for God alone: "Vengeance belongeth unto me; I will recompense, saith the Lord" (Deut. xxxii. 35, quoted in Rom. xii. 19 and Heb. x. 30); as Jesus himself declared, "The Father hath committed all judgement unto the Son" (Jo. v. 22); cf. Acts xvii. 31; Rom. ii. 16, &c.

The objects of the Divine anger were styled in Jer. x. 25 ἔθνη τὰ μὴ εἰδότα σε, and in Ps. lxxviii. 6 ἔθνη τὰ μὴ ἐπεγνωκότα σε; but ἐκδίκησις does not occur in that O.T. connexion (only ὀργή, θυμός), and it may be doubted whether *Gentiles* as such are intended here. If they are (cf. I. iv. 5, and note), the co-ordinate clause, καὶ τοῖς μὴ ὑπακούουσιν τῷ εὐαγγελίῳ κ.τ.λ., must apply, by contrast, to *Jewish* rejecters of the Gospel; but the distinction seems out of place, and would be inadequately expressed for its purpose. Moreover disobedience was a form of sin common to Jewish and Gentile persecutors; with this St Paul taxes rejecters of Christ indiscriminately in Rom. x. 12—16, and even Gentiles specifically in Rom. xi. 30 (cf. Acts xiv. 2, xix. 9); the fundamental Isaianic passage—see note above on v. 7—speaks of "the disobedient" without distinction. On the other hand, ignorance of God can be with equal force ascribed to *Jewish* misbelievers: see Jo. viii. 54 f., and *passim*; Tit. i. 16; 2 Cor. iv. 4—6. In a Hebraistic strain like this, despite the distinguishing articles, the conjoined, parallel datives may be read as synonymous, the second enhancing upon the first. So conceived, the two form one extended category including, with the Thessalonian oppressors, all who in their estrangement from God (cf. Eph. iv. 18) disobey His message conveyed in the Gospel of Christ, their disobedience being the consequence and full expression of a wilful ignorance. If it be insisted, however, that the double article marks off distinct categories, these must be represented by the Gentile and Jewish elements respectively of the anti-Christian agitation at Thessalonica. Rom. i. 18—25 shows how Gentile idolatry sprang from a self-chosen ignorance of God, and brought on itself a "revelation of wrath" in the frightful immorality of contemporary Paganism; in I. ii. 14 ff., it was indicated how Jewish resistance to the Gospel, by its spitefulness, was bringing down a great ἐκδίκησις on the nation: this text pursues the penal consequences of those sins to the Last Day. Supposing τὰ μὴ εἰδότα θεόν to designate *Gentile* idolaters, it is not meant that Divine "vengeance" will fall on the heathen as such and for the mere fact of their "not knowing God" as Christians do; St Paul speaks quite otherwise in Rom. ii. 14. It is due to men who "do not think God worth having in their knowledge" (Rom. i. 28), and who show their hatred toward Him by their hatred of His children (cf. Jo. xv. 24; 1 Jo. iii. 13). Each will be judged according to his personal responsibility and share in the common offence (see 2 Cor. v. 10); this we may argue from δικαία κρίσις (v. 5). The men denounced at Thessalonica (v. 6) definitely *refused* to know God. For μή with participles, see note on I. ii. 15.

"The gospel (good news)" is a "call," a summons of God as well as a message from God (cf. I. ii. 2 and 12, &c.); therefore faith in it takes the form of *obedience*, which is faith in exercise; see Rom. i. 5, xvi. 19, 26, vi. 16; 1 Pet. i. 2, 14, &c. Such obedience had for its testing point the acknowledgement of Jesus as "Lord" (1 Cor. viii. 6, xii. 3; Ph. ii. 10; Acts ix. 5 ff.). In the First Epistle the Apostles spoke repeatedly of "the gospel of God"; here it is "the gospel *of our Lord Jesus*," partly to balance the parallel expression referring to "God" (see v. 1, &c.), and partly in keeping with the eschatological context (see v. 7, and note on I. iii. 13). "Of our Lord Jesus" is *subjective*, while "of God" is *objective* genitive in this connexion; see note on I. ii. 2, and Rom. i. 1 f.

9. οἵτινες δίκην τίσουσιν ὄλεθρον αἰώνιον, *who shall pay a just penalty, even eternal destruction*. Ὅστις, generic and qualitative, implying a reason in stating the fact—"qui (quum ita sint) poenam pendent." Δίκη means first *right, legality*, in the abstract; then *a suit for right, an action at law*; then *the right determined* or *exacted, penalty*, &c. It connotes *justice* in the penalty, punishment determined by a lawful process; whereas κόλασις (Matt. xxv. 46; Acts iv. 21; 2 Pet. ii. 9; 1 Jo. iv. 18) denotes *chastisement* of the wrong-doer, remedial or otherwise; and τιμωρία (Heb. x. 29), *satisfaction* demanded by the injury. Punishment is δίκη from the point of view of the dispassionate judge; κόλασις from that of the criminal; τιμωρία from that of the injured party. Acts xxviii. 4 and Jud. 7 (δίκην πυρὸς αἰωνίου) furnish the only other N.T. examples of a word exceedingly common in Greek. Τίνω is also a judicial term, a N.T. *hap. legomenon*; ἀπο-τίνω is preferred, with finesse, in Phm. 19.

St Paul uses the term ὄλεθρος respecting the σάρξ of a gross sinner in 1 Cor. v. 5; in 1 Tim. vi. 9, along with ἀπώλεια (the commoner word, marked by the intensive ἀπο-), of the "*destruction* and perdition into" which riches "plunge" those resolved at all costs on having them. Here, and in I. v. 3, ὄλεθρος signifies the *ruin* falling on the ungodly at Christ's coming. As αἰώνιος, affecting the man *for ever*, this ὄλεθρος exceeds any πρόσκαιρος, or "temporal ruin," that might befall in this fleeting visible world (see the antithesis in 2 Cor. iv. 18). The phrase ὄλεθρος αἰώνιος is found in 4 Macc. x. 15, where the "eternal destruction" inflicted on a heathen tyrant is contrasted with "the happy death" of a martyr. St Paul does not contemplate under ὄλεθρος the *annihilation* of the reprobate; the sinner of 1 Cor. v. 1—5 was not to suffer "destruction of the flesh" in such a way that his "saved spirit" would be *bodiless* in its future state. Nor does αἰώνιος suggest any periodic limitation (*age-long destruction*); it lifts the ὄλεθρος out of time-conditions; like the κόλασις αἰώνιος of Matt. xxv. 46, this ὄλεθρος αἰώνιος is the antithesis of ζωὴ αἰώνιος.

ἀπὸ προσώπου τοῦ κυρίου καὶ ἀπὸ τῆς δόξης τῆς ἰσχύος αὐτοῦ, *from the face of the Lord and from the glory of His strength.* 'Aπό is ambiguous in its connexion with ὄλεθρος: (*a*) If the sense be determined by Isai. ii. 10, &c. (cf. Rev. vi. 15 f.), from which this double phrase is manifestly borrowed, then ἀπό is *local* and pregnant in use, representing the ruin as consisting in "*being driven from,*" or in "*exclusion from,* the face of the Lord," &c. (cf. ii. 2, below, and note); but the verb of Isaiah (LXX), viz. κρύπτεσθε, "hide yourselves," connotes *motion from* as ὄλεθρος does not. The preposition loses its contextual force by its severance from the original context; the idea of *separation* is not obviously relevant here. (*b*) Others give to ἀπό a *temporal* sense, "from (the time of) the Lord's appearance" (cf. Rom. i. 20): this is easier grammatically, but does not suit πρόσωπον and is pointless in sense. (*c*) The preposition is most appropriate in the *causal, semi-local* significance it bears in *v.* 2 and so often— "*proceeding from* the face of the Lord and from the glory of His strength"—thus recalling in a striking figure, and with impressive repetition, the διδόντος ἐκδίκησιν of *v.* 8; cf. Acts iii. 20, καιροὶ ἀναψύξεως ἀπὸ προσώπου τοῦ κυρίου. The aptness of τῆς ἰσχύος αὐτοῦ is evident on this construction. "The strength" of the Judge, glorious in itself, by supplying executive force to His decisions doubles the terror that His "face" wears for the condemned; cf. Jo. xix. 37, Rev. vi. 16. To the enemies of Christ, by whom He was "crucified in weakness," His return as Judge in glorious strength must be inexpressibly dreadful (cf. Matt. xxvi. 64). Ἰσχύς is *strength* resident in a person; δύναμις, *power* relevant to its use. For the (hostile)

"face of the Lord," cf. Ps. xxxiv. 16, lxxvi. 7: "Who may stand in Thy sight, when once Thou art angry?" Estius remarks: "Si enim daemones praesentiam Christi versantis in terris non sustinebant, quanto minus praesentiam ejus cum tanta majestate venientis ad judicium impii sustinere poterunt!"
The "affliction" of the persecutors and the "relief" of the persecuted, contrasted in themselves (*vv.* 6 f.), are identified in their occasion; for justice will overtake the former—

10. ὅταν ἔλθῃ ἐνδοξασθῆναι ἐν τοῖς ἁγίοις αὐτοῦ καὶ θαυμασθῆναι ἐν πᾶσιν τοῖς πιστεύσασιν, *when He comes to be glorified in His saints and wondered at in all those who believed*. Ἐνδοξασθῆναι, bare infin. of *purpose*, common after verbs of *coming* and the like (Winer-Moulton, pp. 399 f.). Ἐνδοξάζω, to make ἔν-δοξος, a compound only found besides in LXX. Is. xlix. 3, or Ezek. xxviii. 22, is running in the writer's mind; perhaps along with Isai. iv. 2 f., which combines δοξάζω (relating to God) and ἅγιοι in one context; cf. also Ps. lxxxviii. 8 (a Messianic Psalm, of which other traces might be noted in the context), ὁ θεὸς ἐνδοξαζόμενος ἐν βουλῇ ἁγίων. Ἐν τοῖς ἁγίοις...θαυμασθῆναι, with its context, reflects the magnificent close of Ps. lxvii. (LXX), *vv.* 35 f.: δότε δόξαν τῷ θεῷ· ἐπὶ τὸν Ἰσραὴλ ἡ μεγαλοπρέπεια αὐτοῦ, καὶ ἡ δύναμις αὐτοῦ ἐν ταῖς νεφέλαις· θαυμαστὸς ὁ θεὸς ἐν τοῖς ὁσίοις αὐτοῦ. To this δόξα of the Lord Jesus (see Jo. xvii. 10) *v.* 12 reverts (cf. note also on ii. 14). For ἐν τοῖς ἁγίοις αὐτοῦ, see note on I. iii. 13.

With the latter phrase ἐν πᾶσιν τοῖς πιστεύσασιν is synonymous; they run in Hebraistic parallels, like the double ἀπό clauses of *v.* 9, and like the double dative and articular clauses of *v.* 8 (cf. note on τοῖς μὴ εἰδόσιν κ.τ.λ.). "In all that *believed*," not "believe" (as in I. ii. 10, &c.), for we anticipate in imagination "that day"; the beholder, as he views the glory won by the Lord Jesus in His saints, traces it back to the *faith* which was its source; he wonders at the mighty growth from so small a seed, and gives the praise to Christ (cf. Matt. xiii. 31 f.; Jo. v. 24, vii. 38, &c.). If the "glory of His strength" is terrible to the persecutors (*v.* 9); in His saints "the glory of His *grace*" is seen (*v.* 12: cf. Eph. i. 3—14; also Rom. viii. 28—30, marking the steps of its progress). Their character as "saints" redounds to the Redeemer's honour: see I. iii. 13, v. 23 f.; and cf. Rom. viii. 29; Col. i. 22, 28 f.; Eph. v. 27 (ἵνα παραστήσῃ...ἔνδοξον τὴν ἐκκλησίαν); Rev. i. 5 f., vii. 14; Heb. ii. 10; 2 Cor. viii. 23; Tit. ii. 10, &c. The θαυμάζοντες St Paul would find in the ἀρχαὶ κ. ἐξουσίαι ἐν τοῖς ἐπουρανίοις, who are represented in Eph. iii. 10 as learning "now through the Church" lessons of "the manifold wisdom of God,"—lessons which will "on that day" be finished; cf. also 1 Pet. i. 12.

The last clause of the verse, ἐν τῇ ἡμέρᾳ ἐκείνῃ, belongs to ἐνδοξασθῆναι καὶ θαυμασθῆναι: for the phrase itself, identically recurring in 2 Tim. i. 18, iv. 8, see note on I. v. 4; and for its emphatic detachment, cf. Rom. ii. 16. The intervening sentence, ὅτι ἐπιστεύθη κ.τ.λ., is difficult. Some critics would strike it out as a marginal gloss; but there is nothing to allege against it on textual grounds. It can only be read as a parenthesis,—an interjectional outburst of the author occurring as he dictates to his secretary, or possibly a note inserted on re-reading the Letter by way of comment on τοῖς πιστεύσασιν, and thrown in without strict regard to grammatical connexion. The conspicuous success of the Gospel at Thessalonica had, for various reasons (see *Introd.* pp. xxxiii., lxii.), given extreme satisfaction to St Paul; as he imagines the glory accruing to his Lord "in that day" from the multitude of sanctified believers, the joyous thought rises in his breast, that "*our* testimony addressed *to you*" (Thessalonian heathen) contributed to bring about this result! The parenthesis is an echo of I. ii. 13, iii. 13, ii. 19 f.,—τίς ἡμῶν...στέφανος καυχήσεως...ἢ οὐχὶ καὶ ὑμεῖς; Very similarly in Ph. ii. 16 St Paul identifies his personal καύχημα with the ἡμέρα and δόξα Χριστοῦ; cf. 1 Pet. v. 4, for this association of ideas. We must remember that the whole passage is a *thanksgiving*, swelled at the outset by a *glorying* (*v.* 4) on the writers' part. It is as though they said: "Admired in all that *believed*: yes, for the testimony we brought to you won your *faith*; and in your faith, bearing fruit in holiness, we see the pledge of Christ's glorification." In I. i. 8, it is "the faith" of the Thessalonians that has "gone abroad," and vindicates the Apostles' mission; such faith inspires the confidence respecting the final outcome, which is explicitly stated in Ph. i. 6 and is tacitly implied here.

τὸ μαρτύριον ἡμῶν ἐφ' ὑμᾶς presents a unique construction: πρός, *of address*, is usual in such connexion (cf. iii. 1; I. ii. 2), or the dative (as in Matt. viii. 4, xxiv. 14, &c.). In Lk. ix. 5 μαρτύρ. ἐπί is "a witness *against*," coming "upon" its hearers by way of accusation (cf. Acts xiv. 15 ff.): here it signifies a "testimony *accosting*" (assailing, challenging) you"; cf. 1 Tim. i. 18, Eph. ii. 7, Rev. xiv. 6, where the use of ἐπί is more or less parallel to this; also I. ii. 2, where ἐπαρρησιασάμεθα ...ἐν πολλῷ ἀγῶνι describes the effort and struggle hinted at in μαρτύριον ἐπί. For the non-repetition of the article, see note on πίστεως ἐν, *v.* 4, and cf. I. iv. 16. Μαρτύριον ἡμῶν, in respect of its *medium*; but μαρτύριον τοῦ χριστοῦ, 1 Cor. i. 6, in respect of its *contents*; μαρτύριον τοῦ θεοῦ, 1 Cor. ii. 1, in respect of its *authorship*: the synonymous εὐαγγέλιον shows the same variety of usage (I. i. 5, ii. 2, *v.* 8 above).

Hort (in Westcott-Hort's *N.T. in Greek*, Appendix, p. 128) finds ἐπι-στεύθη in this passage (to which he needlessly attaches ἐφ᾽ ὑμᾶς) so impracticable, that he proposes the conjectural emendation ἐπιστώθη (see Textual Note above), *was confirmed* (*made good, verified*) *toward you* (cf. I. i. 5, ii. 13). This verb is synonymous with ἐβεβαιώθη of 1 Cor. i. 6; and it is found with τὰ μαρτύρια for subject, and a similar context, in Ps. xcii. 4 f. (LXX); also with ἐπί as complement in 1 Paral. xvii. 23, 2 Paral. i. 9; but nowhere in N.T. This smooths out the sentence, but loosens its connexion with the foregoing πιστεύσασιν, and makes it a tame observation. Bengel renders ἐπί locally, "*ad vos* usque, in occidente" (cf. 2 Cor. x. 14), a construction that strains the preposition and gives an irrelevant sense.

11. **Εἰς ὃ καὶ προσευχόμεθα πάντοτε περὶ ὑμῶν.** *To which end we are also praying always about you*: see notes on I. i. 2, v. 17; and for the contents of the prayer, cf. I. iii. 12 f., v. 23, and ii. 16 f. below. Prayer rises out of *thanksgiving* (v. 3), as in ii. 16; I. iii. 11; Eph. i. 17; Ph. i. 9; Col. i. 9. The καί indicates that the μαρτύριον is carried on into προσευχή.

Εἰς ὅ (cf. Col. i. 29; also εἰς τοῦτο in Rom. xiv. 9, 2 Cor. v. 5, 1 Pet. iv. 6) points to the Divine end of Christ's advent (v. 10), ἐνδοξασθῆναι κ.τ.λ., which is again recalled in v. 12; but it embraces the whole of vv. 5—10, looking back through the immediate context to the δικαία κρίσις εἰς τὸ καταξιωθῆναι ὑμᾶς of v. 6. It is only through Christ's verdict at the Judgement that God's approval of the readers (ἵνα ὑμᾶς ἀξιώσῃ ὁ θεός) will be made duly manifest: "we pray that God may deem you worthy, so that you may contribute to the glory of the Lord Jesus, when He comes in judgement and finds you amongst God's approved saints."

ἵνα ὑμᾶς ἀξιώσῃ ὁ θεὸς ἡμῶν τῆς κλήσεως, *that our God may count you worthy of* (*His*) *calling*. For ἵνα after a verb of *praying*, cf. iii. 1; 1 Cor. xiv. 13; Ph. i. 9; Mk xiii. 18; and see note on I. iv. 1. For the sense of ἀξιόω,—"to reckon," not to make, "worthy"—see note on καταξιόω, v. 5; and cf. 1 Tim. v. 17; Lk. vii. 7; Heb. iii. 3, x. 29. Καλέω, κλητός, κλῆσις, elsewhere (see particularly note on I. ii. 12; also iv. 7, v. 24; 1 Cor. i. 2, 26, vii. 18—24; Rom. viii. 28, xi. 29; Gal. i. 6, 15; Eph. iv. 1; 2 Tim. i. 9) point not to the Christian "vocation" as a continued state, but to the "call" of God which first makes men Christians, the invitation and summons to enter His kingdom. Of this "high calling" (Ph. iii. 14) those who receive it are, to begin with, utterly unworthy (Gal. i. 13—15); henceforth it is the rule of their life to "walk worthily" of it (I. ii. 12); their own highest aim, and the best hope of those who pray for them, is that "God may count" them "worthy," through His grace taking effect in them (see the next clause). To be "reckoned worthy of God's calling" is in effect to be "reckoned worthy of His kingdom" (v. 5), to which He "calls" men from the first (I. ii. 12); and this "kingdom and glory of God" are realized in the glorification of the Lord Jesus, the goal now immediately in view: see note on εἰς ὅ above; and cf., in view of the identity assumed, 1 Cor. xv. 24 and Ph. ii. 9 ff. The Thessalonian believers have been called *to glorify their Saviour* on the day of His appearing by the final outcome of their faith; "from the beginning God chose" them to be participators in the glory and honour won by the Lord Jesus (ii. 13 f.), and thus to add lustre to His triumph (see v. 12): this is a privilege of which the Apostles pray that "God may count" their disciples "worthy." This estimate—God's tacit judgement on the desert of individual men—precedes Christ's public and official verdict pronounced at His coming (see I. ii. 4 b; and cf. 1 Cor. iv. 5 with 2 Cor. v. 10 f.).

The emphatic ὑμᾶς at the beginning of the clause explains the added ἡμῶν at the end. The personal relation of writers and readers prompts the prayer: cf. the juxtaposition of ἡμῶν ἐφ' ὑμᾶς in v. 10; and the play on these pronouns in I. i. 5 f., ii. 13, 17—20, iii. 6—13; also Ph. iv. 19; 2 Cor. iii. 2, xii. 21.

καὶ πληρώσῃ πᾶσαν εὐδοκίαν ἀγαθωσύνης καὶ ἔργον πίστεως ἐν δυνάμει, *and may fulfil every good pleasure of goodness and work of faith in power*: in other words, "May God mightily accomplish in you all that goodness would desire, all that faith can effect." This second half of the prayer links together the κλῆσις and the ἀξίωσις of the first. By the ἔργον πίστεως, in which they "walk worthily" (I. ii. 12 f.), Christian men carry out the call of God received in the Gospel, so that He counts them worthy of having received it and fit to contribute to the glory of His Son. But this very εὐδοκία and ἔργον of theirs, their consent and effort of obedience, are wrought in them by God—He must "fulfil" it all; see Ph. ii. 12 f. For πληρόω with objects of this kind, cf. Ph. ii. 2; Matt. iii. 15; Acts xiii. 25. The best commentary on this prayer is the Collect for Easter Week: "That as by Thy special grace preventing us Thou dost put into our minds good desires, so by Thy continual help we may bring the same to good effect."

The contents of the *worth* to be approved by God, as above implied, are defined by the parallel terms, πᾶσαν εὐδοκίαν ἀγαθωσύνης καὶ ἔργον πίστεως. Πᾶσαν covers both εὐδοκίαν and ἔργον; the latter interprets the former. Εὐδοκία is not therefore, as in most other places, *God's "good pleasure"* (so the older commentators generally), but (as in Rom. x. 1; Ph. i. 15) the "good-will" or "delight" of the readers,— of "goodness" itself in them. The parallelism suggests, if it does not require, that ἀγαθωσύνης be read as a subjective genitive (of source, cause)—"every delight of goodness," rather than "delight in welldoing" (as Lightfoot, e.g., would have it, referring by contrast to Rom. i. 32); cf. ii. 12 (εὐδοκέω); Eph. i. 5: in Sirach xviii. 31, εὐδοκίαν ἐπιθυμίας, "desire of lust," supplies an apposite parallel (cf. πάθος ἐπιθυμίας, I. iv. 5 above). The Apostles thankfully recognize the "goodness" of their readers (see vv. 3 f.; I. i. 3, ii. 13, iv. 9 f.), and could say of them what St Paul afterwards says to the Romans (xv. 14), πέπεισμαι...περὶ ὑμῶν, ὅτι...μεστοί ἐστε ἀγαθωσύνης; they pray that every desire which such goodness prompts may by God's help be realized. See also note on εὐδοκέω, I. ii. 8; εὐδοκία connotes a *hearty consent, good will* added to good feeling. Ἀγαθωσύνη—used by St Paul besides in Rom. xv. 14, Gal. v. 22, Eph. v. 9—in each instance denotes a human quality; it is a broad N.T. expression for *moral excellence*, like the ἀρετή of the philosophers (once in St Paul, Ph. iv. 8), but implies specifically an active beneficence; goodness is the expression of *love*. More narrowly taken, ἀγαθωσύνη, *bonitas*, is distinguished from χρηστότης, *benignitas* (cf. Gal. v. 22; see Trench's *Syn.* § 63), which denotes the kindly temper of the ἀγαθός. The abstract ἀγαθωσύνη becomes in the concrete πᾶν ἀγαθὸν τὸ ἐν ἡμῖν, τὸ ἀγαθόν σου, of Phm. 6, 14.

For ἔργον πίστεως, see note on I. i. 3. This double parallel repeats the triple parallel of that passage, with the order reversed, "goodness" balancing "faith," as "love" and "hope" there balance it together. Ἐν δυνάμει belongs to πληρώσῃ, indicating the manner and style of God's working in this behalf: see I. i. 5 (and note), ii. 13 (ἐνεργεῖται); Col. i. 29; Rom. i. 4; 1 Cor. iv. 20. The prayer is addressed τῷ δυναμένῳ...ποιῆσαι (Eph. iii. 20).

12. **ὅπως ἐνδοξάσθῃ τὸ ὄνομα τοῦ κυρίου ἡμῶν Ἰησοῦ ἐν ὑμῖν**, *so that the name of our Lord Jesus may be glorified in you*: the purpose of the prayer just uttered; ὅπως κ.τ.λ. (avoiding the repetition of ἵνα: cf. 1 Cor. i. 28 ff.; 2 Cor. viii. 14) expounds the εἰς ὅ of v. 11 (see note). "The glory of our Lord Jesus" was the aim of the Father in the entire dispensation of the Gospel (see Ph. ii. 9—11, and ii. 14 below), and is therefore the governing object of the Apostle's prayer and work (Ph. i. 20). For ἐνδοξάζω, see note on v. 10.

To "glorify *the name* of the Lord Jesus" is to exalt Him to the height of His character and attributes, or, more definitely, to show that "Jesus is *Lord*," giving Him τὸ ὄνομα τὸ ὑπὲρ πᾶν ὄνομα (Ph. ii. 9 ff.). In the final revelation (*v.* 7), His redeemed people will supply the best reason for calling Jesus "Lord": cf. 1 Pet. i. 7; Rev. i. 5 f., v. 9 f., &c. The general description of the ground of Christ's Advent glory in *v*. 10—ἐν τοῖς ἁγίοις αὐτοῦ, ἐν πᾶσιν τοῖς πιστεύσασιν—is now translated into the specific and consoling ἐν ὑμῖν (cf. 1 Pet. i. 4 f.). The Thessalonian Church was to supply its missionaries with their δόξα καὶ χαρά (I. ii. 20)—nay, it will supply this to the Lord Jesus Himself; all beholders will praise Him, on seeing His completed work "in you"!

καὶ ὑμεῖς ἐν αὐτῷ is added, since the glory accruing to the name of Jesus in the Thessalonians will shine in their own character, now that they are "presented perfect" in Him (see Col. i. 22, 28; Eph. v. 26 ff.; Rom. viii. 29 f., τούτους καὶ ἐδόξασεν), so that His highest glory carries with it *theirs*. They will be not merely "glorified *with* Him" (cf. I. v. 11; 2 Tim. ii. 11 f.; Rom. viii. 17), but "*in* Him" (see note on ἐν Χριστῷ, I. i. 1 and iv. 16; and cf. 1 Cor. i. 30, Gal. i. 20): this implies the intrinsic union of Christ and His own, set forth by St Paul in his next Epistle under the figure of *the body and its members* (1 Cor. xii. 12—27)—a union brought to its consummation in the Second Advent (1 Cor. xv. 23, 45—49; Col. iii. 1—4; Ph. iii. 21), which the Apocalypse represents under the emblem of "the marriage of the Lamb" (Rev. xix. 7; cf. Jo. xiv. 3, xvii. 24).

Ὅπως ἐνδοξασθῇ τὸ ὄνομα τοῦ κυρίου...ἐν ὑμῖν is part of the web of O.T. prophetic sayings woven into this section. The writer of Is. lxvi. 5 (as in the LXX; cf. the references under *v.* 8 above, and *Introd.* pp. lx. f.) comforts the persecuted and fearful **remnant of Israel** with the anticipation, ἵνα τὸ ὄνομα κυρίου δοξασθῇ καὶ ὀφθῇ ἐν τῇ εὐφροσύνῃ αὐτῶν. See, besides, Isai. xlix. 3, Ezek. xxviii. 22, xxxviii. 23, xxxix. 21,—in which last passage ἐν ὑμῖν appears, and the verb ἐνδοξάζομαι (with *God, the Lord*, for subject) in the other three. That the δόξα κυρίου is to be manifested to the whole world in Israel's redemption from her oppressors, was the grand consolation of exilic prophecy.

The adjunct **κατὰ τὴν χάριν** κ.τ.λ. belongs to the entire qualified predicate, ἐνδοξασθῇ...ἐν αὐτῷ; it is *in accordance with the grace of our God* (*ours*, as thus caring for *us*) *and the Lord Jesus Christ*, that the glorification of Christ and Christians in each other should come about. That Christ should find His glory in men, and share His glory with them, is the greatest conceivable *favour* (χάρις)—a favour on God's part to begin with, since "He gave up His own Son" (Rom. iv. 24 f., viii. 32; Jo. iii. 16; 1 Jo. iv. 9, &c.) for this end: for ἡ χάρις τοῦ θεοῦ in this connexion, see particularly ii. 16 below; Rom. iii. 24 f., v. 15—21; Eph. i. 6—14, ii. 4—10; 2 Tim. i. 9; Tit. ii. 11, iii. 7; Heb. ii. 9 f.; 1 Pet. i. 13. As to ἡ χάρις τοῦ κυρίου, see 2 Cor. viii. 9: "You know the grace *of our Lord Jesus Christ*, how that on your account He became poor when He was rich, that you through His poverty might become rich." In *His* grace our Lord prayed to *the Father's* grace for His disciples, "that they may be with me where I am, that they may behold my glory" (Jo. xvii. 23 f.). To ask this was the highest possible mark of regard that our Lord could pay to His servants.

Grammatically, ἡμῶν and κυρίου Ἰησοῦ Χριστοῦ might be parallel complements to τοῦ θεοῦ,—*God of us and of the Lord*, &c.; but Pauline usage forbids this construction (cf. *vv.* 1 f., I. i. 1, &c.). The grand expression "our Lord Jesus Christ" (in full style and title) heightens the emphasis of χάρις. More plausible, in view of the anarthrous κυρίου and the rule prescribing the reference of two co-ordinate nouns prefaced by a single article to the same subject (A. Buttmann's *Gram. of N.T. Greek*, pp. 97—101), is the rendering (*grace*) *of our God and Lord, Jesus Christ*, adopted by Hofmann (cf. 2 Pet. i. 1, 11; Tit. ii. 13). The Apostle Paul appears to call Jesus Christ explicitly θεός in Rom. ix. 5 and Tit. ii. 13 (cf. Jo. xx. 28), as he does implicitly in Col. i. 15 ff., ii. 9, Ph. ii. 6, &c.; but his habitual discrimination between "the Father" as θεός and "Jesus Christ" as κύριος (*vv.* 11, 12 *a*, ii. 16, &c.; also 1 Cor. viii. 6; Eph. iv. 5; Ph. ii. 11) makes the identification improbable in point of usage; the context in no way suggests it. The absence of the article is accounted for by St Paul's frequent use of κύριος as a proper name of Jesus Christ (Winer-Moulton, p. 154).

For χάρις, see note on I. i. 1, to which the following observations are added:—(1) The radical sense of χάρις is *pleasingness*. From the artistic feeling of the Greek nature, this came to be synonymous with *loveliness, gracefulness*, which was variously personified in the three Χάριτες, divinities idealizing all that is charming in person and in social intercourse. Such was the connexion of the term with religion in classical Greek. (2) Ethically applied, χάρις denoted *pleasingness of disposition, favour*—both (*a*) in the active sense of *obligingness, graciousness*; and (*b*) in the passive sense of *acceptableness*: Ps. xliv. 3 (LXX) illustrates the former use, similarly Col. iv. 6; while (*b*) is exemplified in the familiar phrase, to "find grace in the eyes of" so and so (cf. Lk. ii. 52). On (2)(*a*) is based the specific

N.T. signification of χάρις, so conspicuous in St Paul. It denotes, therefore, (3) *the favour of God towards mankind* revealed in Jesus Christ, which stands *in contrast with human ill-desert*, and seeks to overcome and displace sin (see Rom. v. 20 f., &c.). It proceeds from the fatherly nature of God Himself (*v*. 2, ii. 16; Jo. i. 14, &c.); His grace is His redeeming love to sinners. *Mercy* (not *grace*) is the nearest O.T. counterpart to the N.T. χάρις: the former expresses God's pitiful disposition towards man as weak and wretched; the latter, His loving, forgiving disposition toward man as guilty and lost. Χάρις acts in the way of *forgiveness* (cf. the use of χαρίζομαι in Eph. iv. 32, &c.), and makes *a free gift* of the blessings of salvation (Rom. iii. 24, v. 17, &c.). Hence it is opposed, in Pauline teaching, not only to *sin* which it abolishes, but to *human merit* which it sets aside—to "works of law" regarded as means of salvation, and to everything that would make God's benefits, conferred in Christ on mankind, matter of "debt" on His part: see Rom. iii. 19—21, iv. 4—15; Gal. ii. 15—21; Eph. ii. 1—10. (4) Χάρις may signify a specific *act* or *bestowment of Divine bounty*, "grace" in some concrete form (Rom. i. 5; Eph. iii. 8, &c.); with this application is connected the use of χάρισμα for a specific *endowment*, or *function*, imparted in the order *of Divine grace* (1 Cor. vii. 7, xii. 4 ff., &c.). (5) Sometimes, again, χάρις denotes *a state of grace* in man,— God's grace realized and operative in the Christian, as in Rom. v. 2; 2 Tim. ii. 1; 2 Pet. iii. 18. (6) Lastly, χάρις bears in the N.T., as in common Greek, the sense of *thanks, gratefulness*; so in 2 Tim. i. 3.

CHAPTER II.

1. The first ημων (after κυριου) is wanting in B and syr[hcl]. It may have come in from I. iii. 13, v. 23, &c.: ημων appears slightly to weaken the collocation of παρουσια του κυρ. Ιησ. Χρ. and ημων επισυναγ. επ' αυτον, and is better left out.

2. For μηδε (θροεισθαι) the T.R., after the Syrian uncials (**KLP**), has μητε by assimilation to the context. *Per contra*, some Western copies read μηδε for μητε in the sequel. B 37 present the itacistic θροεισθε (-αι); cf. note on iii. 14, also on I. v. 13.

The latest uncials (**D**^c**K**) and most minn. substitute (η ημερα) του κυριου by του χριστου; cf. Phil. ii. 16. **GP** omit του.

3. της ανομιας, in ℵB with ten minn., cop sah arm, Tert Amb Ambrst: της αμαρτιας, **ADGLP** &c., latt vg syrr. The consistency of the former reading with της ανομιας and ο ανομος in *vv*. 7 f., which are not very likely to have influenced the copyist at this *earlier* point (as these expressions might have done if preceding our text), lends intrinsic probability to the well-attested reading of ℵB and the Egyptian versions. If ανομιας be rightly preferred, αμαρτιας must be set down as a Western paraphrase; it is curious that the three Latin Fathers above-named here oppose themselves to the reading of the Latin versions. Aνομια is a comparatively rare word in the N.T.

4. The gloss ως θεον is interpolated before καθισαι in D^cF^{gr}GKL and most minn., in syr^{pesh} and g [lat]; it was incorporated on this quite insufficient evidence in the T.R. **G*** employs in this phrase the extraordinary Latinism ινα θεον (g* *ut*, in the sense of *quasi, deum*).

AG 37 put αποδεικνυοντα for -νντα.

5. D* Ambrst, ετι εμου οντος, for ετι ων.

6. αυτου, in ℵ*AKP 17 37, and some others: εαυτου, **BDGL** &c.— The latter seems to be a Western and Syrian emendation: or is αυτου an assimilation to αυτον occurring just above?

8. Ιησους, after ο κυριος, is wanting in B and the Syrian witnesses, followed by the T.R. WH query the word, despite the almost unanimous support of the pre-Syrian witnesses (including the versions), to which other editors defer. WH rely on the authority of B, and on the preferability, high in the case of the *names* of Christ, of the *brevior lectio*. The O.T. complexion of the passage favours the bare κυριος; see Expos. Note. Moreover the frequency of ο κυριος Ιησους in 1 and 2 Thess. would prompt insertion on the part of copyists; cf. second note on I. v. 9 above. The Fathers quote this sentence somewhat loosely: "Christ," "the Lord Christ," "the Lord Jesus Christ," but oftenest "the Lord Jesus."

ανελει in ABP and some minn.; αναλοι, ℵ* Or (probably); ανελοι, D*G 17 67**—latt and vg, however, have *interficiet*, which points to ανελει; αναλωσει in D^cKL &c.; the cop and syrr indicate αναλοι or -λωσει. On the whole, αναλοι commends itself as the mother reading, from which αναλωσει sprang by way of grammatical emendation, and ανελει partly by itacism, or paraphrase, and partly by correction after Isai. xi. 4. See Expository Note.

10. To the Syrian editors appear to be due the article with αδικιας, and εν before τοις απολλυμενοις. D also reads της.

Χριστου after αληθειας, in D*, is an example of Western license.

11. πεμψει in ℵ^cD^cEKLP, most minn., and the verss. (except am fu cf the Vulgate)—a tame correction of πεμπει (ℵ*ABD^{gr*}G^{gr} 17 67** cat^{txt}, Or Bas Cyr Dam, &c.)—originating perhaps with the versions.

12. απαντες, ℵAG; παντες, BDKLP &c. The peculiar force of άπαντες does not lie on the surface (see Expos. Note); there was no obvious temptation to copyists to insert the ά-, otherwise rare in N.T.

εν is prefixed to τη αδικια by AK and the Syrians, conforming to the ordinary construction: see 1 Cor. x. 5; 2 Cor. xii. 10.

13. ειλετο, for -ατο: grammatical correction of K and the minuscules; see note on προειπαμεν (-ομεν), I. iv. 6.

απαρχην, in BG^{gr}P 17, f vg syr^{hcl}, Did Euthal Cyr Dam (ωσπερ απαρχην) Amb: certainly a favourite expression of St Paul's, and not inappropriate, nor out of keeping with I. i. 4. απ' αρχης, which is strongly attested by ℵDKL (A latet) &c., d e g syr^{pesh} cop arm aeth, Chr Thdrt Ambrst Vig, is a *hap. leg.* for St Paul; it well accords with the parallel representation in I. i. 4 ff.: cf. Ph. i. 5 and iv. 15; and see Expository Note.

14. και is inserted between εις ο and εκαλεσεν in אGP 37 and several minn., latt syr—a group resembling that which reads απαρχην in v. 13; against ABDKL &c., for omission. On the other hand, as Weiss points out, the conjunction in its contracted form might easily slip out in writing ΕΙϹΟΚ,ΕΚΑΛΕϹΕΝ, as it did between καθως and εκληθητε in Eph. iv. 4 (B). Cf. Textual Note on I. iv. 8 above. ABD* and several minusco. mechanically conform υμας to ευαγγ. ημων, writing ημας.

16. For Ιησους Χριστος, A 47 read Ιησους ο χριστος; and B, Χριστος Ιησους—an order of the names found seven times in B where no other MS. presents it.

BDK 17 omit ο before θεος—a letter easily overlooked in uncial writing before θ. Instead of ο πατηρ ημων A and the Syrian uncials, with latt and vg, read και πατηρ ημων, squaring with I. i. 3, iii. 11, 13, &c.

17. στηριξαι υμας, in the latest uncials, and cop; cf. iii. 3.

εργω και λογω, transposed by G and the Syrians, in conformity with Rom. xv. 18; 2 Cor. x. 11; Col. iii. 17, &c. Lk. xxiv. 19 gives the only N.T. parallel to the order of this passage.

§ 3. ii. 1—12. THE REVELATION OF THE LAWLESS ONE.

In this Epistle, as in the First, the principal aim of the Letter discloses itself in the second chapter, after the opening act of praise. The writers' thoughts gravitate towards it in their thanksgiving, from i. 5 onwards. *The near coming of Christ* preoccupies both themselves and their readers (see §§ 8, 9 of Epistle I., and pp. xxvii. ff. of *Introd.*). To the preceding section this is related (see *Introd.* to § 2) as I. v. 1—11 to iv. 13—18; in each instance the writers pass, by the contrastive δέ, from consideration of the import of the Parousia to that of its time,—there insisting on its uncertainty of date as a reason for watchfulness, here giving a premonitory sign as evidence that "the day" is not yet in sight and by way of dissuasive from premature excitement on the subject. Cf. *Introd.* pp. lii., lxiii. f. Chapters 1 and 2 are closed by Prayer and Thanksgiving, as they commenced with Thanksgiving and Prayer (cf. Eph. i.—iii.), being thus rounded off into a whole by themselves, like chaps. i.—iii. of Epistle I. (cf. τὸ λοιπόν, iii. 1 below, with λοιπὸν οὖν, I. iv. 1); but the secondary topic of Epistle I. becomes the primary topic of Epistle II.,—a reversal due to the increased acuteness of the questions connected with the Parousia. The Thessalonian Church was too eager and credulous in its expectation of the Lord's advent; the Apostles beg them "for the sake of [that] advent" to be cautious (*v.* 1). Some went so far as to declare that "the day of the Lord is already come" (*v.* 2). To enable the readers to "prove the prophesyings" (I. v. 20 f.) addressed to them on this matter, they are furnished with a token, or omen, of the Second Advent, which indeed St Paul had virtually supplied beforehand (*v.* 5). Preceding Christ's return in judgement (i. 5 ff.), there must be *a supreme manifestation of evil* (*vv.* 3—10). This development, as it seems to be represented, will be twofold, producing (1) "the apostasy"; and (2) "the revelation of the man of lawlessness" (or "of sin"), in whom the sin of humanity will culminate, assuming an absolutely Satanic character (*vv.* 3, 4, 9, 10). This gigantic impersonation of evil is exhibited as the antagonist and antithesis of Christ in such a way that, while St Paul does not give to his conception the name *Antichrist*, yet this designation correctly sums up his description; the term ἀντίχριστος (the climax of the ψευδόχριστοι of Matt. xxiv. 24), subsequently made familiar by St John's use of it (1 Jo. ii. 18 ff.), was not improbably derived in the first instance from this passage. Meanwhile, we are told, there exists (3) a "withholding" influence, which delays the appearance of Antichrist, though the lawlessness that comes to its height in him "is already at work" (*vv.* 6 f.). When the "revelation" of this "mystery" at last takes place, while it heralds the return of the Lord Jesus (*v.* 8), at the same time it will prove for His rejecters a signal means of judgement, captivating by its magical delusions all who are not armed against them by "the love of the truth" (*vv.* 9 ff.).

This paragraph is the most obscure in the whole of the Pauline Epistles. It is composed in a reserved, elliptical fashion and bears reference to St Paul's oral communications, without which indeed he does not expect what is here written to be understood. In their recollection of his spoken words the Thessalonian readers had a key, which was soon lost, to the words of the Letter. We must grope for the interpretation as well as we can. Considerable light is, however, thrown on this dark passage by its relation to O.T. prophecy, and by the historical events and current ideas of the apostolic age. An *Appendix* will be added on the subject. See Milligan's *Commentary*.

1. Ἐρωτῶμεν δὲ ὑμᾶς, ἀδελφοί, ὑπὲρ τῆς παρουσίας τοῦ κυρίου [ἡμῶν] Ἰησοῦ Χριστοῦ καὶ ἡμῶν ἐπισυναγωγῆς ἐπ' αὐτόν. *But we ask you, brothers, on behalf of the coming of the* [or *our*] *Lord Jesus Christ and our gathering together to* (*meet*) *Him.* By δέ of contrast we pass from the certainty and blessedness of the παρουσία (i. 5 ff.) to the

state of disquiet about it into which this Church is in danger of falling.

For ἐρωτάω in *requests*, see I. iv. 1, v. 12, and note on the former verse; as in the above instances, ἀδελφοί is naturally interjected where common Christian interests and sentiments are involved. Ὑπέρ may be nothing more than an equivalent for περί (*about, concerning*), stating the matter of request (see, for περί in like connexion, I. v. 10, and note; 1 Cor. vii. 1; Phm. 10, &c.); but it may be questioned whether ὑπέρ in St Paul ever quite loses the stronger meaning, *on behalf of*: cf. I. iii. 2; 2 Cor. i. 6, xiii. 8; Ph. ii. 13. "In the interest of" that very advent, in which their future happiness is wrapped up (ἡμῶν ἐπισυναγωγῆς), the Apostles warn their readers against deception. The Latin rendering, followed by the A.V., *per adventum*, is certainly erroneous : this ὑπέρ *obtestationis*, frequent in Homer after λίσσομαι (see e.g. *Iliad* xv. 660), is rare otherwise. The full title, "our Lord Jesus Christ," heightens the solemnity of the appeal; see note on I. i. 1, also I. v. 9; and, for παρουσία, I. ii. 19.

The writers add καὶ ἡμῶν ἐπισυναγωγῆς ἐπ' αὐτόν, remembering what they had said in I. iv. 17 and v. 10 concerning the reunion of departed and living saints at Christ's coming; perhaps also under the painful sense of continued separation from their "brothers" in Thessalonica and the uncertainties of meeting in "this present evil world": see I. ii. 17 ff., iii. 6, 11, II. i. 4 f.; and the pathetic "rest *with you*" of i. 7. Ἐπισυναγωγή (the noun in Heb. x. 25, δὶς λεγόμενον in N.T.; also 2 Macc. ii. 7, ἐπισυναγωγὴν τοῦ λαοῦ) recalls the prophetic words of Jesus in Matt. xxiv. 31 f., Mk xiii. 27, ἀποστελεῖ τοὺς ἀγγέλους κ. ἐπισυνάξει τοὺς ἐκλεκτοὺς ἐκ τῶν τεσσάρων ἀνέμων κ.τ.λ., which rest on the promise of Deut. xxx. 4 respecting the διασπορά of Israel; cf. the echoes of our Lord's sayings on the Last Things noted in I. iv. 13—v. 11. The ἐπι- in this compound—a word of the κοινή, which loved cumulative prepositional compounds—implies "convening *upon*" some centre: *Christ* supplies this mark,—ἐπ' αὐτόν (as in Mk v. 21); cf. note on ἐφ' ὑμᾶς, i. 10. Under the single article, παρουσία and ἐπισυναγωγή form one object of thought, the latter accompanying the former (I. iv. 14—17); cf. εἰς τὴν βασιλείαν...καὶ δόξαν, I. ii. 12.

2. In I. v. 12 ἐρωτάω was construed, in the regular classical way, with the infinitive; in I. iv. 1, according to commoner N.T. usage with verbs of *asking*, it was followed by ἵνα and subjunctive; here, more loosely, by εἰς τό with infin., stating the matter of the request as its *aim*: see notes on this usage, I. ii. 12, 16.

εἰς τὸ μὴ ταχέως σαλευθῆναι ὑμᾶς ἀπὸ τοῦ νοὸς μηδὲ θροεῖσθαι, *to* the end you be not quickly shaken from your mind (out of your wits: *ut non cito moveamini a sensu vestro*, Vulg.; *ne cito a mente dimoveamini*, Beza; *præcipitanter* for ταχέως, de Wette—more vividly), nor be kept in agitation. Σαλεύω (see Lk. xxi. 25, σάλος θαλάσσσης, "*tossing* of the sea") denotes a rocking motion, a shaking up and down: cf. Matt. xi. 7; Lk. vi. 48; Acts xvi. 26; Heb. xii. 26 f. Lightfoot quotes in illustration from Plutarch's *Moralia* II. 493 D, ὄρεξιν τοῦ κατὰ φύσιν ἀποσαλεύουσαν...ὡς ἐπ᾽ ἀγκύρας τῆς φύσεως σαλεύει, suggesting that St Paul's σαλευθῆναι ἀπό (ἀπο-σαλεύειν) is the opposite of σαλεύειν ἐπί (ἀγκύρας), so that the figure intended would be that of a ship loose from her anchor and at the mercy of the waves. But νοῦς scarcely holds the office of an *anchor* to the soul (in Plutarch, as above, the ὄρεξις, not the man himself, ἀποσαλεύει; and the verb is intransitive); it signifies rather the mental poise and balance, *off* (ἀπό) which the Thessalonians might be thrown by the shock of sensational announcements. Ταχέως does not require a *terminus a quo* in point of time (cf. Gal. i. 6); it implies a *speedy* disturbance, a startled movement. For νοῦς, the regulative intellectual faculty, cf. Rom. vii. 25, xii. 2; 1 Cor. i. 10; Ph. iv. 7; Tit. i. 15: it is here virtually contrasted with πνεῦμα (see next clause) as its check and counterpart, much as in 1 Cor. xiv. 14 f., 19. The δοκιμάζειν of I. v. 19—21 involves the application of νοῦς to "prophesyings." Νοός, νοΐ (1 Cor. xiv. 15, 19) are 3rd declension forms, such as were assumed, on the analogy of βοῦς, by two or three 2nd decl. nouns in later Greek (cf. πλοός, Acts xxvii. 9), and to some extent in the earlier vernacular; see Winer-Moulton, p. 72.

Θροεῖσθαι (the verb found besides in Mk xiii. 7, in like connexion; cf. Lk. xxiv. 37, Cod. B) signifies in the present tense an excited condition of mind following the shock of agitating news (σαλευθῆναι, aorist). The former clause describes the overthrow of mental equilibrium, this the nervous, fluttered state supervening. Hence μηδέ, "nor indeed": some might have already experienced a σάλευσις, but even they should not be kept in θρόησις, in *continued discomposure*. Θροεῖσθαι may be used of any agitating emotion (cf. Cant. v. 4, LXX)—not *fear* in this instance—"*terreamini*" of the Vulg. is misleading; in classical Greek, where the verb is chiefly poetical, it signifies *to cry* or *tell aloud*.

μήτε διὰ πνεύματος μήτε διὰ λόγου μήτε δι᾽ ἐπιστολῆς ὡς δι᾽ ἡμῶν, *neither through spirit, nor through word, nor through letter as (coming) through us.* The writers suppose three various means by which the report about the Advent may have been set on foot. It could not be traced to a definite and single source; the information forthcoming led the Apostles to think that each of these causes may have been at work. If e.g. it were believed in some part of the Church—through misunderstanding either of Epistle I. or of some other Letter of the Apostles, or from some Letter falsely circulated in their name —ὅτι ἐνέστηκεν ἡ ἡμέρα, both prophets and teachers would be found to enforce, and probably exaggerate, the epistolary statement or inference.

Πνεῦμα and λόγος are distinguishable in the light of 1 Cor. xii. 8—11, xiv. 6, 26 : they denote the agencies by which ἀποκάλυψις and διδαχή respectively are communicated; λόγος σοφίας and λόγος γνώσεως are there contrasted with προφητεία, which was the mark of possession by the πνεῦμα in the highest sense (1 Cor. xiv. 1, &c.). While λόγος means "discourse of reason," the expression of rational thought and judgement (proceeding in this case upon the data of revelation), πνεῦμα applies to the ecstatic or prophetic utterances of supernaturally inspired persons.

Ὡς δι' ἡμῶν—parallel to δι' ἐπιστολῆς, or to διὰ λόγου (see ii. 5) and δι' ἐπιστολῆς together (cf. ii. 15)—indicates not a fact *per se*, but as subjectively conceived (cf., for the use of ὡς, Rom. ix. 32; 2 Cor. ii. 17; Eph. vi. 5; Phm. 14),—"*supposing that* it is through us," viz. that the announcement of the arrival of "the day" comes from the Lord through His Apostles and has their authority. The deception in the case is implied not by the adverb ὡς, but by the context. Whether this impression was derived from an actual Apostolic Letter, or from a supposititious Letter, either circulated in the Church or only alleged to be in existence, it is impossible to say; the curious ambiguity of the words suggests that the writers were at a loss on this point. The language of iii. 17 suggests that spurious Letters of St Paul were in existence; the mere suspicion of this would be enough to dictate the precaution there taken. On the other hand, judging from the words of I. v. 27, it appears to have been possible that some members of the Church knew the First Epistle only by report and at second-hand, in which case its expressions on the subject might be distorted to the effect described. The plainest words will be misinterpreted by prepossessed minds.

ὡς ὅτι ἐνέστηκεν ἡ ἡμέρα τοῦ κυρίου, *supposing that the day of the Lord is now present*. For ὡς ὅτι, cf. 2 Cor. v. 19, xi. 21; "the idea of misrepresentation or error is not necessarily inherent in this combination of particles; but the ὡς points to the subjective statement as distinguished from the objective fact, and thus the idea of untruth is frequently implied" (Lightfoot) : the Thessalonians are being alarmed and distracted "under the idea that the day of the Lord has arrived" (see note on ὡς δι' ἡμῶν above : cf. also Rom. v. 16; 1 Cor. iv. 7, viii. 7 ; 2 Cor. x. 14 ; Col. ii. 20). For ἡ ἡμέρα τοῦ κυρίου, see note on I. v. 2. Ἐνέστηκεν, the perfect, with present sense, of ἐνίστημι, signifies more than *nearness*, more even than *imminence* (ἐπίσταται, I. v. 3); it means *to be in place, in course*—not merely approaching but *arrived*—and is regularly contrasted with μέλλω (see Rom. viii. 38; 1 Cor. vii. 26; Gal. i. 4 ; Heb. ix. 9). "The day," it was affirmed, had so come that while it was not actually visible, its hour had struck, and its light might break any moment on the eyes of men : "Christ has come," was the cry—ὁ κύριος πάρεστι, though His παρουσία is not manifest (cf. Matt. xxiv. 26 f., xxv. 6).

3 a. **μή τις ὑμᾶς ἐξαπατήσῃ κατὰ μηδένα τρόπον.** *Let no one deceive you in any kind of way*—i.e. in the way of πνεῦμα, λόγος, ἐπιστολή, or otherwise. The warning conveyed by μή...ἐξαπατήσῃ seems to be directed against a wilful, dishonest deception : cf. *v.* 10 ; also (for this verb) Rom. vii. 11, xvi. 18 ; 2 Cor. xi. 3. Κατὰ...τρόπον (cf. Rom. iii. 2 ; Acts xxvii. 25) differs slightly from ἐν...τρόπῳ, iii. 16, the former implying a more definite "way" or "ways" before one's mind. For like warnings, from St Paul, cf. 1 Cor. vi. 9, xv. 33 ; Gal. vi. 7 ; Col. ii. 4, 8 ; 1 Tim. iv. 1 ; 2 Tim. iii. 13 ; Tit. i. 10 ; from our Lord on this very subject, Matt. xxiv. 4 f., 11, 24 ; Lk. xxi. 8.

WH, in the *margin* of their text, place a comma, instead of the full stop, after κυρίου, thus connecting *v.* 3 *a* (elliptically) with *v.* 2, through the μή of *apprehension* : (*I say this*) *lest any one should, in any kind of way, deceive you*; cf. I. iii. 5, upon the common construction of the μή in that passage ; see Moulton's *Proleg.*, p. 178.

3 b. **ὅτι ἐὰν μὴ ἔλθῃ ἡ ἀποστασία πρῶτον—**, *because (it will not be) unless there come the apostasy first* : "first," i.e. before the Lord comes. Πρῶτον, for πρότερον, of *two* events, in I. iv. 16 ; Lk. vi. 42, &c. The ellipsis is natural, the matter of deception, stated in *v.* 2 *b*, being in every one's mind ; after *v.* 3 *a*, a formal contradiction of the announcement ἐνέστηκεν ἡ ἡμέρα is needless. Probably the writer meant to insert the contradiction after the ἐάν clause ; but this sentence so runs on that its intended apodosis drops out of mind. We shall find a similar lapse in *v.* 7. St Paul is liable to grammatical *anacolutha* (incoherences) in passages of excited feeling : cf. Gal. ii. 4, 6, v. 13 ; Rom. iv. 16, v. 12 ff. ; see Winer-Moulton, p. 749. His style is that of a speaker, not of a studied writer ; such broken sentences are inevitable, and explain themselves, in animated conversation.

Judging from the difference of contents in the two members of the ἐὰν μή clause, it seems likely that the Apostles conceived of two distinct and closely connected historical conditions precedent to the Lord's παρουσία, both of which St Paul had set forth in his original teaching at Thessalonica (*v.* 5). First, the "coming" of "the apostasy": the definite article marks this out as a *known* futurity, defined by evidence either from the O.T. or from current Christian prophecy,—the latter, if we must be guided by analogy (cf. i. 8—12), being grounded upon the former. Ἀποστασία in classical Greek denotes *a military* or *political revolt, defection*; in the O.T., specifically, *a revolt from the theocracy* (from "the Lord"): see e.g. Jos. xxii. 22 (ἐν ἀποστασίᾳ...ἔναντι τοῦ κυρίου, בְּמָרְד...בַּיהוה); also 1 Macc. ii. 15 (οἱ καταναγκάζοντες τὴν ἀποστασίαν...ἵνα θυσιάσωσιν); so in Acts xxi. 21, "thou teachest apostasy from Moses"; and the verb ἀφίσταμαι in 1 Tim. iv. 1; Heb. iii. 12 (τὸ ἀποστῆναι ἀπὸ θεοῦ ζῶντος). Correspondingly, in the Christian Church the term (here first appearing) signifies *revolt from Christ,* the defection of men "denying the Lord that bought them" (2 Pet. ii. 1). "*The* apostasy" is surely no other than that foretold by Jesus in His great prophetic discourse (so much in St Paul's mind when he wrote these Letters): see Matt. xxiv. 10—13, 24: "Then shall many stumble...Many false prophets shall arise (cf. διὰ πνεύματος above), and shall mislead many...Because iniquity (ἡ ἀνομία) shall abound, the love of the many shall wax cold...There shall arise false Christs and false prophets...so as to lead astray, if possible, even the elect"; cf. Matt. xiii. 24—30, the parable of the Wheat and Tares. This sad forecast of their Lord weighed on the hearts of the early Christians; the presentiments arising from it grew in distinctness in St Paul's mind as time went on, and were expressed with increasing emphasis: see Rom. xvi. 17—20; Acts xx. 29 f.; Eph. iv. 14. In his last Letters (1 Tim. iv. 1—3; 2 Tim. iii. 1—9, iv. 3 f.) he defines "the apostasy" as it took shape toward the close of his own career, in language portending a full development, which he seems to have thought might not be far distant. The false teachers portrayed in the Pastoral Epistles as belonging to "the last times," supply a link between St Paul's ἡ ἀποστασία and the ἀντίχριστοι πολλοί of St John (see *Appendix,* pp. 223 f.). Such words as those of 1 Cor. xii. 3, xvi. 22, Col. ii. 19, show that, in the Apostle's view, personal loyalty to Christ was the safeguard of Christianity. "Apostasy" leads the way in the supreme manifestation of evil here predicted, as though the infidelity of Christians supplied the occasion for the final eruption of wickedness; see, by contrast, Matt. v. 13—16. Ἡ ἀποστασία gave the Latin translators much trouble: *abscessio* (Tertullian); *discessio* (Vulg.); *defectio* (Ambrosiaster, Beza, Estius); *refuga* (Augustine), as if for ἀποστάτης.

3 c, 4. καὶ ἀποκαλυφθῇ ὁ ἄνθρωπος τῆς ἀνομίας, ὁ υἱὸς τῆς ἀπωλείας, ὁ ἀντικείμενος καὶ ὑπεραιρόμενος ἐπὶ πάντα λεγόμενον θεὸν ἢ σέβασμα: *and there be revealed the man of lawlessness, the son of perdition, the adversary and exalter of himself against every one called god or (that is) an object of worship* (*aut numen*, Beza). The emphatically prefixed ἀποκαλυφθῇ (substituted for ἔλθῃ of the parallel clause), which is repeated in *vv*. 6 and 8 (see notes; and cf. note on ἀποκάλυψις in i. 7), gives to the coming of ὁ ἄνθρωπος τῆς ἀνομίας a superhuman stamp (cf. *v.* 9). He is identified in *v.* 7 (see note) with τὸ μυστήριον τῆς ἀνομίας; he comes κατ᾽ ἐνέργειαν τοῦ Σατανᾶ—ἄνθρωπος τὴν φύσιν, πᾶσαν ἐν ἑαυτῷ τοῦ διαβόλου δεχόμενος τὴν ἐνέργειαν (Theodore)—and attended with manifold miracles (*v.* 9). The terms describing his appearance and action are borrowed throughout from those belonging to the Parousia of the Lord Jesus, whose ἀντικείμενος he is to be,—a Satanic parody of Christ, His counterpart in the realm of evil.

This fearful personality is described by three epithets, the last of the three consisting of a double participle, and all three Hebraistic in form: (*a*) ὁ ἄνθρωπος τῆς ἀνομίας (see Textual Note)—"the man" in whom "lawlessness" is embodied, "in quem recapitulatur sex millium annorum omnis apostasia et injustitia et dolus" (Irenæus), who takes this for his rôle (cf. "man of God," "man of Belial [worthlessness]," "man of war," &c., in O.T. idiom); more simply named ὁ ἄνομος in *v.* 7. As "*the* man of lawlessness," Antichrist concentrates into himself all that in human life and history is most hostile to God and rebellious to His law; he is the *ne plus ultra* of τὸ φρόνημα τῆς σαρκός (Rom. viii. 7). (*b*) The first epithet refers to the *nature*, the second to the *doom* of Antichrist; he is ὁ υἱὸς τῆς ἀπωλείας: cf. υἱὸς θανάτου, 1 Sam. (Kingd.: LXX) xx. 31; similarly in Deut. xxv. 2 the man "worthy of stripes" is called, in Hebrew, "a son of smiting"; in Isai. lvii. 4 the LXX reads τέκνα ἀπωλείας, σπέρμα ἄνομον, for "children of transgression, a seed of falsehood" (in the Hebrew). To Judas Iscariot alone this name is elsewhere given in Scripture (Jo. xvii. 12); but "whose end is perdition" (Ph. iii. 19), and "he goeth to perdition" (εἰς ἀπώλειαν ὑπάγει, Rev. xvii. 8, 11; said of the seven-headed Wild Beast), affirm virtually the same thing. (*c*) Of the two terms of the third title, ὁ ἀντικείμενος (cf. 1 Cor. xvi. 9, 1 Tim. v. 14) is familiar, being equivalent to הַשָּׂטָן, ὁ Σατανᾶς, *Satan*, whom this "man of lawlessness" is to represent and whose power has its ἐνέργεια in him (*vv.* 9 f.): see note on I. ii. 18; cf. also Zech. iii. 1

(LXX), ὁ διάβολος εἱστήκει...τοῦ ἀντικεῖσθαι αὐτῷ. This participle might be complemented, along with the following ὑπεραιρόμενος, by ἐπὶ πάντα κ.τ.λ.; but it is a quasi-substantive, with a recognized and complete sense of its own. It is Christ to whom "the adversary" ἀντίκειται. In the second and extended participial clause of (c)—identified with ὁ ἀντικείμενος by the single article—ὑπεραιρόμενος has a parallel in 2 Cor. xii. 7 ("exalted above measure": St Paul is fond of ὑπερ-compounds). ᾿Επί as distinguished from ὑπέρ, and in this context, is *against*. Πάντα λεγόμενον θεόν (illustrated by 1 Cor. viii. 5 b) embraces the entire Pan-theon of mankind, deposed by this Great Usurper in favour of himself; while καὶ σέβασμα extends the previous term, already so wide, by way of including every conceivable object of religious reverence. So σεβάσματα in Acts xvii. 23 embraces the religious monuments and emblems of Athens generally—shrines, altars, images, and the like: the only other N.T. instance of the word, which occurs besides in Wisd. xv. 17.

4 (*continued*). **ὥστε αὐτὸν εἰς τὸν ναὸν τοῦ θεοῦ καθίσαι, ἀποδεικνύντα ἑαυτὸν ὅτι ἔστιν θεός,** *so that he takes his seat within the temple of God, showing himself off* (to the effect) *that he is God!* ῞Ωστε (with infin. of result) brings in the climax of the self-deification of the Antichrist. Καθίσαι (the verb is here intransitive, as in 1 Cor. x. 7, Matt. v. 1, and commonly) is the aorist of the single (inceptive), not continuous, act (cf. Matt. xix. 28, &c.); εἰς is suitable to the aorist, as implying *motion towards,*—putting himself "into" God's seat in the ναός. By their several positions αὐτόν and καθίσαι are both emphasized: "*He* in the temple of God *takes his seat,*" as though that throne were his! Ναός, as distinguished from ἱερόν, is the temple proper, the inner shrine of Deity. For ἀποδεικνύναι, cf. 1 Cor. iv. 9; it implies a public display, a *show—spectandum aliquid proponere* (Winer); but the verb, as Lightfoot proves, bears in later Greek the technical sense, *to nominate* or *proclaim* one who accedes to office: so e.g. Philo, *in Flaccum*, § 3, Γαΐου δὲ ἀποδειχθέντος αὐτοκράτορος. The verb thus read is construed with ὅτι quite easily—" proclaiming himself that he is God"—with attraction of the dependent subject (see Winer-Moulton, p. 781). The present participle, qualifying the aorist infinitive (for indicative), denotes a course of conduct that attends and centres in the principal act. On the ordinary rendering of ἀποδεικνύντα, the ὅτι clause forms a second explanatory object, by a kind of synizesis: "showing himself off, (declaring) that he is God." The rendering of Beza, "præ se ferens se esse Deum," corrects the Vulg. translation, "ostendens se tanquam sit Deus," which misses the essential point: ἀντίθεός τις ἔσται (Chrysostom).

The latter part of the description of the Antichrist, from καὶ ὑπεραιρόμενος onwards, is based on Dan. xi. 36 f.: καὶ ὑψωθήσεται ἐπὶ πάντα θεὸν καὶ ἐπὶ τὸν θεὸν τῶν θεῶν ἔξαλλα λαλήσει...καὶ ἐπὶ τοὺς θεοὺς τῶν πατέρων αὐτοῦ οὐ μὴ προνοηθῇ...ὅτι ἐν παντὶ ὑψωθήσεται; cf. Dan. vii. 25, ix. 27; Isai. xiv. 13 f.; Ezek. xxviii. 2 (ὑψώθη σου ἡ καρδία, καὶ εἶπας Θεός εἰμι ἐγώ, κατοικίαν θεοῦ κατῴκηκα...καὶ ἔδωκας τὴν καρδίαν σου ὡς καρδίαν θεοῦ). In the above prophetic sketches the monarchic pride of the ancient world-rulers is seen rising to the height of self-deification; these delineations adumbrate the figure which St Paul projects on to the canvas of the Last Times. That *self-deification* forms the governing feature in this description of Jesus Christ's Satanic counterfoil, presupposes the assumption of Divine powers on the part of Jesus; cf. note below on ὁ ναὸς τοῦ θεοῦ.

St Jerome gave the two possible interpretations of εἰς τὸν ναὸν τοῦ θεοῦ, writing in *Epist.* 121: "in templo Dei—vel Ierosolymis, ut quidam putant [so the older Fathers—Irenæus, Hippolytus, &c.]; vel in ecclesia, ut verius arbitramur" (so the later Greek interpreters). Chrysostom presents the latter view less exactly (for St Paul refers to the *entire* Church as ὁ ναὸς τοῦ θεοῦ in 1 Cor. iii. 16 f., 2 Cor. vi. 16; cf. Eph. ii. 21; Rev. iii. 12, vii. 15), when he says, καθεδήσεται εἰς τὸν ναὸν τοῦ θεοῦ, οὐ τὸν ἐν Ἱεροσολύμοις ἀλλὰ καθ' ἑκάστην ἐκκλησίαν. When the Apostles speak of "the sanctuary of God" without other qualification, they might be supposed to refer to *the existing Temple at Jerusalem* (cf. the usage of the Gospels, as respects ὁ ναός and the wider τὸ ἱερόν, which includes the courts and precincts; similarly in Acts, τὸ ἱερόν), to which the kindred passages in Daniel (xi. 31, xii. 11), cited in our Lord's prophecy (Matt. xxiv. 15; Mk xiii. 14), unmistakably apply. Attempts have been made to show that their words were practically fulfilled soon after this date by certain outrages committed by Nero, or Vespasian, upon the sacred building. But this is not clearly made out; and even the worst of the Emperors was but an adumbration of St Paul's Antichrist. On the other hand, we have learnt from I. ii. 16 that St Paul believed national Judaism to be nearing its end,—the Temple presumably with it. Our Lord had predicted the speedy destruction of the Jerusalem Temple (see Lk. xxi. 6, 32, &c.), which, forsaken by the Son of God, could no longer be viewed by Christians as properly His "Father's house" (see Matt. xxiii. 37—39, xxi. 13; Jo. ii. 16). Along with the terms ἐκκλησία τοῦ θεοῦ (I. ii. 14), Ἰσραὴλ τοῦ θεοῦ (Gal. vi. 16), οἱ ἅγιοι and the like (cf. Phil. iii. 3; 1 Pet. ii. 4—10), the presumption is that ὁ ναὸς τοῦ θεοῦ belonged stately, in Pauline dialect, to the new kingdom of God and had its "foundation" in "Jesus Christ"; this transference of the ναός-conception is assumed in 1 Cor. iii. 10—17, the next Epistle to ours in point of date, as a recognized fact (οὐκ οἴδατε ὅτι ναὸς θεοῦ ἐστε; v. 16); the true ναός is marked out by the indwelling of "the Spirit of God" (cf. I. iv. 8 above). It is true that there is nothing in our context to identify ὁ ναός with ἡ ἐκκλησία; but we must remember that we have an incomplete context before us; the paragraph is throughout allusive to previous teaching (v. 5). The doctrine that the Christian community constitutes the veritable shrine of God on earth, may have been as familiar to the Thessalonian as it certainly was a few years later to the Corinthian Christians. Granted this equivalence, the connexion between ἀποστασία and ἄνθρωπος τῆς ἀνομίας becomes exceedingly close : the Lawless One, in superseding all forms of religion except the worship of himself, assumes to sit within the Church of God, abetted by its apostates, and proclaims himself its supreme Head, thus aping the Lord Jesus and playing his anti-Christian part to the uttermost,—"quasi quia ipse sit Christus" (Theodore).

FURTHER NOTE on *vv*. 3, 4: The premonition of the Lord's advent the Apostle finds, therefore, in a previous counter-advent, and this is twofold: the coming (*a*) of "the apostasy," (*b*) of "the man of lawlessness, &c."—(*a*) a movement, (*b*) a personality. The former element in the representation remains in shadow, and is developed by the Apostle in later Epistles; the image of "the lawless one" dominates this passage, but forthwith vanishes from the Pauline writings, to reappear, considerably altered, in St John's Apocalypse. Three chief factors go to furnish the conception these verses give of the final manifestation of evil: (1) Its foundation lies in *the data of O.T. prophecy*, more particularly in *the Apocalypse of Daniel*, to which our Lord attached His own predictions of the Last Things and with whose "son of man coming in the clouds of heaven" He identified Himself. "The apostasy" and "the lawless one," since they embody ideas from this source, appear to signify two distinct but co-operating agents, as distinct as were e.g. the apostates of Israel from the heathen persecutor, Antiochus Epiphanes, for whose coming their appearance gave the signal at the Maccabean epoch. The distinction is one pervading Pauline thought and teaching, viz. that existing between Jew and Gentile (Israel and the nations), which are reconciled on the true basis in the Church of Jesus Christ; the corresponding evil powers unite to form the conspiracy of Satan. The new Messianic community, of Jews and Gentiles in one body, has become "the Israel of God" (Gal. vi. 16), defection from which is "apostasy" (see 1 Tim. iii. 15—iv. 1: ἀποστήσονται ἀπὸ τῆς πίστεως); the old antagonism of Jew and Gentile has been resolved into the opposition of the people of God and the world—the antithesis, in short, of Christian and un-Christian. St Paul, to speak in modern phrase, appears to foresee the rise of an apostate Church paving the way for the advent of an atheistic world-power. So it is "out of the" restless, murmuring "sea" of the nations and their "many waters" that "the Wild Beast" of Rev. xiii. 1, xvii. 1, 15, "comes up." This combination Dan. viii. 23 already presents: "When the transgressors are come to the full, a king of fierce countenance...shall arise"; cf. 1 Macc. i. 10—15, for the parallel earlier situation. (2) While, for Christian believers, "apostasy" means *revolt from Christ*, by the same necessity the figure of the atheistic world-king, transmitted from the Book of Daniel and from the struggle with Antiochus, is clothed with an *Antichristian* character; "the lawless one" becomes from point to point the antithesis of the Lord Jesus,—a Satanic caricature of the Messiah-king, a mock-Christ. But (3) *contemporary history* supplied a powerful stimulus to the prophetic spirit of the Church, which already dimly conceived its Antichrist as the counterpart in the kingdom of darkness to the true Christ reigning in God's kingdom of light. The deification of the Roman emperors, from Julius Cæsar downwards, was the religious portent of the times. This cultus must have forced itself on the notice of St Paul and his companions in their recent journey through the north-west of the peninsula of Asia Minor (Acts xvi. 6—10), where it already flourished; not improbably, their route led through Pergamum, a city which boasted, in its magnificent Augusteum, the chief seat of Cæsar-worship in the whole empire (cf. Rev. ii. 13: ὅπου ὁ θρόνος τοῦ Σατανᾶ). The attempt of the mad emperor Gaius (Caligula), made in the year 40, to place his statue in the temple of Jerusalem for Divine worship, an attempt only frustrated by his death, compelled the attention of the entire Jewish people whom it filled with horror, and of the Christian Church with them, to this blasphemous cult. The event was typical, showing to what lengths the intoxication of supreme power in an atheistic age might carry a man inspired by Satan. This attempt was, in Caligula's case, but the last of a series of outrages upon "every so-called god." Suetonius relates that this profane monster transported the statue of Olympian Zeus to Rome, displacing its head for the image of his own; also, that he built his palace up to the temple of the old Roman gods Castor and Pollux, and made of this a vestibule where he exhibited himself standing between the twin godships to receive the adoration of those who entered (*De Vita Cæsarum*, IV. 22). The Apostles are only projecting into the future the development of a "mystery of lawlessness"—a tendency of inscrutable force, springing from unsounded depths of evil in human nature—that was "already at work" before the eyes of all men, masquerading in the robes of Godhead on the imperial stage at Rome. So far-reaching was the impression produced by the Emperor-worship, that Tacitus represents the German barbarians speaking in ridicule of "ille inter numina dicatus Augustus" (*Ann.* I. 59). The effect of this new Government cultus on what remained of natural religion in the rites of Paganism is indicated in the pregnant words of Tacitus (*Ann.* I. 10), the first clause of which might have been borrowed from St Paul: "Nihil deorum honoribus relictum, cum se templis et effigie numinum per flamines et sacerdotes coli vellet [Augustus]." Nor was the exaltation of the emperors to deity an act of mere autocratic blasphemy and pride of power. Rome and the provinces spontaneously gave Divine honours to Julius Cæsar at his death; and Augustus promoted the new worship out of policy, to supply a religious bond to the Empire and to fill up the void created by the decay of the old national religions, the very want which Christianity was destined to meet. In relating the obsequies of Julius Cæsar Suetonius says (*Ibid.* I. 84, 88): "Omnia simul ei divina atque humana decreverat [senatus]... Periit sexto et quinquagesimo ætatis anno, atque in deorum numerum relatus est, non ore modo decernentium sed *et persuasione volgi*." The unconscious irony of the above passage is finely pointed by the exclamation which the same historian puts into the mouth of the dying Vespasian (VIII. 23): "Vae, puto deus fio!" Cf. the tragic scene of Acts xii. 20—23, ὁ δῆμος ἐπεφώνει· Θεοῦ φωνὴ κ. οὐκ ἀνθρώπου...καὶ γενόμενος σκωληκόβρωτος ἐξέψυξεν (Herod Agrippa I.). The shout of the Cæsarean δῆμος shows the readiness of a sceptical and servile heathenism to deify its human rulers, while the language of St Luke reflects the loathing stirred thereby in Christian minds. The Apostle Paul realized the significance of the Cæsar-worship of his time; he saw in it τὸ μυστήριον τῆς ἀνομίας at work in its most typical form. Antiochus Epiphanes and Gaius Caligula have sat as models for his Antichrist; the Emperor Elagabalus (218—222 A.D.), in more Oriental fashion, subsequently reproduced the type. The struggle between heathen Rome and Christianity was to turn, in reality, upon the alternative of κύριος Καῖσαρ (*Martyr. Polycarpi* 8) or κύριος Ἰησοῦς (1 Cor. xii. 3),—the point already raised, with a strange instinct (like that of Caiaphas respecting the Atonement, Jo. xi. 50 ff.), by the Jews when they cried to Pilate, "If thou let Him [Jesus] go, thou art not

Cæsar's friend" (Jo. xix. 12). Cæsar-worship being the state-religion, and the worship of Christ admitting of no sharer, Christianity became a *religio illicita* and its profession, constructively, high treason. Ὅμοσον τὴν Καίσαρος τύχην was the test put to Polycarp by the Proconsul of Asia in the stadium of Smyrna (*Martyr.* 9); and this challenge, with the martyr's reply—πῶς δύναμαι βλασφημῆσαι τὸν βασιλέα μου;—is typical of the entire conflict of the Christian faith with its ἀντικείμενος, the veritable θεὸς τοῦ αἰῶνος τούτου enthroned on the Palatine. Cæsar's titular name Σεβαστός, the Greek rendering of *Augustus* (cf. ὁ ὑπεραιρόμενος ἐπὶ πᾶν...σέβασμα above)—to which *Divus* was added at death—was itself a blasphemy to Jewish and Christian ears. With σεβαστός the title υἱὸς θεοῦ was associated in popular use and even in business documents (see Deissmann's *Bible Studies,* pp. 166 f., and Dalman's *Words of Jesus*, p. 273), a circumstance that gave additional point to the rivalry, which forced itself on Christian thought, between the deified Cæsar and Christ.

5. **Οὐ μνημονεύετε ὅτι ἔτι ὢν πρὸς ὑμᾶς ταῦτα ἔλεγον ὑμῖν;** *Do you not remember that when I was still with you, I used to tell you these things?* cf. 1 Cor. xi. 23, xv. 1 f.; Ph. iii. 18. With οὐ μνημονεύετε (wrongly rendered in Vulg. "Num retinetis?"—Ambrose, Beza, "**Annon** meministis?") cf. in Pauline usage I. ii. 9; Acts xx. 31. For ὢν πρὸς ὑμᾶς, see note on I. iii. 4, also iii. 1 below. Ἔτι ὢν implies that St Paul had spoken of these matters, as we should expect, toward the end of his ministry, when he had not "as yet" left them; cf. Acts xviii. 18, Jo. xx. 1, &c., for ἔτι. On the probable duration of the mission in Thessalonica, see *Introd.* p. xx. Ἔλεγον, imperfect, of repeated discourse; cf. I. iii. 4.

The *first person singular* in this reminder interrupts the plural pervading the Letter, and only appears again in iii. 17. St Paul's self-consciousness comes to the surface. What had been said on this mysterious and awful subject came from the principal writer (see i. 1), who had dealt with it on his own distinct authority; whereas in I. iii. 4 and in I. iv. 15—passages in different ways parallel to this—the communicative plural was used, no such personal distinctiveness of teaching being implied: cf. notes on the singular of I. ii. 18, iii. 5, v. 27; and *Introd.* pp. xxxix. f.

The reminder gently reproves the readers, who should not have been so easily disturbed by the alarmists, after what the Apostle had told them; it obviates further explanation in writing on a subject bordering upon politics, the more explicit treatment of which might have exposed the missionaries to a renewal in more dangerous form of the charges that led to their expulsion from Thessalonica: see Acts xvi. 6 f.; *Introd.* pp. xxix. f. St Paul's enemies would be quick to seize on anything calculated to compromise him with the Roman Government.

6. καὶ νῦν τὸ κατέχον οἴδατε. *And for the present, you know the thing that withholds.* Καὶ νῦν might be construed with οἶδα, or the like, describing a present knowledge due to past instruction, whether immediate or more distant: cf. Jo. viii. 52, xvi. 30; Acts xii. 11, xx. 25; also I. iii. 8. At the same time, νῦν τὸ κατέχον does not stand for τὸ νῦν κατέχον, as some read it (ὁ κατέχων ἄρτι, v. 7, is different); but practically the same sense is arrived at by reading καὶ νῦν as equal to καὶ τὰ νῦν (cf. Acts iii. 17 with iv. 29, v. 38; xx. 22 with 32; τὰ νῦν is never found in St Paul), *and for the present,* in contrast with the future ἀποκάλυψις ἐν τῷ καιρῷ αὐτοῦ of vv. 3, 6, 8. The stress thrown by v. 7 on the actual, contemporary working (ἤδη, ἄρτι; see notes) of τὸ μυστήριον τῆς ἀνομίας points decidedly to this rendering of the emphatically placed temporal adverb (cf. Jo. iv. 18); see Lightfoot and Bornemann *ad loc.*

Τὸ κατέχον οἴδατε,—not "you know *what it is* that withholds"; but "you know *the withholding thing*": the restraint is something within the range of the readers' experience; they are *acquainted with it,* apart from their having been told of it by the Apostle; cf. I. ii. 1 f., iii. 4; 1 Cor. xvi. 15, &c. We have not, therefore, to look far afield for the bar then in the way of the Man of Lawlessness. Further definition is needless, and might have been dangerous on the writers' part; *verbum sapientibus sat.* Τὸ κατέχον becomes ὁ κατέχων in v. 7—here a principle or power, there a personal agency, as with τὸ μυστήριον and ὁ ἄνθρωπος τῆς ἀνομίας. For the interpretation of the phrase, see the next verse. For the *adverse* sense of κατέχω, see note on I. v. 21 (otherwise applied in that passage); cf. Rom. i. 18, vii. 6. The classical use of the neuter participle as a substantive is elsewhere confined to St Luke in the N.T.; see Lk. i. 35, ii. 27, iv. 16, &c.

εἰς τὸ ἀποκαλυφθῆναι αὐτὸν ἐν τῷ αὐτοῦ καιρῷ, *to the end that he* (viz. ὁ ἄνθρωπος τῆς ἀνομίας, vv. 3 f.) *may be revealed in his season.* For εἰς τό with infinitive, blending purpose and result, cf. v. 2, and note on I. ii. 16. For καιρός, see I. v. 1, and note: "the Lawless One" has "his season," the time fit and appointed for him in the development of events and in the counsels of God—one of the series of καιροί of which the Thessalonians had vainly desired to have the chronology. Antichrist has his set time, corresponding to that τῆς ἐπιφανείας τοῦ κυρίου ἡμῶν Ἰησοῦ Χριστοῦ, ἣν καιροῖς ἰδίοις δείξει ὁ μακάριος καὶ μόνος δυνάστης, 1 Tim. vi. 14 f. The restraining power so operates as to hold back and put bounds to human lawlessness, until the hour strikes for its final outbreak in the Man of Lawlessness and the revelation of all its hidden potencies. This order of things belongs to God's purposes. If He allows moral evil to exist in His creatures (and its possibility is inseparable from moral freedom), yet He knows how to control its activity, till the time when its full manifestation will best subserve its overthrow and judgement. The Jewish Law had also been in the Apostle's view, and under the same theory of a Divine control and overruling of sin for its final extinction, a κατέχον and yet a δύναμις τῆς ἁμαρτίας for its sphere and age, preparing for and leading up to the καιρὸς τοῦ χριστοῦ: see Gal. iii. 19—24; Rom. v. 13, 20 f.; 1 Cor. xv. 56. The καιρὸς τοῦ ἀνόμου will be the last and worst of many such crises, chief amongst which was that of Lk. xxii. 53: "This is your hour (ὑμῶν ἡ ὥρα) and the power of darkness"; cf. again 1 Tim. iv. 1.

7. τὸ γὰρ μυστήριον ἤδη ἐνεργεῖται τῆς ἀνομίας. *For the mystery is already working* (or *set in operation*)—*(that) of lawlessness*. For ἐνεργεῖται, see note on I. ii. 13. Verse 7 explains (γάρ) *v.* 6; at present the Lawless One is held back till the fit time, "for he is *already* here in principle, *operative as a mystery* awaiting revelation, and checked so long as the withholder stands in the way" (see notes on *v.* 6). Νῦν is *nunc, now, at this time*; ἤδη, *jam, already, by this time*; ἄρτι, *in præsenti, just now* or *then, at the moment*: for ἤδη, cf. further 1 Cor. iv. 8, v. 3; Phil. iii. 12; 2 Tim. ii. 18, iv. 6; 1 Jo. iv. 3. The sentence identifies the present hidden with the future open and unrestrained working of the forces embodied in ὁ ἄνομος.

Τὸ μυστήριον, correlative with ἀποκαλυφθῆναι (as in Rom. xvi. 25; 1 Cor. ii. 7—10, xiv. 2; Eph. iii. 3, 9 f.; Col. i. 26; Rev. i. 1, 19 f.), is, like that, a term proper to the things of God and the manifestation of Christ, appropriated here to the master-work of Satan and the appearing of the Man of Lawlessness; cf. note on *v.* 3 (ἀποκαλυφθῇ). Τὸ μυστήριον, in St Paul's dialect, is not something strange and hard to understand; nor is it some secret reserved, like the Mysteries of Greek Paganism or of Jewish Alexandrian or Essenic esoteric systems, for the initiated few; it denotes that which is by its nature above man's reason, and is therefore known only as and when God is pleased to reveal it (*vv.* 6, 8); 1 Cor. ii. 6—16 sets the Pauline use of the word in a full light: see the Note *ad rem* in J. A. Robinson's *Ephesians*, pp. 234 ff. In the Book of Daniel, μυστήριον (LXX: rendered "secret") first appears in its distinct Biblical sense;

then in Wisdom ii. 22, vi. 24, &c. In the Gospels (Matt. xiii. 11 and parallels) the word is once cited from the lips of Jesus, referring to the truths conveyed to disciples but veiled from others by His parables. So monstrous and enormous are the possibilities of sin in humanity, that with all we know of its working the character of the Man of Lawlessness remains incomprehensible beforehand. The history of Sin, like that of Divine Grace, is full of surprises.

μόνον ὁ κατέχων ἄρτι ἕως ἐκ μέσου γένηται : *only (there is) the withholder for the present, until he be taken out of the way.* Again a hiatus in the Greek, as in *v.* 3, an incoherence of expression very natural in a letter written by dictation, and due seemingly to the excitement raised by the apparition of ὁ ἄνθρωπος τῆς ἀνομίας before the writer's gaze. Ἄρτι qualifies ὁ κατέχων : the restraint *at present* in exercise *holds down* (κατέχω, as in Rom. i. 18) *lawlessness*, and veils its nature by limiting its activity, until ὁ καιρὸς τοῦ ἀνόμου (*v.* 6) shall arrive. Ἄρτι (see note on ἤδη above; also on I. iii. 6) indicates a particular *juncture*, or *epoch*; it suggests a brief transitional period, such as St Paul, without claiming certain knowledge, was inclined to suppose the current Christian dispensation to be; see note on I. iv. 15, also 1 Cor. vii. 29, &c. Ἕως and synonymous conjunctions, often in classical Greek and more often than not in the N.T., dispense with ἄν in governing the subjunctive of contingency : see Moulton's *Prolegomena*, pp. 165—9; also Winer-Moulton, p. 371, A. Buttmann, *N. T. Grammar*, pp. 230 f. For ἐκ μέσου, cf. 1 Cor. v. 2; 2 Cor. vi. 17; Col. ii. 14 (ἐκ τοῦ μέσου, classical) ; and contrast I. ii. 7.

On ὁ κατέχων, see note to τὸ κατέχον, *v.* 6. While the restrainer and the object of restraint are each expressed in both personal and impersonal form, it is noticeable that the former appears as primarily *impersonal*, while the latter is predominantly *personal*: the writers contemplate the power of lawlessness in its ultimate manifestation, as embodied in a supreme human antagonist of Christ; whereas the restraint delaying Antichrist's appearance appears to be conceived as an influence or principle, which at the same time may be personally represented. It is better therefore to render ὁ κατέχων "ho that restraineth," rather than "one that restraineth" (R.V.); the expression seems to signify a class, not an individual : cf. Eph. iv. 28.

Where then are we to look, amongst the influences dominant at the time and known to the readers, for the check and bridle of lawlessness? where but to law itself,—*Staat und Gesetz* (J. A. Dorner)? For this power the Apostle Paul had a profound respect; he taught that αἱ οὖσαι ἐξουσίαι were ὑπὸ θεοῦ τεταγμέναι (Rom. xiii. 1—7). Silvanus and himself were citizens of Rome, and had reason to value the protection of her laws; see Acts xvi. 35—39, xxii. 23—29, xxv. 10—12. About this time he was finding in the upright Proconsul Gallio a shield from the lawlessness of the Jewish mob at Corinth; the Thessalonian "politarchs" at least made some show of doing him justice (Acts xvii. 5—9). St Paul's political acumen, guided by his prophetical inspiration, was competent to distinguish between the character and personal action of the Emperor-god and the grand fabric of the Roman Empire over which he presided.

As head of the civil State, the reigning Augustus was the impersonation of law, while in his character as a man, and in his assumptions of deity, he might be the type of the most profane and wanton lawlessness (witness Caligula, Nero, Elagabalus). Roman law and the authority of the magistrate formed a breakwater against the excesses of autocratic tyranny as well as of popular violence. The absolutism of the bad Cæsars had after all its limit; their despotic power trampled on the laws, and was yet restrained by them. Imagine a Nero master of the civilized world and adored as a god, with all respect for civil justice destroyed in the action of the powers of the State, and St Paul's "mystery of lawlessness" would be amply "revealed." Despite τὸ κατέχον ἄρτι, the reign of Nero, following in a few years the writing of this Letter, showed to what incredible lengths the idolatry of a wicked human will may be carried, in the decay of religion and the general decline of moral courage which this entails. This monster of depravity, "the lion" of 2 Tim. iv. 17, stood for the portrait of "the wild beast" in St John's Apocalypse, which carried forward St Paul's image of "the lawless one," even as the latter took up *Daniel's* idea of the godless king impersonated in Antiochus Epiphanes. Döllinger, seeing in Nero St Paul's ὁ ἄνθρωπος τῆς ἀνομίας, regarded *Claudius*, the reigning emperor, as ὁ κατέχων— *scil. preventing*, while he lived, Nero's accession—because of the resemblance of his name to *claudens*, a Latin equivalent for κατέχων: but this ascribes to the Apostle an unlikely kind of foresight; and it credits him with a pun (made in Latin too, though he is writing in Greek) quite out of keeping with the solemnity of the subject. (Askwith identifies Claudius and his policy with ὁ κατέχων, τὸ κατέχον, inasmuch as he rescinded the edict of Caligula.) Nero fell; and the Roman State remained, to be the restrainer of lawlessness and, so far, a protector of infant Christianity. Wiser rulers and better times were in store for the Empire. Through ages the κατέχον of the Apostolic times has proved a bulwark of society. In the crisis of the 8th century "the laws of Rome saved Christianity from Saracen dominion more than the armies.... The torrent of Mohammedan invasion was arrested" for 700 years. "As long as Roman law was cultivated in the Empire and administered under proper control, the invaders of Byzantine territory were everywhere unsuccessful" (Finlay, *History of Byzantine Empire*, pp. 27 f.). Nor did Roman Law fall with the Empire itself, any more than it rose therefrom. It allied itself with Christianity, and has thus become largely the parent of the legal systems of Christendom. Meanwhile *Cæsarism* also survives, a second legacy from Rome and a word of evil omen, the title and model of illegal sovereignty. The lawlessness of human nature holds this "mystery" in solution, ready to precipitate itself and "to be revealed at the last season." The mystery betrays its working in partial and transitional manifestations, until "in its season" it crystallizes into its complete expression. Let reverence for law disappear in public life along with religious faith, and there is nothing to prevent a new Cæsar becoming master and god of the civilized world, armed with immensely greater power. For other interpretations given to ὁ κατέχων, see the *Appendix*.

8. **καὶ τότε ἀποκαλυφθήσεται ὁ ἄνομος.** *And then* (not before) *shall be revealed the Lawless One:* this sentence resumes vv. 3, 4, in the light of v. 7 b. Καὶ τότε,—by contrast with the foregoing νῦν, ἤδη, ἄρτι, as in 1 Cor. iv. 5 (note also the previous ἕως), xiii. 12; with νῦν following, Rom. vi. 21, Gal. iv. 8 f., 29. Ὁ ἄνθρωπος τῆς ἀνομίας (v. 3), the principle of whose existence operated in τὸ μυστήριον τῆς ἀνομίας (v. 7), is briefly designated ὁ ἄνομος, just as the heathen, generically, are οἱ ἄνομοι (Acts ii. 23; 1 Cor. ix. 21, &c.). For ἀποκαλυφθήσεται, see notes on vv. 3, 6; and in its relation to μυστήριον, v. 7. *Thrice,* with persistent emphasis, ἀποκαλύπτεσθαι is asserted of ὁ ἄνομος, as of some portentous, unearthly object holding the gazer spell-bound. His manifestation will be signal, and unmistakable in its import to those whose eyes are not closed by "the deceit of unrighteousness" (v. 10); "the mystery of lawlessness" will now stand "revealed."

ὃν ὁ κύριος [᾽Ιησοῦς] ἀνελεῖ (or ἀναλοῖ) **τῷ πνεύματι τοῦ στόματος αὐτοῦ,** *whom the Lord* [*Jesus*] *will slay* (or *consume*) *by the breath of His mouth.* So that ὁ ἄνομος has scarcely appeared in his full Satanic character and pretensions, when he is swept away by the Redeemer's advent. The sentence is a reminiscence of Isai. xi. 4, where it is said of the "shoot from the stock of Jesse," πατάξει γῆν τῷ λόγῳ τοῦ στόματος αὐτοῦ (Heb. בְּשֵׁבֶט פִּיו, "by the rod of His mouth") καὶ ἐν πνεύματι διὰ χειλέων ἀνελεῖ ἀσεβῆ (LXX)—the ἀσεβής of that passage becomes the ἄνομος of this: cf. Job iv. 9, ἀπὸ πνεύματος ὀργῆς αὐτοῦ ἀφανισθήσονται; also Isai. xxx. 33, נִשְׁמַת יהוה כְּנַחַל גָּפְרִית

("the breath of Jehovah, like a stream of brimstone"), Ps. xviii. 8, xxi. 9, for theophanies of fiery destructiveness. Later Jewish teaching identified the ἀσεβής of Is. xi. 4 with *Armillus* (or *Armalgus*), the Anti-messiah; see Appendix, pp. 218 f. The terrible metaphor is in keeping with the language of i. 7 f. above, ἀποκάλυψις...ἐν πυρὶ φλογός. Τὸ πνεῦμα (synon. with λόγος of Isai. xi. 4) τοῦ στόματος αὐτοῦ is not conceived as a physical agent: "the word" or "breath" —the judicial sentence—issuing "from the mouth" of the Lord, has an annihilating effect on the power of the ἄνομος, even as the O.T. λόγος Κυρίου, or πνεῦμα τοῦ στόματος αὐτοῦ (Ps. xxxii. 6, LXX; cf. Ps. ciii. 30), operated creatively in the making of the world. As the *sight* of the Lord Jesus brings punishment on the cruel persecutors of His saints (i. 9), so *the breath of His mouth* suffices to lay low the Titanic Antichrist; "a word shall quickly slay him."

καὶ καταργήσει τῇ ἐπιφανείᾳ τῆς παρουσίας αὐτοῦ, *and will abolish by the apparition of His coming*. Ἐπιφάνεια denotes a signal, often a sudden appearance, the coming into sight of that which was previously, or commonly, hidden. The word recurs in the Pastoral Epp., applied once to the First Advent, 2 Tim. i. 10; and four times to the Second (in place of παρουσία), 1 Tim. vi. 14, Tit. ii. 13, 2 Tim. iv. 1, 8. Ἐπιφανής, in Acts ii. 20 (from the LXX, Joel ii. 31), is rendered "notable"; the verb ἐπιφαίνομαι occurs in Tit. ii. 11, iii. 4, in like connexion. Bengel paraphrases the expression, "prima ipsius adventus *emicatio*,"—"*the first dawn* of the advent." This noun belongs to later Greek: it is used of the "*dawning* of day" (Polybius), of the *starting into sight* of an enemy, of the *apparition* of gods to their worshippers, &c.; "dictum de Imperatoris, quasi dei apparitione, accessione ad regnum" (Herwerden, *Lexicon Græcum suppletorium*); much employed by the Greek Fathers in application to the various appearances of Christ. The Latin translators see in ἐπιφάνεια the *brightness* of the Advent (cf. ἐν πυρὶ φλογός, v. 7): "illustratione adventus sui" (Vulg.), "illuminatione præsentiæ suæ" (Augustine); similarly Erasmus, "ut accipias claritate Christi advenientis obscuratum iri Antichristum." For παρουσία, see note on I. ii. 19.

καταργέω, a favourite word of St Paul's—found once in Euripides, then in Polybius, four times in 2 Esdras (LXX)—signifies by etymology *to make idle* (ἀργός, ἀ-εργός), *inoperative*, so *to bring to nought, destroy*, a thing or person in respect of power and efficacy, *to make void, annul*: cf., besides instances above, Lk. xiii. 7; Heb. ii. 14; 1 Cor. xv. 24; Gal. v. 11. Severianus aptly says, recalling Col. iii. 4, ζωῆς οὐρανόθεν φανερουμένης, ἀδύνατον μὴ καταργηθῆναι τὸν τοῦ θανάτου πρόξενον. For the whole verse, cf. the description of Christ in Rev. i. 16 f.: ἐκ τοῦ στόματος αὐτοῦ ῥομφαία δίστομος ὀξεῖα ἐκπορευομένη, καὶ ἡ ὄψις αὐτοῦ ὡς ὁ ἥλιος φαίνει ἐν τῇ δυνάμει αὐτοῦ· καὶ ὅτε εἶδον αὐτὸν ἔπεσα...ὡς νεκρός; for the former part of it, Rev. xix. 15. St Paul may be thinking here, as in i. 7 f. (see note), of the sudden light and arresting voice by which the Lord Jesus was revealed to himself (Acts ix. 3, xxii. 6). Theodore paraphrases the verse in a striking fashion: ἐξαίφνης ἀπ᾽ οὐρανῶν φανεὶς ὁ χριστὸς καὶ μόνον ἐπιβοήσας παύσει τῆς ἐργασίας, ὅλον αὐτὸν ἀναλώσας (cf. ἀναλοῖ in text above).

9. οὗ ἐστὶν ἡ παρουσία κατ᾽ ἐνέργειαν τοῦ Σατανᾶ, *whose coming is* (or *who has his coming*) *according to Satan's working*. The παρουσία of the Lord Jesus (*v.* 8 *b*) recalls the παρουσία of His "adversary" and false counterpart (see *v.* 4 and notes), which is further set forth in its manner (κατά), and accompaniments (ἐν), as "in accordance with (in the way or fashion of) a working of Satan"—being such a παρουσία as might be expected from such a source—and "in all manner of power and signs and wonders...and in all deceit," &c. The ἐνέργεια τοῦ Σατανᾶ (in respect of its agent) is an ἐνέργεια πλάνης in respect of its method, *v.* 11; Antichrist's παρουσία is, on the part of "the god of this world," a kind of mocking prelude to Christ's. This noun and the corresponding verb ἐνεργέω (-έομαι, I. ii. 13 : see note) frequently have *God* or *Divine* powers for subject: see 1 Cor. xii. 6; Gal. ii. 8, iii. 5; Eph. i. 11, 19 f., iii. 20; Phil. ii. 13, &c. As distinguished from δύναμις and ἰσχύς (see note on *v.* 9), ἐνέργεια means *power in operation* ("efficacia Satanæ," Beza). "Satan" holds toward Antichrist a relation analogous, in a shocking sense, to that of God toward Christ; the systematic and, as one might suppose, calculated adoption by Antichrist of the attributes of Christ is the most appalling feature in the whole representation. Even as God ἐνήργηκεν ἐν τῷ χριστῷ (Eph. i. 20), "by powers and wonders and signs" crowned in His resurrection (Acts ii. 22—24), Satan will find his supreme ἀποκάλυψις in the Antichrist ("diabolicam apostasiam in se recapitulans," Irenæus; "medius inter Satanam et perditos homines," Bengel), and will furnish him with δύναμις καὶ σημεῖα κ.τ.λ. to match. With ὁ Σατανᾶς we must associate ὁ ἀντικείμενος of *v.* 4 ; see note.

The series of terms in which the counterfeiting of Christ by Antichrist is indicated (see ἀποδεικνύντα ἑαυτὸν ὅτι ἔστιν θεός, ἀποκαλυφθῆναι, μυστήριον, ἐνεργεῖται, παρουσία) concludes ἐν πάσῃ δυνάμει καὶ σημείοις καὶ τέρασι,—the three expressions applied to the miracles of our Lord and His Apostles: see Mk vi. 2; Lk. xix. 37; Jo. iii. 2;

Acts ii. 22; Rom. xv. 19; 2 Cor. xii. 12; Heb. ii. 4, where they are variously combined. Of the three, σημεῖον is commonest, esp. in St John's Gospel; occasionally σημεῖα and τέρατα are coupled together, somewhat frequently in Acts—τέρατα is never used in the Gospels of the actual works of Jesus; δύναμις (-εις, rendered in the plur., by R.V., "mighty works") is most frequent in the Synoptics. Δύναμις names the miracle from its *cause*, the supernatural force acting in it; σημεῖον from its *meaning*, its *significance*; τέρας, *portentum, prodigium, miraculum*, from its abnormal nature and the astonishment it arouses. It is unfortunate that the "miracles" of Divine revelation have taken their modern name (through the Latin) from the last, which is the rarest and least characteristic of these synonyms; see Trench's *Syn*. § 91, also *On the Miracles*, chap. i. The three terms might constitute a collective idea, with πάσῃ at the beginning indicating the number and variety of Antichrist's "signs," and ψεύδους at the end qualifying them unitedly (Lightfoot); but—since δύναμις is singular, and rarely has this concrete sense except in the plural—we may better render the phrase: *in all power—both signs and wonders of falsehood* (cf. Rom. xv. 19, ἐν δυνάμει σημείων καὶ τεράτων; also i. 11, I. i. 5, Rom. i. 4, Col. i. 11, 29, for ἐν δυνάμει). Ψεύδους, the genitive noun of quality, does not (like ψεύδεσιν) stigmatize these as "false," i.e. pretended miracles (with no supernatural δύναμις behind them); but as "of falsehood," belonging to this realm, to the sphere of him who is ψεύστης καὶ πατὴρ αὐτοῦ (Jo. viii. 44), and serving his ends; they are signs attesting and suitable to a ψεῦδος, as our Lord's miracles attest and are suitable to ἡ ἀλήθεια: cf. Jo. iii. 2, x. 32, xiv. 10 f., xx. 30 f. These marks of Antichrist's coming were predicted by Jesus of the ψευδόχριστοι and ψευδοπροφῆται (Matt. xxiv. 24 f.; Mk xiii. 22),— σημεῖα μεγάλα καὶ τέρατα ὥστε πλανῆσαι, εἰ δυνατόν, καὶ τοὺς ἐκλεκτούς. The Apocalypse ascribes them, in ch. xiii. 11—14, to the second Wild Beast with his "lamb-like horns" and his dragon-like speech,—the Dragon aping the Lamb. Miracles are never in Scripture made as such—apart from their moral character and aim—the proof of a Divine mission; see Deut. xiii. 1—5. This weighty ἐν clause must be attached to ἐστίν, **not to** ἐνέργειαν, and forms indeed its principal complement.

10*a*. Already cumulative, the predicate is further extended **by καὶ ἐν πάσῃ ἀπάτῃ ἀδικίας τοῖς ἀπολλυμένοις** (this clause belongs to *v.* 9), *and in all deceit of unrighteousness for the perishing*,—words describing the subjective effect, as ἐν πάσῃ δυνάμει κ.τ.λ. describes the objective nature, of Satan's working in the Antichrist. Πάσῃ indicates a manifoldness of deception corresponding to the manifold forms of the deceiving agency, πάσῃ δυνάμει κ.τ.λ. 'Απάτη ἀδικίας, construed similarly to εὐδοκία ἀγαθωσύνης in i. 11 (see note), means such "deceit" as belongs to "unrighteousness," as it is wont to employ—*subjective* genitive, not unlike σημεῖα...ψεύδους above. 'Απάτη is the active and concrete "deceit," not " deceivableness " (A. V.), nor "deceitfulness" (elsewhere in A.V.): see Matt. xiii. 22; Eph. iv. 22 ; Col. ii. 8; Heb. iii. 13. On ἀδικία, the comprehensive term for *wrong*, *wrong-doing*, as between persons—synon. with ἀνομία (*v.* 8), which is wrong as committed against sovereign law—see further *v.* 12; it is connected with ψεῦδος, as violation of conscience with perversion of intellect, and opposed to ἀλήθεια here, much as in Rom. i. 18, ii. 8; 1 Cor. xiii. 6.

Τοῖς ἀπολλυμένοις is the dative to ἀπάτῃ, of the persons concerned; cf., for the construction, 1 Cor. i. 18, τοῖς ἀπολλυμένοις μωρία ἐστίν. For the sense of ἀπόλλυμαι, cf. i. 8 f.; also 1 Cor. xv. 18; 2 Cor. iv. 3 f. (ἐν οἷς ὁ θεὸς τοῦ αἰῶνος τούτου ἐτύφλωσεν τὰ νοήματα τῶν ἀπίστων); Ph. iii. 19. Οἱ ἀπολλύμενοι (see εἰς τὸ σωθῆναι following), the opposite of οἱ σωζόμενοι (1 Cor. i. 18; 2 Cor. ii. 15); the *present* participle connotes their perdition as commenced and going on, in the loss of the sense for truth and right and of receptiveness for God: cf. Rom. i. 18 ff., 28 ff.; Eph. iv. 18 ff.; 1 Tim. vi. 5; 2 Tim. iii. 8; Tit. i. 15 f.; Heb. x. 26 f.; Jude 10—13. They follow the guidance of ὁ υἱὸς τῆς ἀπωλείας (*v.* 3), and share his ruin. Satan's devices are *deceit for the perishing*, for men without the life of God, whose spiritual perceptions are destroyed through sin; while the children of God escape the deception, knowing how to "prove all things" (I. v. 21): cf., as to this contrast, I. v. 4 f.; 2 Cor. iv. 2—6; 1 Jo. iv. 1—6.

10 *b*. ἀνθ' ὧν τὴν ἀγάπην τῆς ἀληθείας οὐκ ἐδέξαντο εἰς τὸ σωθῆναι αὐτούς, *because they did not receive the love oj the truth to the end they might be saved*; or "in requital of their refusal to entertain the love of the truth," &c. For ἀνθ' ὧν (*pro eo quod*, Calvin), see Lk. i. 20, xii. 3, xix. 44; Acts xii. 23 (also 3 Kingd. xi. 11, Joel iii. 5, in LXX; Xenophon); for ἀντί of *correspondence* ('tit for tat'), cf. I. v. 15, &c. The dupes of Antichrist are treated after their kind; as they would not love truth, they shall not have truth, lies must be their portion : cf. the *lex talionis* in i. 6 f. ; also Ps. xviii. 26, cix. 17 ff.; Rev. xvi. 6, and Matt. xxv. 29. For δέχομαι, implying *welcome*, the opening of the heart to what is offered, cf. I. i. 6, ii. 13, describing the opposite conduct of the Thessalonian readers.

Ἡ ἀλήθεια is not the moral quality, "truth" as sincerity in the person, but the objective reality—"the truth" coming from God in Christ, viz. the Gospel, &c.: see *vv.* 12 f.; Rom. i. 18, 25, ii. 8; 2 Cor. iv. 2; Gal. v. 7; Eph. iv. 24; Col. i. 5; 1 Tim. iii. 15; Jo. viii. 32, &c. Ἡ ἀγάπη τῆς ἀληθείας is the bent of the mind toward the truth, the setting of the heart upon it (cf. Prov. ii. 2 ff., iv. 6, 13, &c.); this affection those condemned οὐκ ἐδέξαντο, inasmuch as they refused to entertain it,—they had no predilection for truth; "they loved the darkness rather than the light" (Jo. iii. 19). Ἀγάπη in this connexion is synonymous with εὐδοκία (i. 12 : cf. εὐδοκήσαντες τῇ ἀδικίᾳ, *v.* 12 below), but denotes the principle of affection, the radical disposition of the mind, while εὐδοκία signifies its consent and expressed inclination; cf. Rom. i. 32. For εἰς τό κ.τ.λ., see notes on *v.* 6 and on I. ii. 16: "that they should be saved" (see note on σωτηρία, I. v. 9) is the result of that embracing of "the truth" offered in the Gospel, which these men refused to give; and such refusal marks them out as οἱ ἀπολλύμενοι.

Verses 11, 12 draw out the consequence of the criminal unbelief described in ἀνθ᾿ ὧν κ.τ.λ., affirming the terrible delusion above described to be a visitation on God's part, and a δίκαιον παρὰ θεῷ (cf. i. 6)—in fact *a judicial infatuation.* And since this fatal and wide-spread deception is effected by the παρουσία of Antichrist, that coming, while it is the consummate manifestation of human sin and Satanic power, is brought within the scope of the Divine counsels; it proves to be an instrument in God's sovereign hand. Cf. the conclusion of Rom. ix.—xi., setting forth the judicial πώρωσις of Israel : Ὦ βάθος πλούτου καὶ σοφίας καὶ γνώσεως θεοῦ· ὡς ἀνεξεραύνητα τὰ κρίματα αὐτοῦ καὶ ἀνεξιχνίαστοι αἱ ὁδοὶ αὐτοῦ.

11. καὶ διὰ τοῦτο πέμπει αὐτοῖς ὁ θεὸς ἐνέργειαν πλάνης. *And on this account God sends them a working of error.* For διὰ τοῦτο, and its backward reference, cf. I. ii. 13, iii. 5; καί consecutive,— almost "*so for this cause*" (Ellicott). Πέμπει, *present* (see Textual Note), by anticipation of the predicted certainty; or rather, as the affirmation of a principle already at work (see *v.* 7)—what takes place in the victims of Antichrist is seen every day on a smaller scale. Αὐτοῖς is dative of *persons concerned* : πρός (or εἰς) with accus., in such connexion, denotes *motion towards.* Ὁ θεός is emphatic by position ; see note below. Ἐνέργεια πλάνης is parallel to ἐνέργεια τοῦ Σατανᾶ, *v.* 9, "Satan" being ὁ πλανῶν τὴν οἰκουμένην (Rev. xii. 9, xiii. 14, xx. 10; cf. Jo. viii. 44). On πλάνη, see I. ii. 3; it is an active principle, the opposite in its "working" of the λόγος θεοῦ (I. ii. 13); for ἐνέργεια, see note on *v.* 9. This πλάνη is the ἀπάτη ἀδικίας of *v.* 10

operative and taking effect,—the poison running in the veins; it is the ψεῦδος of Antichrist (see next clause) believed and followed. What "God sends" is not "error" as such, but error used for correction and with the train of moral consequences included in its ἐνέργεια. This effectual delusion God sends on wicked men to the very end, foreseen by Him, **εἰς τὸ πιστεῦσαι αὐτοὺς τῷ ψεύδει**, *that they should believe the lie*. The question of Is. lxiii. 17 is inevitable : "O Lord, why dost Thou make us to err from Thy ways?" Τὸ ψεῦδος—the opposite of ἡ ἀλήθεια (*v.* 10), the truth of God in the Gospel (cf. Eph. iv. 25; 1 Jo. ii. 21)—in Rom. i. 25 taking the form of idolatry, is here "*the* lie" *par excellence*, the last and crowning deception practised by Satan in passing off the Lawless One as God (*vv.* 4, 9 f.). This passage, in fact, ascribes to God the delusion that we have hitherto been regarding as the masterpiece of Satan (cf. the contradiction of 2 Sam. xxiv. 1 and 1 Chron. xxi. 1). Three things must be borne in mind in reflecting upon this: (1) that Satan is never regarded in Scripture as an independent power or rival deity of evil, like the Ahriman of Parsism. However large the activity allowed him in this world, it is under Divine control; see Job i., ii.; 1 Cor. v. 5, x. 13, &c. (2) St Paul teaches that sin works out its own punishment. In Rom. i. 24 ff. he represents the loathsome vice of the Pagan world as a Divine chastisement for its long-continued idolatry: "For this cause *God sends* effectual delusion," is parallel to "For this cause *God gave them up* to vile passions." In each case the result is inevitable, and comes about by what we call a natural law. That a persistent rejection of truth destroys the sense for truth and results in fatal error, is an ethical principle and a fact of experience as certain as any in the world. Now he who believes in God as the Moral Ruler of the universe, knows that its laws are the expression of His will. Since this delusion, set on foot by Satan, is the moral consequence in those who receive it of previous and wilful refusal of the light of truth, it is manifest that God is here at work; He makes Satan and the Lawless One instruments in punishing false-hearted men; cf. Ezek. xiv. 9, and 1 Kings xxii. (3) The advents of Christ and of Antichrist are linked together (*vv.* 3, 9); they are parts of the same great process and drama of judgement, and the deceivers will suffer heavier punishment than the deceived: cf. Rev. xx. 10. God, who "sends a working of error" in the Antichrist, will quickly send the Christ to put a stop to the delusion and to "destroy" its author by His sudden and glorious coming (*v.* 8, i. 7—9).

12. **ἵνα κριθῶσιν πάντες**, *that they might be judged, all (of them)*—

or, all (of them) together (ἅπαντες). "Ἵνα κριθῶσιν is parallel to εἰς τὸ εἶναι...ἀναπολογήτους of Rom. i. 20 (this whole passage, as Bornemann points out, is full of parallels—some manifest, others recondite —with Rom. i. 18—32, both in expression and thought). For the opposite purpose on God's part, see *vv*. 13 f., i. 10; I. v. 9, &c. All God's dispensations, in dealing both with good and evil men, have this aim, and find their terminus in "the day of the Lord": cf. Rom. ii. 5—16, xiv. 10 f.; 1 Cor. iv. 5; 2 Cor. v. 9 f.; Acts xvii. 30 f., &c.

Πάντες: "late ergo et diu et vehementer grassatur error ille" (Bengel). If the ἐνέργεια πλάνης and the ψεῦδος in question belong specifically to the παρουσία of Antichrist, Bengel's *diu* is scarcely justified: Antichrist is but "revealed," when his destruction comes (*v*. 8); his appearance signals to the Church her Lord's approach (*v*. 3). Granting ἅπαντες the true reading (see Textual Note), then this judgement comes sweepingly, it descends on the deceived *all together, in a body*; for the delusion of Antichrist takes effect everywhere; this is the one thing in which the enemies of Christ agree, and serves as a crucial test of their character: cf. τὸ χάραγμα τοῦ θηρίου (Rev. xiii. 3, 16, &c.), and its universal currency.

"Judgement" implies here condemnation, as in Rom. ii. 1, 3, iii. 7, 1 Cor. xi. 31 f., &c.; the point of the statement lies not in the nature of the sentence passed, but in *the judicial purpose* of God's controlling action in the case. The subjects of this judgement of God are defined almost in the terms of *v*. 10: **οἱ μὴ πιστεύσαντες τῇ ἀληθείᾳ** recalls τῆς ἀληθείας; **τῇ ἀδικίᾳ** repeats τῆς ἀδικίας of that passage; while **ἀλλὰ εὐδοκήσαντες** κ.τ.λ. echoes οὐκ ἐδέξαντο τὴν ἀγάπην: *who did not believe the truth, but had a good-will toward unrighteousness*. Cf. with the two clauses respectively, Rom. i. 18, 28, and 32 (εὐδοκήσαντες κ.τ.λ., the climax of the denunciation); also Rom. ii. 8, for the whole expression. Εὐδοκέω is construed elsewhere with ἐν, importing the element *in* which the satisfaction lies; here only in N.T. with dative (*scil.* of interest, i.e. *favour, inclination to*, being parallel to πιστεύσαντες τῇ ἀληθ.): the same construction is found in 1 Macc. i. 43, and in Polybius. "*Obedience to* unrighteousness," instead of "truth" (Rom. ii. 8), is the practical expression of "*favour* (inclination) *toward* unrighteousness," which excludes "faith in the truth."

The men described are such as sin not through force of passion or example or habit, but out of delight in wrong; "the light that is in" them has "become darkness"; evil is their good. They are credulous of what falls in with their inclination: "the Man of Lawlessness" is welcomed as their Messiah and God; his advent is the Avatar of their hopes. Their reception of "the adversary" is itself a terrible judgement upon misbelievers, proving a touchstone of their falsehood of heart and leaving them open, without excuse, to the speedy condemnation of Christ's tribunal. Men without love of truth naturally believe the lie when it comes; there is nothing else for them. As Christ came at first "for judgement into this world" (Jo. ix. 39, &c.), by His presence discriminating the lovers of truth and falsehood, so will it be, in the opposite sense, at Antichrist's coming. He attracts his like; and the attraction is evidence of character. This is not, however, as yet the Last Judgement; it is possible that some, under this retribution, may repent even at the eleventh hour, seeing how shameful is the delusion into which they have fallen by rejecting Christ.

§ 4. ii. 13—iii. 5. Words of Comfort and Prayer.

Solatium post prædictionem rerum tristium (Bengel). Turning from the awful apparition of Antichrist, the writers with a sigh of relief join in thanksgiving for those who will " prevail to escape all these things that shall come to pass, and to stand before the Son of man " (Lk. xxi. 36). (*a*) *Thanksgiving* for the happier lot awaiting the Christian readers (*vv.* 13 f.) passes (*b*) into *exhortation* that they should hold fast the treasure they possess (*v.* 15), which is followed (*c*) by *prayer to this effect* (*vv.* 16 f.). With this supplication the Letter, in its main intent, is complete and might have appropriately closed at the end of chap. ii. But in praying for their readers the Apostles are reminded (*d*) of their need for *prayer on their own behalf*, to which they exhort the readers in turn (iii. 1 f.); and this appeal for prayer throws the writers' thoughts (*e*) upon *the fidelity of God* to His purpose of grace in the readers (*vv.* 3 f.), for whom (*f*) *the Apostles' intercession* is renewed (*v.* 5). Discursiveness is natural in the free outpouring of heart between friends and friends; it is a sign of unstudied epistolary genuineness. There is nothing incoherent, nor an irrelevant word. The passage grows out of the last section, to which it forms a counterpart, beginning with δέ of contrast and marked by a train of expressions antithetical to those there occurring. The contrast delineated between the followers of Antichrist (*vv.* 10—12) and of Christ (*vv.* 13 f.) is parallel to that exhibited in I. v. 1—11.

13. Ἡμεῖς δὲ ὀφείλομεν εὐχαριστεῖν τῷ θεῷ πάντοτε περὶ ὑμῶν. *But, for our part, we are bound to give thanks to God always for you:* a nearly verbatim reproduction of the opening words of the Epistle; see notes on i. 3. The repeated ὀφείλομεν betrays in the missionaries

a keen sense of personal debt for the support given them at this juncture by the faith of the Thessalonian Church; cf., in explanation of this, I. i. 8, iii. 8 f. Hence also the emphatic ἡμεῖς prefacing ὀφείλομεν, where we might have looked for περὶ δὲ ὑμῶν at the head of the sentence, to supply the main subject of the paragraph in contrast with οἱ ἀπολλύμενοι, οἱ μὴ πιστεύσαντες κ.τ.λ., of the foregoing: cf. I. v. 4; Eph. iv. 20; also Heb. vi. 9. Contemplating the revelation of the Lawless One and the multitude of his dupes, the Apostles realize their deep obligation to God for the certainty that their Thessalonian brethren are of another disposition and have a happier destiny assured them. Περὶ ὑμῶν is emphasized by the terms that follow:—

ἀδελφοὶ ἠγαπημένοι ὑπὸ Κυρίου, *brethren beloved by the Lord*. In the εὐχαριστία of I. i. 2—4, &c.—and precisely at the same point, viz. in grounding their position as Christians upon the Divine ἐκλογή (εἵλατο...ὁ θεὸς...εἰς σωτηρίαν)—the Thessalonians were addressed as "brethren beloved *by God*." "The Lord" is *Christ*, as distinguished from "God" in the adjoining clauses; see notes on I. ii. 1, and i. 12 above. Appalled by the thought of Antichrist, the Church finds in the love of Christ her refuge (cf. Rom. viii. 35—39); since He is κύριος, His love has at its command Divine power (i. 7 f.); to "the Lord" (Jesus), their strong Protector, the Apostles forthwith commit these persecuted "brethren" (see *vv.* 16 f., iii. 3, 5). St Paul is probably reminding himself in this expression of the ancient blessing upon Benjamin, his own tribe, pronounced in Deut. xxxiii. 12: "The beloved of the Lord (ἠγαπημένος ὑπὸ Κυρίου, LXX) shall dwell in safety by Him; He covereth him all the day long, and he dwelleth between His shoulders."

ὅτι εἵλατο ὑμᾶς ὁ θεὸς ἀπ' ἀρχῆς (or ἀπαρχὴν) εἰς σωτηρίαν, *in that God chose you from the beginning* (or *as a firstfruit*) *unto salvation*: a reaffirmation of εἰδότες...τὴν ἐκλογὴν ὑμῶν, I. i. 4; see notes. Εἵλατο is used of the "choice" of Israel for Jehovah's people in Deut. vii. 6 f. and x. 15 (προείλετο); in xxvi. 18 f. (LXX) it stands, Κύριος εἵλατό σε σήμερον γενέσθαί σε αὐτῷ λαὸν περιούσιον...εἶναί σε λαὸν ἅγιον Κυρίῳ τῷ θεῷ σου. Deut. vii. 8 accounts for this in the words, παρὰ τὸ ἀγαπᾶν Κύριον ὑμᾶς (cf. previous note). As respects the *purpose* of the choice (εἰς σωτηρίαν), the verse is parallel to I. v. 9, οὐκ...εἰς ὀργὴν ἀλλὰ εἰς περιποίησιν σωτηρίας; see the note there on σωτηρία. Hence those whom "God chose for salvation" are set in contrast with "the perishing," with those to whom "God sends an ἐνέργειαν πλάνης in order that they may be judged" (*vv.* 10 f.). Cf. with this also the paragraph on "God's elect" in Rom. viii. 33—39. For ὅτι after εὐχαριστέω, cf.

i. 3, I. ii. 13; for the hybrid aorist εἴλατο—with its *strong* stem and *weak* ending—see note on προείπαμεν, I. iv. 6.

It is doubtful whether ἀπ' ἀρχῆς looks further back than to the time when God's call in the Gospel reached the Thessalonians (cf. Ph. iv. 15, ἐν ἀρχῇ τοῦ εὐαγγελίου; also 1 Jo. ii. 7, 24, iii. 11; Jo. vi. 64, xv. 27, xvi. 4); without some indication in the context, the readers would hardly think here of a *pretemporal* election. The ἐκλογή of I. i. 4 was associated with the arrival of the Gospel at Thessalonica (I. i. 5, 9). Then, practically and to human view, "God chose" this people—i.e. *took them for His own out of the evil world in which they moved*: cf. the εἴλατο σήμερον of Deut. xxvi. 18. Such "choice" is intrinsically, and as the act of God's loving will, ἀπ' αἰῶνος (Acts xv. 18). Hence in later Epp. the "beginning" is traced to its spring, and its origin is seen in the Divine love "predestinating" its chosen "before the foundation of the world" (Eph. i. 4, &c.); the relative is grounded in the absolute ἀπ' ἀρχῆς (1 Jo. i. 1): cf. the double ἀπ' ἀρχῆς of 1 Jo. ii. 7, 13 f., 24. But the Apostles speak here in the language of grateful remembrance, not of theological contemplation. The marginal reading of WH, ἀπαρχήν (*primitias*, Vulg.; see Textual Note), gives a thoroughly Pauline word—applied to *persons* in Rom. xi. 16, xvi. 5, 1 Cor. xv. 20, 23, xvi. 15 (also in Jam. i. 18, Rev. xiv. 4)—and is quite suitable to the Thessalonian Christians, since they were along with the Philippians the "firstfruit," in comparison with Achaia and Corinth (cf. I. i. 7 ff.), of the present mission.

ἐν ἁγιασμῷ πνεύματος καὶ πίστει ἀληθείας, *in sanctification of spirit* (or *of the Spirit*) *and faith in* (*the*) *truth*: an adjunct not to εἴλατο, but to σωτηρίαν (for similar ἐν clauses attached to verbal nouns, see I. i. 1, iv. 16, v. 2; and i. 7 f. above). "Salvation" is defined in its subjective ground and factors—"God chose you to a salvation operative and realized in sanctification and faith": by the same signs the Apostles "know the election" of their Thessalonian converts (I. i. 3—7; cf. iv. 7); on these conditions rests the σωτηρία spoken of in I. v. 9. Ἐὰν μείνωσιν ἐν πίστει...καὶ ἁγιασμῷ, 1 Tim. ii. 15, presents the same conditions in the reverse order. For ἁγιασμός, see notes on I. iii. 13 (ἁγιωσύνη) and iv. 3, 7.

Πνεύματος may be (*a*) *subjective* genitive—"sanctification proceeding from (wrought by) the Spirit (of God)": cf. I. iv. 7 f., Rom. xv. 16, 1 Cor. iii. 16 f.; and the formal parallel in 1 Pet. i. 2. See I. i. 6, Rom. v. 5, viii. 2, 23, 1 Cor. vi. 11, xii. 3, 13, 2 Cor. i. 22, Gal. iii. 3, Eph. i. 13, iv. 30, Tit. iii. 5, for the offices of the Holy Spirit in the initiation and first movements of the Christian life. But (*b*) the word gives a sense equally good in itself if understood as *objective* genitive—"sanctification of (your) spirit": thus read, the phrase recalls the memorable prayer of I. v. 23, ὁ θεὸς...ἁγιάσαι ὑμᾶς...καὶ... ὁλόκληρον ὑμῶν τὸ πνεῦμα κ.τ.λ. ἀμέμπτως...τηρηθείη; on this construction, sanctification is viewed as an inward state of the readers, leading them to complete salvation at the coming of Christ, just as "unbelief of the truth and delight in unrighteousness" (v. 12) will bring "the perishing" to ruin through the fascination of Antichrist. This patent antithesis inclines one, after Estius ("anima, in qua sanctitatis donum principaliter residet"), to adopt (b), notwithstanding the preference of most commentators for (a): contrast μολυσμοῦ σαρκὸς καὶ πνεύματος, 2 Cor. vii. 1; and cf. Eph. iv. 23. Add to this ruling consideration the probability that the writer, if intending the Holy Spirit by πνεύματος, would for clearness have prefixed the article or attached to the generic noun some distinguishing term; and observe the fact that the genitive is objective in the parallel πίστει ἀληθείας. This ἁγιασμὸς πνεύματος is complementary to the ἁγ. σαρκός implied in I. iv. 3—8. The objection that (interior) "sanctification of spirit" should follow and not precede "faith in the truth," applies with equal force to "sanctification by the Spirit" (cf. Gal. iii. 2); on the other hand, "faith in the truth" in this context involves more than the initial faith of conversion (I. i. 8, &c.), or "the *reception* of the truth on the part of the person influenced" (Lightfoot); it signifies that habit of faith by which one adheres to the truth and so escapes the ἀπάτη ἀδικίας and ἐνέργεια πλάνης (vv. 10 f.), and includes the ὑπομονὴ καὶ πίστις (i. 4) by virtue of which believers (οἱ πιστεύοντες) "stand fast": see next verse; and cf. 2 Cor. i. 24, Col. ii. 5, &c. Such abiding faith leads to ultimate salvation; it is co-ordinate with, not anterior to, sanctification.

14. εἰς ὃ ἐκάλεσεν ὑμᾶς διὰ τοῦ εὐαγγελίου ἡμῶν, *to which end He called you through our good tidings*, i.e. "through the good news we brought": cf., for this genitive, I. i. 5, and i. 10 above; also I. ii. 13, λόγον ἀκοῆς παρ' ἡμῶν τοῦ θεοῦ. Since "through *our* gospel" the Thessalonians were called to salvation, "*we* are bound to give thanks" on this behalf (v. 13: see note). For the thought of God as "caller" of men in the Gospel, see I. ii. 12, v. 24, and notes. God's *summons* gives expression and effect to His *choice* (εἵλατο, v. 13); see note on ἐκλογή, I. i. 4; also Rom. viii. 30, 1 Cor. i. 26 f., for the connexion of *election* and *call*. Εἰς ὅ resumes εἰς σωτηρίαν ἐν ἁγιασμῷ κ.τ.λ., having the whole of this for its antecedent; the Divine call that brings men into the fellowship of Christ (1 Cor. i. 9) includes "sanctification" among its primary objects (see I. iv. 7, v. 23 f.).

εἰς περιποίησιν δόξης τοῦ κυρίου ἡμῶν Ἰησοῦ Χριστοῦ, *unto the securing of the glory of our Lord Jesus Christ*: cf. 1 Pet. v. 10, ὁ καλέσας...εἰς...δόξαν ἐν Χριστῷ; and 2 Tim. ii. 10, σωτηρίας τῆς ἐν Χ. Ἰ. μετὰ δόξης αἰωνίου. This is an end not lying beyond or arising out of σωτηρία (*v.* 13), but virtually identical with it, so that the second εἰς clause is explicative of the first (*v.* 13) and represents objectively what εἰς σωτηρίαν (εἰς ὅ) states subjectively; the Christian's ultimate salvation lies in the "glory" won by his Redeemer, wherein he shares: see Rom. viii. 17, ἵνα συνδοξασθῶμεν; 2 Tim. ii. 11 f.; Rev. iii. 21. Εἰς περιποίησιν δόξης τοῦ κυρίου κ.τ.λ. is therefore identical in substance with εἰς περιπ. σωτηρίας, I. v. 9: see note there on περιποίησις. The "δόξα of our Lord Jesus Christ" is the "glory" proper and due to Him as *our Lord*, to be received on "the day of the Lord," when the winning of His kingdom is complete (see Matt. xix. 28, xxv. 31; Lk. xxiv. 26, &c.; Phil. ii. 9—11; Tit. ii. 13); its chief matter will be found "in His saints" (i. 10). God intends the glory of Christ in all that He does for men through Him; and Christ's glory is in turn the heritage of those who are Christ's (οἱ τοῦ χριστοῦ ἐν τῇ παρουσίᾳ, 1 Cor. xv. 23: cf. συγκληρονόμοι, Rom. viii. 17; also Jo. xii. 26, xiv. 3; Rev. xxii. 3 ff.). To this end "God called" them in calling them to their own salvation; cf. notes on ἐνδοξασθῆναι κ.τ.λ., ἐνδοξασθῇ, i. 10, 12 above; also on I. ii. 12 *b*. The δόξα is already won in principle, and its περιποίησις is guaranteed: see i. 7—12, *v.* 8 above; Matt. xxiv. 30; Phil. iii. 20 f.; Eph. v. 26 f.; Col. i. 22, iii. 4; Rom. viii. 18 f.; 1 Cor. xv. 24—28; Jo. xvii. 24; Rev. i. 5—7, &c.

15. Ἄρα οὖν, ἀδελφοί, στήκετε. *So then, brothers, stand firm:* the practical conclusion of all that has been said, from *v.* 2 onwards. "Since the Lord's return is delayed and its date uncertain, and in prospect of the coming of Antichrist whose deceptive influence is already at work,—inasmuch as God by our means has made you heirs of His kingdom and sharers in the promised glory of Christ, we bid you STAND FAST!" For ἄρα οὖν, see note on I. v. 6. Στήκω, formed from ἕστηκα (cf. γρηγορέω, I. v. 6), is a derivative of the κοινή. The verb occurs seven times in Paul, thrice in John (including Rev.), twice in Mk; cf. note on I. iii. 8, also its hortatory use in 1 Cor. xvi. 13; Gal. v. 1; Phil. iv. 1: the opposite of σαλευθῆναι, *v.* 2. Similarly in 1 Cor. xv. 58, Col. i. 23, *hope* is the incentive to steadfastness.

καὶ κρατεῖτε τὰς παραδόσεις ἃς ἐδιδάχθητε, *and hold fast the traditions which you were taught.* Παραδόσεις (cf. iii. 6, for one particular here included; 1 Cor. xi. 2; also Rom. vi. 17, 1 Cor. xi. 2, 23, xv. 3, for St Paul's use of παραδίδωμι in referring to his teaching) embraces all that the readers "had been taught" of the Gospel received through St Paul and his companions, whether on points of faith or conduct (cf. I. i. 5, ii. 1 f., 9—14, iii. 3 f., iv. 1 f.; ii. 5 above). The παράδοσις (-σεις) of earlier Epp. becomes the παραθήκη, *deposit*, of the Pastorals; it is, on its practical side, a παραγγελία (-αι) : see I. iv. 2, and note. On παράδοσις, see Lightfoot's note *ad loc*. He observes that this term in the N.T. connotes "an authority external to the teacher himself." What these Apostles "hand on" to the Thessalonians is not their own doctrine as such, but the facts and teachings about Christ coming from Himself and belonging to all Christians. For the *accusative of thing* retained with passive of a verb governing two accusatives, see Winer-Moulton, p. 286, and the ordinary *Greek Grammars*.

For κρατέω (κράτος)—*to have* or *apply strength, to grip, master, hold firmly*—with like object, cf. Mk vii. 3; Rev. ii. 14 f. Elsewhere in St Paul the synonymous κατέχω, as in I. v. 21; 1 Cor. xi. 2, xv. 2.

εἴτε διὰ λόγου εἴτε δι' ἐπιστολῆς ἡμῶν, *whether through word or through letter of ours*—ἡμῶν qualifies both nouns; in *v.* 2 the pronoun has, less certainly, the same twofold reference. The writers put their "epistle" on the same level with their spoken "word"; they bid the readers hold by what they had learned from their fathers in Christ, whether through this channel or that, thus guarding themselves against every attempt to "deceive" them (*v.* 3): cf. 1 Cor. xi. 2, for the emphasis thrown on adherence to Apostolic teaching; similarly in Rom. vi. 17; Eph. iv. 20 f.; Phil. iv. 9; Col. ii. 6 f.; 2 Tim. ii. 2; 1 Jo. ii. 24; Matt. xxviii. 20, &c. For the importance now beginning to be attached to St Paul's Letters, see notes on *v.* 2 and iii. 17; and for the possibility that an *epistle* might be undervalued at Thessalonica, see note on I. v. 27.

16. Αὐτὸς δὲ ὁ κύριος ἡμῶν Ἰησοῦς Χριστὸς καὶ [ὁ] θεὸς ὁ πατὴρ ἡμῶν—. *But may our Lord Jesus Christ Himself and God our Father*—. For αὐτὸς δέ, and this form of prayer, cf. I. iii. 11, v. 23, and notes. This invocation corresponds in its position to that of I. iii. 11 ff., completing the Epistle in its first and main part, the sequel in each case being appended by (τὸ) λοιπόν (see iii. 1 below). But while the corresponding petition of Ep. I. bears on *love and holiness* as needed for the Church's perfectness at Christ's coming, this bears on *strength and steadfastness of heart* as needed for present duty; στηρίξαι (*v.* 17) is common to both passages. Here *Christ's* name precedes the Father's (as later in the benediction of 2 Cor. xiii. 13), which leads Chrysostom to exclaim, Ποῦ νῦν εἰσιν οἱ τὸν υἱὸν ἐλαττοῦντες; "Our Lord Jesus

Christ" is foremost in the writers' thoughts; He in whose "glory" the readers were "called" by God to take part at the "winning" of His kingdom, is invoked to help them toward this end. Christ and the Father are one in love to this Church (I. i. 4, and v. 13 above), and in all saving action; so the singular predicate, παρακαλέσαι κ.τ.λ. (v. 17), is natural, as in I. iii. 11. There is a *chiasmus*, or crossing, in the arrangement of the parallel names, ὁ πατὴρ ἡμῶν balancing ὁ κύριος ἡμῶν, while ὁ θεός is set over against Ἰησοῦς Χριστός.

ὁ θεὸς ὁ πατὴρ ἡμῶν is described as ὁ ἀγαπήσας ἡμᾶς καὶ δοὺς παράκλησιν αἰωνίαν καὶ ἐλπίδα ἀγαθὴν ἐν χάριτι, *who has loved us and given (us) eternal encouragement and good hope, in grace.* The readers have just been told that they are "beloved by the Lord" (Jesus: v. 13); that reference is complemented by their inclusion, along with the Apostles, in the special love *of God the Father.* Now God's love, in view of His "call" and its purpose stated in v. 13, carries with it a παράκλησιν and ἐλπίδα which minister the very strengthening of heart the readers require. Ἀγαπήσας and δούς are bound in one by the single article, the second being, as the case stands, the necessary outcome of the first. For God's *loving and giving,* cf. Jo. iii. 16, 35, 1 Jo. iv. 10; also Matt. vii. 11, Lk. xii. 32, for the *fatherly* regard which prompts God's gifts; similarly of Christ, in Gal. ii. 20, Eph. v. 2, 25. These parallels support Lightfoot's observation, that "the aorist ἀγαπήσας (not ἀγαπῶν) refers to the act of God's love in giving His Son to die for us": this is borne out by ἐν χάριτι, qualifying δούς; for it is in this act above all that "God commends His own love to us," and in it "the grace of God, and His gift in grace, overflowed" (Rom. v. 8, 15). From the supreme evidence of God's love an "*eternal* comfort" is derived; see the way in which St Paul draws out this παράκλησις, and builds up this ἐλπίς, in Rom. viii. 31—39. Though the cross of Christ is never mentioned in the two Letters, and His death but twice (I. iv. 14, v. 10) in cursory fashion, "the grace of God" therein displayed furnishes the basis and fulcrum of the entire system of doctrine and life implied in the Epp.; cf. the notes on I. v. 9 f., to the same effect. In the passage just referred to the essential connexion is assumed, that is latent here, between God's purpose of salvation for men and the death of Jesus Christ on their behalf.

For the term παράκλησις, see note on I. ii. 3. For *God* as ὁ παρακαλῶν, cf. Rom. xv. 4 f.; 2 Cor. i. 3—7; Phil. ii. 1; Heb. vi. 18, xii. 5; Acts ix. 31. God's παράκλησις follows up His κλῆσις (v. 14). The "comfort" is "eternal," inasmuch as it continues unshaken by the losses and sorrows of life, rising above all temporal conditions and defying death: see Rom. viii. 35—39, 1 Cor. xv. 55—58, 2 Cor. iv. 16—v. 8, for the scope of the Christian consolation. Here only and in Heb. ix. 12, in N.T., has αἰώνιος a distinct feminine ending; also in Num. xxv. 13, and elsewhere in LXX; otherwise, according to rule for adjectives in -ιος, the -ος is common in gender.

The added καὶ ἐλπίδα ἀγαθήν shows that the Divine cordial here held out lies in the *prospect* of faith: see the parallels above given; to which add I. ii. 19, v. 8—11; Rom. v. 2—5, 17, 21, viii. 17—25, xv. 13; Tit. i. 2; Heb. iii. 6, vi. 17—20, vii. 19; 1 Pet. i. 3—9, v. 4, 10, &c. A hope is "good" (ἀγαθήν; cf. note on I. v. 15) as it is sound in itself and salutary in its effect—a hope which it is good to have. This is amongst the best of God's "good gifts" (Lk. xi. 13; Jam. i. 17). The same adjective is attached by St Paul to πίστις (Tit. ii. 10), and to συνείδησις (1 Tim. i, 5, 19; Acts xxiii. 1), as human faculties. For χάρις as the sphere and basis of God's gifts in the Gospel (ἐν χάριτι qualifies δούς, not ἐλπίδα), see note on this word in i. 12: along with ἀγαπάω (see previous note), χάρις points to the work of Divine Redemption, on which Christian "hope" specifically rests; see Rom. v. 2, 15—21; Eph. i. 7; Tit. ii. 11 ff., iii. 7; &c.

17. παρακαλέσαι ὑμῶν τὰς καρδίας καὶ στηρίξαι ἐν παντὶ ἔργῳ καὶ λόγῳ ἀγαθῷ, (*may our Lord Jesus Christ and God our Father...*) *encourage your hearts, and establish* (*them*) *in every good work and word*. For the sense of παρακαλέω, see note on I. ii. 11; for *God* as subject, cf. references under παράκλησις, v. 16; see note on I. iii. 11 for the *singular* predicate. For καρδία, note on I. ii. 4. The emotional sense of "heart" in modern English, and the rendering of παράκλησις by "comfort," suggest *consolation* as the blessing desired in these words; rather it is the rousing and cheering of the whole inner man which the Apostles pray for,—that the Thessalonians may be animated to brave endurance and vigorous activity: see the words στηρίξαι ἐν παντὶ ἔργῳ κ.τ.λ. following; and cf. I. iii. 2 f. above; 2 Cor. xiii. 11; Col. iv. 8, ii. 2. For στηρίζω, see notes on I. iii. 2, 13 (where στηρίξαι ὑμῶν τὰς καρδίας was anticipated), also iii. 3 below. St Paul uses this word four times in these two Letters, and only in Rom. i. 11, xvi. 25 besides. The phrase στηρίζειν τὴν καρδίαν occurs in Jam. v. 8, and somewhat frequently in the LXX—Ps. ciii. 15, cxi. 8 (ἐστήρικται ἡ καρδία αὐτοῦ, οὐ μὴ φοβηθῇ); Sirach vi. 37, &c. It is the opposite of σαλευθῆναι, v. 2; God's στηρίξειν makes possible the στήκειν and κρατεῖν enjoined in v. 15.

The terms of the antithesis ἔργῳ κ. λόγῳ are usually in the reverse order (Rom. xv. 18; 2 Cor. x. 11; Col. iii. 17); but where the thought of *strength* is present, ἔργον naturally precedes (Lk. xxiv. 19). Λόγος must not be confined to *doctrine*, as when it is opposed to πνεῦμα (*v*. 2) or associated with ἐπιστολή (*v*. 15); coupled with ἔργον, it covers the whole business of life: "May God give you courage and confidence of heart in all the good that you do and say." The Apostles know that their readers are busy in doing good (I. i. 3, iv. 10); they would have them do it with a good and cheerful heart (cf. I. v. 17 f.; Rom. ii. 7; Col. i. 10; 2 Tim. ii. 21, iii. 17).

CHAPTER III.

3. For ο κυριος, **AD*G** 71, with some latt, Ambrst, have ο θεος—conformed to I. v. 23; 1 Cor. i. 9, &c.

Baljon proposes for υμας the emendation ημας (cf. 2 Tim. iv. 18), which gives a smoother sense after *v.* 2 (see Expository Note); he quotes Bentley in favour of the change. The confusion of these pronouns being so very common, it is curious that no MS. evidence is forthcoming for the 1st plural here, where it is plausible.

4. D^cG, verss. (except d e vg), add υμιν to **παραγγελλομεν** (cf. *v.* 2).

The double form of ποιεω has occasioned a crop of various readings:

(*a*) **ποιειτε και ποιησετε**, in ℵ*A d e; (*b*) ποιειτε και ποιησατε, **D***^{gr};
(*c*) και ποιειτε και ποιησετε, ℵ^cD^c**KLP** &c., f vg *et facitis et facietis*;
(*d*) και εποιησατε και ποιειτε και ποιησετε, **B**; cop *fecistis et facitis*;
(*e*) και εποιησατε alone, G^{gr}, several minn.; g *et fecistis et facietis*.

The early (itacistic) corruption of **ποιησετε** into ποιησατε (**D**) appears to have bewildered the copyists. Is it not just possible, however, that BG cop have preserved a true reading, and that in (*a*) ποιειτε was an assimilation of και εποιησατε to *v.* 1 above (and to I. iv. 10?). εποιησατε is commended by its difficulty (after πεποιθαμεν), and by the fact that its priority might best explain the genesis of the other readings. The initial και of **B** and **G** seems original.

5. την before υπομονην in all uncials; omitted in a few minn.

6. ημων, after κυριου, supplied by ℵAD^cGKLP &c., is wanting in BD*, Cyp: a suspicious complement; cf. ii. 1.

(*a*) **παρελαβετε**, in BG 43 73 80 go syr^{hcl}, Or Thdrt Ambrst;
(*b*) **παρελαβοσαν**, ℵ*A, D* (without παρ-), } The Latin Versions
    17, Bas; WH *margin.*   } and Fathers, generally,
(*c*) παρελαβον, ℵ^cD^{b,c}KLP;   } read the 3rd plural;
(*d*) παρελαβε, in a few minn., syr^{pesh}, Oec.

παρελαβοσαν (see Expos. Note on the grammatical ending) is the *hardest* reading, and best accounts for the others. Weiss, however, says it "betrays the Alexandrian emendators."

παρελαβετε, obvious in itself, may have been further suggested by I. iv. 1. On the other hand, WH, who agree with Weiss in preferring (a), think that -οσαν may be due to an "ocular confusion with -οσιν (παραδοσιν) in the line above" (Appendix, p. 165).

For παρ' ημων B has αφ' ημων, which Weiss deems original, explaining παρ' as an assimilation to the verb, and to I. ii. 13, iv. 1.

8. νυκτος και ημερας, אBG and six minn.; νυκτα και ημεραν, ADKLP &c. See Expository Note.

12. The Syrian text reads δια του for εν (κ. I. X.), after I. iv. 2.

13. ενκακησητε in B* (εγκ-אA 37 39 47), ενκακειτε in D*; εκκακησητε in DᶜGKLP &c., with εκκακειτε in Dam. Cf. note on ενκαυχασθαι, i. 4.

14. B and a number of minuscules read (λογῳ) υμων for ημων; Thphyl quotes Chr, seemingly by error, to the same effect. B makes the same senseless mistake in 2 Cor. vi. 11.

σημειουσθαι, in אD*GP 17, cop go. The confusion of -ε and -αι is the commonest of itacisms ("innumeris locis promiscue ponuntur," Tischdf); the spelling of such verb-forms is no index to their grammatical meaning.

συναναμιγνυσθαι: so in אABGʳ 17 (Dᵍʳ*), which must be peculiar, -μισγεσθαι); -σθε, in Dᵇ·ᶜKLP &c., and versions. Dᵍʳ*GKLP &c. introduce και before μη συναναμ., understanding the verb surely as *imperative*, despite the -σθαι of D* and G. Cf. the notes on ii. 2 and I. v. 13 above, and the Expository Note on this verse below.

16. For τροπῳ A*D*G 17, latt vg, Chr Ambrst, read τοπῳ, after I. i. 8: cf. 1 Cor. i. 2; 2 Cor. ii. 14; 1 Tim. ii. 8.

18. The liturgical αμην is appended in אᶜADGKLP, and most verss., due to the Western and Syrian copyists, as in Ep. I.

SUBSCRIPTION: אB* read προς Θεσσαλονικεις β̄ (B* -νεικεις).

---

1. The introductory phrase τὸ λοιπόν, *For the rest* (see note, I. iv. 1), indicates that the writer, though he may afterwards digress, is drawing to a close. The main purpose of the Epistle is accomplished (see *Introd.* pp. xxxvii. f., and the special *Introd.* to this section); what follows, however important, is comparatively incidental. But the thoughts immediately following are suggested by those of ii. 13—17; and ii. 13—iii. 5 forms in substance a single paragraph: cf. *inter alia στηρίξει ὑμᾶς* (v. 3) with ii. 17; v. 4 with ii. 15; *εἰς τὴν ἀγάπην τοῦ θεοῦ* (v. 5) with ii. 16. The request **προσεύχεσθε, ἀδελφοί, περὶ ἡμῶν**—*Pray, brothers, for us* (who have prayed for you)—arises out of the prayer of ii. 16 f., as in the case of I. v. 23—25: see note on the last-mentioned passage.

The intercession requested by the Apostles has two specific objects in view: first, **ἵνα ὁ λόγος τοῦ κυρίου τρέχῃ καὶ δοξάζηται**, *that the word of the Lord may run on and be glorified* (*may have a triumphant career*, Lightfoot). "The word of the Lord" (see notes on this expression in I. i. 8, and on Κύριος, ii. 13 above) is the word of Christ, proclaimed by His messengers far and wide (as *e.g.* in Acts i. 8; cf. Jo. xvii. 8, 18); the expression is synonymous, from a different point of view, with τὸ εὐαγγέλιον τοῦ θεοῦ, I. ii. 2, &c. To "the Lord" the writers are servants (cf. 2 Cor. iv. 5)—four times in *vv.* 1—5 Christ bears this name (cf. v. 6 besides); and they desire prayer for themselves on His business, in the service of His kingdom.

The figure of the λόγος τρέχων comes from Ps. xviii. 5 f. (LXX: v. 5 quoted in Rom. x. 18); cf. cxlvi. 15 (cxlvii. 4), ὁ ἀποστέλλων τὸ λόγιον αὐτοῦ τῇ γῇ, ἕως τάχους δραμεῖται ὁ λόγος αὐτοῦ; also Is. lv. 11; Acts xii. 24. Cf. Vergil's splendid lines on *Fama* (*Æneid* IV. 173 ff.), "Mobilitate viget, viresque adquirit eundo," &c. The spread of the Gospel was remarkably rapid in Macedonia (cf. I. i. 8 f., and the impression given by Acts xvi. 11—xvii. 12); but a check ensued at Athens, and in the early weeks of the mission at Corinth. The great success finally achieved in the latter city, from which the Apostles write, cost eighteen months to win (Acts xviii. 11). The metaphor of τρέχειν is complementary to that of the θύρα ἀνεῳγμένη used in 1 Cor. xvi. 9; 2 Cor. ii. 12. This "glorifying" of "the word of the Lord" is not subjective—the lauding, exalting of it by men—as in Acts xiii. 48; but objective—the display of its glory by its saving effects: cf., for this use of the verb, 2 Cor. iii. 10, Matt. v. 16, Jo. xii. 28, xvii. 10 &c.; also i. 10, 12, and ii. 14 above; and I. i. 7 ff., ii. 13 f., 20, for the "glory" thus achieved in *Thessalonica*. The "glory" of God's word shines in the character and worth of those who have received it, and who "adorn the teaching of our Saviour God" (Tit. ii. 5, 10, &c.). Observe the *present* tense of the two subjunctives: a *continuously* swift advance and rich illustration of the Gospel is to be prayed for. For ἵνα in this connexion, see notes on i. 11 and I. iv. 1.

καθὼς καὶ πρὸς ὑμᾶς, *as indeed* (*is the case*) *with you*. In both the above respects—in the swift progress and fair fruit of the Gospel—

the Thessalonian mission was conspicuous; see note on the last clause and references there given, to which add i. 3 f. above, I. iii. 6—9, iv. 9 f.; and cf. Phil. i. 5—7; 2 Cor. ii. 14—16, iii. 2 f.; 1 Cor. i. 4—7; Rom. i. 8; Col. i. 5 f.

2. **καὶ ἵνα ῥυσθῶμεν ἀπὸ τῶν ἀτόπων καὶ πονηρῶν ἀνθρώπων**, *and that we may be delivered from the perverse and wicked men*: the second object of the prayers solicited; διπλῆ μὲν ἡ αἴτησις εἶναι δοκεῖ, μία δὲ ὅμως ἐστίν· τῶν γὰρ πονηρῶν ἀνθρώπων ἡττωμένων, ἀκωλύτως καὶ ὁ τοῦ κηρύγματος συντρέχει λόγος (Chrysostom) Cf. Rom. xv. 31, ἵνα ῥυσθῶ ἀπὸ τῶν ἀπειθούντων κ.τ.λ., both passages recalling Is. xxv. 4, ἀπὸ ἀνθρώπων πονηρῶν ῥύσῃ αὐτούς. Τῶν points to a definite body, or class, of such men: these were, in chief, the Jewish enemies of the Gospel in Corinth, from the outset violent opponents of St Paul's work (Acts xviii. 6, 12—17), from whom the Apostles were in fact "delivered" by the sentence of the Proconsul Gallio. Of the same breed were the adversaries who in vain combated the progress of the Gospel in Macedonia (Acts xvii. 5, 13; cf. I. ii. 14—16, and notes). *Ἄ-τοπος* is *hap. leg.* in N.T. as applied to *persons*; of *things*, Lk. xxiii. 41; Acts xxv. 5, xxviii. 6: it signifies *place-less, out-of-the-way, out of court*; and so *eccentric, absurd, ineptus*; then, in a moral sense, *ill-bred* or *ill-conditioned, stupid, perverse, importunus* (Vulg.)—the common meaning of ἄτοπος in later Greek (Lightfoot): cf. Demosthenes 439. 26, ἄτοποι καὶ δυσχερεῖς. For πονηρός, see note on I. v. 22; πονηροὶ ἄνθρωποι appear in 2 Tim. iii. 13 in company with γόητες; see also note on ὁ πονηρός in next verse.

For ῥύομαι, see I. i. 10, and note; the word points to enemies who seemed to have the Apostles in their grasp: cf. also 2 Tim. iv. 17; and the catalogue of perils in 2 Cor. xi. 23—33.

οὐ γὰρ πάντων ἡ πίστις, *for not to all does the faith belong.* Cf., for the form of the sentence, the proverb, Οὐ παντὸς ἀνδρὸς ἐς Κόρινθόν ἐσθ' ὁ πλοῦς. This expression does not refer, like the similar denunciation of Acts viii. 21 ff., to pretended Christian believers, but to those "who do not obey the Gospel" and have become in consequence its bitter, unscrupulous opponents (i. 6—10),—the ἄπιστοι of Corinth (2 Cor. iv. 4, vi. 14 f.; 1 Tim. v. 8), and such as the ἀπειθοῦντες of Rom. xv. 31. Ἡ πίστις, in this context, signifies not the moral quality of *faithfulness, fidelity* (a very questionable sense for πίστις in the N.T.: cf. note on i. 4), but "the (Christian, true) faith"; cf. ἡ ἀλήθεια in ii. 10, and the πίστις ἀληθείας of ii. 13. The Apostles put their meaning in a pathetically softened way (cf. note on "not pleasing," I. ii. 15): "Alas, all do not share our faith (cf. Acts xxvi. 29); many are its enemies and bear us a fierce hatred on its account. Will you pray that we may be delivered from their power?" There is a like sad *litotes* in Rom. x. 16: οὐ πάντες ὑπήκουσαν τῷ εὐαγγελίῳ. Their unbelief in Christ brought out the ἀτοπία and πονηρία of the Corinthian opposers, who "loved the darkness rather than the light, for their deeds were evil" (Jo. iii. 19): hence the explicative γάρ clause. Schmiedel gives a different explanation: "Only deliverance from them is to be prayed for, *since their conversion is hopeless.*" For *the genitive of the possessor*, with similar subject, cf. Acts i. 7; Heb. v. 14.

3. Πιστὸς δέ ἐστιν ὁ κύριος. But *faithful is the Lord—scil.* Jesus (see note on *v.* 1): from the un-faith of men the Apostles turn to the fidelity of Christ their Lord, who has sent His servants into a hostile world and will stand by them. Observe the fine coincidence between this verse and Acts xviii. 9 f.: " The Lord said to Paul in the night by a vision" (under the discouragement of his early experiences at Corinth), "Fear not, but speak on and be not silent; for I am with thee, and none shall set upon thee to do thee hurt; for I have a numerous people in this city." This probably happened before Ep. II. was written. Cf. also I. v. 24; 1 Cor. i. 9, x. 13; 2 Tim. iv. 17; for the contrast implied, Rom. iii. 3, 2 Tim. ii. 13. St Paul plays on the kindred (not identical) senses of πίστις—πιστός (resembling our *faith—faithful, trust—trusty*): cf. *v.* 11, Eph. iii. 14 f., Gal. iv. 17, 1 Cor. iii. 17, for Pauline word-plays; also Jo. ii. 23 f. (πιστεύω).

ὃς στηρίξει ὑμᾶς καὶ φυλάξει ἀπὸ τοῦ πονηροῦ, *who shall establish you and guard (you) from the evil one* (or *from evil*). After *v.* 2, one expects ἡμᾶς (see Textual Note) as the object of protection (this object would not be, however, so congruous with στηρίξει); but St Paul characteristically forgets his own peril in that of his flock, as Calvin observes: "Ceterum de aliis magis quam de se anxium fuisse Paulum, ostendunt hæc ipsa verba. In eum maligni homines improbitatis suæ aculeos dirigebant, in eum totus impetus irruebat; curam interea suam ad Thessalonicenses convertit, ne quid hæc illis tentatio noceat." For στηρίξει, see notes on ii. 17; I. iii. 13. For the connexion of the two clauses, cf. 1 Cor. x. 13: πειρασμὸς ὑμᾶς οὐκ εἴληφεν εἰ μὴ ἀνθρώπινος· πιστὸς δὲ ὁ θεός, ὃς οὐκ ἐάσει κ.τ.λ.

Φυλάξει ἀπὸ τοῦ πονηροῦ recalls Matt. vi. 13, ῥῦσαι...ἀπὸ τοῦ πονηροῦ (cf. ἵνα ῥυσθῶμεν just above, *v.* 21), a sentence which in all likelihood was in the writers' mind. If so, the question of the *gender* of the adjective turns on its interpretation in the Lord's Prayer. Ch. ii. 17 and I. v. 22 are not decisive for the *neuter*; against Rom. xii. 9, in

St Paul, may be set Eph. vi. 16, where τοῦ πονηροῦ is certainly masculine and a designation of Satan; so Matt. xiii. 38 f., 1 Jo. ii. 13, v. 18 f. In Lk. xii. 15, 1 Jo. v. 21—the only other N.T. examples of φυλάσσειν ἀπό—the object of precaution is impersonal. On the other hand, the prayer of Ps. cxxxix. 5 (LXX: cf. Ps. cxl. 9), φύλαξόν με, κύριε, ἐκ χειρὸς ἁμαρτωλοῦ, ἀπὸ ἀνθρώπου ἀδίκου ῥῦσαί με, in view of the parallel ἵνα ῥυσθῶμεν ἀπὸ τῶν...πονηρῶν ἀνθρώπων of v. 2, suggests a *personal* enemy—as though the Apostles meant: "We have asked you to pray that we may be rescued from the power of wicked men; and we trust that our faithful Lord will guard you from the Wicked One" ("improborum omnium capite," Calvin); cf. Rom. xvi. 20, ὁ θεὸς... συντρίψει τὸν Σατανᾶν κ.τ.λ. Satan overshadowed the recent context (ii. 9), as the instigator and inspirer of Antichrist. The passage depicts a personal conflict, not a war of principles. On the whole, the masculine rendering seems the more fitting. See Lightfoot's full note *ad loc.*, referring to Matt. vi. 13, also his *Fresh Revision of the Eng. New Test.*[3], pp. 269 f.; and the exhaustive discussion of the subject by F. H. Chase, *The Lord's Prayer in the Early Church*, in *Texts and Studies*, I. 3, pp. 70—167.

4. The Apostles, trusting for the safety of their flock to "the Lord," are at the same time well assured of the faithfulness of the Thessalonians themselves: πεποίθαμεν δὲ ἐν κυρίῳ ἐφ' ὑμᾶς, *But we confidently rely, in the Lord, upon you.* Πεποιθέναι ἐπί with accusative occurs besides (for the N.T.) only in 2 Cor. ii. 3 and Matt. xxvii. 43 (the better reading): cf. ἐπί with dat., 2 Cor. i. 9, Heb. ii. 13, Lk. xi. 22, xviii. 9; and εἰς with accus. after the same verb, Gal. v. 10. The preposition signifies—as after πιστεύω, πίστις, in Acts ix. 42, xi. 17, Heb. vi. 1; or ἐλπίζω in 1 Tim. v. 5, 1 Pet. i. 13; or χρηστότης in Eph. ii. 7—a confidence directed *towards* and resting *upon* its object. The simple dative, according to classical regimen, follows this verb in 2 Cor. x. 7, Phil. i. 14, Phm. 21; dative with ἐν in Phil. iii. 3 f.; πέποιθα has much the same variety of construction as πιστεύω. The perfect is of the type of οἶδα, ἕστηκα, κ.τ.λ.: "I have got the persuasion," so "I have confidence"; cf. πέπεισμαι, Rom. viii. 38, xiv. 14, &c. Ἐν κυρίῳ is related to πεποίθαμεν...ἐφ' ὑμᾶς, as to its sentence in I. iv. 1 (see note): "the Lord (Jesus Christ)" and His service supply the sphere of all Christian relationships; St Paul's confidence toward the Thessalonians is grounded ultimately in Christ: cf. Gal. v. 10, ἐγὼ πέποιθα εἰς ὑμᾶς ἐν κυρίῳ.

The matter of confidence is thus stated: ὅτι ἃ παραγγέλλομεν [καὶ] ποιεῖτε [or ἐποιήσατε] καὶ ποιήσετε, *that the things which we charge (you), you (both) are doing* [or *have done*] *and will do.* For παραγγέλλω, thrice repeated in the sequel, see notes on I. iv. 2 (παραγγελία) and 11. Under the *present* tense the verb brings forward no general directions respecting the Christian life, such as were included in the παραδόσεις of ii. 15, nor does it recall the παραγγελίαι of I. iv. 1—12; it urges the injunctions presently given—in the first place, the appeal of *v.* 1 f., and then the charge immediately to follow in *vv.* 6—15: cf. 1 Cor. vii. 10, xi. 17. The reading ἐποιήσατε (for ποιεῖτε: see Textual Note) would imply assurance on the writers' part that their commands *had been* obeyed in time past, and accordingly *will be* in time to come. For the fact stated by ποιεῖτε, cf. I. iv. 10; also Rom. xv. 14. Πεποίθαμεν bears specially on the *future*, ποιήσετε; had the *present* (or *past*) only been in view, the writers might have used οἴδαμεν: see 2 Cor. ix. 2; εἰδὼς ὅτι...ποιήσεις, however, of *certain* expectation, in Phm. 21; cf. also Phil. i. 6, 19, and I. v. 24 above.

5. **Ὁ δὲ κύριος κατευθύναι ὑμῶν τὰς καρδίας εἰς τὴν ἀγάπην τοῦ θεοῦ καὶ εἰς τὴν ὑπομονὴν τοῦ χριστοῦ.** *But may the Lord direct your hearts into the love of God and into the patience of Christ.* A prayer significantly interjected between *vv.* 4 and 6: one might expect the important παραγγελία of *vv.* 6 ff. to follow at once upon the παραγγέλλομεν of the last sentence. But the Apostles' confidence in their readers' obedience is grounded "in the Lord." They know how critical the charge they have to give will be for the temper of this Church. So another word of prayer must be uttered before the admonition is delivered. Under the sense of "God's love" and in the spirit of "Christ's patience" matters of Church discipline are fitly undertaken. The Apostles have given directions to their Thessalonian flock,—"but" above both is the Supreme Director of hearts, whose guidance they invoke. For the verb κατευθύνω, and for the transitional δέ, see note on I. iii. 11. The idiom κατευθύνειν τὴν καρδίαν (πρός: Heb. הֵכִין לֵבָב אֶל) occurs in the LXX—1 Paral. xxix. 18; 2 Paral. xii. 14, xix. 3, xx. 33, &c.; Sir. xlix. 3, li. 20 (τὴν ψυχήν)— where the phrase implies an inward movement of the soul drawn to seek and find its Divine object: cf. also Ps. lxxvii. (Heb. lxxviii.) 8, cxviii. 5; Prov. xxi. 2. "The Lord" is Christ throughout this passage; see note on *v.* 3.

In the latter of the two parallel clauses of direction (εἰς...καὶ εἰς), the genitive τοῦ χριστοῦ is certainly subjective: ὑπομονή is misrendered "patient waiting for" (A.V., after Beza, "patientem exspectationem"; so Erasmus, Calvin, Estius; although the Vulg. had "patientiam Christi"; Chrysostom is undecided), as though the noun represented ἀναμένω (I. i. 10). Ὑπομονή is used over thirty times in the N.T.—fifteen times by St Paul; in every case it means *endurance* (of trial, evil), as e.g. in i. 4; I. i. 3 (see note); so in classical Greek, with the additional sense of "remaining behind." "The endurance of Christ," or "the Christ," includes more than the patience *of Jesus* historically viewed (cf. Rev. i. 9; Heb. xii. 2f.; Gal. vi. 17; see note on Ἰησοῦς, I. iv. 14); ὁ χριστός is "the" patient "Christ," who in enduring the cross and the contradiction of sinners, and the whole burden of His mission, fulfilled the prophetic ideal of Jehovah's suffering Servant (Isai. liii.): cf. the allusions of Rom. xv. 3; 1 Pet. ii. 21—25; Matt. xi. 29 f., &c. The previous genitive has the same kind of signification; ἡ ἀγάπη τοῦ θεοῦ denotes "God's love (to you)," not "(your) love to God": so everywhere else in St Paul,—Rom. v. 5, viii. 39; 2 Cor. xiii. 13. It is in the deepened sense of God's love and in the following of Christ's patience that the admonitions of the context will be rightly received and carried into effect; so from "God who loved us" comfort and hope were expected in ii. 16 f.

§ 5. iii. 6—15. THE CASE OF THE IDLERS.

This section contains the chief matter pointed to in τὸ λοιπόν of *v.* 1 (see note above). But the added homily is no afterthought; it is of only second importance to the topic of ii. 1—12. In the former Ep. the writers had occasion to exhort their readers to a quiet life and to the continued pursuit of their secular avocations (I. iv. 11 f.). The call to enter the kingdom of God and seek its glory brought men of a naturally idle or restless disposition under temptation upon this score. To such natures the rumours current about the Day of the Lord (ii. 1 f.) would appeal with particular force. "If Christ is on the point of appearing and the end of this evil world is so near, of what use are worldly occupations?" they would say; "to prepare to meet Him is the only business now worth minding. How can a Christian man interest himself any longer in the market or the field, in the tradesman's books or the craftsman's tools, when to-morrow the Lord may be here and the whole 'fashion of this world' may have passed away?" (cf. 1 Cor. vii. 29—31). Their conduct tended to general disorder (*v.* 11), and brought reproach on the Christian community at Thessalonica. Moreover they did the Church a material injury, by throwing the burden of their maintenance on their industrious brethren, who would not see them starve. These ἀτάκτως περιπατοῦντες were called οἱ ἄτακτοι in I. v. 12 ff. (see note introductory to § 10); they had given trouble to the προϊστάμενοι, whom the body of the Church were bidden loyally to support. The mild and somewhat indirect reproofs of the former Epistle had been insufficient to check this mischief, which was subsequently aggravated by the false announcements about the Parousia. Such wild reports were calculated to disturb even those most regular and conscientious in following their daily duties. So the Apostles, having calmed the agitation of the readers by what they have said in ch. ii., proceed to rebuke in strong terms the irregularity thus unhappily stimulated.

The παραγγελία runs as follows : (1) First, and last, *the avoidance is enjoined of those persistent in disorder* (who are, notwithstanding, "brethren" still, *vv.* 6, 15), *vv.* 6, 14; (2) the missionaries recall their *personal example and instructions* bearing upon this matter, *vv.* 7—10 ; (3) the "*idlers and meddlers*" *are solemnly required to amend*, and the rest to avoid their example, *vv.* 11—13 ; (4) the Church is urged, while *eschewing fellowship* with the wrong-doers, *to seek their reformation, vv.* 14, 15. It is to be observed, in comparing this instruction with I. v. 12 ff., that no further mention is made in this connexion of the προϊστάμενοι (Elders); the Church as a whole is charged with the discipline necessary; the disorder has grown to larger proportions and become more acute: cf. 1 Cor. v. 4 ff.; 2 Cor. ii. 6, ἡ ἐπιτιμία...ἡ ὑπὸ τῶν πλειόνων.

6. **Παραγγέλλομεν δὲ ὑμῖν, ἀδελφοί, ἐν ὀνόματι τοῦ κυρίου [ἡμῶν] Ἰησοῦ Χριστοῦ.** *But we charge you, brothers, in the name of the* [or *our*] *Lord Jesus Christ*. The general ἃ παραγγέλλομεν (v. 4 : see note) is particularized ; and the confidence in the loyalty of the readers there expressed is put to proof. The charge is addressed to "brothers"; it is not the mere command of a superior, but appeals to the sense of a common duty in the readers. At the same time, it *is* a command— not a personal wish, nor advice open to debate and qualification; it is delivered ἐν ὀνόματι τοῦ κυρ. Ἰησοῦ Χριστοῦ—on the authority of "Jesus Christ" as "Lord" of His people, by those who have the right to speak "in" His "name": see note on ἐν κυρίῳ Ἰησοῦ, I. iv. 1, and cf. *v.* 12 below; also Rom. i. 5; 1 Cor. v. 4; Ph. ii. 9 ff.; Col. iii. 17; Jam. v. 10. After the disregard of their admonition in Epistle I., the writers feel they must speak in the most peremptory and solemn tone; they pronounce as judges in the Sovereign's name. They speak collectively, since the action taken devolves on them in their joint responsibility for the well-being of the Church.

στέλλεσθαι ὑμᾶς ἀπὸ παντὸς ἀδελφοῦ ἀτάκτως περιπατοῦντος, *that you hold aloof from every brother walking in disorderly fashion.* Παραγγέλλω takes the regular infin., as in 1 Tim. i. 3 and often in St Luke; construed with ἵνα of the thing commanded in Mk. vi. 8; with ὅτι in v. 10, by way of apposition to the immediate object τοῦτο. The verb στέλλομαι (middle)—synon. with μὴ συναναμίγνυσθαι (v. 14)—signifies (transitively) to avoid in 2 Cor. viii. 20, the only other N.T. example; cf. however ὑποστέλλομαι, ὑποστολή, Heb. x. 38 f., Acts xx. 20, 27. Apparently this meaning, to contract, to draw within oneself—sometimes to shrink, flinch—is derived from the maritime figure of furling or shortening sail—ἱστία στέλλειν (lit. to set, fix in position) or στέλλεσθαι (Homer, &c.: see examples in Liddell and Scott); it is complemented by ἀπό also in Mal. ii. 5 (LXX). 'Απὸ...ἀδελφοῦ: for this is a matter between "brethren" (cf. v. 15; 1 Cor. v. 11 f.). The general avoidance of the man will be at once a punishment for him and a safeguard to the rest (v. 13), who might be infected by his company. This implies surely exclusion from Church-meetings, including the Agapé and the Lord's Supper; but it is not an absolute bar to personal intercourse: cf. v. 15. For ἀτάκτως, see note on I. v. 14—the adverb is a N.T. hap. leg.—also vv. 7, 11 below; for περιπατεῖν, I. ii. 12. Bengel observes on ἀτάκτως, "Igitur Ordo mendicantium non est ordo, sed gravat rempublicam ipsam" (v. 8).

καὶ μὴ κατὰ τὴν παράδοσιν ἣν παρελάβετε [or -οσαν] παρ' ἡμῶν, and not in accordance with the tradition which you [or they] received from us. Μὴ (περιπατοῦντος) κατὰ τὴν παράδοσιν κ.τ.λ.—not οὐ—for this is an assumed condition of the στέλλεσθαι: see Winer-Moulton on μή with participles, pp. 606 ff. (μή encroaches on οὐ in this connexion in later Greek: cf. i. 8, ii. 12); for οὐ with participles, cf. 2 Cor. iv. 8, Col. ii. 19, &c. For περιπατεῖν κατά κ.τ.λ. (Hebraistic), cf. Mk vii. 5; the phrase is elsewhere only Pauline in N.T.—Rom. viii. 4, xiv. 15, 1 Cor. iii. 3, 2 Cor. x. 2, Eph. ii. 2. For παράδοσις, see note on ii. 15; this includes παραγγελία as well as διδαχή: cf. 1 Cor. iv. 17, xi. 2; I. iv. 1 above.

The irregular παρελάβοσαν is strongly attested (see Textual Note): the harshness of the concord (the third plural referring to παντὸς ἀδελφοῦ), beside the anomalous ending, makes the substitution of -οσαν for -ετε on the part of copyists unlikely. At the same time the 3rd plural -οσαν, for imperfect and strong aorist indicative (also for optatives), is established in the κοινή (LXX; rare in Papyri: see J. H. Moulton's Prolegomena, pp. 51, 52); Rom. iii. 13 (from LXX) and Jo. xv. 22, 24, in the critical texts, afford examples. The termination is an Æolic (Bœotian) contribution to the mixed vernacular κοινή, favoured perhaps by the tendency to parisyllabic inflexional endings. On παραλαμβάνω, see I. ii. 13.

7. αὐτοὶ γὰρ οἴδατε. *For you know of yourselves*—"without our needing to tell it again": see notes on καθὼς οἴδατε, I. i. 5 f., ii. 1, &c.

πῶς δεῖ μιμεῖσθαι ἡμᾶς, *in what manner you ought to imitate us*—"an abridged expression for πῶς δεῖ ὑμᾶς περιπατεῖν ὥστε μιμεῖσθαι ἡμᾶς" (Lightfoot). Πῶς (*quali ratione*, Bengel) qualifies μιμεῖσθαι rather than δεῖ (cf. I. iv. 1; Eph. v. 15; 1 Tim. iii. 15): not urging the grounds of this duty, but showing the direction in which it lies, the true *line of imitation*. For μιμεῖσθαι, see notes on I. i. 6, and v. 9 below.

ὅτι οὐκ ἠτακτήσαμεν ἐν ὑμῖν, *for we did not act a disorderly part among you.* Ἠτακτήσαμεν is misrendered in the Vulg. "inquieti fuimus"; Erasmus better, "praeter ordinem viximus"; Beza, "inordinate nos gessimus"; Calvin, "inordinate egimus." Another meiosis (cf. οὐ πάντων ἡ πίστις, v. 2; and θεῷ μὴ ἀρεσκόντων, I. ii. 15): how far the Apostles were from conduct like this! Ἀτακτέω (=ἀτάκτως περιπατέω, v. 6; cf. ἀτάκτους, I. v. 14)—*hap. leg.* in N.T.—a military term, applied e.g. to soldiers *out of rank*: cf. Col. ii. 5, τὴν τάξιν ὑμῶν καὶ τὸ στερέωμα κ.τ.λ., "your order and the solid front of your faith in Christ." Officers are as much subject tò discipline as the rank and file; it was due to their Churches that the Apostles should set an example of a strictly ordered life; with this example before them, which bore exactly upon the point in question, the readers "know" what the nature of their "imitation" should be. Ὅτι governs along with οὐκ ἠτακτήσαμεν the following οὐδέ clause, which should have been included in the same verse, for it brings out the kind of disorder reproved:—

8. οὐδὲ δωρεὰν ἄρτον ἐφάγομεν παρά τινος, *nor indeed ate bread for nought at the hand of any one*: whereas the ἄτακτοι would not work for their bread, and expected the Church to support them. For δωρεάν (advbl. accus.), *gratis, by way of gift,* cf. 2 Cor. xi. 7; Matt. x. 8; Exod. xxi. 2; Isai. lii. 3 (LXX); in Gal. ii. 21, &c., the phrase gets a further meaning. Ἄρτον ἐσθίειν (Matt. xv. 2; Mk iii. 20; Lk. xiv. 1) renders the Heb. אָכַל לֶחֶם (Gen. xliii. 15; 2 Sam. [Kingd.] ix. 7, &c.), *to get food, have one's maintenance* (τρέφεσθαι); similarly ἐσθίειν alone in v. 10, 1 Cor. ix. 4. For παρά τινος, "acceptum a quoquam" (Beza)—"*from*" *of the bestower*—cf. Eph. vi. 8; Ph. iv. 18; Acts ii. 33, &c. There was a manly pride about St Paul in this matter; cf. 2 Cor. xi. 10 f., ἡ καύχησις αὕτη οὐ φραγήσεται.

ἀλλ' ἐν κόπῳ καὶ μόχθῳ νυκτὸς καὶ ἡμέρας ἐργαζόμενοι, *but in toil and travail, by night and day working.* Ἐν κόπῳ καὶ μόχθῳ forms one adjunct, νυκτὸς...ἐργαζόμενοι another, both qualifying ἐφάγομεν and negativing δωρεάν (cf. the connexion in v. 12). Along with the clause that follows, this reminder is almost a repetition of I. ii. 9 : see notes on that verse for the identical words. With hard, exhausting labour the Apostle Paul earned his daily bread ; " tent-making " (Acts xviii. 3) was a poorly paid handicraft. His companions, if not pursuing the same trade, acted on the same principles.

πρὸς τὸ μὴ ἐπιβαρῆσαί τινα ὑμῶν, *in order not to put a burden on any one amongst you.* For πρός with infinitive, and for ἐπιβαρέω, see notes on I. ii. 9.

9. οὐχ ὅτι οὐκ ἔχομεν ἐξουσίαν, *not that we are without right* (to act otherwise, to claim our maintenance: *scil.* ἐξουσίαν τοῦ δωρεὰν ἄρτον φαγεῖν· τοῦ φαγεῖν καὶ πεῖν, τοῦ μὴ ἐργάζεσθαι—see 1 Cor. ix. 4, 6. For this elliptical, corrective use of οὐχ ὅτι (*non quasi*, Vulg.; rather *non quod*, Beza)—"it is not the case that," or "I do not mean that"—cf. 2 Cor. i. 24, Phil. iii. 12, iv. 11, &c. This ἐξουσία St Paul carefully demonstrates, on behalf of the ministry of the Gospel, in 1 Cor. ix. 3—14, tracing it back to the Lord's ordinance (Lk. x. 7) ; cf. also Heb. xiii. 10. Ἐξουσία is *moral power, right, authority (jus,* Beza correctly ; not *potestatem*, as in Vulg.), in distinction from δύναμις (i. 7, 11, ii. 9), *actual power, force.*

ἀλλ' ἵνα ἑαυτοὺς τύπον δῶμεν ὑμῖν εἰς τὸ μιμεῖσθαι ἡμᾶς, *but* (*we did this*—ἐν κόπῳ κ.τ.λ....εἰργαζόμεθα, v. 8 ; or, *we waived this right*—τῇ ἐξουσίᾳ οὐκ ἐχρησάμεθα, 1 Cor. ix. 15), *that we might give ourselves to you by way of example, so that you might imitate us.* The ellipsis after ἀλλά resembles that following ὅτι in ii. 3, or μόνον in ii. 7 (see notes). Ἑαυτούς (for its use in 1st person, see I. ii. 8) is thrown forward with emphasis—the writers would *themselves* exemplify the life they preach ; from the first they impressed their message on the Thessalonians in this living, practical fashion (I. i. 6): cf. 1 Cor. iv. 17; Ph. iii. 17, where τύπος appears in the same connexion—for this word, see note on I. i. 7. To "*give* oneself (as) an example " is more than to "*make* oneself an example " (as though δίδωμι had the twofold sense of Heb. נתן) ; it implies sacrifice, self-surrender, resembling μεταδοῦναι...τὰς ἑαυτῶν ψυχάς, I. ii. 8: cf. ὁ δοὺς ἑαυτὸν ἀντίλυτρον, 1 Tim. ii. 6; Eph. i. 22, v. 2; Rom. vi. 16. On εἰς τό with infinitive, see I. ii. 12: the εἰς τό clause (of *issue*) is consecutive to the ἵνα clause (of *purpose*), as in I. ii. 16 ; the consecution of ii. 11 f. above was the reverse of this (εἰς τό..., ἵνα).

In *vv.* 8 and 9 the Apostles give *two* reasons for their practice of manual labour,—the former alone stated in I. ii. 9. The second reason

—less complimentary to the readers, but on which the conduct of the ἄτακτοι now compels insistence—was however half implied in the context of the parallel passage (Ep. I.), *scil.* in μεταδοῦναι...τὰς ἑαυτῶν ψυχάς (ii. 8) and ὡς...δικαίως...ὑμῖν...ἐγενήθημεν,...ὡς πατὴρ τέκνα ἑαυτοῦ ...μαρτυρόμενοι κ.τ.λ. (*vv.* 10 f.) : cf. 2 Cor. xi. 11 f., xii. 14 f. (St Paul an example of self-denial) ; see note on I. ii. 9 above.

10. καὶ γὰρ ὅτε ἦμεν πρὸς ὑμᾶς, τοῦτο παρηγγέλλομεν ὑμῖν. *For indeed when we were with you, we used to give you this charge*: cf. I. iv. 11. Καὶ γάρ is parallel to the γάρ of *v.* 7; it sets the Apostolic παραγγελία side by side with the Apostolic τύπος in the matter of ἐργάζεσθαι καὶ ἐσθίειν (cf. γάρ...καὶ γάρ in I. iv. 9 f.) : together these constitute ἡ παράδοσις of *v.* 6. This sentence almost repeats I. iii. 4, only substituting τοῦτο παρηγγέλλομεν (after *v.* 6) for προελέγομεν. On the use of πρός, see note to I. iii. 4, and ii. 5 above.

ὅτι εἴ τις οὐ θέλει ἐργάζεσθαι μηδὲ ἐσθιέτω. '*If any one refuses* (*nonvult,* Vulg.) *to work, neither shall he eat!*' a Jewish proverb, based upon Gen. iii. 19. For the apodosis, thrown into the lively imperative mood, cf. 1 Cor. xi. 6. For the ὅτι recitative of direct narration, cf. Gal. i. 23, Acts xiv. 22; and see Winer-Moulton, p. 683, *note*. For τοῦτο...ὅτι, cf. I. ii. 13, iv. 15. Οὐ θέλω is not the mere contradictory, but the contrary of θέλω—" if any one *won't* work "—not a negative supposition (εἰ μή), but the supposition of a negative : see Winer-Moulton, pp. 597, 599 ; cf. Rom. vii. 19 f., 1 Cor. vii. 9, 1 Tim. iii. 5, &c., and *v.* 14 below. "*Nolle,* vitium est" (Bengel). Note the *present* of continuous action (*habit* or *rule*) in the verbs: cf. for the last verb, 1 Cor. x. 18, 25, &c., xi. 22—34. The neglect of this stern but necessary rule makes charity demoralizing. This law of Christ touches the idle rich as well as the poor ; it makes that a disgrace which one hears spoken of as though it were a privilege and the mark of a gentleman,—" to live upon one's means," *fruges consumere natus*: see *v.* 12. This rule is forcibly applied in the following direction of the *Didaché,* xii. 2—5 : εἰ θέλει [πάροδιος ὁ ἐρχόμενος] πρὸς ὑμᾶς καθίσαι, τεχνίτης ὤν, ἐργαζέσθω καὶ φαγέτω· εἰ δὲ οὐκ ἔχει τέχνην, κατὰ τὴν σύνεσιν ὑμῶν προνοήσατε πῶς μὴ ἀργὸς μεθ' ὑμῶν ζήσεται Χριστιανός· εἰ δὲ οὐ θέλει οὕτω ποιεῖν, χριστέμπορός ἐστιν· προσέχετε ἀπὸ τῶν τοιούτων. Cf. the quotation cited below, on *v.* 12.

11. ἀκούομεν γάρ τινας περιπατοῦντας ἐν ὑμῖν ἀτάκτως. *For we hear of certain persons walking amongst you in disorderly fashion.* On the last word, see *v.* 6. Ἐν ὑμῖν (cf. οὐκ ἠτακτήσαμεν ἐν ὑμῖν, *v.* 7),— for their relations *with the Church* were irregular. Not "that there are some" (A.V.; after the Vulg., "inter vos quosdam ambulare inquiete"; Beza, "inordinate"): the Apostles do not simply know that such people are to be found in this Church; they *know about them*—who they are, and how they are behaving. For ἀκούω with accus. of the *content* or *matter* of report, cf. Gal. i. 13, Eph. i. 15, iii. 2, Acts xvii. 32, &c.; and for τινές relating to persons known but not named (*quosdam*), 2 Cor. ii. 5, x. 2, 12, Gal. i. 7, ii. 12, Col. ii. 8, 1 Tim. i. 3, Tit. i. 12. The writers state this on *hearsay* (cf. 1 Cor. i. 11, v. 1, xi. 18); the matter was not officially communicated to them, though probably letters had passed to and fro (see *Introd*. p. xxxv., and note on I. v. 2). This verse gives the reason (γάρ) for recalling the severe maxim of *v*. 10, or perhaps for the entire reproof (*vv*. 6—10). In the *Didaché* (i. 10—12), probably the oldest Post-apostolic document extant, there is a warning addressed both to givers and receivers of alms, which shows how prevalent was the danger of similar abuse of Church charities: Μακάριος ὁ διδοὺς κατὰ τὴν ἐντολήν...οὐαὶ τῷ λαμβάνοντι· εἰ μὲν γὰρ χρείαν ἔχων λαμβάνει τις, ἀθῷος ἔσται· ὁ δὲ μὴ χρείαν ἔχων δώσει δίκην, ἱνατί ἔλαβε καὶ εἰς τί· ἐν συνοχῇ δὲ γενόμενος ἐξετασθήσεται περὶ ὧν ἔπραξεν, καὶ οὐκ ἐξελεύσεται ἐκεῖθεν μέχρις οὗ ἀποδῷ τὸν ἔσχατον κοδράντην· ἀλλὰ καὶ περὶ τούτου δὴ εἴρηται· Ἱδρωτάτω ἡ ἐλεημοσύνη σου εἰς τὰς χεῖράς σου, μέχρις ἂν γνῷς τίνι δῷς—" let thine alms sweat into thine hands, till thou knowest to whom thou shouldst give."

μηδὲν ἐργαζομένους ἀλλὰ περιεργαζομένους, *working at nothing, but being busybodies*; or—to imitate the play on ἐργάζομαι—" whose one business is to be busybodies," "minding every body's business but their own." Lightfoot quotes the same verbal play from Demosthenes, *Philip*. iv., p. 150. 21 f., σοὶ μὲν ἐξ ὧν ἐργάζει καὶ περιεργάζει τοὺς ἐσχάτους ὄντας κινδύνους; the like appears in Quintilian's Latin, *Instit. Orat*. vi. 3. 53: "Afer venuste Mallium Suram, multum in agendo discursantem, salientem, manus jactantem, togam dejicientem et reponentem, non *agere* dixit sed *satagere*." So Calvin and Beza here: "nihil agentes, sed curiose (inaniter) satagentes"; Vulg., "nihil operantes, sed curioso agentes." The verb περιεργάζομαι is hap. leg. in N.T.; but the adj. περίεργος—associated with ἀργαί, φλύαροι and περιερχόμεναι—is applied in 1 Tim. v. 13, in its well-established sense, to good-for-nothing, gossiping women; τὰ περίεργα, in Acts xix. 19, signifying *impertinent, superfluous*, describes the magic ("curious") practices prevalent in Ephesus. So, in Polybius xviii. 34. 2, Antiochus protests against the Romans "meddling" (πολυπραγμονεῖν) with affairs in Asia, οὐδὲ γὰρ αὐτὸς περιεργάζεται τῶν κατὰ τὴν Ἰταλίαν ἁπλῶς οὐδέν, "for he does not on his part *interfere* in the least with Italian politics." In earlier Greek the verb meant to *overdo* things. For similar epigrams of St Paul, cf. *vv.* 2 f. above (πίστις, πιστός), Rom. i. 20, 1 Cor. vii. 31, 2 Cor. vi. 10, Phil. iii. 2 f.; see also Heb. v. 8. This troublesome activity of the ἄτακτοι was probably connected with the agitation about the Parousia censured in ii. 2. Having thrown up their proper work, the mischief-makers went about ventilating the latest sensational rumours on this subject, and thus disturbing the quiet of the Church and interrupting their diligent brethren.

12. **τοῖς δὲ τοιούτοις παραγγέλλομεν καὶ παρακαλοῦμεν ἐν κυρίῳ Ἰησοῦ Χριστῷ.** *But those that are such we charge and exhort in the Lord Jesus Christ*: the παραγγελία of *v.* 6 was given to the Church respecting the offenders; now the Apostles turn to address, in the same authoritative and solemn manner, the ἄτακτοι and περιεργαζόμενοι themselves. With the definite τοῖς τοιούτοις—" the men of this sort," "those who answer to the above description"—cf. Rom. xvi. 18; 1 Cor. v. 11, xvi. 16; 2 Cor. ii. 6; Gal. v. 23; Ph. ii. 29; Tit. iii. 11: it is the qualitative of τινές above (*v.* 11). The third instance of παραγγέλλω in this homily (*vv.* 6, 10). But παρακαλοῦμεν is added (see I. ii. 11 on the word) with a softening force; cf. the transition in Phm. 8 f., also the combinations of I. ii. 11, iv. 1, and 2 Tim. iv. 2. For ἐν κυρίῳ ʼΙ. Χ., see note on the threefold Name, I. i. 1; also on ἐν ὀνόματι κ.τ.λ., *v.* 6.

ἵνα μετὰ ἡσυχίας ἐργαζόμενοι τὸν ἑαυτῶν ἄρτον ἐσθίωσιν, *that with quietness, keeping to their work, they eat their own bread*: cf. I. iv. 11 (and notes), closely echoed here. Μετὰ ἡσυχίας (=ἡσυχάζοντες, I. iv. 11)—in contrast with περιεργαζόμενοι (*v.* 11)—appears to qualify the whole clause, while ἐργαζόμενοι stands in the same relation to ἐσθίωσιν as to ἐφάγομεν in *v.* 8: "that they eat their own bread quietly, by working," not by going about in idleness and taxing the community. For τὸν ἑαυτῶν ἄρτον, see *v.* 8—"*their own* bread," not the bread of others received δωρεάν (*v.* 8); "a Rabbinical phrase" (Lightfoot). For the use of ἵνα after παρακαλέω and the like, see note on I. iv. 1. For μετά of the attendant disposition, cf. I. i. 6; Eph. iv. 2, 1 Tim. ii. 15, &c.; cf. ἐν ἡσυχίᾳ, 1 Tim. ii. 11 f.

13. **Ὑμεῖς δέ, ἀδελφοί, μὴ ἐνκακήσητε καλοποιοῦντες.** *But for yourselves, brothers, do not falter in right-doing*. The writers turn from the offending section to the body of their readers: cf. the (supposed) opposite transition in παρακαλοῦμεν δὲ ὑμᾶς, ἀδελφοί, I. v. 14, and note. Ἐν-κακέω (not ἐκ-κακέω) is a favourite Pauline term— 2 Cor. iv. 1, 16; Gal. vi. 9; Eph. iii. 13, also Lk. xviii. 1—*to become*

κακός, *to flag, fail in* a thing. Καλο-ποιοῦντες (*hap. leg.* for the compound; Rom. vii. 21, 2 Cor. xiii. 7, Gal. vi. 9, Jam. iv. 17 exhibit the components) points to a quality of conduct—"doing the fair, noble thing"—as distinguished from ἀγαθο-ποιεῖν, "benefiting," Mk iii. 4; cf. notes on ἀγαθός and καλός, I. v. 15, 21. Phil. iv. 8 supplies a rich enumeration of the Christian καλά. The above rebuke of περιεργάζεσθαι and the commendation of ἡσυχία, if not thus guarded, might have damped the ardour of some whose activity was praiseworthy. The misconduct of the unruly was of a nature to discourage zealous friends of the Gospel.

The present participle with ἐνκακήσητε is of the type of that following παύομαι (cf. Eph. i. 16, &c.) and other verbs signifying a moment of action, the participle stating that *in the course of which* the condition denoted by the principal verb arises. Μή is construed in prohibitions with subjunctive aorist (but impv. *present*; see v. 15); cf. ii. 3; see Moulton's *Proleg.*, pp. 122—4. Another paronomasia (see v. 11) is traceable in ἐν κ α κήσητε—κ α λ ο ποιοῦντες: cf. Rom. vii. 21, Gal. vi. 9, Heb. v. 14; also Gal. iv. 18, 1 Tim. iii. 13, Matt. xxi. 41.

14. εἰ δέ τις οὐχ ὑπακούει τῷ λόγῳ ἡμῶν διὰ τῆς ἐπιστολῆς. *But if any one is disobeying our word* (sent) *through this letter.* Remembering the neglect of the former admonition (I. iv. 11 f.), the writers anticipate that this remonstrance may be disregarded by some of the offenders. The matter is put, according to Greek epistolary idiom, from the readers' standpoint—in *present* time. The Letter has been read in the assembly; the ἄτακτοι have received the Apostolic message; the Church appeals to them; some acknowledge their fault and promise amendment; one or more, it is feared, will prove refractory, giving no sign of obedience: the Church must now deal with these. Εἰ with present indicative assumes an existing case; see note on εἰ τις οὐ θέλει, v. 10—also on the use of οὐ rather than μή: the stronger particle assumes a positive *refusal* of obedience.

Διὰ τῆς ἐπιστολῆς qualifies the verbal noun λόγῳ—"our word (spoken, addressed to him) through the Epistle": cf. note on the two nouns in ii. 15. The λόγος in question is specifically the pointed command and appeal of the last verse. Ἡ ἐπιστολή, "*the* (present) letter," as in I. v. 27; Rom. xvi. 22; Col. iv. 16, &c.

Διὰ τῆς ἐπιστολῆς is attached by some of the older commentators to σημειοῦσθε—"note this man through letter (*scil.* to us)," as though the Thessalonians were instructed to send to the Apostles the names of recusants in writing; "eos vult apud se deferri" (Calvin). But the position of the clause, the use of the definite article, and the scope of the context are against this reading of the verse. The purpose of the σημειοῦσθαι is not to inform the Apostles at a distance, but to prevent συναναμίγνυσθαι on the spot. The διά clause insists that the "word conveyed *by letter*" shall take effect just as though it were directly uttered; see again note on εἴτε διὰ λόγου εἴτε δι' ἐπιστολῆς ἡμῶν, ii. 15.

τοῦτον σημειοῦσθε, μὴ συναναμίγνυσθαι αὐτῷ, *take note of this man, not to associate with him*—literally, " not to mix-up-along with him ": the same double compound is used in 1 Cor. v. 9, 11; ἀναμίγνυσθαι is classical Greek in this sense; συναναμίγνυσθαι appears in the κοινή. Σημειοῦσθαι (middle), N.T. *hap. leg.*—" to put a mark upon", or " make a note of, for oneself "—is another word of the κοινή (Attic ἀποσημαίνεσθαι). The "noting", one imagines, would be effected by publicly *naming* the culprit in the Church as thus under censure.

ἵνα ἐντραπῇ, *that he may be abashed.* Ἐντρέπομαι (cf. 1 Cor. iv. 14; Tit. ii. 8; Lk. xviii. 2, &c.) is passive, signifying "to be turned in (upon oneself)"; the idiom only appears in later Greek. This is all the punishment desired, at least in the first instance; the door is left open for repentance. The direction of 1 Cor. v. 13 is far sterner, as the offence was more heinous. Cf. the treatment of the later case of discipline (surely different from that of 1 Cor. v.) at Corinth in 2 Cor. ii. 6—8.

15. καὶ μὴ ὡς ἐχθρὸν ἡγεῖσθε, ἀλλὰ νουθετεῖτε ὡς ἀδελφόν. *And do not regard (him) as an enemy, but admonish (him) as a brother.* The R.V. retains the intruded "yet" (after "and," καί) of the A.V.; but the contrast thus implied was not in the writers' thoughts any more than in their language. The action dictated in v. 14 is kindly and *saving* in intent; the man who could be " put to shame " by censure was not lost to the Church. This added sentence deprecates any hostile manifestation, such as would provoke sullenness instead of compunction, thus defeating the Apostles' purpose. Νουθεσία is a friendly act, associated with brotherhood and tenderness: see e.g. Acts xx. 31; 1 Cor. iv. 14; Eph. vi. 4. For the verb νουθετέω, see note on I. v. 12; and for ἡγέομαι, on I. v. 13: cf. ἡγεῖσθαι ὥσπερ in Job xix. 11, xxxiii. 10. For ἀδελφόν in this connexion, cf. 1 Cor. viii. 11; Gal. vi. 1; 1 Tim. v. 1; Jam. iv. 11; 1 Jo. iii. 15; Matt. vii. 3 ff., xviii. 21—35.

The general instruction of v. 6, στέλλεσθαι ὑμᾶς κ.τ.λ., which applied to any kind of ἀταξία, is thus combined with the direction of I. v. 14, νουθετεῖτε τοὺς ἀτάκτους; and the combined injunctions are enforced in the instance of those Thessalonian idlers who shall after the reproof now given persist in their misconduct. In such a case the disorder takes the form of open disobedience to Apostolic command, and must be dealt with publicly and put an end to. But even so *expulsion* is not so much as named.

§ 6. iii. 16—18. CONCLUSION OF THE LETTER.

This brief but pregnant conclusion consists of *prayer* (v. 16 a); *benediction* (v. 16 b); and autograph *salutation*, with precaution against forgery (v. 17), including a second *benediction* (v. 18).

16. Αὐτὸς δὲ ὁ κύριος τῆς εἰρήνης δῴη ὑμῖν τὴν εἰρήνην διὰ παντὸς ἐν παντὶ τρόπῳ. *But may the Lord of peace Himself give you peace continually in every way.* For Αὐτὸς δέ, cf. ii. 16 above—the fourth recurrence of this phrase in the prayers of the two Epistles: from their own attempts to preserve the Church's peace and to remedy disorder the Apostles turn to the Author and Disposer of peace, invoking this all-comprising blessing from His hand. For εἰρήνη, cf. I. i. 1; with ὁ κύριος τῆς εἰρήνης cf. ὁ θεὸς τῆς εἰρήνης, I. v. 23, and note: similarly in II. ii. 13 the ἠγαπημένοι ὑπὸ θεοῦ of I. i. 4 become the ἠγαπημένοι ὑπὸ Κυρίου. "The Lord of peace" is surely *Christ*, as in the whole context (see note on κύριος, v. 1 above), and regularly with St Paul. The previous context—v. 14 especially—suggests this prayer; the "peace" desired has reference to the Church troubles of the hour. But the supplication is broadened to its widest extent by διὰ παντός κ.τ.λ., including e.g. peace with heathen neighbours and relief from persecution (see i. 4, I. ii. 14, iii. 3 f., contrasting I. v. 3; Acts ix. 31); and it comprises beneath all this the "peace with God" which is the basis of Christian happiness (I. i. 1; II. i. 2; Rom. v. 1, &c.), whereof Christ is administrator and "Lord": see Eph. ii. 13—18, where peace amongst brethren (between Jew and Gentile) centres in Christ and is grounded on the peace between God and man effected by the cross; also Jo. xiv. 27, xx. 19, 21, 26; Rom. xv. 5 ff., 13, illustrates the double reference of εἰρήνη. Cf. Num. vi. 26, Κύριος.. δῴη σοι εἰρήνην,—the high-priest's blessing upon Israel.

Διὰ παντός, "through all," is better rendered (as in Lk. xxiv. 53, Heb. ix. 6, xiii. 15) "continually"—lasting unbroken, despite trouble —than "at all times" (R.V.), which represents πάντοτε (i. 3, &c.). For ἐν παντὶ τρόπῳ, cf. ii. 3; also Ph. i. 18, παντὶ τρόπῳ,—a form of phrase sufficient here but for the foregoing διὰ παντός, suggesting the corresponding ἐν: for such *balanced* prepositions, cf. I. iv. 14;

Eph. iv. 6, &c. This phrase impresses on τὴν εἰρήνην the *manifold* aspect above described.

Nor is it the Lord's "peace" alone, but "the Lord" Himself, in His personal presence and authority (see Matt. xxviii. 18, 20), and protection (see v. 3 above), whom the Apostles invoke: ὁ κύριος μετὰ πάντων ὑμῶν, (*May*) *the Lord* (*be*) *with you all* (cf. Rom. xv. 33)—as in v. 18—not excluding the ἀδελφοὶ ἄτακτοι, who even more than others need the control of "the Lord" and the calming effect of His "peace." In the Benedictions of 1 Cor. xvi. 24, 2 Cor. xiii. 13, πάντων has the like pointed significance. See also note on I. v. 27.

17. Ὁ ἀσπασμὸς τῇ ἐμῇ χειρί—ΠΑΥΛΟΥ. *The salutation with my own hand—of PAUL.* In the last word the Apostle Paul's formal signature is attached, which endorses the Epistle as proceeding from him and expressing his mind, though another hand had held the pen (cf. Rom. xvi. 22), and although his two companions were partners in the Letter and may, either or both of them, have personally contributed to it; see *Introd.*, pp. xlviii.—lii., liv. In Gal. vi. 11 and Phm. 19 St Paul again notifies the inscribing of certain words *sua manu*, implying that the body of the Epistle was indited through an amanuensis. This was, presumably, the Apostle's habit. In other Epistles we find the autograph conclusion (ὁ ἀσπασμός) serving as signature without the *name*, which in ancient writing was given at the head of the letter. There was no reference to this signature at the close of the former Epistle; but since its dispatch the written authority of the Apostles has been quoted for statements they repudiate (ii. 2; see note). St Paul is now guarding against such misrepresentation.

St Paul calls attention in penning the attestation to his handwriting, and gives notice that no document claiming his authority will be genuine without this seal: ὅ ἐστιν σημεῖον ἐν πάσῃ ἐπιστολῇ· οὕτως γράφω, *which is a token* (*sign*) *in every letter—so I write*. In St Paul's extant Letters, while it is the exception for him to sign his name in the closing salutation, he appears regularly to have written out the ἀσπασμός with his own hand. There was something peculiar and noticeable in the Apostle's script. Some infer from Gal. vi. 11 that he wrote an unusually large, bold hand; but the γράμματα μεγάλα of that passage may have been employed there for emphasis. His handicraft of tent-cloth stitching would inevitably make his fingers stiff and inapt for the use of the pen.

18. ἡ χάρις τοῦ κυρίου ἡμῶν Ἰησοῦ Χριστοῦ μετὰ πάντων ὑμῶν. *The grace of our Lord Jesus Christ* (*be*) *with you all*: cf. note on I. v. 28, to which only πάντων is added (see concluding note on v. 16).

APPENDIX.

THE MAN OF LAWLESSNESS ('Ο ἄνθρωπος τῆς ἀνομίας).
2 Thessalonians ii. 1–12.

A full account of the exegesis of 2 Thess. ii. 1–12 would embrace the history of the critical epochs and decisive conflicts of Christendom. This prophecy has constantly recurred to the mind of the Church and its meaning has been anxiously scanned in hours of trial. To such seasons, indeed, we should look for its interpretation. History is the expositor of prophecy. The seeds of the future lie in the past; and not the seeds alone, its buddings and forthputtings are there; for "that which is hath been already, and that which is to be hath already been." "First the blade," said Jesus, "then the ear, then the full corn in the ear." The development of God's kingdom, and of Satan's, is in either case continuous until full ripeness. "Let *both* grow together until the harvest."

It may be worth our while, therefore, to trace in its historical outline the development of the doctrine of Antichrist—as it appears in Scripture, and as it has been unfolded in the belief of the Church.

1. THE APOCALYPSE OF DANIEL.

The origin of St Paul's conception of ὁ ἄνθρωπος τῆς ἀνομίας, with that of the kindred visions of St John, is to be found in the Book of Daniel[1]. Daniel's Apocalypse has its starting-point in the dream of Nebuchadnezzar (ch. ii.): *the fourfold metal image*, with its feet of mixed iron and clay, broken in pieces by the "stone cut out without hands," which "becomes a great mountain." This dream takes an enlarged form in Daniel's first Vision, that of *the four wild beasts* (ch. vii.). Amidst the "ten horns" of the fourth Beast there shoots up "a little horn," before which "three of the first horns were plucked up by the roots," having "eyes like the eyes of a man, and a mouth speaking great things" (v. 8). In a moment the scene

---

[1] See the penetrating and suggestive article in Smith's *Dictionary of the Bible*, by Westcott; also Hastings' *Dict. of the Bible*, on the *Book of Daniel*; and Driver's *Daniel* in the *Cambridge Bible for Schools*.

changes: the "thrones" of the Last Judgement are "placed"; the "Ancient of Days" is beheld sitting; and there is "brought near before Him" the "one like unto a son of man, coming with the clouds of heaven," with whom the Lord Jesus at the High Priest's tribunal identified Himself. To this true king the prophet assigns universal and ever-during dominion (*vv.* 9–14). As the Judgement proceeds, and before the appearance of the glorified Son of Man, the fourth Wild Beast is slain, and "his body destroyed and given to be burned with fire" (*v.* 11), "because of the voice of the great words which the [little] horn spake." The idea is here presented of a cruel, haughty, and triumphant military power, to be overthrown suddenly and completely by the judgement of God, whose fall, apparently, will give the signal for the establishment of the kingdom of heaven; and this kingdom, in contrast with the previous monarchies symbolized by the "wild beasts," is to be ruled by "one like unto a son of man"—a king of ideal human character, yet clad with Divine glory and "brought near before" God Himself.

In the next Vision, ch. viii., that of *the duel between the Ram and the He-goat*, the Little Horn reappears (*vv.* 9 ff.), and assumes a distinct personal shape. He becomes "a king of fierce countenance and understanding dark sentences," who will destroy (or corrupt) the people of the saints...and stand up against the Prince of princes; but he shall be broken without hand" (*vv.* 22–25).

The third Vision, ch. xi., viz. of *the wars of North and South*, leads to a further description of the great Oppressor looming through the whole apocalypse, in which his atheism forms the most important feature: "Arms shall stand on his part, and they shall profane the sanctuary...and they shall set up the abomination that maketh desolate....And the king shall do according to his will; and he shall exalt himself, and magnify himself above every god, and shall speak marvellous things against the God of gods; and he shall prosper till the indignation be accomplished" (*vv.* 31–36).

This series of tableaux, notwithstanding the obscurity of their details, gives in broad outline a continuous view of a polity or empire evolved out of the warring kingdoms of this world, from which emerges at last a monster of wickedness armed with all earthly power and bent on the destruction of Israel's God and people, who is suffered by God in His anger to bear rule for a brief space, but in whose person the realm of evil suffers a conclusive judgement and overthrow.

2. The Messianic Times and Jewish Apocalyptic.

Antiochus Epiphanes[1], it is agreed, was the primary subject of the Visions of judgement on the great enemy of Israel contained in the Book of Daniel. In his overthrow, and in the Maccabean resurrection of the Jewish nationality, this Apocalypse received its proximate fulfilment. But when the period of the Maccabees was past and the nation fell again under a foreign yoke, while no further sign appeared of the Messiah, it was plain to believing readers that the revelation had some further import. In this faith the sufferings of the people of God under the Herodian and Roman oppression were endured, as "birthpangs of the Messiah"; it was felt that Israel's hope was even at the doors.

In this expectation the patriotism of Israel lived and glowed; it is vividly expressed in the extant Apocryphal literature of the pre-Christian times,—in the *Sibylline Oracles*; the *Book of Enoch*, ch. xc.; the *Psalms of Solomon*, especially xvii., xviii. Of less importance in this respect are the *Assumption of Moses* and the *Book of Jubilees*, contemporaneous with the Christian era. The 2nd (Latin 4th) *Book of Esdras*, and the kindred *Apocalypse of Baruch*, though dating probably from the close of the first century A.D., reflect the eschatology of Jewish nationalists during the struggle with Rome[2]. These witnesses confirm and illustrate the indications of the Gospels as to the keenness and intensity of the Messianic outlook at the time of the appearance of Jesus, and as to the political and materialistic nature of the popular ideal, which was animated by antipathy to Rome on the one side, and to sceptical or heretical movements within Judaism upon the other. Our Lord in assuming the title Son of Man appealed to, while He corrected, the anticipation of those who "looked for Israel's redemption"—an expectation largely founded upon the Apocalypse of Daniel and coloured by its imagery. Before long, as He foretold, "the abomination of desolation, spoken of by Daniel the prophet," would again "stand in the Holy Place"

---

[1] Antiochus IV., or Antiochus Epiphanes—i.e. the Illustrious or Manifest (scil. θεὸς ἐπιφανής), nicknamed *Epimanes*, the *Madman*—was the seventh king of the Græco-Syrian dynasty of the Seleucids, and reigned from 175 to 164 B.C. His father was Antiochus III. (*the Great*), after whose defeat by the Romans in the year 188 he was given to them as a hostage, and brought up at Rome. He returned to take his father's throne, full of wild ambition and of reckless impiety and prodigality. On the career of Antiochus IV., see Stanley's *History of the Jewish Church*, vol. III.; Ewald's *History of Israel*, vol. V. (Eng. Trans.); Smith's, and Hastings', *Dict. of the Bible*; Driver's *Daniel*, Introd. § 2.
[2] See, on the whole subject, Schürer's *The Jewish People in the Time of Christ* (Eng. Tr.), Div. II. Vol. II. pp. 128 ff., *The Messianic Hope*.

(Matt. xxiv. 15); thereafter "the sign of the Son of Man" would be "seen in heaven," and at last the Son of Man Himself was destined to "come with the clouds of heaven" (Matt. xxiv. 30, xxvi. 64).

The Messianic forecasts of our Lord's time, being drawn from the above Danielic source, could not fail to bring along with them as their counterpart, and in their shadow, the image of Daniel's Antichrist; it may be seen in the παράνομος-Βελίαρ of the *Sibylline Oracles* (cf. St Paul's ὁ ἄνομος, and the Βελίαρ-Antichrist of 2 Cor. vi. 15). The direct evidence of this fact is only slight; the existence of the Jewish doctrine of Antichrist anterior to the Christian era depends for proof, as appears in M. Friedländer's recent monograph on the subject (*Der Antichrist in den vorchristlichen jüdischen Quellen*), upon the data of the Midrash and Talmud, from which one has to argue back to antecedent times (see also Weber's *Jüdische Theologie*, 4te *Abtheilung*). Bousset has however shown, by the researches summarized in his Essay on *Antichrist*[1], that the roots of this conception run far back into esoteric pre-Christian Jewish teaching; and Gunkel, in his striking work, *Schöpfung und Chaos in Urzeit und Endzeit*, has even attempted to find its origin in primitive Babylonian cosmogony. This last theory would carry us into very distant and speculative regions. In later Judaism—certainly before the eighth century—Antichrist became a familiar figure under the name *Armillus* (? = Romulus: the designation is aimed at *Rome*, which was also cryptically known as *Edom*). Under this name he figures in the Jewish fables of the Middle Ages, in a variety of forms partly analogous and partly hostile to the Christian doctrine. "Armillus" appears in the *Targum of Jonathan* upon Isai. xi. 4, the passage quoted by the

---

[1] *Der Antichrist in der Ueberlieferung des Judentums, des neuen Testaments, und der alten Kirche* (Göttingen, 1895). Following Gunkel, Bousset writes (p. 93): "In the literature of the O.T., and in some passages of the New, we find abundant traces of a primeval Dragon myth, which in later times took the form of an eschatological anticipation. There subsisted in popular Jewish belief the expectation, which can be recognized in the Apocalypse, of an uprising at the end of the days of the old Sea-monster with whom God strove in the creation, who will assault heaven in his war with God... The legend of Antichrist appears to me to be no more than an anthropomorphic recasting of this myth...The Dragon is replaced by the Man, armed with miraculous powers, who deifies himself. For the Jews, this personality was necessarily identical with the Pseudo-Messias." See also Gunkel, *op. cit.*, pp. 221 f.: "It is well known that Judaism expected a great and general apostasy in the last times. After the age of Daniel it was understood that this consummation of wickedness would incorporate itself in a man, who would wantonly assail everything holy, and even the temple of God in Jerusalem...The ἄνομος proclaims himself God, in the temple of God; and this deification of a man is the crowning sin which Judaism imputes to the kings of the Gentiles...The ἄνομος-prophecy of 2 Thessalonians is no arbitrary invention of an individual; it gives expression to a belief which had behind it a long historical development, and was at that time universally diffused."

Apostle in II. ii. 8: "With the breath of his lips shall he (Messiah) slay Armillus, the wicked one." The currency of an archaic Jewish doctrine, or legend, of Antichrist makes it easier to understand the rapid development which this conception received in the New Testament, and the force with which it appealed to the mind of the Apostolic Church.

The words of Christ fixed the attention of His disciples upon the prophecies of *Daniel*, and supplied the ἀφορμή from which proceeded the revival of Old Testament Apocalypse in the prophecies of St Paul and St John, where this movement took a direction and an ethical character very different from that of non-Christian Judaism. Beside His express citations of Daniel, there were other traits in our Lord's pictures of the Last Things—the predictions of national conflict, of persecutions from without and defections within His Church (Matt. xxiv. 3-13)—which reproduced the general characteristics of this prophet's visions, and which lent emphasis to His specific and deliberate references thereto. The use made by Jesus Christ of this obscure and suspected Book of Scripture has raised it to high honour in the esteem of the Church.

3. Antichrist in the Book of Revelation.

St Paul treats the subject of Antichrist's coming incidentally in this passage, and never again in his extant Letters does he revert to it. But his language, so far as it goes, is positive and definite. There is scarcely a more matter-of-fact prediction in the Bible. While the Apostle refuses to give any chronological datum, and posits the event in question as the issue of an historical development—as the unfolding of "the mystery of iniquity already working," whose course is in the nature of things contingent and incalculable in its duration—his delineation of the personality of Antichrist, in whom he sees the culmination of Satanic influences upon humanity, is vividly distinct. He asserts the connexion between the appearance of this monster and the reappearance of the triumphant Christ from heaven with an explicitness which leaves no room for doubt. It may suit us to resolve these realistic figures and occurrences into a pictorial dramatization, to see in them no more than an ideal representation under conventional symbols of the crucial struggle between the Christian and the Antichristian principle operative in mankind; but the Apostle was not dealing with abstract principles and ethical forces—he knew these in their actuality and conceived them, alike in the present and in the future, as they take shape in

personal character and action and display themselves, under the
Divine order of human history, in living encounter and full-bodied
antagonism upon the field of history, where they fight out their duel
to its appointed end.

St John's Apocalypse was cast in a different mould from that of
St Paul. Like that of the Book of Daniel, his revelation came
through *visions*, received apparently in a passive and ecstatic mental
state, and clothed in a mystical robe of imagery through which at
many points it is impossible certainly to distinguish the body and substance of truth, which one feels nevertheless to be everywhere present
beneath it. St John's visions border upon those ἄρρητα of "the
third heaven," which the soul may descry in rare moments of exaltation, but which "it is not allowed to utter" in discourse of
reason (2 Cor. xii. 2-4). The prophecy of 2 Thessalonians, on the
other hand, was given in sober waking mood, and states what is to
the writer matter of assured foresight and positive anticipation.

The visions of the Wild Beast contained in Revelation xiii.—xx.
present, however, a tolerably distinct and continuous picture; and it
is just in this part of the Apocalypse that it comes into line with
the Apocalypses of Daniel and of St Paul, and, as at least it seems
to us, into connexion with contemporary secular history. It is
characteristic of the two seers, that St John's mind is possessed by
the symbolic idea of the Horned Wild Beast of Daniel vii. and viii.,
while St Paul reflects in his Man of Lawlessness the later and more
concrete form assumed by the Danielic conception of the enemy of
God in ch. xi. But the representations of the two Apostles coincide
in some essential features. The first Wild Beast of St John, seven-
headed and ten-horned, receives "the power and throne of the Dragon
and great authority" from "him that is called Διάβολος καὶ ὁ Σατανᾶς,
the deceiver of the whole world" (Rev. xii. 9, xiii. 1, 2), just as
St Paul's Lawless One comes "according to the working of Satan"
and "in all deceit of unrighteousness" (II. ii. 9 f.). He "opens his
mouth for blasphemies against God, to blaspheme His name and His
tabernacle" and everything Divine; and "all that dwell upon the
earth will worship him," whose names were "not written in the
book of life of the slain Lamb"; and "torment" is promised to
them, who "worship the Beast and his image" and "receive the
mark of his name" (Rev. xiii. 5-8, xiv. 11): so the Man of Lawlessness "exalts himself against all that is called God or worshipped";
he "takes his seat in the temple of God, displaying himself as God";
and men are found to "believe the lie," who will thus "be judged"
for their "pleasure in unrighteousness," being of "them that perish"

THE JOHANNINE APOCALYPSE. 221

(2 Thess. ii. 4, 10-12). Again, the authority of the Wild Beast is vindicated by means of "great signs," through which "they that dwell on the earth are deceived" (Rev. xiii. 13 f.); and by this means "the kings of the whole earth" are to be "gathered for the war of the great day of God the Almighty" (xvi. 14): similarly, with our Apostle, Satan's great emissary "comes in all power, and signs and wonders of falsehood," deluding all those who have not "the love of the truth" and leading them to ruin under the judgement of God (2 Thess. ii. 9 ff.). The same token, that of false miracles, was ascribed by our Lord to the "false Christs and false prophets" predicted by Him (Matt. xxiv. 24). The name of "faithful and true" given to the Rider on the White Horse in Rev. xix. 11 ff., the "righteousness" in which "He judges and makes war," and "the righteous acts of the saints" constituting the "fine linen, clean and white," that clothes His army, are the antithesis to the picture of Antichrist and his followers in 2 Thess. ii. 10-12. Finally, having "come up out of the abyss," the Wild Beast "is to go away εἰς ἀπώλειαν" (Rev. xvii. 8), like the Lawless One, with his παρουσία κατ' ἐνέργειαν τοῦ Σατανᾶ, who was introduced as ὁ υἱὸς τῆς ἀπωλείας (2 Thess. ii. 3, 9).

The ten-horned Wild Beast of John is set forth as the secular antagonist of the Man-child, Son of the Woman[1], who was born "to rule all the nations," as His would-be destroyer and the usurper of His throne; by whom at last, when He appears as conqueror upon the "white horse," the Beast is taken and cast with his followers "into the lake that burneth with fire and brimstone" (comp. Rev. xii. with xiii., and then see ch. xix. 11-21). This battle-picture expands and translates into Johannine symbolism the conflict between the Lord Jesus and the Lawless One, which animates the condensed and pregnant lines of 2 Thessalonians ii. The outlines etched in rapid strokes by St Paul's sharp needle are thrown out upon the glowing canvas of the Apocalypse in idealized, visionary form; but the same conception dominates the imagination of the seer of Patmos which haunted the writer of this measured and calm Epistle.

The first Wild Beast of Rev. xiii. forms the centre of a group of symbolical figures. There "comes out of the earth another Wild

---

[1] W. H. Simcox with good reason sees in *the woman* who brings forth the royal man-child, and then "flies into the wilderness unto her place" till the appointed time, *the Jewish Church*: see his Notes in *Camb. Greek Test.* on Rev. xii. Cf. Rom. ix. 5, ἐξ ὧν ὁ χριστὸς τὸ κατὰ σάρκα. Gunkel however, in *Schöpfung und Chaos*, pp. 173 ff., contests this application, deriving this scene from Jewish mythology, as representing an attack of the Ancient Dragon on *the pre-existent Messiah*.

Beast" kindred to the former, called afterwards "the false prophet," who acts as his apostle and re-establishes his power after the "deadly wound" he had received, performing the "signs" by which his worship is supported and enforced. To this second actor, therefore, a *religious* part is assigned, resembling that of a corrupt Church serving a despotic State. The False Prophet of St John supplies a necessary link between the Apostasy and the Lawless One of 2 Thess. ii. 3 (see notes above, *ad loc.*); by his agency the "lying miracles" of *v.* 10 appear to be performed—in other words, superstition is enlisted in the service of atheism.

While St John's first Wild Beast has the False Prophet by his side for an ally, he carries on his back the Harlot-woman, who is the antithesis to the Church, the Bride of Christ. She is identified, in the plainest manner, with *the imperial city of Rome.* On her forehead is the legend, "Mystery; Babylon the great, the mother of the harlots and the abominations of the earth." This is but St Paul's "mystery of iniquity" writ large and illuminated. What Babylon was to Old Testament prophecy, that Rome became to the prophets of the New and to the oppressed Jewish Church, being the metropolis of idolatry, the active centre of the world's evil and the nidus of its future development. Further than this, *the imperial house of Rome—Nero* in particular for St Paul, and Domitian (possibly, as *Nero redivivus*) for St John—held to the prophetic soul of the Apostles a relation similar to that of the Syrian monarchy and Antiochus Epiphanes toward the prophecy of *Daniel*, serving as a proximate and provisional goal of its presentiments, the object around which the Satanic forces were then gathering and the fittest type of their ulterior evolution. But as history pursued its course and the Church passed beyond the Apostolic horizon, the new Apocalypse, like the old, was found to have a wider scope than appeared at its promulgation. The Wild Beast has survived many wounds; he survived the fall of the great city, mistress of the earth—the Woman whom St John saw riding upon his back. The end was not yet; the word of prophecy must run through new cycles of accomplishment.

It is only in bare outline that we may pursue the later history of the doctrine of Antichrist[1]. It has passed through four principal stages, distinguished in the sequel.

---

[1] For the history of this question, see the articles *Antichrist* in vol. I. (2nd ed.) of Smith's *Dictionary of the Bible*, and in Hastings' *DB.*, also in Herzog's *Real-Encyklopädie* (3rd ed.). There are valuable dissertations on "the Man of Sin": by Lünemann, in Meyer's *N.T. Commentary* (earlier edd.), Riggenbach in Lange's *Commentary*, Olshausen in his *Commentary, ad loc.*; also in Alford's *Prolegomena* to the Thess. Epp. Döllinger elucidates the subject with learning

PATRISTIC INTERPRETATION. 223

4. ANTICHRIST IN THE EARLY CHURCH.

During the earliest age of the Church's History, ending with the dissolution of the Western Empire in the fifth century, one consistent theory prevailed respecting the nature of Antichrist,—viz. that he was *an individual destined one day to overthrow the Roman Empire and to establish a rule of consummate wickedness, which would quickly be terminated by the appearance of the Lord Jesus from heaven, coming to effect the Last Judgement.* After the downfall of Rome, Greek theologians saw in *the Eastern Empire*, with its Christian capital of Constantinople (the New Rome), the fabric which Antichrist would destroy. In later ages this *rôle* was assigned to *the Holy Roman Empire*, resuming the part of imperial Rome in the West. The Eastern Empire succumbed in the fifteenth century; but this remained the most imposing bulwark of society. When the Western Empire in its turn became a shadow, its office was transferred—especially by Roman expositors—to *the Christian State* in general. Here "the withholder" (ὁ κατέχων, τὸ κατέχον) was found by the Fathers, in the power of the Roman government and the civil polity of the Empire— *Romanus status,* as Tertullian says; its dissolution imported the end of the world to the mind of the Church of the first three centuries. The above view was not inconsistent, however, with the recognition of the features of Antichrist in particular imperial rulers. Chrysostom probably echoes a popular belief when he speaks of Nero as "a type of Antichrist," and as embodying "the mystery of iniquity already working." The resemblance of Nero to St John's first θηρίον probably favoured this identification. The idea of Nero's return and re-enthronement, so long current in the East, was associated with this tradition and kept it alive.

Many leading Patristic writers however—including Theodore of Mopsuestia, Theodoret, Augustine, Pelagius, John of Damascus—sought τὸ μυστήριον τῆς ἀνομίας not in the political but in the religious sphere, following the intimation of 1 Jo. ii. 18—22; they saw it continuously working in the progress of *heresy* and *schism*;

and exactness in Appendix I. to his *First Age of the Church* (translated); and Eadie in the Appendix to his Commentary on *Thessalonians*. For the interpretation of the parallel texts in the Apocalypse, see Simcox's *Notes* in *Camb. Greek Test.*, and his interesting *Introduction;* also C. A. Scott's *Revelation*, in the *Century Bible*. As to the bearings of this topic on Eschatology at large, see the profound remarks of Dorner in his *System of Christian Doctrine*, vol. IV., pp. 373—401 (Eng. Trans.); also H. A. A. Kennedy, *St Paul's Conceptions of the Last Things*, pp. 207—221. We find ourselves in agreement, as to the main lines of interpretation, with Dorner, Olshausen, Riggenbach, Alford, Ellicott, Eadie. Bornemann, in Meyer's *Kommentar*[6], discusses the subject comprehensively; also Milligan, in his Commentary on *Thessalonians*.

some attempted to combine the two factors, detecting a common leaven of Satanic evil in civil and in ecclesiastical rebellion. Greek interpreters made *faith*, or *the gifts of the Spirit*, the κατέχον. As to the meaning of ἡ ἀποστασία in this context, opinions were divided upon much the same lines. It was *revolt from the Catholic Church*, or *from the Imperial State*, or from both at once. Immorality was a feature regularly attached to doctrinal aberration by orthodox exegetes in their treatment of this point; and contemporary illustration was not wanting. The ναὸς τοῦ θεοῦ of II. ii. 4 was usually regarded as *the Christian Church*; but a few scholars (Cyril of Jerusalem, Pelagius; and in later days, Nicolas de Lyra and Cornelius a Lapide) adhered to the literal reference of this expression to the Jewish Temple, supposing that this must be *rebuilt*, to become Antichrist's seat, before the end of the world. In connexion with the latter opinion, a *Jewish* origin, from the tribe of Dan (Gen. xlix. 17)[1]— the genealogy of Antichrist suggested by Rabbinical interpreters—was assigned to the Man of Lawlessness. Many patristic and medieval interpreters confess themselves at a loss on this subject.

5. Antichrist in the Middle Ages.

The old Rome and its vast dominion in the West were submerged under the tide of barbarian conquest. But the framework of civilized society held together; the rude conquerors had already been touched by the spell of the Græco-Roman civilization, and by the breath of the new Christian life. Amid the wreck and conflagration of the ancient world, precious and vital relics were spared; a "holy seed" survived, in which the elements of faith and culture were preserved, to blossom and fructify in the fresh soil deposited by the deluge of the northern invasions. Out of the chaos of the early Middle Ages there slowly arose the modern polity of the Romanized European nations, with the Papal See for its spiritual centre, and the revived and consecrated Empire of Charlemagne—*magni nominis umbra*—taking the leadership

---

[1] From this text, in conjunction with Deut. xxxiii. 22 and Jer. viii. 16 (Lev. xxiv. 10 ff. and Jud. xviii. 30 f. helped to blacken Dan's character), an astonishing vein of Jewish speculation and allegory has opened out. Dan has served as the *bête noire* of Rabbinism, being made to play amongst the sons of Jacob a part resembling that of Judas amongst the twelve Apostles. With its ensign of *the serpent*, Dan stood for the antithesis and would-be supplanter of the royal tribe of Judah; it belonged to the dark *north* of the land, and supplied the seat of Jeroboam's apostate and idolatrous worship. Dan, to be sure, is wanting in the Apocalyptic list of the Tribes (Rev. vii.). See Friedländer's work above cited, ch. ix., *Die Abstammung des Antichrist aus Dan*; also Bousset's *Antichrist*, pp. 112 ff. Amongst the Fathers, this tradition goes back to Irenæus and Hippolytus.

of the new world (800 A.D.). Meanwhile the ancient Empire maintained a sluggish existence in the *altera Roma* of Constantine upon the Bosphorus, where it arrested for seven centuries the destructive forces of Muhammadanism, until their energy was comparatively spent. This change in the current of history, following upon the union of Church and State under Constantine, disconcerted the Patristic reading of prophecy. The συντέλεια τοῦ αἰῶνος appeared to be indefinitely postponed, and the clock of time put back once more by the Overruling Hand. After the fifth century, moreover, the interpretation of Scripture, along with every kind of human culture, fell into a deep decline. Things present absorbed the energy and thought of religious teachers to the exclusion of things to come. The Western Church was occupied in Christianizing the barbarian hordes; the Eastern Church was torn by schism, and struggling for its very existence against Islam; while the two strove with each other, covertly or openly, for temporal supremacy. Medieval theologians did little more than repeat and systematize the teaching of the Fathers respecting Antichrist, which they supplemented from Jewish sources and embroidered with fancies of their own, often childish or grotesque.

Gradually, however, fresh interpretations came to the front. The Greeks naturally saw ὁ υἱὸς τῆς ἀπωλείας and ὁ ἄνομος in *Muhammad*, and ἡ ἀποστασία in the falling away of so many Eastern Christians to his delusions. In the West, the growing arrogance of the Roman bishops and the traditional association of Antichrist with Rome combined to suggest the idea of *a Papal Antichrist*, which had been promulgated here and there, and yet oftener whispered secretly, long before the Reformation. This theory has, in fact, high Papal authority in its favour; for Gregory I. (or the Great), about 590 A.D., denouncing the rival assumptions of the contemporary Byzantine Patriarch, wrote as follows : " Ego autem fidenter dico quia quisquis se universalem sacerdotem vocat, vel vocari desiderat, in elatione sua Antichristum præcurrit "; he further stigmatized the title of Universal Priest as " erroris nomen, stultum ac superbum vocabulum...nomen blasphemiæ." By this just sentence the later Roman Primacy is marked out as another type of Antichrist.

In the 13th century, when Pope Gregory VII. (or Hildebrand, 1073 —1085 A.D.) and Innocent III. (1198—1216 A.D.) had raised the power of the Roman See to its climax, this doctrine was openly maintained by the supporters of the Hohenstaufen Emperors. Vindicating the divine right of the civil state, they stoutly resisted the claims to temporal suzerainty then asserted by the Pope in virtue of his spiritual authority over all nations as the sole Vicar of Jesus Christ, who is "the ruler of the kings of the earth." The German Empire claimed to succeed to the office ascribed by the Fathers to the old Roman State as "the restrainer" of the Man of Sin. Frederic II. of Germany and Pope Gregory IX. bandied the name of "Antichrist" between them. That century witnessed a revival of religious zeal, of which the rise of the Waldenses, the theology of Thomas Aquinas, the founding of the Dominican and Franciscan Orders, the immortal poem of Dante, and the wide-spread revolt against the corruptions of Rome, were manifestations in different directions. This awakening was attended with a renewal of Apocalyptic study. The numbers of Daniel xii. 6—13, Rev. xii. 6, &c., gave rise to the belief that the year 1260 would usher in the final conflict with Antichrist and the end of the world; while the frightful invasion of the Mongols, and the intestine divisions of Christendom, threatened the latter with destruction. Simultaneously in the East by adding 666, "the number of the Wild Beast" in Rev. xiii. 18, to 622, the date of the Hejira (the flight from Mecca, which forms the starting-point of Mussalman chronology), it was calculated that Muhammadanism was approaching its fall. This crisis also passed, and the world went on its way. But it remained henceforward a fixed idea, proclaimed by every dissenter from the Roman See, that Antichrist would be found upon the Papal throne. So the Waldenses, so Hus, Savonarola, and our own Wyclif taught[1].

6. THE LUTHERAN DOCTRINE OF ANTICHRIST.

Martin Luther's historic protest *adversus execrabilem bullam Antichristi* inaugurated the Reformation in 1520 A.D. It was one of Luther's firmest convictions, shared by all the leading Reformers of the 16th century, that Popery is the Antichrist of prophecy; Luther expected that it would shortly be destroyed by Christ in His second advent. This belief was made a formal dogma of the Lutheran Church by the standard Articles of Smalkald in 1537 A.D.[2] It has a place in the English Bible; the translators in their address to James I. credit that monarch with having given, by a certain tractate he had published against the Pope, "such a blow unto that Man of Sin, as will not be healed." Bishop Jewel's *Exposition of the*

---

[1] We must distinguish, however, between *an* Antichrist and *the* Antichrist. A sincere Roman Catholic might assign to this or that unworthy Pope a place amongst the "many Antichrists."
[2] Melanchthon admitted a *second* Antichrist in Muhammad. He distinguished between the Eastern and Western Antichrists. The conjunction of Pope and Turk was common with our Protestant forefathers.

THE OLDER PROTESTANT THEORY. 227

Thessalonian Epistles, delivered in the crisis of England's revolt from Rome, is the most characteristic piece of native Reformation exegesis, and gives powerful expression to the Lutheran view. In the 17th century, however, this interpretation was called in question amongst English Divines. The late Christopher Wordsworth, in his *Lectures on the Apocalypse*, and in his *Commentary on the New Testament*, has contributed a learned and earnest vindication of the traditional Protestant position.

This theory has impressive arguments in its favour, drawn both from Scripture and history. It contains important elements of truth, and applied with great cogency to the Papacy of the later Middle Ages. But many reasons forbid us to identify the Papal system with St Paul's ἄνθρωπος τῆς ἀνομίας. Two considerations must here suffice: (1) the Apostle's words describe, as the Fathers saw, *a personal Antichrist*; they cannot be satisfied by any mere succession of men or system of Antichristian evil. (2) His Man of Lawlessness is to be *the avowed opposer and displacer of God*, and had for his type such rulers as Antiochus Epiphanes and the worst of the deified Cæsars. Now however gross the idolatry of which the Pope has been the object, and however daring and blasphemous the pretensions of certain occupants of the Papal Chair, Romanism does not, either openly or virtually, exalt its chief ἐπὶ πάντα λεγόμενον θεὸν ἢ σέβασμα; one must seriously weaken and distort the language of the Apostle to adjust it to the claims of the Roman Pontiff. The Roman Catholic system has multiplied, instead of abolishing, objects of worship; its ruling errors have not been those of atheism, but of superstition. At the same time, its adulation of the Pope and the priesthood has debased the religious instinct of Christendom; it has nursed the spirit of *anthropolatry*—the man-worship, which St Paul believed was to find in the Man of Lawlessness its culminating object.

7. ANTICHRIST IN MODERN TIMES.

It would occupy several pages barely to state the various theories advanced upon this mysterious subject in more recent times.

Not the least plausible is that which saw τὸ μυστήριον τῆς ἀνομίας in the later developments of *the French Revolution* at the close of the 18th century, with its apotheosis of an abandoned woman in the character of Goddess of Reason, and which identified ὁ ἄνομος with *Napoleon Buonaparte*. The empire of Napoleon was essentially a restoration of the military Cæsarism of ancient Rome. He came within a little of making himself master, like Julius Cæsar, of the civilized world. This unscrupulous despot, with his superb genius and insatiable egotism—the offspring and the idol, till he became the scourge, of a lawless democracy—is, surely, in the true succession of Antiochus Epiphanes and Nero Cæsar. Napoleon has set before our times a new and commanding type of the Lawless One, which has had, and may have hereafter, its imitators.

Nor is the godlessness of St Paul's υἱὸς τῆς ἀπωλείας wanting in a bold and typical modern expression. Following upon the negative and destructive atheism of the 18th century, the scientific, constructive atheism of the 19th century has built up an imposing system of thought and life. The theory of Positivism, as it was propounded by its great apostle, Auguste Comte, culminates in the doctrine that "Man is man's god." God and immortality, the entire world of the supernatural, this philosophy abolishes in the name of science and modern thought. It sweeps them out of the way to make room for *le grand être humain*, or *collective humanity*, which is to command our worship through the memory of its heroes and men of genius, and in the person of woman adored within the family. This scheme of religion Comte worked out with the utmost seriousness, and furnished with an elaborate hierarchy and ritual based on the Roman Catholic model. Although Comte's religion of humanity is disowned by many positivists and has only come into practice upon a limited scale, it is a phenomenon of great significance. It testifies to the persistence of the religious instinct in our nature, and indicates the direction which that instinct is compelled to take when deprived of its rightful object (see the Apostle's words in Rom. i. 23). Comte would have carried us back, virtually, to the Pagan adoration of deified heroes and deceased emperors, or to the Chinese worship of family ancestors. Positivism provides in its Great Being an abstraction which, if it should once take hold of the popular mind, must inevitably tend to realize itself in concrete individual shape. It sets up a throne of worship within "the temple of God," which the man of destiny will be found "in his season" to occupy.

Since the time of Hugo Grotius (1583—1645 A.D.), the famous Dutch Protestant scholar, theologian, and statesman, numerous attempts have been made to demonstrate the fulfilment of N.T. prophecy within the Apostolic or post-Apostolic days, upon the assumption that the παρουσία of Jesus was realized in the judgement falling upon the Jewish nation and by the destruction of Jerusalem in the year 70 A.D. This line of interpretation was adopted by Romanist theologians, as by Bossuet in the 17th century and Döllinger in the 19th, partly by

PRÆTERIST VIEWS. 229

way of return to the Patristic view and partly in defence against Protestant exegesis. These *præterist* theories, restricting the application of St Paul's prediction to the first age of the Church, in various ways strain and minimize his language by attempting to bring it within the measure of contemporary events. Or else they assume, as rationalistic interpreters complacently do, that such prophecies, proceeding from a subjective stand-point and being the product of the passing situation, were incapable of real fulfilment and have been refuted by the course of history. Almost every Roman Emperor from Caligula down to Trajan—some even of later times—has been made to serve for the Man of Sin, or the Restrainer, by one or other of the commentators; Nero has figured in both capacities; so has Vespasian[1]. Others hold—and this theory is partly combined with the last, as e.g. by Grotius—that *Simon Magus*, the traditional father of heresy, was ὁ ἄνομος; while others, again, see τὸ μυστήριον τῆς ἀνομίας in the Jewish nation of St Paul's time[2]. Outside the secular field, *the power of the Holy Spirit, the decree of God, the Jewish law, the believing remnant* of Judaism, and even *Paul himself*, have been put into the place of τὸ κατέχον by earlier or later authorities. But none of these suggestions has obtained much acceptance. A small group of critics—Bahnsen, Hilgenfeld, Pfleiderer—who date 2 Thessalonians in the reign of Trajan and after the year 100 (see *Introd.* p. xlv.), explain τὸ μυστήριον τῆς ἀνομίας as the heretical Gnosticism of that period, and τὸ κατέχον as the Episcopate, or the like. Apart from the assumed *date*, Bahnsen's interpretation is a return to the view of Theodore and Augustine.

The tendency of recent critical interpretation is to ascribe to this passage, and to the prophetic eschatology of the N.T. generally, a purely ideal or "poetic" and parænetic value[3]. The rise of Antichrist, along with the παρουσία of the Lord Jesus and the judgement-

---

[1] On the relation of contemporary Emperors to 2 Thess. ii. 3 ff., see Askwith's *Introduction to the Epp. to the Thessalonians*, pp. 130 ff.
[2] So Lightfoot: "It seems on the whole probable that the Antichrist is represented especially by Judaism" (Smith's *DB*., art. 2 *Thessalonians*).
[3] C. L. Nitzsch (in his Essays *De revelatione*, 1808) was the first to give this theory systematic expression. The following sentences, quoted by Bornemann, indicate his position: the παρουσία "est factum ideale, non certo loco ac tempore, sed ubicumque et quandocumque opus fuerit ad confirmanda pietatis studia, cum fiducia exspectandum." The prediction of the Parousia is "mere moralis qua materiam, et poetica qua formam...Apostolus, cum illa scriberet, parum curavit aut sensiit discrimen quod poeticæ rerum divinarum descriptioni cum historia intercedit. Ex instinctu morali ac divino docebat omnia, accommodate ad usum practicum; non ut scholæ præceptis atque ita ut theologicis usibus inserviret." As to the Man of Sin: "Homo iste malus, cujus futura revelatio describitur, nusquam quisquam fuit nec in posterum futurus esse videtur." As much as to say, the Apostle Paul aimed at edification in his prophecies, with very little regard to fact and truth!

scene of the Last Day, are taken to be no literal occurrences of the future, but "super-historical" events of the kingdom of God—in other words, to be imaginative representations, under their symbolic Biblical dress, of spiritual conflicts and crises which will find their issue in modes determined by conditions remote from those existing in the first ages and far beyond the horizon of the New Testament. The N.T. fulfilment, it is pointed out, set aside in what appeared to be essential particulars the concrete terms of O.T. prophecy, so that the interpreters of the latter were thrown quite off the track in their forecast of the Messianic days; and the like fate, it is said, will overtake the expositors of N.T. eschatology, who moreover are at complete discord amongst themselves. No doubt, the Apostles expected, and that shortly, a visible return of the glorified Jesus and the gathering of mankind in judgement before Him. But this mode of conceiving the consummation belonged to the mental furniture of their times; it was supplied them by the prophetic imagery of the Old Testament and by Jewish Apocalyptic; only the spiritual ideas expressed under this conventional dress were truly their own, and are essential to the Christian faith and of unchanging worth.

The above mode of treating N.T. prophecy falls in with the spirit of our times, and escapes the difficulties pressing on those who maintain a belief in definite prediction. But, in consistency, it must be applied to the words of our Lord as well as to those of His Apostles, and to the *thoughts* which lay behind His words. The Day of the Lord and the Second Coming were matter of positive expectation on His part. However mistaken Jewish eschatology had been in respect to the circumstances of His first coming, that proved a matter-of-fact event and not a mere regulative or edifying idea; it realized in historical form the deeper sense and true burden of O.T. prophecy. Ancient Israel was right in the main fact. The Church should be wiser by the experience of Judaism; it has been cautioned by the failure of so many presumptuous deductions from the words of Christ and His Apostles respecting the last days. To evacuate their predictions of all definite meaning because that meaning has been over-defined, to suppose that what they foresaw was a mere exaggerated reflexion of the circumstances of their own age and is without objective warrant or reality, is an act of despair in the interpreter. The ideal and the abstract, if they be living forces, are bound to take a real, determinate shape. History requires another coming of Jesus in His glory to crown human development, and to complement His first coming in lowliness and for rejection. On the other hand, the powers of evil at work in humanity tend, by a secret law, to gather themselves up at one crisis after another into some dominant and representative personality. The ideal Antichrist conceived by Scripture, when actualized, will mould himself upon the lines of the many Antichrists whose career the Church has already witnessed. Like other great prophecies of Scripture, this word of St Paul has a progressive fulfilment. It is carried into effect from time to time, under the action of Divine laws operating throughout human affairs, in partial and transitional forms, which prefigure and may contribute to its final realization. For such predictions are inspired by Him who "worketh all things after the counsel of His own will"; they rest upon the principles of God's moral government, and the abiding facts of human nature. We find in Antiochus IV. and in Gaius Caesar examples, present to the minds of inspired writers, of autocratic human power animated by a demonic pride and a desperate spirit of irreligion. We accept, with Chrysostom, an earnest of the embodiment of St Paul's idea in the person of Nero, who furnished St John with an apt model for his more extended and vivid delineations. We recognize, with the later Greek Fathers and Melanchthon, plain Antichristian tokens and features in the polity of Muhammad. We recognize, with Gregory I. and the Protestant Reformers, a prelude of Antichrist's coming and conspicuous traits of his character in the spiritual despotism of the See of Rome; and we sorrowfully mark throughout the Church's history the tares growing amid the wheat, the perpetuation and recrudescence in manifold forms of "the apostasy" which prepares the way of Antichrist and abets his rule. We agree with those who discern in the Napoleonic idea an ominous revival of the lawless absolutism and worship of human power that prevailed in the age of the Caesars; while positivist and materialistic philosophy, with sensualistic ethics, are making for the same goal[1].

[1] The following extract from Comte's *Catéchisme Positiviste* is a striking proof of the readiness with which scientific atheism may join hands with political absolutism: "Au nom du passé et de l'avenir, les serviteurs théoriques et les serviteurs pratiques de L'HUMANITÉ viennent prendre dignement la direction générale des affaires terrestres, pour construire enfin la vraie providence, morale, intellectuelle, et matérielle; en excluant irrévocablement de la suprématie politique tous les divers esclaves de Dieu, Catholiques, protestantes, ou déistes, comme étant à la fois arriérés et perturbateurs."—The true Pontifical style! It is not a very long step from these words to the situation which the Apostles describe in 2 Thess. ii. 4 and Rev. xiii. 16 ff. It is significant that Comte issued his Catechism of the new religion just after the *coup d'état* of Louis Napoleon, whom he congratulates on "the happy crisis"! In the same preface he glorified the Emperor Nicholas I. of Russia, as "the sole truly eminent chief of which our century can claim the honour, up to the present time." Comte's ignorance of politics is some excuse for these blunders; but the conjunction remains no less portentous. Faith in God and faith in freedom are bound up together. See Arthur's *Physical and Moral Law*, pp. 231—237; and his *Religion without God*, on Positivism generally.

APPENDIX.

The history of the world is one. The first century lives over again in the twentieth. All the factors of evil co-operate, as do those of good. There are but two kingdoms behind the numberless powers contending throughout the ages of human existence, that of Satan and that of Christ; though to our eyes their forces lie scattered and confused, and we distinguish ill between them. But the course of time quickens its pace, as if nearing some great issue. Science has given an immense impetus to human progress in almost all directions, and moral influences propagate themselves with greater speed than heretofore. There is going on a rapid interfusion of thought, a unifying of the world's life and a gathering together of the forces on either side to "the valley of decision," that seem to portend some worldwide crisis, in which the glorious promises or dark forebodings of revelation, or both at once, will be anew fulfilled. Still Christ's words stand, as St Augustine said, to put down "the fingers of the calculators[1]." *It is not for us to know times or seasons.* What backward currents may arise in our secular progress, what new seals are to be opened in the book of human fate, and through what cycles the evolution of God's purpose for mankind has yet to run, we cannot guess.

[1] "Omnes calculantium digitos resolvit"; on Matt. xxiv. 36.

I. GENERAL INDEX.

Such references are omitted as are sufficiently indicated by chapter and verse of the two Epistles. To other Books of Scripture only the principal references are indicated, and those involving quotation.

Achaia, 141, 189
Acts of Apostles; compared with 1 and 2 Thess., xiv—xxxix *passim*, lxii, 15 f., 25, 28, 50, 59, 198; other reff., x, 35, 41, 44 f., 51, 64, 71, 98, 109, 121, 129, 147, 150, 167, 169, 173, 178, 200, 207
address of Epp., 15—18, 139
advent of Christ (see *coming* and παρουσία)
Ægean Sea, xi
Æschylus, 28, 57
affection, mutual, of Paul and Thess., lxii, 42 ff., 57 ff, 70 ff.
Agrapha of our Lord, 98, 109, 130
Alexandrian readings of Text, lxvii, 62 f., 78, 79, 106
Ambrose, St, xii, 174
Ambrosiaster, 139
Ammonius, 107
Amos, Bk of, 108
Amphipolis and Apollonia, xvi
anacolutha in Pauline style, lix, 46 f., 166, 177
analysis of the Epp., lxix ff.; of their sections, 34, 49 f., 57, 69 f., 79 f., 94, 106 f., 120 f., 126, 139, 142 f., 161 f., 187, 203 f.
Antichrist, of Paul, xxx, li, 162,
168—187; of John, 167, 219—223; of Daniel, 170 ff., 215—219; of the Early Church, 223 f.; of the Middle Ages, 224 ff. ; of modern times, 227—232; bearing on date of 2 Thess., xlv—liv
Antioch, Pisidian, sermon at, xxiii, xxv f., 55
Antioch, Syrian, 141
Antiochus IV. (Epiphanes), xlviii, 171 f., 217 f., 222, 228, 231
Apocalypse, of Daniel (see *Daniel*); of John (see *Revelation*); of Paul, 29 ff., 94—103, 161—187, 215 ff. (Appendix)
Apocalyptic, of the O. T., lvii, lx, 100, 143, 146; Jewish and Christian, 1 f., 217 ff.
apostle, apostleship (see ἀπόστολςs)
Apostolic Constitutions, 135
Aquila and Priscilla (Prisca), xix, 27
Aristarchus, xxi
Aristophanes, quoted, 19, 53, 122
Aristotle, quoted, 39, 124
Armillus (Armalgus), 180, 218 f.
Arthur, W., on Positivism, 231
Asia, province of, xiv, 172

I. GENERAL INDEX.

Askwith, E. H., liv, 178, 229
Assumption of Moses, 217
asyndeton, 27
atheism, 228
Athens, xxxii f., xxxix, 64; discourse at, xxv, 51
atonement, doctrine of, xxvi f., 31, 117 f., 193
Augustine, St, quoted or referred to, 32, 42, 95, 104, 135, 168, 180, 229, 232
Augustus, the Emperor, 173
Augustus, the title, 174
Aurelius, Marcus, quoted, 46
authenticity of Epp.: 1 Thess., xliii ff.; 2 Thess., xlv—liv
authorship, plural, xxxix ff., 15, 67

Babylon, and Rome, 222
Bacon, Francis, 29
Bahnsen, F., xlv, 229
Baljon, J. M. S., on Text, 196
Barnabas, Ep. of, xlii, 84, 137
Baruch, Apoc. of, 115, 217
Baur, F. Chr., xxxviii, xlii, xlv
Beasts, the Wild, of Daniel, 215 f.; of Revelation, 178, 220 ff.
Bengel, J. A., quoted, 20, 37, 42, 43, 46, 57, 60, 91, 98, 99, 114, 137, 140, 153, 180, 181, 186, 187, 205, 208
Berœa, xxxii f., 25, 26, 54, 59, 91
Beza, Th., quoted or referred to, 13, 58, 66, 74, 92, 98, 110, 116, 164, 169, 174, 202, 206, 209
Biblical Greek, lvii
Bion, quoted, 118
Blass, F., quoted or referred to, 15, 20, 59, 68, 88
body, the human, sanctification of, 82—90, 133
Bornemann, W., quoted or referred to, xxvii, xxviii, xlix, liv, 39, 46, 56, 59, 68, 69, 77, 86 f., 103, 143, 223

Bossuet, J. B., on Antichrist, 228 f.
Bousset, W., on Antichrist, 218, 224
brotherly love (see φιλαδελφία), xxxi, xxxvi
Buttmann, A., *Grammar of N. T. Greek*, 40, 54, 142, 157, &c.
Byzantine Empire, 179 f., 223

Cæsarism, xxx, 227, 231
Cæsar-worship, xix f., 172 ff., 178, 228
Caligula, Emperor Gaius, xlviii, 172 f., 231
Calvin, John, quoted, 19, 35, 37, 43, 72, 74, 75, 115, 123, 143, 200, 201, 202, 206, 209, 212
Canticles, Bk of, 164
Cassander, ix f.
Charlemagne, the Emperor, 224 f.
Chase, F. H., quoted or referred to, 131, 201
chastity, xxxi, xxxvi, 82—90
Chronicles (Paralipomena), 1 and 2 Bk of, 153, 185, 202
Chrysostom, St John, quoted, 26, 37, 40, 42, 43, 84, 102, 107, 113, 114, 124, 127, 169, 170, 192, 199, 223, 231
church (see ἐκκλησία), 16 f.
church-officers and organization, xliv, liii, 120 ff.
Cicero at Thess., xii; quoted, xi, 44
Claudius, the Emperor, xix, xxxix, 178
Clemens Romanus, 24, 73, 137
Clementine Recognitions, 94
Codices, Greek, of Epp., lxv ff., and Textual Notes *passim*
Colossians, Ep. to, xxii, 15, 30, 38, 48, 84, 86, 93, 103, 118, 137, 156, 206
coming, the second, of Christ (see παρουσία), xxvii—xxx, xxxvi ff., lxiii f., 29 ff., 95—103, 146—152, 162 f., 165 f., 179 ff., 229 f.

I. GENERAL INDEX. 235

Comte, A., his new religion, 228; *catéchisme positiviste*, quoted, 231
conflate readings, lxvi, 62, 63
Constantinople, 223, 225
Conybeare and Howson, *Life of St Paul*, xvi
Coptic Version, xvii, lxvi, Textual Notes
Corinth, Paul at, xxxiii, 71, 140 f., 178, 189, 199 f.; Thess. Epp. written from, xxxix
Corinthians, 1 Ep. to, xxi, xxvii, xxviii, lvii, lxiii, 15, 16, 23, 27, 30, 42, 45, 46, 47, 51 f., 60, 62, 65, 83, 84, 85, 90, 91, 95, 96 f., 98, 99, 102, 114, 118, 119, 120, 128, 129, 134, 139, 147, 149 f., 153, 156, 164 f., 170 f., 176, 183, 200, 207, 212, 214
Corinthians, 2 Ep. to, xxi, xxvi, li, lviii, lxiv, 15, 23, 37, 40, 41, 43, 45, 47, 60, 65, 71, 72, 87, 91, 99, 102, 118, 133, 137, 141, 165, 169, 183, 190, 204, 206, 214, 218
cross of Christ, the, preached at Thess., xxvi f.
Council of Jerusalem, xiv, xxxix
Cyril of Alexandria, 130

Dalman, G., *Words of Jesus*, 174
Dan, associated with Antichrist, 224
Daniel, Bk of, lx f., 101, 170 ff., 176 ff., 219 f., 226; the Visions of, 215 f.
date of Thess. Epp., xxxix, xlii f., xliv, xlv—liii
Davidson, S., liv
day of the Lord (see $\dot{\eta}\mu\acute{\epsilon}\rho\alpha$), xxxvii, 108 f.
death of Christ and human salvation, xxv ff., 117 f., 193
deification of Cæsars, xxx, 172 f.
Deissmann, G. A., *Bible-Studies*, lxi, 48, 174

delusion, punitive purpose of, 185 ff.
Demas, xxii
Demetrius, St, xiii, xxii
Demosthenes, 18, 199, 209
Deuteronomy, Bk of, lxi, 29, 88, 147, 148, 163, 182, 188 f., 224
De Wette, W. M. L., xlii
Dichotomists and Trichotomists, 133
Dick, Karl, on *plural authorship*, xxxix ff.
Didaché XII Apostolorum, xlii, 41, 208 f.
diligence, duty of, xxxi, xxxvi, 92 f., 208 ff.
Dio Cassius, 93
Diodorus Siculus, x, 55
Diogenes Laertius, 66
discipline, need of (see *indiscipline*)
divinity of Christ, 17, 74 f., 157, 170
Döllinger, J. J. I., 178, 222 f., 228 f.
Domitian, the Emperor, 222
Dorner, J. A., 177, 223
doublets, verbal, in 2 Thess., lix

Elagabalus, the Emperor, 173
Ellicott, C. J., quoted or referred to, 37, 56, 89, 99, 111, 133, 184
ellipses, in Pauline style, lix, 97 f.
Emperors, the Roman, 170, 178, 222, 229
Empire, the Roman, xi, xv, xix f., 174 f., 178, 223 f.
Enoch, Bk of, 217
Ephesians, Ep. to, lix, 20, 22, 33, 35, 42, 73, 83, 87, 96, 112, 113, 116 f., 122, 143, 151, 189, 213
Epictetus, quoted or referred to, lxi, 65, 89
episcopate, the (supposed) withholder, xlv, 229

epistle to Paul from Thess., xxxvi, 108, 209
Epistles of Paul, their origin, xxxv f.; arrangement of, 13; style of, lviii, lxi; reading of, enjoined, 136 f.; authenticity of, guarded, 214; signature of, 214; written by secretary, 137, 214; share of companions in, xxxix ff., 50, 141; (possible) abuse of, 165
epistolary formulæ, lxi
Erasmus, Desid., quoted, xliii, 26, 108, 123, 145, 180, 202, 206
eschatology of Paul (see παρουσία, Antichrist, Apocalypse, ἡμέρα Κυρίου), xx, xxvii ff., xxxvii f., li f., lxiii f., &c.
Esdras, 4 (2) Bk of, lx, 217
Estius, G., quoted or referred to, 19, 26, 72, 89 f., 108, 123, 143, 151, 190, 202
ethics (see morals)
Europe, Pauline mission to, xv
Eustathius, Bp of Thess., xii
Ewald, H., xxxviii
Exodus, Bk of, 29, 58, 100, 102, 138 f., 147
Ezekiel, Bk of, lx f., 60, 87, 90, 109, 151, 156, 170, 185

Fathers, the ancient, on Antichrist, 223 ff., 231; as textual witnesses, lxvi, and Textual Notes passim
Finlay, G., on Roman law, 178 f.
forgiveness of sins, xxv f., 30 f.
Frederic II., German Emperor, 226
French Revolution and Antichrist, 227 f.
Friedländer, M., on Antichrist, 218, 224

Gabriel, the archangel, 101
Galatia, xiv f., 141
Galatians, Ep. to, xv, xxvi, xlix, lviii, 15, 16, 20, 23, 29, 30, 41, 47, 52, 55, 68 f., 86, 118, 137, 142, 171, 176, 201, 214
Gallio, the Proconsul, 178, 199
Genesis, Bk of, lx, 31, 48, 56, 85, 206, 208
Gentiles, the Epp. addressed to, xxv, lx, 28 f., 53, 55
Gnosticism and Thess. Epp., xlv, 229
God, doctrine of, xxiv f., 28 ff., 83 f.
Gospel, the, its coming to Thess., xiv ff.; Pauline, at Thess., xxiii ff., 96 f., 117 f.; of Christ's second coming, xxvii f., xxx, 30 f. (See εὐαγγέλιον)
gospel, a, to Paul from Thess., xxxiii, 70
Gregory I., Pope, on Antichrist, 225, 231
Gregory VII., Pope, 225
Gregory IX., Pope, 226
Grotius, Hugo, xxxviii, 88, 102; on Antichrist, 228 f.
Gunkel, H., 218

hapax legomena, lv ff., 26, 36, 53, 91, 100, 106, 118, 130, 149, 160, 199, 205, 206, 211
Harnack, A., xlv
Harris, J. Rendel, xxxv, lxi, 108
harlot-woman, the, of Revelation, 222
Hase, K., xlv
Hausrath, A., liv
Hebraisms, of grammar or expression, in Thess. Epp., lvii, 17, 30, 41, 48, 59 f., 93, 102, 112, 116, 141, 148, 168, 179
Hebrews, Ep. to, 18, 33, 51, 60, 82, 85, 88, 98, 130, 131, 137, 163, 167, 182
Hejira, the, of Muhammad, 226
heresy and Antichrist, xlv, 223 f., 229
Hermas, Shepherd of, 84
Herodotus, ix, 19

I. GENERAL INDEX. 237

Herwerden, *Lexicon Græcum suppletorium*, 180
Hesychius, quoted, 58
Hilgenfeld, A., xliii, xlv, 229
Hippolytus of Rome, 224
history and prophecy, xxix f., 215, 229—232
Hofmann, von, J. C. K., quoted or referred to, xlvii, 16, 47, 67, 69, 77, 100, 116, 132
Hohenstaufen Emperors, 225 f.
holiness, holy (see ἅγιος, κ.τ.λ.); holiness and bodily purity, 82—90; holiness and love, 76 f.
Holsten, C., xliii
Holtzmann, H. J., xliii, xlv f.
holy living, directions for, 126—135
Holy Roman Empire, 223
HOLY SPIRIT, THE (see πνεῦμα ἅγιον), 23
Homer, quoted, 29, 43, 69, 163, 205
homœoteleuta, 33, 79, 106, 138
hopelessness of Pagan world, 95 f.
Horace, 58
Horn, the Little, in Daniel, 215 f., 220
Hort, F. J. A., quoted or referred to, 41, 90, 121, 139, 153
humanity, worship of, 228
Hus, John, 226
Huxtable, E., 41

idealistic eschatology, 219 f., 229 ff.
idleness at Thess., xxxviii, 203—213
idolatry, xxiii ff., 28 f.
Ignatius, St, 113
indiscipline at Thess., xxxvi, xxxviii, xliii, liii, 124, 204 ff., 211 ff.
Innocent III., Pope, 225
inscriptions, Greek, xvi, lvii
interpolation, in 2 Thess., theory of, liii f.
Irenæus, 168, 181, 224

irony in Paul, 92, 108, 209
Isaiah, Bk of, lx f., 22, 29, 31, 60, 83, 91, 96, 100, 108 f., 110, 112, 115, 135, 138, 146, 147, 150, 156, 160, 170, 179 f., 185, 203, 218 f.
itacism, lxvii, 63, 105, 159, 160, 197

James, Ep. of, xxxvi, 20, 76, 189, 194
Jason of Thess., xviii f., xxxii f., 45
JEHOVAH (*Jahveh*), the name, 29
Jeremiah, Bk of, 29, 38, 57, 86, 91, 109, 116, 146, 148, 224
Jerome (Hieronymus), St, quoted or referred to, 87, 108, 170
Jerusalem, 15, 52, 141; fall of, xxxix, 50, 56 f., 228; temple of, 170
JESUS, words of, used by Paul, lxi, 95 f., 98, 107, 109 f., 112, 113, 130, 163, 164, 167, 182
Jewel, Bp, on Antichrist, 226 f.
Jewish Antichrist, 218 f.
Jewish nation, attitude of, to the Gospel, xvi ff., 50, 53 ff.
Jews, the, in Thess., xi, xv—xviii, xxxiv f., 50, 60
Job, Bk of, lx, 131, 146, 179, 185
Joel, Bk of, 100, 108, 129, 180
John, Apocalypse of (see *Revelation*)
John, 1 Ep. of, 30, 47, 60, 76, 87, 90, 111, 162, 167, 189, 223; 2 Ep. of, 17, 91; 3 Ep. of, 48
John, Gospel of, xix, 23, 29, 41, 53, 60, 72, 75, 76, 80, 86, 91, 95 f., 101, 108, 109, 111, 112, 118, 133, 148, 170, 173, 182, 189, 213
Josephus, quoted, 15, 55, 131
Joshua, Bk of, 167
Jowett, B., quoted, xxvii, 18, 53
Jubilees, Bk of, 217

I. GENERAL INDEX.

Judæan Churches, 52 f.
Judaistic controversy, xxxiv, 41
Judas Iscariot, 168
Jude, Ep. of, 101
Judenhasse, 55
Judgement, the Last, Paul's preaching of, xxviii ff.; doctrine of, in Thess. Epp., 30 f., 108 ff., 145—151, 179—187
Judges, Bk of, 224
Jülicher, A., xliii, xlv
Julius Cæsar, 173
Justin Martyr, xlii
Juvenal, quoted, 54

Kennedy, H. A. A., 223
Kern, F. H., xlii, xlv ff.
Kingdom of God, of Christ (see $\beta\alpha\sigma\iota\lambda\epsilon\acute{\iota}\alpha$), xix f., 48 f.
kiss, the holy (see $\phi\acute{\iota}\lambda\eta\mu\alpha$)
Klöpper, A., xlvii
Kühner, R., *Grammatik der griech. Sprache*[2], quoted, 24, 131

Lactantius, 108
Lamentations, Bk of, 146
Later Greek ($\kappa o\iota\nu\acute{\eta}$), language of, lvi f., 23, 41, 87, 105, 111, 117, 164, 191, 205, 212
Latinisms in Greek text, lxvi f., 63, 105, 159
law, the withholder, 177 ff.
Leviticus, Bk of, 48
Lightfoot, J. B., quoted or referred to, x, liv, 18, 31, 36, 39, 41, 46, 51, 60, 74, 81, 82, 90, 108, 109, 110, 111, 113, 114, 117, 118, 122, 135, 136 f., 140, 147, 155, 165, 182, 190, 201, 206, 229
litotes (or *meiosis*), 54, 199 f.
liturgical rhythm, lvii, 143
Livy, quoted, x
Lock, W., 108
Lucian, quoted, x, 19
Lucifer of Calaris, quoted, 13
Luke, St, associated with Paul, xv

Luke, Gospel of, lxi, 23, 30, 49, 53, 54, 55, 57, 74, 77, 84, 108, 109, 110, 130, 135, 143, 175, 176
Lünemann, G., 69
Luther, Martin, on Antichrist, 226 f.

Maccabean times, 171, 217
Maccabees, 1 Bk of, 59, 123, 167, 172, 186
Maccabees, 2 Bk of, 96, 163
Maccabees, 4 Bk of, 150
Macedonia, Province of, ix, x, xv, xxi, 198 f.; see *map*
Macedonian Churches, xxi, xliii f., lxii, 91 f.
Malachi, Bk of, lxi, 109, 116, 205
Manen, van, xliii
manual labour, 44 f., 93 f., 207 f.
manuscripts, Greek, of the Epp. (see *uncial, minuscule*)
Mark, Gospel of, 53, 61, 74, 113, 163, 164, 182
Matthew, Gospel of, lxi, 22, 30, 35, 42, 49, 53, 54, 56, 61, 67, 74, 75, 77, 87, 100, 102, 108, 113, 125, 127, 150, 163, 167, 170, 182, 200, 217 f., 218, 221, 232
Melanchthon, Philip, on Antichrist, 226, 231
Messiah, the suffering, xviii
Meyer, H. A. W., 84
Micah, Bk of, 100, 109
Michael, the archangel, 101
military metaphors, 100 114 f.
Milligan, G., 103, 223, &c.
ministry of Church, xliv, 120—5
minuscule mss., lxv, and Textual Notes *passim*
miracles of Antichrist (see $\sigma\eta\mu\epsilon\hat{\iota}o\nu$)
Moffatt, J., xliii, xlv
morals, Christian, xxx f.; defective at Thess., 79 f.
Moulton, J. H., lxvii, 56, 69, 117

I. GENERAL INDEX

Muhammadanism and Antichrist, 225

Napoleon Buonaparte, 227 f., 231
Nehemiah, Bk of, 59
Nero, the Emperor, xlvi f., 178, 222, 223, 228, 231; *redivivus*, xlvi f., liii f.
Nestle, Eb., on Greek Text of N.T., 60
Nitzsch, C. L., quoted, 229
number, the, of the Wild Beast, 226
Numbers, Bk of, lxi, 135, 194, 213

Obadiah, Bk of, 146
Œcumenius, 132
Old Testament, use of, in Thess. Epp., lvii, lx f.
Olympus, Mt, xi f.; see *map*
Origen, quoted, 13, 32, 42

Paganism, condition of, xxv, xxviii, 83, 86, 96, 173 f., 178
Papacy, the, and Antichrist, 225 ff., 231
Papyri, the Egyptian-Greek, lvii, lxi, 205
paronomasia and *word-plays*, lix, 200, 209
pauperism, danger of, at Thess., 208 ff.
Pergamum, 172
persecution at Thess., xviii—xxi, xxxvii f., 52 ff., 66 f.; at Berœa, xxii, 54; at Philippi, xv, 36; at Corinth, 71, 199 f.
Peter, 1 Ep. of, 15, 17, 66, 67, 83, 84 f., 113, 114, 116, 126, 133, 191
Peter, 2 Ep. of, 17, 108, 147, 167
Pfleiderer, O., xliii, xlv, 229
Philemon, Ep. to, xxi, xxii, 149, 155, 214
Philippi, xv f., xxix, 36, 91, 144; bounty from, sent to Paul, xxxiv, 45

Philippians, Ep. to, its relation to Thess. Epp., lviii f., lxii; other reff., xxii, xxxiv, lx, lxii, lxiv, 15, 30, 42, 45, 51, 53, 59, 60, 65, 96, 102, 103, 108, 131, 143, 155, 168
Philo Judæus, 64, 84, 132, 169
Pindar, quoted, 57 f.
Plato, quoted or referred to, 19, 28 f., 46, 53, 64, 92 f., 131
Pliny the younger, *Nat. History* of, x, 44
Plutarch, 132, 164
Politarchs, the, at Thess., x, xviii f., xxxii, 60, 178
Polybius, *Histories* of, x, 46, 180, 209 f.
Polycarp, St, *Ep.* of, xlii; *Martyr.* of, 173 f.
Pompey, at Thess., xii
Positivism and Antichrist, 228, 231
præterist theories of Antichrist, 229
prayer and thanksgiving, 127, 135, 153, 161
preaching, Paul's, at Thess., xvii —xx, xxiii—xxxi, 23 f., 28 f., 35—49, 51, 67, 80 f., 174, 191 f., 205, 208
prophecy (see προφητεία), in Apostolic Church, 98, 128; progressive fulfilment of, 231 f.
Prophet, the False, of Revelation, 222
proselytes, Jewish, and Christianity, xvii
Proverbs, Bk of, lx, 60, 88, 100
Psalms, Bk of, lx f., 22, 29, 31, 40, 72, 74, 76, 83, 86, 100, 112, 135, 147, 148, 151, 180, 183, 194, 198, 201, 202
Psalms of Solomon, 91, 217
purity of motive, Paul's, xxxiv f., 36—40

Quintilian, quoted, 209

I. GENERAL INDEX.

Rabbinical phrases, 85, 210; teaching on Antichrist, 224
Ramsay, W. M., quoted or referred to, xv, xvii, xx, xxviii, xliii
Raphael, the archangel, 101
readings of Greek text, the more noticeable, lxvi f.
Reformers, the Protestant, on Antichrist, 226 f.
relative attraction, 142
resurrection, the Christian, xxiv, 30, 97, 101; of Jesus, 30, 96 f., 117 f.
retaliation forbidden, 125
retribution, Divine, 145 f., 184 ff.
revelation (see ἀποκάλυψις)
Revelation, Bk of, its relation to 2 Thess., xlii f., xlvi f., liii f., 219—222; other reff., 17, 19, 30, 100, 108, 109, 143, 145, 147, 150, 156, 168, 172, 181, 184, 186, 224, 226
right of maintenance, Apostolic, 40 f.
riot at Thess., xviii ff.
Ritschl, A., 50
Robinson, J. A., on *Ephesians*, quoted, 52, 117, 176
Roman law and Christianity, 179
Romans, Ep. to, xxvi, xxix, li, lviii, lx, 20, 22, 23, 27, 31, 41, 46, 50, 51, 56, 84, 86, 91, 96, 115, 116, 118 f., 121, 131, 148, 149, 167, 176, 177, 182, 184, 185, 186, 188, 193, 199, 200, 201, 213, 221
Rome, city of, ix, xix, 27, 218, 222
Ruth, Bk of, 85

Sabatier, A., quoted, xxxiv
Sahidic Version, lxvi, 33
Saint Sophia, mosque of, at Thess., xiii
saints, the (see ἅγιοι)
Sallust, *Catilina*, 96
Saloniki, ix

Samuel, 1 and 2 Bks of (1 and 2 Kingdoms in LXX), 38, 45, 70, 83, 133, 168, 185, 206
Saracens, masters of Thess., xiii; assault on Eastern Empire, 178 f.
Savonarola, 226
Schmidt, J. C. Chr., xlii
Schmidt, P. W., liii f.
Schmiedel, P. W., in *Handcommentar*, xliii, xlv ff., 35, 38, 50, 132, 200
Schrader, K., xlii
Schürer, E., 41
self-defence of Paul, xxxiv f., 34—48, 57—61
Severianus, 180
Shakespeare, quoted, 55, 85
Sibylline Oracles, 217 f.
Silas (Shila, Silvanus; see also Σιλουανός), xiv f.; xxxii f., 15 f., 28, 50, 52, 98, 141; his possible share in 2 Thess., xl f., xlix f.
Simcox, W. H., on Revelation, 221
Simon Magus, and Antichrist, 229
Sirach, Bk of, 21, 54, 76, 85, 146, 155, 194, 202
Sophocles, 44, 60, 123
soul, the (see ψυχή)
spirit (see πνεῦμα)
SPIRIT, THE HOLY (see πνεῦμα ἅγιον, and HOLY)
Spitta, F., xlvii f., 1, 67 f.
Steck, R., xliii
Stephen, St, 54, 144
Strabo, quoted, x
style of the Epp., lviii ff.; of 2 Thess., xlviii ff., lvii, lix f., 143
subscription to Epp., xxxix
Suetonius, *De vita Cæsarum*, xix, 172 f.
synagogue, the Jewish, its Gentile adherents, xvi f.; Paul preaching in, xvii f.
Syrian readings and recension of

I. GENERAL INDEX.

Text, lxvi f., 33, 62 f., 78 f., 104, 159, 161, 197

Tacitus, quoted, 54, 173
Tafel, *de Thessalonica ejusque agro*, xii
Tancred, the Crusader, xii
Targum of Jonathan, 218 f.
Tarsus, 44
'tendency' school of criticism, xlii f., xlv
tent-making, Paul's trade of, 44 f., 206 f., 214
Tertullian, quoted or referred to, 84, 104, 135, 223
Theocritus, 119
Theodore of Mopsuestia, 84, 122, 168, 171, 181, 229
Theodoret, xi, 75, 145
Theodosius the Great, Emperor, xii
Theophylact, 33
Therma, ix
Thermaic Gulf, xi; see *map*
Thessalonian Christians, character of, xliii f., 19 ff., 28 f., 45, 51, 60 f., 74, 81, 91 f., 95, 112, 140—145, 164, 187—191, 198 f., 201 f., 210 f.; sufferings of, xviii, xxxiii, xxxvii, lxii f., 21, 25, 49 ff., 67, 125, 126 f., 141—146
Thessalonians, 1 and 2 Ep. to, mutual relations of, xxxvii ff., xlviii ff., 161, 164 f.; order of, xxxviii f. ; general character of, lxi ff.
Thessalonica, history of, ix, xii f.; position of, xi f., xvi, 92, 198, —see *map*; Paul's connexion with, xiv—xxii, xxxii—xli, lxi ff., 16, 28, 34 ff., 72 ff., 152 f., 174, 190 f.; his wish to return to, xxxiv ff., 57 ff., 71; Paul's sermon at, xvii f. (see *preaching*)
Thucydides, quoted, 39, 87, 123
Timothy, with Paul at Thess., xiv ff., 15 f., 64; his visit to

Thess. and report, xxxiii, 57, 63—73, 79 f., 140; his share in the Epp., xl f., xlviii—lii; other reff., 28, 64, 65, 141
Timothy, 1 Ep. to, xxi, 37, 91, 93, 117, 118, 121, 143, 149, 167, 172, 175 f., 180, 209
Timothy, 2 Ep. to, lxiv, 33, 60, 82, 91, 109, 167, 178, 180, 191, 199
Tischendorf, C., quoted, 63, 197
title of Epp., 13
Titus, Ep. to, lxiv, 29, 86, 180, 189
Tobit, Bk of, 101
treason, charge of, against Paul, xviii ff., 174 f.
Trench, R. C., on *N.T. Synonyms, passim*
Troas, port of, xiv f.
Turks, at Thess., xi, xiii

uncial MSS., the Greek, lxv ff., and Textual Notes *passim*
union with Christ, 102 f., 117 f., 156, 191

Van Manen, xliii
Vergil, quoted, 198
versions, ancient, of Epp., lxv ff., Textual Notes *passim*
Vespasian, the Emperor, 173, 229
Via Egnatia, x, xvi, xxix
vocabulary, the Greek, of 1 and 2 Thess., lv ff.
Vulgate version, the Latin, quoted or referred to, xvii, 47, 58, 87 f., 89, 107, 122, 123, 130, 163, 164, 169, 174, 180, 202, 209

Waldenses, the, on Antichrist, 226
Weber, F., on Antichrist, 218
Weiss, B., on Text of Thess. Epp., 32, 63, 79, 105, 161, 197; on Apocalyptic, xlvii
Weizsäcker, C., 41
Wesley, C., quoted, 97
Westcott, B. F., on *Daniel*, 215

Westcott-Hort, *N.T. in Greek* (WH), lxv ff., 32 f., 60, 160, 166, 197, and Textual Notes generally
Western readings of Greek Text, lxvi f., 63, 78 f., 104, 106, 159, 160, 197
Winer-Moulton, *Grammar of N.T. Greek*, passim
Winer-Schmiedel, *Grammatik d. n.-t. Sprachidioms* (incomplete), 32, 110
Wisdom, Bk of, 110, 115, 150, 169, 177

women of Thess., the Greek, xvii
word-plays (see *paronomasia*)
Wordsworth, Chr., 227
worship, objects of (see $\sigma \acute{\epsilon}\beta \alpha \sigma \mu \alpha$)
Wrede, W., on authenticity of 2 Thess., xlvi, xlix

Xenophon, quoted, 82, 85
Xerxes at Thess., ix

Zahn, Th., xliii, xlviii, 15
Zechariah, Bk of, 38, 100, 109, 168 f.
Zephaniah, Bk of, 109

II. INDEX OF GREEK WORDS AND PHRASES.

Words specially defined or discussed are marked with an asterisk, with the specific reference in thicker type.

ἀγαθός, 70, 125 f., 194 ; -ωσύνη, lvi, 154 f.
ἀγαπάω, ἀγάπη, 20 f., 70, 91, 114 f., 122 f., 188, 193, 202 ;
ἀγαπητός, 44
ἄγγελος, 101, 147
ἀγιάζω, *-σμός, 76, **83**, 89, 131 f., 189 f. ; *ἅγιος, -ωσύνη, lvi, **46**, 76, 90 ; ἅγιοι (οἱ), 77, 151
ἀγνοεῖν, οὐ θέλω..., 94 f.
ἄγω, 97
ἀγών, 36
ἀδελφός (ὁ), -οί, 21, 57, 87, 107, 135, 163, 188, 198, 205, 212
ἀδιαλείπτως, lvi, lxi, 19, **126**
ἀδικία, 183, 186
ἀήρ, 102
*ἀθετέω, **89**
αἱρέομαι, 188
αἰφνίδιος, 110
*αἰώνιος, **150**, 193 f.
*ἀκαθαρσία, **37**, 88 f.
ἀκοῆς, λόγος, 51
ἀκούω, 209
*ἀκριβῶς, **108**
*ἀλήθεια (ἡ), 183 f., 186, 189 f.
ἀληθινός, 29
ἀληθῶς, 51 f.
ἀλλήλους, 75, 103, **125 f.**
ἁμαρτία, 56

ἅμα σύν, 101, 118 f.
ἄμεμπτος, -ως, lvi, 46, 76 f., **134**
ἀμήν, 63, 106, 197
ἀναγινώσκω, 136 f.
*ἀνάγκη, **71**
ἀναιρέω, or ἀναλίσκω, 160, 179, 181
ἀναμένω, lvi, 29 f.
ἀναπληρόω, 56
*ἄνεσις, **146**
ἀνέστη ὁ Ἰησοῦς, 96 f.
ἀνέχομαι, 142
ἄνθρωπος (see ἀρέσκω)
*ἄνθρωπος (ὁ) τῆς ἀνομίας (ἁμαρτίας), xxxvii f., xlv f., li, 159, **168–174**, 175 ff., 179 ff., 186 f.; the Appendix
ἀνθ᾽ ὧν, 183 f.
ἀνίστημι, 96 f., 101
ἀνομία (ἡ), ἄνομος (ὁ), xlviii, 176 f., 179-183; the Appendix
ἀνταποδίδωμι, 72, 145 f.
ἀντέχομαι, 124
ἀντί, 125
ἀντικείμενος (ὁ), xlv f., 168 ff.
ἄξιος, -ως, 48, 140 ; ἀξιόω, 38, 153 f.
ἀπάντησιν, εἰς, lvii, 102
ἅπαξ καὶ δίς, 59
ἀπαρχή, 160, 188 f.
ἀπ᾽ ἀρχῆς, 160, 188 f.

ἅπας, 160, 185 f.
*ἀπάτη, 183, 220
ἀπέθανεν ὁ 'Ιησοῦς, 96 f., 117 f.
ἀπέχομαι, 82, 130 f.
ἀπό, 58, 147, 150, 164; ἀπό—ἐκ, 40
ἀποδείκνυμι, 169
ἀποδίδωμι, 105, 125
ἀποκαλύπτω, *-ψις, 61, 146, 168, 175 f., 179
ἀπολλύμενοι (οἱ), 182, 184, 220
ἀπορφανίζω, lvi, 57 f.
*ἀποστασία (ἡ), 167, 224
*ἀπόστολος, 41
ἀπώλεια (see υἱός)
ἆρα οὖν, lvi, 113, 191
ἀρέσκω ἀνθρώποις, θεῷ, 38, 54, 81
ἁρπάζω, 101 f.
*ἄρτι, 70, 176, 177
ἄρτον ἐσθίω, 206, 210
ἀρχάγγελος, 100 f.
ἀσθενής, 124
ἀσπάζομαι, -σμός, 135, 214
ἀσφάλεια, 109 f.
ἀτακτέω, -τος, -τως, lvi, 124, 204 ff., 213
*ἄτοπος, 199
αὐτοί...οἴδατε, 34, 66, 107, 206; αὐτὸς ὁ θεός, ὁ κύριος, 74, 99, 131, 192, 213

*βάρος, 40 f.
*βασιλεία (ἡ) τοῦ θεοῦ, 48, 49, 60 f., 144 f.
Βελίαρ, 218

γαστρί, ἐν, ἔχουσα (ἡ), 110
γίνομαι εἰς, 23, 68; *— ἐν, 39 ff.
γινώσκω, 68, 86
*γρηγορέω, 113, 118

δέ, 58, 75, 95, 104, 106, 162, 202
δεῖ, 81, 206
δέομαι, 73
δέχομαι, 25, 51, 183
διά, with genitive, 71, 82, 97, 211 f.; with accus., 24, 73; διὰ παντός, 213; διὰ τοῦτο, 50 f., 67, 71

διάκονος, 62 f., 64 f.
διαμαρτύρομαι, 88
δίδωμι, 148, 193, 207; δίδωμι εἰς, 90
*δίκαιος, -ως, 46, 145
*δίκην τίνω, 149
διό, 63 f., 119
*διότι, 44, 58, 88
δίς, 59
διωγμός, 142
διώκω, 125
*δοκιμάζω, 37 f., 106, 129 f.; δοκιμάζων (ὁ) τὴν καρδίαν, lvii, 38
δόξα, 40, 48 f., 61; — Χριστοῦ, 151, 155 f., 191
δοξάζω, 198
δουλεύω, 29
δύναμις, 147, 155, 181 f.; δύναμις— πνεῦμα, 23
δωρεάν, 206

ἑαυτούς (1st person), 43, 207; (2nd person), 123
ἐγὼ Παῦλος, 59
ἔθνη (τά), 55
εἰ, 96; — οὐ (οὐχ), 208, 211; εἴπερ, 145
*εἶδος, 130 f.
*εἴδωλον, 28, 29
εἰρηνεύω, 123
*εἰρήνη, 17 f., 109 f.; εἰρήνης (τῆς), ὁ θεός, ὁ κύριος, 131, 213
εἰς, 91, 128, 169, 191; εἰς τό (infinitive), 48, 56, 73, 91, 144, 163, 183 f., 207
εἷς—εἷς, 119; εἷς ἕκαστος, 47, 140
εἴσοδος, 28, 35
εἴτε—εἴτε, 118
ἐκ (ἐξ), 37, 40; ἐκ μέσου, 177
*ἐκδίκησις, ἔκδικος, lvi, 88, 147 f.
ἐκδιώκω, lvi, 54
*ἐκκλησία, 16 f.
*ἐκλογή, 21 f.
ἔλεγον (προ-), 67, 174
ἐλπίς, 19 ff., 60, 96, 115 f., 193 f.
ἔμπροσθεν τοῦ θεοῦ, 19, 73, 76
ἐν, 37, 77, 89, 100, 102, 103, 122 f., 134, 141, 147, 181, 194; ἐν Θεῷ, Κυρίῳ, Χριστῷ,

GREEK WORDS AND PHRASES. 245

κ.τ.λ., 16 f., 52, 72, 80, 101, 127 f., 201, 204, 210; ἐν μέσῳ, 42
ἐνάντιος, 54 f.
*ἔνδειγμα, lvi, 144
ἐνδοξάζω, lvii, 151, 155 f.
ἐνδύω, 114 f.
*ἐνεργέω (in passive), *-γεια, 52, 176, 181, 184
ἐνέστηκα, 165 f.
ἐνέχω, 138, 142
*ἐνκακέω, 211
ἐνκαυχάομαι, lvi, 141
*ἐνκόπτω, 59
ἐνορκίζω, xl, lvi, 106, 136 f.
ἐντρέπω, 212
ἐξαπατάω, lvi, 166
ἐξέρχομαι, 27
ἐξηχέω, lvi, 26
ἐξουθενέω, 128 f.
*ἐξουσία, 207
*ἔξω (οἱ), 93, 96
ἔπειτα, 101
ἐπί, with genitive, 19; with dative, 71, 73, 89; with accusative, 152 f., 163, 201
ἐπιβαρέω, lvi., 45, 207
*ἐπιθυμία, 58, 85 f.
ἐπιποθέω, 71
ἐπίσταμαι (ἐφίσταμαι), 104, 110
ἐπιστολή, 136, 164 f., 192, 211, 214
ἐπιστρέφω, 28
ἐπισυναγωγή, 163
*ἐπιφάνεια, -ης, lvi, 61, 180, 217
ἐργάζομαι, 44, 93, 207, 208, 209
ἔργον, 123; — καὶ λόγος, 194 f.; — πίστεως, 20, 154
ἔρχομαι, 31, 108
*ἐρωτάω (in requests), 80, 121, 163
ἐσθίω, 208; see ἄρτον
ἔτι, 174
εὐαγγελίζομαι, 70
*εὐαγγέλιον (τό), 23, 38, 65, 148 f., 190; — τοῦ θεοῦ, 35, 43, 45
*εὐδοκέω, -ία, 43, 64, 154 f., 186
εὐσχημόνως, lvi, 93
εὐχαριστέω, -ία, lxi, 18 f., 72, 126 f., 140, 187

ἐχθρός, 212
ἕως, 177

ζάω, 72, 98 f., 101, 117 ff.

*ἡγέομαι ἐν, 122 f.; — ὡς, 212
*ἤδη, 176
ἡμεῖς—ὑμεῖς, 24, 57 f., 61, 71, 73, 75, 152, 154, 187 f., 190, 207
*ἡμέρα, 112, 114 f.; *— Κυρίου, 108 f., 111, 152
ἤπιος, lvi, 32 f., 42
ἡσυχάζω, ἡσυχία, 92 f., 210

θάλπω, 42
θαυμάζω, 151
θέλημα (τοῦ) Θεοῦ, 82 f., 127 f.
*θέλω, 58 f.
θεοδίδακτος, lvii, 91
Θεός (ὁ), 65, 169–174, 193, 202
θηρίον (τό), of the Apocalypse, 220 ff.
θλίβω, -ψις, 25, 145 f.
*θροέω, 164
θώραξ, 114 f.

ἴδια (τά), 92
Ἰησοῦς, 17, 30 f., 53, 97
ἵνα, 55, 78, 81, 111 f., 153, 210
Ἰουδαία (ἡ), 52
Ἰουδαῖοι (οἱ), 53
*ἰσχύς, 150

καθάπερ, 47, 71, 75, 86
καθεύδω, 113, 118
καθίζω εἰς, 169
καί, 135, 212; doubled, 53, 59
*καιρός, 58, 107, 175 f.
κακόν (τό), 125
καλέω, 48, 89, 134 f., 190
καλόν (τό), 130; *καλοποιέω, lvi, 211
*καρδία, 38, 58, 76, 194, 202
κατά, 181
καταλαμβάνω, 111
καταλείπω, 64
*καταξιόω, 144
*καταργέω, 180
*καταρτίζω, 74

κατευθύνω, 74, 202
κατέχω, 129 f.; *κατέχον (τό), κατέχων (ό), 175, 177—179, 223 f., 229
κεῖμαι, 66
*κέλευσμα, lvi, 100
*κενός, εἰς κενόν, 35, 68 f.
κηρύσσω, 45
κλέπτης—κλέπτας, 104, 108, 111
κλῆσις, 153 f.
*κοιμάομαι, οἱ κοιμώμενοι, xliv f., 95-98
κοινή (see later Greek)
κολακία, lvi, 39
κοπιάω, *κόπος, 21, 44, 68 f., 121, 206 f.
κρατέω, 191 f.
κρίνω, -σις, 143, 186
*κτάομαι (σκεῦος), 84 f.
Κύριος (ό), 17, 53, 75, 88, 136, 188, 202, 213 f.
κύριος (ό) Ἰησοῦς, 53 f., 77, 82, 105, 146, 149, 155 f., 160, 179
κύριος (ό) Ἰησοῦς Χριστός, 16 f., 116 f., 137, 139, 157, 192 f., 204, 210
κωλύω, 55

λαλέω, 28, 36, 55
λεγόμενος θεός, 29, 169
λόγος θεοῦ, 51; — (τοῦ) κυρίου, 26 f., 98, 198; λόγος—δύναμις, 23; λόγος—πνεῦμα, 165; λόγος —ἐπιστολή, 164, 192, 194 f., 211; see ἔργον
*λοιποί (οἱ), 96, 113; λοιπόν (τό), 78, 80, 197
λυπέω, 95

*μακροθυμέω, 125
μᾶλλον, 80 f., 92
*μαρτύριον (τό) ἐπί, 152 f.
*μαρτύρομαι, 47
μάρτυς, 39 f., 45
*μεθύσκω, *μεθύω, 114
μέλλω, 67
μέν, 59
μετά, 25, 77, 146, 210
μεταδίδωμι, 43

μή, with participles, 64, 205; with subjunctive, 166, 211; μή πως, 68 f.; μηδέ, μήτε, 159, 164
μηκέτι, 64, 67
μιμέομαι, μιμητής, 25, 206 f.
μνεία, lvi, 19, 70
*μνημονεύω, 19, 44, 174
μόνον, μόνος, 64, 177
*μόχθος, lvi, 44, 206 f.
*μυστήριον, 176 f.; μυστήριον (τό) τῆς ἀνομίας, xlviii, 162, the Appendix

*ναός (ό) τοῦ θεοῦ, 169—171, 224
νεκροί (οἱ), 101
νεφέλη, 101 f.
νήπιοι—ἤπιοι, the various reading, 32 f.; interpretation of, 42
νήφω, 113 f.
*νουθετέω, 122, 124, 212
νοῦς, 164
*νῦν, 72, 175, 176
νύξ, 112 f.; νυκτὸς καὶ ἡμέρας, 44, 73, 206 f.

οἶδα, 121, 175; with infin., 84; —Θεόν, 86, 148 f.; οἴδατε, 24, &c.
οἰκοδομέω, 119
οἶος—ὁποῖος, 24, 28
ὄλεθρος, lvi, 149 f.
ὀλιγόψυχος, lvi, 124
*ὁλόκληρος—*ὁλοτελής, lvi, 132
ὁμείρομαι, lvii, 42 f.
ὄνομα τοῦ κυρίου Ἰησοῦ (Χριστοῦ), 155 f., 204
ὅπως, 155
ὁρᾶτε μή, 125
*ὀργή (ἡ), 31, 56 f., 116
*ὁσίως, lvi, 46
ὅστις, 149
ὅτι, 22 f., 53, 70 f., 169, 208
οὐ θέλω, 94 f., 208; οὐ—μή, 64, 205; οὐ μή, 99; οὐχ ὅτι, 207
*οὐρανοί (οἱ), οὐρανός, 30, 147
οὕτως γράφω, 214; οὕτως καί, 97; καὶ οὕτως, 102
ὀφείλω, 140, 187 f.

*πάθος, 85 f.

GREEK WORDS AND PHRASES.

πάντοτε, 56, 70, 126
παρά, with genitive, 51, 80 f., 206; with dative, 206
*παραγγέλλω, *-λία, 82, 93, 201 f., 204 f., 208
παραδίδωμι, παράδοσις, 191 f., 205
*παρακαλέω, 47, 65, 80, 92, 103, 119, 124, 210; *παράκλησις, 36 f., 193
παραλαμβάνω, 51, 81, 205
*παραμυθέομαι, 47, 124
παράνομος (ό), 218
*παρουσία (ή), xxvii f., lxiv, 60, 77, 95–103, 134, 180 f.;—τοῦ ἀνόμου, 181 ff.
*παρρησιάζομαι, 34 f.
πᾶς, 112, 125, 127, 136 f., 182, 199, 213 f.
πάσχω ὑπέρ, 145; — ὑπό, 53
πατήρ, 47; πατήρ (ό), ὁ θεός, 16 f., 74 f., 139, 157, 192 f.
Παῦλος, 16, 214
πειράζω, -σμός, 38, 68; πειράζων (ὁ), 59, 68 f.
πέποιθα, 201 f.
περί, 117, 163; περὶ δέ, 90, 107
*περιεργάζομαι, lvi, 209 f.
περικεφαλαία, ivi, 115
περιλειπόμενοι (οἱ), xliv, lvi, 98 f., 101
περιπατέω, 48, 81, 93, 204 f.
*περιποίησις, 116 f., 191
περισσεύω, 75, 92
περισσοτέρως, 58
πιστεύοντες (οἱ), 26, 52; πιστεύσαντες (οἱ), 151; πιστεύω, 38, 96 ff., 152, 186; πίστις (ή), 20, 27, 68, 70, 71, 74, 114 f., 140, 141 f., 154, 189 f., 199
πιστός, 134 f., 200
*πιστόω, 139, 153
πλάνη, 37, 184
πλεονάζω, 75
πλεονεκτέω, *-ξία, xxxiv, lvi, 39, 87
*πληροφορία, 23
πληρόω, 154
*πνεῦμα, 133, 164 f., 179 f., 189 f.; πνεῦμα (τό), 128 f.; πνεῦμα ἅγιον, 90; see δύναμις; also λόγος

ποιέω, 91 f., 135, 201 f.
πονηρόν (τό), 131; πονηρός, 199; πονηρός (ὁ), 59, 200
πορνεία, 82 f.
*πρᾶγμα (τό), 87 f.
πράσσω τὰ ἴδια, 92
*προϊστάμενοι (οἱ), xliv, lvi, 121 f., 135 f.
προλέγω, -εῖπα, lvi, 67, 88
προπάσχω, lvi, 36
πρός, 27, 45, 93, 198, 207
πρός, εἰμί, 67, 174, 208
προσευχή, 19; προσεύχομαι, 126 f., 135, 198
πρόσωπον, 58, 73
πρόφασις, 39
*προφητεία, 129
προφῆται (οἱ), 54
πρῶτον, 166; πρῶτον—ἔπειτα, 101
πῦρ, 147
πῶς, 28, 81, 206

ῥύομαι, 199; *ῥυόμενος (ὁ), 31

*σαίνω, lvii, 66
σαλεύω ἀπό, 164
*σάλπιγξ, 100
Σατανᾶς (ὁ), 59 f., 168 f., 181, 220 f.
σβέννυμι, 105, 128
σέβασμα, 169, 174
Σεβαστός (ὁ), 174
*σημεῖον, 182, 214, 221
σημειόω, lvi, 212
Σιλᾶς, Σιλουανός, 15 f., 138
*σκεῦος, 84 f.
σκότος, 111 f.
σπουδάζω, 58 f.
*στέγω, lvi, 64, 67
στέλλομαι ἀπό, lvi, 204 f.
στέφανος καυχήσεως, lvii, 60
στήκω, 72, 191
στηρίζω, 65, 200;—τὴν καρδίαν, lvii, 76, 194
συμφυλέτης, lvi, 53
σύν, 97, 102 f.; see ἅμα
συναναμίγνυμαι, 212
συνεργός, 62 f., 64 f.
σώζω, 55; σωτηρία, 115, 188 f.

II. GREEK WORDS AND PHRASES.

*σῶμα, 133
ταχέως, 164
τέκνον, 42, 47
τέλος, εἰς, 56 f.
*τέρας, 182, 221
τηρέω, 134
τίθεμαι εἰς, 116
τιμή, 84 f.
Τιμόθεος, 15
τινές, 209
τίνω, lvi, 149
τοιγαροῦν, 89
τοιοῦτος (ὁ), 210
τόπῳ, ἐν παντί, 27
τότε, 110, 179
*τρέχω, 198
τρόπος, 166, 213
τροφός, 42 f.
τύπος, 25 f., 207

ὑβρίζω, 36
υἱὸς (ὁ) τῆς ἀπωλείας, 168; — ἡμέρας, κ.τ.λ., lvii, 112; υἱὸς (ὁ) τοῦ θεοῦ, 29 f.
ὑπακούω, 211; — τῷ εὐαγγελίῳ, 148
ὑπέρ, 141, 145; ὑπέρ—περί, 65, 163
ὑπεραίρω, 168 f.
ὑπεραυξάνω, lvi, 140
ὑπερβαίνω, lvi, 87

ὑπερεκπερισσοῦ, -ῶς, lvi, 73
*ὑπομονή, 21, 141 f., 202 f.
ὑστερήματα (τά) τῆς πίστεως, xxvii, xxxv ff., 74

φθάνω, 34, 56 f., 99
φιλαδελφία, 90 f.
φίλημα, 135 f.
*φιλοτιμέομαι, 92
φλόξ, 147
φυλάσσω, 200
*φῶς, 112

χαίρω, χαρά, 61, 73, 126
*χάρις (ἡ) τοῦ θεοῦ, 17 f., 156 f., 157f., 193 f.; — τοῦ κυρίου Ἰησοῦ Χριστοῦ, 137, 156 f., 214
χάρισμα, 158
χειρί, τῇ ἐμῇ, xl, 214; χερσὶν (ταῖς) ἐργάζεσθαι, 93
χρείαν ἔχω, 90, 93 f., 107
Χριστός, 17; χριστός (ὁ), 203; Χριστὸς Ἰησοῦς, 52 f., 127 f.
*χρόνος—καιρός, 107

ψεῦδος, 182, 185, 221
*ψυχή, 43, 133

ὠδίν, 110
ὥρα, 58
ὡς, 47, 165; — ἐάν, 42; — ὅτι, 165 f.
ὥστε, 28, 103, 119, 141, 169